BIOSOCIOLOGY

An Emerging Paradigm

Anthony Walsh

Foreword by Robert A. Gordon

Westport, Connecticut
London

Library of Congress Cataloging-in-Publication Data

Walsh, Anthony.
    Biosociology : an emerging paradigm / Anthony Walsh ;
  foreword by Robert A. Gordon
      p. cm.
  Includes bibliographical references and indexes.
  ISBN 0–275–95328–9 (alk. paper)
  1. Sociobiology. 2. Human behavior. I. Title.
  GN365.9.W36   1995
  303.5—dc20   95–23209

British Library Cataloguing in Publication Data is available.

Library of Congress Catalog Card Number: 95–23209
ISBN: 0–275–95328–9

First published in 1995

Praeger Publishers, 88 Post Road West, Westport, CT 06881
An imprint of Greenwood Publishing Group, Inc.

Printed in the United States of America

The paper used in this book complies with the
Permanent Paper Standard issued by the National
Information Standards Organization (Z39.48–1984).

10 9 8 7 6 5 4 3 2 1

Contents

Tables and Figures

Foreword
by Robert A. Gordon

When I wrote "Prevalence: The Rare Datum in Delinquency Measurement and Its Implications for the Theory of Delinquency" (Gordon, 1976), I was careful not to mention the word "intelligence" in the title. I had two reasons for this. The editor of the book, Malcolm Klein, had requested from me a piece on delinquency measurement, saying, with a confidence in my judgment that I could only hope he would feel was not misplaced, "You'll know what is needed." One of the things I decided was needed was a title that did not affront his conception of what it was I was supposed to do.

The other reason for excluding "intelligence" from the title was that I did not want to risk alienating readers before they had even begun reading the article. After all, a contributor to the *Annual Review of Sociology* admitted several years later, "If you said 'IQ' you drove most sociologists to the barricades" (Simpson, 1980). I did not have direct measures of intelligence in my own data, as Hirschi and Hindelang (1977) did the next year, but had instead inferred the active role of that variable from what I regarded as strong theory and analyses that had to be devised for the purpose.

I had published two articles earlier, each of which rationalized using the epidemiological term *prevalence* for the proportion of individuals in an age cohort who become delinquent, according to some operational definition, by age eighteen. Perhaps Klein knew of those articles and invited me because of them, although that is not as likely as one might think, for both had appeared in journals that were not staple reading for criminologists—one in the *Journal of the American Statistical Association* (Gordon, 1973), the other in the *Journal of Mathematical Sociology* (Gordon & Gleser, 1974). I still smile to myself over these outlets, especially the latter, for I never regarded myself as either a statistician or a mathematical sociologist, and these two journals do carry a certain cachet of rigor.

If Anthony Walsh's bold and stimulating book had been published before that time, I might not have had to place those articles so far afield from mainstream sociology journals because the discipline might have contained more individuals receptive to the findings in them. I had submitted the articles to major sociology journals, but the referee reports came back either angry or suspiciously picky. Each contained a set of race-specific prevalence data that revealed delinquency rates for blacks three or four times higher than those for whites. The term *politically correct* (or "PC") had not yet come into vogue, but that scientifically inappropriate criterion was clearly a source of my problem, for such findings failed the PC test definitively (e.g., Gottfredson, 1994).

Both articles contained rare and important data that would reveal—when coupled with IQ data that had been reported by Jensen (1969)—that the difference between blacks and whites in the prevalence of delinquency was closely commensurate with the difference in their IQ distributions; but I dared not invoke that fact prematurely in dealing with editors, lest they become even more resistant to publishing them. Unveiling the relation with intelligence would have to await an occasion in which I had more space to develop my argument, as Klein's timely invitation, by good luck, was to afford soon afterward.

In view of such considerations, I decided to allow the word "intelligence" to appear late in my article for Klein, where it emerged inductively, partly from the IQ-commensurability property described previously and partly from what would later be called a *meta-analysis* of existing prevalence data. Klein indicated that he thought I was "crazy" to go off in this direction, but that makes even more commendable his willingness to include the article in his book with no interference. I salute him for that intellectual openness so rare in its day.

Because my 1976 article dealt with black–white differences in both delinquency and IQ, it has had a strange citation history. More people have known about it and complimented me on it than have cited it. I have even seen this work listed in an article's references, a gesture of awareness, but with no mention in the text, where the authors would have found it necessary to say something about what my article contained. An informative overview of the surrounding theory to date can be found in Gordon (1986).

Understandably, then, it is a special surprise not only to see my work referred to favorably in Walsh's book—one which makes no concessions to political correctness across a wide range of topics—but also to be invited to write the foreword. Despite the intensification of ongoing campus PC battles, science in some quarters is definitely moving aggressively forward to take account of important biological variables. As I was taught in the army, the best defense is a good offense. Students who use *Biosociology: An Emerging Paradigm* should, therefore, feel especially privileged, as it is a highly informative text that places them, for a change, close to the cutting edge of real explanation rather than decades behind with the usual exclusively sociological and social constructivist treatments of the same topics. Many established scientists, I am sure, will also read this book with profit, as have I.

Preface

While still a graduate student, Lee Ellis (1977) wrote a jarring futuristic polemic in *American Sociologist* entitled "The Decline and Fall of Sociology, 1975–2000." Although the piece described a hypothetical scenario, its message etched itself into my thinking. The substance of Ellis's article was that, since none of sociology's theories of social phenomena or deduced remedies for their ills had produced anything positive (and still have not almost twenty years later), a paradigmatic shift to a more biologically informed sociology was necessary if the discipline was to remain credible and viable. At the time of the appearance of Ellis's article, I was a former biology major who had gone on to do graduate work in sociology because I had decided I was more interested in people than plants. Like many others at the time, I saw a deep division between the life sciences and the "people" sciences; but Ellis convinced me that we should set our sights on building bridges between them. Ellis has done much to help lay the foundations of such bridges for sociologists, and he is perhaps the preeminent figure in biosociology today and the most productive "interpreter" of the biological literature for us.

With some important exceptions, sociology has paid scant attention to Ellis's argument without suffering the dire consequences he predicted. Nevertheless, we have recently witnessed entire sociology departments eliminated (e.g., Washington University in St. Louis and the University of Rochester), others (e.g., Yale, San Diego State University) have been threatened with drastic faculty cuts (Coughlin, 1992), and students declaring sociology majors have declined precipitously since the 1970s (Das, 1989). In these times of tight budgets, sociology may be viewed by administrators as weak, vulnerable, and "expendable."

This is unfortunate, for sociology is a valuable discipline; social inquiry and criticism are indispensable to a free society. But it *is* scientifically weak, and it will remain so unless buttressed by the more basic sciences which are also involved in the study of human behavior. Many social scientists are well aware of the weaknesses inherent in the "contradictory stew of ungrounded, middle-level theories expressed in a babel of incommensurate technical lexicons" that constitute much of social science and of the "growing sense of malaise" generated by this awareness "so that the single largest trend is toward rejecting the scientific enterprise as it applies to humans" (Tooby & Cosmides, 1992:23). If social science is really that bad, then the cure is *more* science, not less. We should make serious attempts to assimilate the basics of those sciences which are already studying "sociological" phenomena such as criminality and sex–gender roles and doing so with "harder" data and methodologies. Data from these studies will greatly enhance our understanding of human behavior if we only let them.

Despite the biophobia that stalks sociology, Melvin Konner (1982:11) believes that "no one in today's behavioral sciences doubts that biology is making, and is destined to continue to make, a massive, profound impact on these sciences." Although biology and the neurosciences are having such an impact, they are having it outside the knowledge or concern of mainstream social scientists. For many sociologists, the intrusion of biology into their domains of interest represents their worst professional nightmares. Data from the biological sciences that do come to the attention of sociologists are largely ignored, for most sociologists "know" that variation in human behavior is almost exclusively accounted for by cultural variations and experiences. A recent poll of 162 American sociologists (Sanderson & Ellis, 1992) found that they assign overwhelming proportions of variance in a variety of behaviors to sociocultural factors and very little to biological factors.

This book was written for those who no longer find such a position tenable. It is a brief introduction to biophysiological systems that are important to the understanding of human behavior genetics, neurophysiology, and the autonomic and endocrine systems. These systems are explored in contexts of sociological importance, such as socialization, learning, gender roles, gender differences, sexuality, the family, deviance, and criminality.

Traditional sociologists will find much in this work that will evoke hostility because I often touch on meaningful differences between the sexes and among races and then attribute at least some of the variability to genetics. Simply exploring gender and racial differences is often construed as "sexist," "racist," "reactionary," or "antihumanist" by a good many social scientists. Such labels are not acceptable substitutes for thought and debate, although for some, their issuance forecloses on discourse. Labelers and labelees alike are often silenced by the chill of name-calling—the former because the application of the label is sufficient reason for doubting anything further the labelee has to say, the latter because of fear of the consequences of being so labeled. When this occurs, labelers miss an opportunity to test their beliefs against contending ones; labelees miss opportunities to rethink their positions; and all remain more ignorant than they would otherwise have been. Science has never, and can never, make progress this way.[1]

I wish to gratefully acknowledge the assistance of the following scientists who read all or part of various drafts of my manuscript and offered many useful suggestions and much constructive criticism. These men and women are specialists in the fields indicated: Dr. Garvin Chastin (neurophysiology), Dr. Alfred Dufty (physiology and endocrinology), Dr. Laura Edles (theory), Dr. Lee Ellis (biocriminality), Dr. Russell Ott (molecular and behavioral genetics), Dr. Mark Snow (cognitive assessment and learning), Dr. Mary Stohr (sex-role sociology), and Professor A. Robert Corbin (evolution of family systems). I have endeavored to incorporate all criticisms and suggestions offered by these scientists into this work. Any errors or inconsistencies that remain are entirely mine.

Special thanks to my wife, Grace Jean, for her constant love and support. Gracie, this book is dedicated to you.

NOTE

1. There are sociologists (e.g., phenomenologists, postmodernists) who do not care whether sociology is, or ever can be, a science. This book is predicated on the belief that sociology is a science and can become a better one; it does not address the concerns of those who think it cannot or, perhaps, even should not.

Chapter 1

The Case for Biosociology

Biology is the key to human nature, and social scientists cannot afford to
ignore its rapidly tightening principles. But the social sciences are potentially far richer in content. Eventually they will absorb the relevant
ideas of biology and go on to beggar them by comparison.
                                                        —E. Wilson (1990:260)

Biosociology is an emerging paradigm seeking to understand human behavior by integrating relevant insights from the natural sciences into traditional
sociological thinking. Biosociology is not a "biological" perspective; it is a
biosocial perspective that recognizes "the continuous, mutual, and inseparable
interaction between biology and the social environment" (Lancaster, Altmann,
Rossi, & Sherrod, 1987:2). Biosociology posits no ultimate causes of human
behavior; rather, it seeks to understand how biological factors interact with
other factors to produce observed behavior. It does not seek to "reduce" complex behavior to the level of biological processes in isolation from environmental influences; it merely insists that such processes must be recognized
and included in any analysis of behavior and that such an analysis be consistent with those processes.
   Biosociology is not sociobiology. Sociobiology has a more ambitious
agenda, it concerns itself with the behavior of all animals, it has a grand theory
(evolutionary theory), and it seeks ultimate causes. Sociobiological explanations are concerned with the ultimate "whys" of a phenomenon in terms of
evolved species traits, and biosociology is concerned with the "hows" of a
phenomenon in terms of less distal and more proximate causes. Biosociology
and sociobiology are only alternative perspectives in the same sense that
proximate and ultimate explanations are alternative (but not competing) ex-

planations. As the grand unifying theory of all life sciences, evolutionary theory provides explanations of ultimate causes and provides directions for the investigation of proximate biosocial causes; and in this sense, it subsumes biosociology. As Allan Mazur (who, as far as I can determine, coined the term *biosociology*) explains, "Sociobiology promises to revolutionize the social sciences at all levels, while biosociology seeks a quiet niche in positivist microsociology" (1981:157).

Sociobiological thinking is useful in that it "grounds" a phenomenon in a broad and general theory, but its very broadness and generality make it less than satisfying to sociologists.[1] Sociologists tend to be "problem" oriented and to conduct research designed more to address and ameliorate social problems rather than to illuminate some ultimate "truth" about human nature. Sociobiologists, on the other hand, are more interested in universals in human nature than differences, a fact that led one of its major proponents to write that sociobiology may be "minimally relevant to social policy decisions" (Symons, 1987:141). For instance, to say that men rape and kill because lust and aggression are male mammalian traits selected in by evolutionary pressures (Thornhill & Thornhill, 1992) may well be true, but it begs an awful lot of questions. Such behavior is the result of phylogenetic characteristics all men share but few express in the normal course of events. If a given man rapes or kills, the distal phylogenetic causes are less useful to us in terms of understanding that behavior than are proximate ontogenetic causes. We would like to know about the offender's unique genotype, the functioning of his nervous system and its usual state of arousal (neurohormonal activation), his developmental experiences, the immediate activating stimuli, and how all these factors permutate and interact.

REDUCTIONISM AND HOLISM IN SCIENCE

Physicist Percy Bridgman maintained that the first and most important step in understanding any system—atomic particles, chemical compounds, cells, individual organisms, societies—is to understand the elementary units comprising the system. The ultimate problem in the social sciences is similar to that of the physical sciences but is more complex.

The ultimate problem is the problem of understanding the functioning of the elementary units of which the systems are built up. The elementary units in the physical sciences are particles. There are only a few kinds of them. It took us a long time to find some of the laws and we haven't got the laws of some of the particles yet. The elementary units of the social sciences are men and the corresponding ultimate problem is to understand the individual human being. (Bridgman, 1955:49–50)

This is not to deny that social phenomena can be explained on their own terms, or that lower-level "elementary units" explanations are necessarily superior to holistic ones. Rather, it is to say that complex social phenomena can be *more fully* understood if their explanations maintain consistency with what we know about the more elementary units—the biology and psychology of the actors in the social drama. Cosmides, Tooby, and Barkow (1992:4) refer to this principle of conceptual consistency as *vertical integration*, explaining that this term refers "to the principle that the various disciplines within the behavioral and social sciences should make themselves mutually consistent, and consistent with what is known in the natural sciences as well." As reasonable as this seems, many sociologists might see it as a call for reductionism, against which there has been a long history of opposition.

When scientists write about the methodologies employed in their disciplines, they typically refer to hierarchically arranged "levels of analysis." These levels serve to organize knowledge within a field of inquiry along manageable lines, albeit artificially discrete ones. The term *reductionism* is often used disparagingly to mean that an inappropriate (lower) unit of analysis has been used to explore, describe, or explain a particular research question. Examining the phenomenon of crime, for instance, one level of analysis might be "society." We could ask questions like "Why is society A more criminogenic than society B?" or "Why is society X more criminogenic today than it was Y years ago?" To ask such questions is to seek a reply from the sociologist (or other social scientist) because it is couched in broad "macro" terms. It is asking for an explanation of the difference in crime rates between two different societies or between the same society at two different times. Being so couched, we need to look for cultural factors that differentiate the two societies or time periods in such a way as to provide a satisfactory explanation for differences in crime rates. A psychologist may also attempt to answer the question using the vocabulary of psychology to indicate that society A produces a different kind of mind-set as it relates to conformity or nonconformity than society B. In doing so, the psychologist has "reduced" the explanation of a question couched in terms of one unit of analysis (whole societies) to a lower unit of analysis (individual mind-sets). A sociologist may consider this inappropriate; the psychologist would beg to differ.

The sociologist need not use the vocabulary of psychology to answer the question as posed, for it does not inquire about "mind-sets." But the psychologist must *necessarily* use the vocabulary of the sociologist because he or she must delineate the nature of the social milieu producing the mind-sets so that the question and its answer maintain consistency; that is, the psychological explanation of the phenomenon requires the use not only of psychological terms but also of specifically sociological, political, economic, and historical terms that do not typically appear in psychology's vocabulary. However, in finding that the culture of society A produces individuals who tend more than individuals in society B to be competitive, aggressive, or hedonistic, for example, and that those possessing such traits tend to be more criminal than those who do not, the psychologist has added a useful dimension to sociological explanation. He or she has not detracted from the sociologist's explanation as long as the cultural conditions associated with the development of the enumerated character traits are acknowledged.

Unlike the psychologist, however, a biologist or chemist could not reply to the question if limited to the vocabulary of biology and chemistry. There are biochemical explanations for why some people are more competitive, aggressive, or hedonistic than others, thereby reducing psychological units of analysis (individual human beings) to biochemical units of analysis (the molecular goings-on within those individuals). But any such biochemical explanation for individual differences says nothing about why such traits apparently translate into criminal behavior more in society A than society B nor why it is that one can be competitive, aggressive, and hedonistic and be perfectly law abiding.

Crime *rates* are emergent properties of sociocultural systems that cannot be deduced from molecular analysis of individuals within them. To assert that they can, a biochemist would have to show that properties of the whole (society) can be deduced from biochemical properties of its constituent parts (individuals) and would have to show that these properties differ between societies A and B. In other words, the biochemist must possess a suitable theory making it possible to analyze the form and nature of the whole as having been derived from the properties of biochemical units of analysis. No such theory exists. Thus, the phenomenon which is to be explained (crime rates) can be adequately explained sociologically, adequately explained psychologically given the proviso that sociocultural variables are acknowledged, and not explained at all by biochemistry. The line separating sociology and psychology is fuzzy with regard to this question, but the line separating sociology and biochemistry is clear and sharp.

Because discipline lines are sharp with regard to some questions, it does not mean that cross-disciplinary lines of communication are closed with regard to other questions. Biosociology believes that the social and behavioral sciences are continuous with biology in the same way that biology is continuous with chemistry and chemistry with physics. Others like to draw sharp lines and erect high fences between "their" science and its neighbors regardless of the form in which a particular research question is posed. The drawers of sharp lines invoke the notion of emergence or holism—the notion that wholes constitute higher levels of organization, the properties of which are not considered predictable from properties found at lower levels of organization. It is undeniable that there are many emergent phenomena possessing properties which are far more complex than the sum of their parts, but what constitutes a "whole" depends on the discipline—one science's holism is another's reductionism. The issue of whether principles relating to one discipline are reducible to the principles of another is entirely an empirical one. To decide the issue on any other basis is to dishonor the spirit of science.

At one time or another in the history of science, representatives of each science on August Comte's "hierarchy of science" ladder, conscious of the emergent nature of the phenomena they study, have attempted to disassociate their science from the "reductionism" of the more basic sciences. As the most basic of the sciences, physics alone has been free of the reductionist phobia. The maturity of this discipline may be gauged from its lack of ambivalence in viewing matter from both the most micro of microsystems (subatomic particles) and the most macro of macrosystems (the cosmos).

Chemistry was the first to suffer and to be cured of antireductionism. Nineteenth-century chemist Benjamin Brodie, fearful of the intrusion of physicists and their new-fangled ideas about things called "atoms" into his discipline, made a case for limiting chemical explanations to qualitative and gravimetric changes in chemical compounds on the grounds that there are emergent properties possessed by those compounds considered not to be predictable a priori from their constituent parts (Harre, 1967:290). Brodie wanted an "atomless" chemistry, and the overwhelming majority of the London Chemical Society of the 1870s were in agreement. But where are the Brodian chemists today? What area, theory, or hypothesis about chemical reactions in any way violates the elegant laws of physics, the very foundation and backbone of modern chemistry?

Biology has a similar history of attempting to maintain discipline autonomy, particularly from the encroachment of molecular biology, whose founders brought with them the arcane methods of physics, their parent discipline. As late as the 1940s, J. H. Woodger (1948) argued, à la Emile Durkheim, that biological phenomena should not be reduced to the concepts of physics and chemistry and that biologists should only use biological facts to explain other biological facts. Life, the subject matter of biology, must surely be the quintessential example of emergence; for the step from the inorganic to the organic is the most momentous discontinuity in all science. Life is certainly something more than the arrangement of amino acid chains wound around the fine symmetry of the carbon atom, and to describe it requires a specific biological vocabulary not found in physics or chemistry. As we know, the decoding of the "language of life" by Watson and Crick was not achieved by adhering to the various doctrines of biological ontological autonomy but rather by an exploration of the structure and chemistry of the DNA molecule.

Early twentieth-century psychology, under the leadership of John Watson and in response to the naïve instinctualism of the time, attempted to exorcise biology from the discipline. It was asserted that behavior could best be examined and explained in its own right with reference to stimulus–response connections and contingencies of reinforcement. Although B. F. Skinner (1966) was the strongest modern advocate of this position, he used the evolutionary model to explain the "whys" behind the acquisition of operant behaviors. He realized that the ease or difficulty of acquiring operant behaviors, and the selection of what stimuli we will pay attention to, has its roots in the biology of the species, particularly in neural structures of the human brain–mind formed overwhelmingly in the 1.5- to 2.0-million-year Pleistocene epoch (Symons, 1992).

Nevertheless, psychology, especially behaviorism, underwent a period in which concepts such as desire, motivation, intelligence, consciousness, and so on were relegated to the realm of metaphysics. But being aware that humans do think, learn, and desire, psychologists soon realized that if they were to comprehend these mechanisms, they would have to open up the "black box" and explore neurophysiological mechanisms underlying these activities. A perusal of modern psychology textbooks will reveal the major shift that has taken place in psychology over the past two decades with respect to integrating biology into psychological theories. Psychology is a more exact science today than it was in the heyday of radical environmentalism because of its marriage to biology, just as biology and chemistry became more exact when they embraced their former scientific bugbears. Many of the new generation of psychologists appear to agree that not to consider evolutionary biology when proposing a psychological concept is to neglect the guidance of a theoretical compass that has elegantly demonstrated its predictive power time and again.[2]

Atop the hierarchy-of-science ladder sits the acrophobic sociologist, afraid to look down. Alone among the sciences, sociology has decided that the path of least resistance lies in ignoring the basic sciences. Like ancient cartographers, sociologists too often draw bad maps delineating social science boundaries "beyond which there be monsters." Jeffery (1979:8) points out that "some of the biggest names in political science, economics, anthropology, psychology, and psychiatry are now involved in biological issues. Only sociology stands out as an opponent of biological systems."[3] The discipline still reveres Durkheim's dictum that explanations of social facts should be sought in other social facts and nowhere else. It was (and is) argued that society is sui generis, uncaused and unrelated by any lower phenomenal levels. Social facts must necessarily be part of the picture explaining other social facts (indeed, some social facts are important to understanding some biological facts), but they cannot shoulder the burden alone. If social science is to become more than a set of ad hoc moral philosophies, we must file Durkheim's dictum alongside Woodger's in the historical archives. As Whitney (1990:144) has pointed out, "Knowledge in general has moved well beyond the point where it was scientifically reasonable to limit causal studies in sociology to social–environmental variables."

While the deductive pyramid of reductionism, a pyramid in which each level incorporates the findings of the level beneath it, appears to be the most fruitful method of scientific progress, it is not without its pitfalls. Just as comprehensive holistic theories have a disconcerting lack of precision, precise reductionist theories have a disconcerting (at least for sociologists) lack of comprehensiveness. There are radical reductionists just as there are radical lovers of holism. A radical reductionist sees an additive chain of causal events running up the causal ladder from molecules to human behavior, even to complex social organizations. One such reductionist has stated emphatically, "Our behavior is controlled by molecules—by nothing else" (Applewhite, 1981:1). Applewhite's claim is made on the basis that we are composed of molecules, that there is no "we" apart from the molecules that compose us, and so our behavior must be the result of some molecules moving around other molecules.

This sort of thinking is just as naïve as the radical environmentalist's claim that our behavior is controlled by our experiences—and by nothing else. Viewing "we," our lives, and our behavior as little more than the movement of molecules conceals higher-order (holistic) explanations that have greater generality and utility. Applewhite's own "we are composed of" argument can be used against itself, for molecules are themselves "composed of." He limits his reductionism to the molecular level because he is a molecular biologist. Were he a physicist, he might have pointed out that molecules are emergent entities composed of two or more atoms (which are themselves "composed of") held together by nonphysical forces. Were a particle physicist so inclined, he or she might claim that our behavior is controlled by nonmaterial cosmic forces—and by nothing else.

Applewhite's extreme reductionism (a kind of reductionism rejected by most philosophers of science today) implies that the DNA molecule is a directions operative that functions in the same rigidly determined way regardless of the organism's experience. Yet we know that genes are "switched" on and off in response to environmental challenges (Kandel, 1983) and that functional connections between brain nerve cells are very much dependent on environmental input (Kalil, 1989). Alterations in structure and function resulting from experience may even occur at the molecular level (Goelet, Castellucci, Schacher, & Kandel, 1986). Although it may sound trite, it is nevertheless true that many phenomena simply cannot be explained at all by reference to reductionist propositions. The meaning of a poem cannot be deduced from an examination of the individual words and letters from which it is composed. While there can be no poem without letters or the sounds they denote, the meaning of the poem lies in their distinctive relationship to one another. On another level, I know that when the sum of the water molecules gyrating in my teakettle at sea level reaches 100 degrees Celsius (212 degrees Fahrenheit), I shall have my cup of tea; but I would lose coherence were I to try to translate this information about temperature (an emergent property of aggregate molecules) into the motion of individual molecules.

The history of science generally shows that higher-order theories and explanations of scientific phenomena were in place before the mechanisms underlying them were discovered and elucidated. Newtonian physics preceded atomic physicics, and Mendelian genetics preceded molecular genetics. Useful observations and hypotheses in these fields now go in both reductionist and emergent directions. Natural scientists have long recognized the complementarity of reductionist and holistic explanations. Cell biologists know that, at bottom, they are dealing with subatomic "energy packets" and seek to understand their properties. But they also know that there are properties of the cell that cannot be deduced from them a priori and that we require functional explanations of the whole cell and even how that cell fits into a network of other cells to form a larger whole (the organism). Science is eclectic by nature, and it can pose questions and offer explanations at several levels of understanding.

Sociology will find it profitable to emulate the more mature sciences and learn from the principles and data offered by them. When and how much to take will be dictated by research agendas. It is realized that even a complete description and understanding of the genetic, hormonal, and neurological bases of complex behavior would not constitute a complete understanding of that behavior-absent knowledge of cultural setting and of motives, purposes, and phenomenolgy of the individual actor. Propositions about genes, hormones, and neurons do not contain terms that help define the human condition at its most meaningful level—terms such as *love, hate, justice, good,* and *evil.* Therefore, biological propositions cannot, by any stretch, be considered the only ones needed to make moral, psychological, or social statements containing such terms. This observation, however, does not disqualify biological propositions from participating in efforts to elucidate the substance of those terms; and social science explanations, even if making no reference to reductionist entities, must not violate them. Stated otherwise, while the old saw, "The whole is greater than the sum of its parts," is almost always true, what we say about the nature of the whole must be consistent with the known nature of the parts.

BIOSOCIOLOGY AND HUMAN NATURE

Every science has its central concepts (e.g., atoms, ions, genes, IQ, social class) and tries to elucidate their nature. These concepts are rarely defined to the satisfaction of everyone, especially in the early stages of development, although broad consensus is eventually reached in the hard sciences. A key concept necessarily shared by all social and behavioral sciences is human nature. When we speak of the "nature" of concepts, we are speaking about the substance of the empirical reality to which they refer. To be aware of the nature of something is to be aware of its essential inherent properties, its constituent parts, the extent and limits of its potentiality, the things it can and cannot do under a variety of conditions, and the distinguishing features that separate it from all other things that are "not it." The nature of everything from asteroids to zebras is open to this kind of matter-of-fact understanding, and, in principle, so should human nature.

Such a statement is anathema for many social scientists among whom it has been fashionable for a long time to embrace the existentialist notion that there is no human nature (thus making human beings the only objects among all animate or inanimate entities in the universe about which this has been said). Exotic anthropological accounts of tribal societies whose practices (at least as reported) were radically at odds with Western practices led to a conception of culture as distinct from nature, that is, free from the reductionist psychobiological influences of its individual members. "Culture" and "society" came to be viewed as supraindividual entities existing sui generis. These reified autonomous entities were seen as shaping human nature by pouring their contents into empty organisms. More precisely, there was no "nature" until this process occurred; and thus, there are as many "human natures" as there are cultures.

Any alternative to this view (e.g., human nature shapes culture) has been stoutly resisted by social scientists against an increasing number of their colleagues who have rejected the sui generis hypothesis. "Whatever the motive may be for resisting the idea that there is a human nature whose features shape culture and society," writes anthropologist Donald Brown, "its intellectual foundations have all but collapsed" (1991:144). Brown, trained in the Boas–Benedict–Mead tradition of cultural relativism, began to question it after he wagered with Donald Symons that he could find exceptions to the panhuman sex differences stressed in Symons's works. Brown lost the bet and "began to think more carefully about human universals, cultural relativism, and, especially, about the role that human biology plays in human affairs" (Brown, 1991:vii).[4]

None of this is to say that culture does not mold individuals in many diverse ways or that cultures and societies are not to some extent autonomous "higher-order" entities. "Culture is not simply psychology, not even evolutionary psychology, 'writ large.' We still need the social sciences" (Barkow, 1991:635). Cultural experiences probably account for the overwhelming proportion of variance in behavioral differences between cultures, and its influence is ubiquitous. But as Barkow (1991:635) further points out, "Psychology underlies culture and society, and biological evolution underlies psychology." Even though human nature is logically prior to culture, it does not follow that culture is "nothing but" the product of evolutionary pressures impinging on individual organisms to form social bonds and to acquire language. This is undoubtedly true at some level, but eons of living in cultures have produced culture's own evolutionary pressures helping to form human nature.

This does not return us to a cultural relativism that asserts that *all* human activities can only be understood relative to the cultural context in which they take place. Human beings, by virtue of the finite range of capacities and potentials imposed by their common physiology and requirements of survival and reproduction, have evolved a set of mechanisms common to all cultures. We call this set of common mechanisms "human nature." The activities that are important to human beings everywhere can be explained via a common human nature; the numerous embellishments accompanying these activities require cultural explanations. Human flexibility means flexibility of means, not ends. For instance, courtship patterns, moral responses to cuckoldry, unwed motherhood, and pre- and extramarital relationships are richly understood in their specifics in terms of cultural history and current environmental contingencies; but the fact that they are ubiquitous concerns obligates us to explore beyond culture to evolved mechanism of human nature. Male–female differences with respect to the attitudes and behaviors enumerated earlier, because they are universal, are also best understood by reference to the evolutionary forces that produced them and the sex-differentiated psychophysiology that perpetuates them.

"BIOLOGICAL DETERMINISM"

The history of science demonstrates time and again that the various disciplines tried to stake out autonomous territory in their infancy, showed a grudging acceptance of the data of the more mature sciences in their adolescence, and came to accept reductionism as a fruitful path to progress in their adulthood. This Hegelian interplay of thesis, antithesis, and synthesis has produced such positive results that one wonders why sociology is so reluctant to follow the example set for it. Perhaps it is because of the confusion surrounding the concepts of reductionism and determinism (Fisher, 1991). Determinism is commonly understood in science to be nothing more sinister than the assumption that every event stands in some causal relationship to other events. To attack determinism in this sense is to attack any theory of causation and the business of science itself. (What would *not* being a determinist imply for a scientist?) Some sociologists do attack determinism in this sense, believing that an ontologically different set of principles (mentalism) is necessary to explain the nature of human behavior. Humanity transcends the "natural" world by virtue of this mentalism, thus placing it beyond the scope of science, which is a method of describing and explaining events as they occur in the natural world. Those with such beliefs would be happier in the humanities.

No scientist qua scientist denies determinism in the cause–effect sense, but we do argue about what the causes are that bring about the events and thus what brand of "determinism" we are for or against. Many sociologists believe that to posit any biological influence at all on a behavioral trait is biological determinism. Critics of biological determinism are not uniform in what they mean when they invoke the label; there are strong and weak meanings attached to it. The strong form is exemplified by Val Woodward, who defined it as "the view that the social practices born out of the view that individual and societal behavior are *direct* outcomes of genetic programs" (1992:227, emphasis added). Woodward is against such a biological determinism, but who would not be? Such a straw-man definition implies that genes absolutely determine an organism's behavior, regardless of environmental input. It also implies that a biosocial scientist would make strong statements such as: "In the presence of biological factor x, behavior y *will* occur" (i.e., $rxy = 1.0$).

Except under circumstances of extreme biological disability (e.g., Down's syndrome, brain tumors, and so forth), he or she would not.

A softer definition is supplied by Gordon Edlin, who defines it as "the idea that the attitudes and behaviors of human society are due more to biology than its cultural history" (1990:375). In contrast to Woodward's deterministic (one might say "fatalistic") definition, Edlin's is more a probabilistic definition in line with reality. A scientist working with this soft definition might make a statement like "In the presence of biological factor x, the *probability* that y will occur increases" (i.e., $rxy > 0 < 1$). This is a proposition to be empirically tested against competing causes of x. It may turn out that indeed "biology" accounts for more variance in a given behavior or trait than "cultural history," but that is an empirical question—a hypothesis to be tested and not something to be assumed. This view of determinism leaves ample room even for the expression of free will ("mentalism"?), a concept that Nobel Prize–winning neuroscientist Gerald Edelman (1992) believes is permitted and predicted from his "reductionist" studies of neuronal development.

Although it is a common misconception, there is no such thing as a single unified "biological approach." David Buss (1990) points out that there are three distinct modes of analysis within the broader biosocial approach to the study of human behavior: the evolutionary, behavioral genetic, and psychophysiological approaches. These approaches employ different methods, have different and often competing (but not logically inconsistent) theories about their observations, and work with different units of analysis and levels of causation (ultimate, distal, and proximate). What they all have in common is the potential to illuminate the study of human nature and the social life that flows from it.

It is not proposed here that biological thinking *replace* traditional social science thinking, only that it can inform and enhance it. A biologically informed sociology no more reduces the discipline to gross biological determinism than an economically informed sociology reduces it to gross economic determinism. Biology will not "cannibalize" sociology and leave it adrift without a role. As has been the case in other sciences, the integration of data from the more basic disciplines will breathe life into sociology and provide it with a cascade of new research questions. We certainly need new research ideas; for unlike most other disciplines claiming scientific status, our direction, concepts, and theories have changed little over the past fifty years, as a perusal of the substance of our textbooks from then and now will attest.[5]

An example of a recent piece of sociological research in which an important issue was illuminated by biology would be useful here. The piece was concerned with the antecedents of adolescent sexual behavior (Udry, 1988). Udry's criterion variable was a seven-item composite measure of sexuality, which included behavioral (coitus) and attitudinal measures. A number of hormonal and social measures were taken from adolescent subjects who were between 13 and 16 years of age. Udry generated three comparative models predicting sexuality: sociological, biological, and biosocial. The adjusted r^2 values for these models for boys and girls are presented in Table 1.1.

In both cases, the sociological model accounted for more variance in sexuality than did the biological model; but the biosocial models represent a considerable improvement in r^2 values over both. The boy's biosocial model is dominated by testosterone (T) and sex hormone–binding globulin (SHBG), although "permissiveness" exerted an independent influence almost as strong as T. Age and pubertal development, serving as proxies in the sociological model for variables now directly measured (T and SHBG), dropped out of the biosocial model for boys. The biosocial model for girls was more complex, although again dominated by hormonal measures. Permissiveness was the most important sociopsychological variable in the girl's model also. A 10-percent increase in explained variance in the biosociological models for both boys and girls over the sociological models is gratifying, as is an illumination of the mechanisms by which age and pubescent development exert their influences via hormone levels.

This example provides evidence that the biosociological perspective produces results that are more interesting and useful than either the sociological or biological perspectives alone. Having said that, let me say that biology is not a nostrum for sociology's ills. No one seriously believes that the dense and messy webs that ensnare the moral, economic, and political nature of many social issues will be unwound by substituting a few nucleotides here and there. However, I am in deep agreement with eminent sociologist Gerhard Lenski's remarks to the effect that sociology's "longstanding opposition to efforts to take biological factors into account in the study of human social systems has become an albatross. If we persist in ignoring or, worse yet, de-

Table 1.1
Summary of Udry's Three Models Predicting Sexuality

	Boys			Girls		
	r^2	N	Number of Variables*	r^2	N	Number of Variables
Sociological	.49	93	5	.32	94	3
Biological	.47	97	2	.14	74	4
Biosociological	.59	97	3	.42	97	7

Source: Adapted from Udry (1988).

*Number of variables retained in the models at p < .05.

nying the powerful influence of genetic and biochemical factors, we jeopardize sociology's credibility in the scientific community" (1977:73).

THE ETHICAL AND MORAL CONCERNS
OF ANTIREDUCTIONISTS

It may be true that most sociologists reject reductionist (biological) explanations not so much on epistomological grounds as on ideological or ethical grounds. Those who reject the encroachment of biology into sociology envision the ghosts of the likes of Lombroso, Spencer, the eugenicists, and the social Darwinists, along with Hitler's hordes of racial purists, marching silently in the data.[6] Because these folks drank from the same well as modern biosociologists, it does not mean that the well is poisoned. Early attempts to link biology to social processes did lead to a number of erroneous and reckless conclusions, either by accident or design. Sociology led the fight against these reckless purveyors of reactionary and racist philosophies that found their theoretical sustenance in the biology of the period. Sociology became the self-appointed conscience of science and took on an advocacy role on the part of the oppressed and underprivileged in society.

Because sociologists tend to view the disadvantaged and the deviant as basically "normal folk" who have fallen afoul of unjust social conditions, they view any kind of biological explanation as diverting attention from the ideological agenda of ameliorating those conditions. Much good has come from their stance, and they are to be applauded for taking it. Such advocacy should and must continue, but it should not be confused with science nor used to stifle ideologically "unapproved" research. Unfortunately, such censorship is apparently alive and well. The Grand Inquisitors of science were successful recently in convincing the National Institutes of Health (NIH) to cancel grant monies for a conference on "Genetic Factors in Crime," sponsored by the University of Maryland. Wheeler (1992:A8) comments on the gloating of the latter-day Lysenkos: "The critics are celebrating the meeting's cancellation but say that many other similar research and policy initiatives by the federal government still need to be halted." This affront to the spirit of science is all the worse, coming as it did from individuals wishing to be called scientists. If these individuals are afraid of following the data wherever they lead them and of the open free-for-all of science, they should get out of the scientific kitchen and take their ideology to the pulpit.

The scientific and social justice agendas should not be considered antagonists: "Ignorance of biological processes," writes Rossi (1987:65), "may doom efforts at social change because we misidentify the targets for change, and hence our means to achieve the change we desire." Scarr and Weinberg (1978:690) augment Rossi, commenting that "naive environmentalism has led us to an intervention fallacy. By assuming that all of the variance in behavior was environmentally determined, we have blithely promised a world of change that we have not delivered, at great costs to the participants, the public, and ourselves." Our efforts will continue to be misdirected (and costly in both human and financial terms) as long as we allow ourselves to be intimidated by those who oppose open inquiry and who have a tendency to substitute ad hominem arguments for reasoned debate. Chilling invectives like "racist" or "sexist" are all too often thrown at anyone daring to write about race and sex differnces from a biological point of view. Yet we must not be intimidated into silence, for "science is in desperate need of good studies that highlight race and gender variables unabashedly" (Scarr, 1988:56). We cannot allow sociology to ossify into a politically correct orthodoxy that places taboos on research that may produce results it may find inconvenient and uncomfortable. Political correctness has no more a place in today's science than religious correctness had in science in the time of Copernicus or Darwin.

We should remind ourselves that radical environmentalism has done more to damage the human spirit than any claims of national or racial superiority buttressed by dishonest science. Gordon (1980) stresses that genocidal behavior has most often been directed against groups who were intellectually superior to their oppressors, and E. Wilson (1978a:301) points out that the belief in the unlimited malleability of human nature has served to support the most reactionary and inhumane of social systems (e.g., communist attempts to forge the "new Russian/Chinese/Cambodian man"). Only pseudoscience is capable of doing the same kind of damage to the human spirit done by advocates of the "empty organism" vision of human nature. History has showed us time and again that the only cure for pseudoscience is honest science but that the cure for ideological infection usually requires bloodshed. To maintain a conspiracy of scientific silence around sensitive issues that have been illuminated by biology is to default to ideologues whose conclusions all too often precede their inquiry.

Lest one has the impression that the question of integrating biology into the social sciences necessarily involves a liberal–conservative split, it should be pointed out that while the political left in the United States has repudiated sociobiology, it has been enthusiastically embraced by the French political left as a sort of neo-Rousseauism (Degler, 1991:319). Degler (1991:310–320) also points out that well-known radicals such as Herbert Marcuse and Noam Chomsky assume an innate human nature; that Karl Marx himself called for an integration of the social and natural sciences; and that social scientists such as Alice Rossi, Melvin Konner, and Alan Mazur, known for their liberal views, are vocal champions of the biosocial approach. Most biosocial scientists began with a traditional social science education and found it wanting. This has nothing to do with political ideology, but it has much to do with wanting to be the best scientist one is capable of being. It is painful to repudiate that which one has spent many years assimilating; those that do so, almost by definition, must be among the most fully committed to the scientific enterprise and to the viability of their discipline. Such scientists are *reformers*, not "apostates" or "heretics."

Alice Rossi (1984), a sociologist with a marked biosocial inclination, called for the integration of biological thinking into sociological theories in her 1983 American Sociological Association (ASA) presidential address. Lester Ward, the first president of the ASA (wisely changed from the American Sociological Society after acronyms became trendy), was a biologist, a Darwinian whose views were diametrically opposed to the social Darwinists and eugenicists. He viewed biology not as limiting individuals, as the social Darwinists and eugenicists did, but as a progressive force which is stifled by the social environment (Degler, 1991). It was Ward who led the fight against the fad of biological analogizing among social thinkers such as Herbert Spencer, Walter Bagehot, and William Graham Sumner; and it was he who so thoroughly discredited the primitive behavioral biology of his time that most sociologists since his time have dismissed all biology as irrelevant.

But sociologist Michael Teitelbaum (1976:17) points out that "the pendulum swung to the other extreme—from facile arguments by analogy to facile dismissal of theory and evidence." Social scientists continue to fight the same old battles against the same old foes, ignoring the fact that the biology of Rossi's time is light years more advanced than it was in Ward's time. Genetics, for instance, is advancing at a dizzying pace. What today's geneticists can contribute to our understanding of human behavior is a far cry from feeling cranial bumps and measuring foreheads. Those who hurl the gauntlet at nineteenth-century biology are fighting battles in wars long ago won: What modern chemist quotes Brodie? What modern geologist resurrects Bishop Ussher as a straw man when discussing plate tectonics? The evidence confronting the detractors of biosocial theory is strong, it cannot be countered with cliches, ad hominem arguments, anecdotes, and straw men. Even Stephen Jay Gould, in many ways an ardent opponent of sociobiology, argues that it is wrong to view it as a theory motivated by a political agenda. He goes on to opine that if the social sciences find sociobiology wanting, "They must find and use a more adequate evolutionary biology, not reject proffered aid and genuine partnership" (Gould, 1991:51). In this "Decade of the Brain, the Human Genome Project, and the Human Genome Diversity Project," writes Sandra Scarr (1993:1350), "it is too late for social scientists to prevent advances in genetic knowledge. Perhaps becoming more educated on the potentially positive uses of such information will allay some fears."

Biosociology is decidedly not about pitting nature against nurture. Rather, it looks at nature *via* nurture, an approach that appears to excite biological scientists more than social scientists. As Rossi (1977:7) remarks, "Researchers in the biological sciences have gone further in incorporating social variables into their research than the social sciences have gone in incorporating physiological variables into theirs, with the ironic consequence that there is more evidence to support the importance of social variables in the biological literature than there is evidence to reject the evidence of physiological variables in the sociological literature." This is a situation that a shift to the biosocial perspective can rectify.

As a social scientist, I must concur with Wilson's (1990:260) epigraph to this chapter: The content of the social sciences is potentially richer than that of biology; but before we can beggar the relevant ideas of biology, we must first absorb them. This does pose problems, not the least of which is the necessity to learn much biology, which may deter many individual social scientists from taking that first step. Those who do hurdle the obstacles of inertia and ideology will find the intellectual challenge most exciting. They will find, as have many others before them, that there is nothing inherently inimical to the social sciences to be found within the framework of biosociology. (There may be an awful lot that is inimical to social ideology, however.) Perhaps the majority of the current cohort of sociologists will remain closed to the arguments for hierarchical integration; but as a discipline, sociology must begin to encourage and require its graduate students to become comfortable with biological science. If we do not and continue to defer to the biological sciences in the study of human behavior, we may find one day that the rest of the scientific community regards us with the same condescension that is today reserved for "scientific" creationists.

NOTES

1. Contrary to its many critics, sociobiology has nothing to do with "genetic determinism." The father of sociobiology penned the epigraph of this paper; and he also wrote, "Human behavior is dominated by culture in the sense that the greater part, perhaps all, of the variation between societies is based on cultural experience. But this is not to say that human beings are infinitely plastic. . . . Assisted by sociobiological analyses, a stronger social science might develop. An exciting collaboration between biologists and social scientists appears to have begun" (E. Wilson, 1978b:xiv).

2. Comte included astronomy and excluded psychology in his hierarchy. He believed the psychology of his time to be in the metaphysical stage of development. Because psychology has long ago embraced positivism and because astronomy has been absorbed by physics, I take the liberty of amending Comte's hierarchy.

3. Indicative of Jeffery's statement are the number of journals born in the late 1970s or early 1980s integrating the biological and sociocultural sciences (e.g., *Ethology and Sociobiology, Human Nature, Behavioral and Brain Sciences, Behavioural Neurology, Journal of Social and Biological Structure, Journal of Biosocial Science, Politics and the Life Sciences*). Also indicative of his statement is the paucity of sociologists contributing to these journals.

4. Brown's (1991) work is an attack on biologically irrelevant notions of culture via the examination of cultural universals. He shows how many of the most prominent arguments that cultural relativists have relied on have been systematically demolished over the years. He concentrates on (1) arbitrary color classification, (2) the nonexistence of stress among Samoan adolescents, (3) sex-role reversal among the Tchambuli, (4) arbitrary facial expressions, (5) the Hopi conception of time, and (6) the nonuniversality of the Oedipus complex. For those of us professionally nurtured on many of these concepts, Brown's book presents a real challenge.

5. Zald (1991:178) points out that other scientists do not read the early "masters" of their disciplines (Newton, Mendel, etc.) as research guides to the solutions to current problems but that sociologists continue to read Marx, Weber, and Durkheim as "sacred texts."

6. Early eugenics programs in the United States and Britain were endorsed as humane and sensible by many moral-minded and progressive individuals such as Karl Pearson, George Bernard Shaw, Sidney and Beatrice Webb, and Oliver Wendell Holmes. "Eugenics" gained its negative connotation when it became associated with the Nazis and their "racial purity" programs.

Chapter 2

Genetics and Human Behavior

> Some people are disturbed by the idea that genes can influence behavior.
> They don't understand the workings of genes and probably picture them
> as master puppeteers within us, pulling our strings.
> —R. Plomin, J. DeFries, & G. McClearn

To assess the degree of literacy among physicists and geologists in scientific
areas other than their own, Hazen and Trefil (1991) asked a number of them
if they could explain the difference between DNA and RNA, a very basic
piece of biological information. Only 12.5 percent could do so. Because DNA
and RNA have no bearing on the phenomena studied by most physical scientists, they can be excused for their ignorance. Such ignorance among those
who study human behavior is less easily excused. Even those who deny genetic influence on complex behaviors should know what it is they are denying; but from the tone of many social science critics of behavioral genetic
research, it is plain that they do not (Cohen, 1987). A reviewer of one of my
works on crime and genetics (Walsh, 1992) rejected my manuscript with the
following words: "It is just not possible for genes to be implicated in socially
defined behavior such as crime. This is blaming the victim and genetic fasism
[*sic*]." This is often the kind of response one gets to "politically incorrect" works
(see Scarr, 1981; Rushton, 1990b, on the politics of publishing such works).

It is a common assumption among behavioral geneticists that their understanding of genetic influences on behavior cannot be fruitful "without considering the complementary influence of the environment" (Goldsmith,
1994:326). Unfortunately, the opposite assumption is not common among
sociologists. Ever since the historic schism between sociology and biology,

most sociologists seem to recoil instinctively when genetics is mentioned. Sociologists seem to labor under the erroneous notion that genetically influenced traits are fixed and immutable; and thus, to acknowlege genetic influence on behavior is to invite programatic nihilism.[1]

The typical social scientist may also be daunted by the intellectually demanding and somewhat arcane nature of genetics. (I wonder how many social scientists could explain the difference between DNA and RNA.) Given the special interests of social scientists, it is neither necessary nor practical to acquire a broad knowledge of genetics to understand how genes influence our behavior. All that is needed is a basic knowledge of elementary molecular genetics and a firm grasp of the concepts and methods of behavioral genetics. I optimistically predict that such knowledge will one day be an integral part of the education of sociologists; for today, "The question is no longer whether but how genes influence behavior" (McGue, Bacon, & Lykken, 1993:107). This chapter provides a brief overview of these subjects with the hope that it will "demystify" this fascinating field.

MENDELIAN GENETICS

The practical principles of heredity have been known for centuries. Plato's *Republic* (1960: book V) contains a dialog pertaining to what we would today call artificial selection, and it even hints that nature might act in the same selective manner on humans. The ancients knew much about breeding, but no one knew how nature managed to maintain such consistency across the generations or what exactly it was that was passed down. This began to change with the work of an Austrian monk named Gregor Mendel (1822–1884), whose painstaking observations of the common garden pea in a monastery garden gave birth to the science of genetics. The principles of heredity discovered by Mendel are elegantly simple.

In his experiments, Mendel noticed that the physical characteristics of his peas (size, color, shape) remained relatively constant over the generations and that a trait occasionally disappeared and reemerged several generations later. He noted that tall plants always produced tall offspring and that short plants always produced short offspring. He also found that if he crossed a tall plant with a short one, all interbred plants were tall. Mendel deduced from this that tallness was *dominant* over shortness in peas. When he interbred his tall–short hybrids he found that about one-fourth of the offspring were short. Further interbreeding revealed that about one-third of the tall hybrids produced only talls, while the other two-thirds produced both short and tall plants in a 3:1 ratio. Crossbreeding two short hybrid plants always produced short offspring. From this, Mendel deduced that the shortness trait is not lost in interbreeding; rather, it is a *recessive* trait that can only be expressed in the absence of the dominant trait.

Mendel concluded that each plant contained two "factors" (one from each parent plant) for a particular trait and that these two factors are transmitted to offspring in statistically predictable ways. We now know that the chromosomes of organisms come in pairs and carry the units of hereditary Mendel called factors, which we now call genes. Each gene on a chromosome has a corresponding gene on the other paired chromosome and are thus said to occupy the same *locus*. Alternate forms of genes that can occupy the same locus are called *alleles*, one of which may be dominant over the other. One such alternate form is the allele for the height trait, one for tallness (T) and the other for shortness (t). When the parent organism produces sex cells during meiosis, the two genes controlling a trait segregate (separate again) and each sex cell receives only one of the genes. When the genes from male and female gametes are combined, the new organism has a new combination of alleles—a new genotype. This separation and recombination process is formalized as Mendel's first law: the principle of segregation.

Since crossbred pea plants receive one gene for a particular trait from each parent plant—height in the present example—there are four possible combinations of alleles produced in a breeding of hybrids: TT, Tt, tT, and tt. The first three pairings will produce only tall offspring because tallness is dominant over shortness; the latter pairing of two recessive alleles will produce, in the absence of the dominant allele (T), only short offspring. Individuals with two identical alleles (TT or tt) are said to be *homozygous*, and those with two variant alleles (Tt or tT) are said to be *heterozygous*.

In addition to the principle of segregation, Mendel gave us the principle of independent assortment. This principle tells us that members of one pair of genes do not influence the way in which other pairs are distributed. They combine and recombine completely independent of one another. In other words, the alleles for one trait (e.g., tallness versus shortness) sort out independent of the alleles for another trait (e.g., smoothness versus wrinkledness). This law also tells us that the units of hereditary are discrete (either–or) and do not blend to produce something intermediary, such as a medium-sized plant that is part smooth and part wrinkled. This nonblending transmission functions to maintain genetic variability.

If we take the two traits of tallness and smoothness and plot them on a Punnett square (Figure 2.1), we see the possible number of genotypes for height and smoothness produced according to the principle of independent assortment. Each cell represents one genotype, that is, what alleles, considered two at a time, the plant has for the two traits. There are sixteen possible genotypes from which we observe four different phenotypes (i.e., the physical appearance of the plant) in a ratio of 9:3:3:1.

This example is an extremely simple one, consisting of only two genes controlling two traits. If we were dealing with alleles for ten different traits, we would have 1,084,576 different genotypes, which, according the Mendel's

Figure 2.1
All Possible Genotypes for Height and Smoothness in a Dihybrid Cross

```
                          Gamete 1.
Gamete 2.
                  TS        Ts        tS        ts

        TS      TTSS      TTSs      TtSS      TtSs

        Ts      TTsS      TTss      TtsS      Ttss

        tS      tTSS      tTSs      ttSS      ttSs

        ts      tTsS      tTss      ttsS      ttss
```

　　　　16 Genotypes　　　　　　　　　　　4 Phenotypes

1 TTSS + 2 TTSs + 2 TtSS + 4 TtSs =　9 tall and smooth
1 TTss + 2 Ttss　　　　　　　　　　 =　3 tall and wrinkled
1 ttSS + 2 ttSs　　　　　　　　　　 =　3 short and smooth
1 ttss　　　　　　　　　　　　　　　 =　1 short and wrinkled

9:3:3:1 ratio, would produce 1,024 different phenotypes. There may be as many as 100,000 genes in the human genome, with a considerable proportion segregating for two or more alleles, thus providing for "astronomical numbers of genotypes" (Plomin, DeFries, & McClearn, 1980:37). Add to this genetic variability the almost unlimited environmental variability affecting the phenotype and we can appreciate the uniqueness of each and every one of us.

CELLS AND CHROMOSOMES

Although Mendel had taken the giant first step in the science of genetics, he had no idea of the chemistry or architecture of the "factors" that were the units of heredity. Until the late nineteenth century, it was not fully appreciated that all living things are made up of cells and the products of cells. Some organisms, such as protozoa, consist of only one cell; human beings have trillions of them. The cell is a chemical factory in which almost all functions essential to life—energy production, growth, reproduction, responsiveness to stimuli—are carried out. With the exception of the sex cells, all cells carry the complete genetic information that an organism possesses. The only parts of the cell that need concern us here are the cytoplasm (a jellylike substance in which the various cell parts float) ribosomes, and the nucleus. The genes are found on chromosomes within the cell nucleus.

A cell, like its parent organism, is born, grows, matures, reproduces, and dies. Cells continually reproduce until their host organism attains maturity, after which they specialize for a particular body task. Cells reproduce in a process called *mitosis*. Human beings have forty-six chromosomes in each cell—twenty-three pairs, one of each pair coming from each parent. Twenty-two of these chromosome pairs are called *autosomes*, or body chromosomes; the other pair are called *sex chromosomes*. The autosomes are homologous ("same-shaped"); the sex chromosomes are homologous in the case of females, who have two X chromosomes (XX), but are not in males, who have one X chromosome paired with a Y (XY). During the process of mitosis, the membranes around the nucleus dissolve and the chromosomes line up in pairs and are then tugged apart as the cell divides. This ensures that each daughter cell gets a complete set of chromosomes that are exact duplicates of the parent cell. Body cells having two of each kind of chromosome are called diploid cells.

The one exception to this process occurs in the sex cells (gametes). Gametes have only half the normal number of chromosomes (sex cells are called haploid, in contrast to diploid). Sex cells reproduce themselves via a process called *meiosis*. During the process of meiosis, genes are randomly exchanged between chromosome pairs as they separate. Meiosis consists of two consecutive cell divisions (which produces four new cells rather than two) but just one chromosomal duplication, with each daughter cell having half the complement of chromosomes of the parent cell. When a sperm fertilizes an egg to produce a zygote, the zygote has a full complement of chromosomes, with each chromosome from the sperm matching up with a virtually identical one from the egg. When this occurs, we have a new organism with a unique genetic makeup.

Thus, chromosomes, like genes, come in pairs; and the pairs, with the exception of the male sex chromosomes, are homologous. As is the case with genes, chromosomes retain their identity in hybrids; and they segregate independently. From the similarities of genes and chromosomes, biologists deduced that the many thousands of genes we possess must lie on the chromosomes; and they now know that each gene has a pair of alleles and that these alternate forms of a given gene lie at the same locus (location) on homologous chromosomes.

GENES

At the molecular level a gene is a segment of DNA (deoxyribonucleic acid) that encodes the amino acid sequence of a protein, or the base sequence of an RNA (ribonucleic acid) molecule. DNA is life itself, having a universal code with each molecule having the same chemical composition and about the same size and shape in every living thing from people to potatoes. It contains all the directions and blueprints, which it issues at the appropriate times to guide and synchronize the organism's operations from conception to death.

The "NA" in DNA and RNA stands for "nucleic acid," so named because it is an acid found in the nucleus of the cell. A single molecule of DNA extends down the entire length of the chromosome and is tightly wrapped around a protein core. The nucleic acids are built from a string of smaller molecules called *nucleotides*. Each nucleotide is built up from a sugar, a phosphate, and a base, which are themselves composed of various combinations of hydrogen, oxygen, phosphorus, and carbon atoms. Nucleotides represent the chemical alphabet of the genetic code, a series of "letters" from which the code will be transcribed. Nucleotides are hooked together by the millions to form a sugar-phosphate spine with a sequence of bases attached to it. The sugar is either ribose (the "R" in RNA) or deoxyribose (the "D" in DNA), with the only chemically structural difference being one less oxygen atom in deoxyribose.

The bases protruding from the sugar–phosphate spine are molecules referred to as nitrogenous bases and are composed of carbon and nitrogen atoms. We can think of these bases—adenine (A), cytosine (C), guanine (G), and thymine (T)—as letters in the alphabet which will be arranged in various ways to form "words" that are chemically read. A and G are purines, and T and C are pyrimidines. The bases can only be arranged according to certain chemical rules that allow hydrogen bonds to form between them. The chemical "shapes" of adenine and thymine are such that they can only bond with each other; the same is true for guanine and cytosine. Thus, there are only four possible bondings for DNA—AT, TA, GC, and CG. Each molecule of DNA contains about 500,000 of these interlocking base pairs. All our traits and characteristics are fashioned from combinations of these four bases because they constitute chemically coded messages that tell the cell how to manufacture protein molecules.

This is the basic chemistry of DNA. The architecture of DNA, the arrangement of the bases giving it the ability to express many genetic messages, is another example of the remarkable efficiency and symmetry of nature. The common metaphor for the DNA model is a spiral staircase, the so-called "double helix" model elucidated by James Watson and Francis Crick in 1952. Think of the paired bases as the "steps" in the staircase, and the sugar–phosphate spine being the "handrails" holding them in place. There is a redundancy of information in the helix; if for some reason the sequence of bases on one side of the chain was to be disturbed, the correct information is still contained in the complementary chain.

All living things must reproduce, and DNA is no exception. DNA replication is much like chromosomal replication during mitosis, and each strand of the helixical staircase contains all the necessary information to replicate the complete staircase. When the DNA is ready to make a copy of itself, the bonds between the bases are pulled apart by enzymes. When enzymes break the base bonds, there are two "handrails" hanging on to unattached bases now exposed to the chemical environment of the cell nucleus, where there are about six billion free-floating nucleotides. When a free-floating nucleotide is attracted to its complement on the exposed handrail, it bonds with it with the help of another kind of specialized enzyme. If the sequence of unbonded bases on the exposed handrail is ATGC, they will be attached to their TACG complements. This process occurs simultaneously on each side of the divided "staircase" so that we end up with two identical double helix molecules in place of one, with each of the old handrails becoming one-half of a new staircase.

The relationship of enzymes to genes should be briefly mentioned. Enzymes are complex proteins made in our cells that produce chemical reactions that either break down or combine other molecules. They are very specialized with respect to the molecules they react with; in general, each enzyme specializes in just one reaction. They work by bringing two specific molecules near each other so that their atoms form bonds. When this is done, the enzyme, which remains unchanged by the process, moves on to repeat the process with another pair of molecules. Just as enzymes are task specialized, they themselves are the products of a single gene coding for a single enzyme. Thus, genes—via enzymes—control the various metabolic activities of the organism.

MAKING PROTEINS

Proteins are large complex molecules composed of chains of amino acids that perform the necessary biological work for all forms of life. Although DNA is confined to inside the cell nucleus, it controls the synthesis of proteins outside the nucleus. The first step in this process is the transcription of DNA into *messenger RNA* (mRNA). Transcription starts with the unwinding of a region of DNA. A molecule of RNA is synthesized by a special enzyme called RNA polymerase in much the same way as new strands of DNA are synthesized. Apart from having ribose instead of deoxyribose as the sugar in its spine, RNA differs from DNA in that it is single stranded and contains far fewer nucleotides. Its nitrogeneous bases are the same except that thymine is replaced by another pyrimidine called uracil (U), which, like T, is complementary to adenine.

When the task of mRNA synthesis is completed, the mRNA leaves the DNA as a faithful transcription of the hereditary code in the nucleus and transmits it to the protein-making machinery in the cytoplasm outside the nucleus. The protein "factory" to which mRNA attaches itself are clusters of tiny particles called ribosomes, which are composed of three different molecules of ribosomal RNA (rRNA). Just as each gene is a chemical code for the production of a specific protein, every ribosome is tailor made for the production of a particular protein. The mRNA is taking the genetic code to the location where this will happen in the form of sequences of nitrogeneous bases. There are twenty "standard" amino acids composed of various arrangements of atoms. Two amino acids combined form a peptide, and longer chains of amino acids are called polypeptides. Each protein made is a precise sequence and number of amino acids, with the "average" protein being a sequence of about 300 of them. Most proteins are enzymes, others are either hormones or the building blocks of cellular structure.

Because there are only four bases, the genetic code must be transmitted according to groupings of bases that can be combined in a rather large variety of ways. Think of this in terms of the Morse code. With just a dot, a dash, and a pause, a Morse code operator can transmit a fully understandable message to someone who knows how to read it. The genetic code is likewise transmitted by a triplet of bases (e.g., CAA, AGC, CCU, etc.). These groupings of three bases are called *codons*, which can be thought of as three-letter words that correspond to particular amino acids. Since there are four bases, there are sixty-four (i.e., $4 \times 4 \times 4$) possible arrangements of triplet bases (codons), more than enough for the coding of the twenty amino acids. A sequence of the codons provides a genetic "sentence," complete with starting and stopping points (capital letters and periods), to make the growing polypeptide.

Just as a Morse code message requires a transmitter and a receiver to translate the message, protein production requires a messenger (mRNA) and translator. Translation of the genetic message requires the cooperation of mRNA, ribosomes, enzymes, and another kind of DNA called *transfer RNA* (tRNA). Like mRNA, tRNA is produced by DNA and migrates from the nucleus into the cytoplasm. There are a number of distinct tRNA molecules, at least one for each of the twenty standard amino acids. With the help of specific enzymes and of an "energizing" molecule called adenosine triphosphate (ATP), molecules of tRNA become attached to specific amino acids. The function of tRNA is to transfer amino acids to the mRNA strands (codons) at the "construction" sites where they will be matched up by ribosomes. The ribosome has already bonded with mRNA and contains chemical "slots" into which tRNA molecules can fit.

A particular mRNA codon can only be matched up with a complementary set of tRNA triplet bases, or its *anticodon*. Visualize the process of manufacturing proteins in terms of zipping up a jacket tooth by tooth. One side of the jacket's teeth is the strand of mRNA, and each tooth is a base-triplet codon. Attached to the teeth on this side of the jacket is the zipper (the ribosome). As yet, there are no teeth on the other side of the jacket. These teeth are brought to the ribosome one at a time by tRNA. With each matching of codon and anticodon, the ribosome zipper moves up one more mRNA codon and another tRNA and its attached amino acid bind on. After transferring its amino acid, the tRNA leaves the site for other tasks. The ribosome moves along in this manner until it encounters a codon for which there is no tRNA with a matching anticodon. This stop signal (an unmatched codon) tells the ribosome that the particular protein has been completed. The completed chain of amino acids is then released by the ribosome, and a new molecule is born. These molecules are then able to carry out their various tasks as enzymes, cell structural proteins, or hormones.

THE ENVIRONMENT AND MODIFICATION OF
ALLELE FREQUENCIES IN POPULATIONS

Molecular genetics stresses the continuity of hereditary information across the generations via the precise self-replication of the DNA molecule. Gene pools have a strong tendency to remain in equilibrium despite the constant shuffling and the different combinations they produce. Yet DNA replication has been going on since life began, and life is infinitely more diverse than it was hundreds of millions of years ago. Human genetic material has undergone a tremendous amount of change over the evolutionary time span, which means that the genetic equilibrium has been frequently disturbed. These genetic changes that provide the variability of life—new species, new kinds of organisms, and new populations—is the domain of population genetics. There are four processes that drive evolutionary change in gene or allele frequencies in living populations: natural selection, mutation, flow, and drift.

Natural selection is the major of the four processes because it causes allelic frequencies in populations to change in response to specific environmental challenges. The other three processes are blind to environmental problems because their action is random with respect to them. Evolution by natural selection acts through genes by selecting traits—which may be physical structures, physiological processes, or behavior patterns—from the existing gene pool that create environmental adaptation. That is, it creates phenotypes better able to survive and reproduce than alternative phenotypes.[2] Small changes that offer greater probabilities of reproductive success will alter the genetic composition of the population over time to arrive at a new equilibrium. Natural selection operates to remove genetic variability, to fix traits in the direction of species uniformity. The more important a trait is to the species phenotype, the more uniform it is among the population (i.e., the less genetic variability there is for that trait).

Natural selection is blind, it cannot see into the future and divine what traits may or may not enhance reproductive success. The features of the environment the organism depends on or uses as input *at the moment* determines whether the organism's genetic traits are advantageous or disadvantageous with regard to reproductive success. If a trait is advantageous to the individual, it will increase the probability that the individual will survive to pass on that trait to more progeny and thus the proliferation of the combination of genes responsible for that trait. Individuals lacking the trait, or with disadvantageous traits, will be less reproductively successful; and their contribution to the gene pool may eventually be lost. Thus, natural selection "selects out" as well as "selects in" but always in response to concurrent environmental challenges.

We should not view evolution through natural selection as having some grand design or as positively progressive such that perfectly adapted phenotypes (i.e., phenotypes that have arrived at "optimal" solutions to all present and future environmental challenges) will someday emerge. To claim that some design is an adaptation is to make a claim about the distant past, not the distant future. Natural selection only "prepares" organisms for the future to the extent that future environments are very much like the past environments that shaped the organism (which, of course, they usually are). Evolution produces nonadaptive as well as adaptive traits, and an adaptive trait in one environment may be nonadaptive or even maladaptive (a lack of "fit" between phenotype and environment) in another. The gene for sickling of hemoglobin cells, for example, was once adaptive in the intensely malarious environments of West Africa; but in nonmalarious environments, it is maladaptive.

This points out that the environment is just as important to natural selection as genes are in producing adapted phenotypes. As Tooby and Cosmides (1990:20) explain, "Over evolutionary time, genetic variation in developmental programs (with selective retention of advantageous variants) explores the properties of the environment, discovering those that are useful sources of information in the task of regulating development and behavior, and rendering those features of the environment that are unreliable or disruptive irrelevant to development." Environments select organisms that are best able to survive and reproduce within them; thus, the "natural" in "natural selection" is nature—the natural environment. It is just as important, however, to realize that the environment cannot act on the organism unless the organism is genetically programmed to recognize and incorporate (react genetically) to those aspects of the environment that are important to it. New adaptations are limited by the genetic material available from previous adaptations, but that genetic material is only available because previous behavior had proved adaptive. It is in this way that genes and environments are locked together as fully interdependent determinants of the traits and characteristics that guide our behavior.

Mutation is a further source of genetic variation. The genetic shuffling occurring at meiosis creates new genetic combinations from existing stock, but it does not create new alleles. Mutation—random mistakes in DNA replication caused by such things as radiation or chemical toxins—introduces entirely new alleles into the gene pool, and as such it is the ultimate source of genetic variability from which nature selects. The form of the human organism today is the result of countless mutations (original form); thus, we are the result of millions of gene mutations caused by random movements of individual atoms. Most mutations are neither harmful nor helpful, some are harmful to the organism (rather like introducing a random connection into a computer), and occasionally some are adaptive. If the new allele somehow makes the organism better able to survive and reproduce than other organisms in the population, the frequency of that allele will increase in the population. The number of progeny produced and raised to sexual maturity by a given organism—not its strength, beauty, health, or intelligence, although these may have a positive influence on reproductive success—is what biologists mean by "fitness" ("reproductive fitness" implies successful nurturing as well as successful breeding). If the mutation is harmful, the organism possessing it may be less fit than it would otherwise be; and its mutant allele will decrease in frequency in the population.

Genetic flow and genetic drift refer to the contributions of immigration and emigration of breeding populations and chance deviations in gene frequency, respectively. Migrating individuals may bring alleles with them that are not represented in the host population (flow). If the allele is advantageous, it will spread among the host population and perhaps other alleles will be lost in the host population. In very small populations the major opportunity for gene change is chance fluctuations (drift) in which certain alleles may be lost forever because of chance matings. Think of flow and drift in terms of sampling: The smaller the sample, the greater influence deviant or "outlier" cases will have. Thus, flow and drift are important sources of change in gene frequency in small populations; but their influence is greatly diminished in larger ones.

It is common to think of endogamous breeding populations (ethnic groups and races) as being genetically quite disparate; and indeed the assumption seems quite reasonable in light of the concepts of genetic drift, flow, and natural selection in local environments (such as that for sickle-celling in West Africa). As Stringer and Andrews (1988:1264) note, though, "As much as 84% of protein polymorphism in human populations results from variation among individuals within populations, a further 6% represents genetic divergence associated with nationality, and only 10% varies between human racial groups." Genetically, then, the groups we humans sort ourselves into are much more similar than different, an observation that makes biological nonsense of "racial purity" and "ethnic cleansing" ideologies and programs. However, a small difference in DNA is not the same as a correspondingly small difference in gene products; there are many differences in allele frequencies among the races at many loci (Whitney, 1990).

ADAPTATIONISM AND EXAPTATIONISM

There has been much criticism of the "adaptationist program" over the past decade (Gould, 1991; Symons, 1992). Adaptationists are accused of positing "genes for" each and every human trait in much the same way that instinctualists used to posit "instincts for" just about anything. Gould (1991) points out that organisms possess many features that are useful but did not arise as adaptations for their present roles, and he calls such features *exaptations*. Adaptations promote their own frequency via an extended period of selection because of their effectiveness in their current roles; exaptations, on the other hand, are said to have "seized" or "co-opted" characteristics built by natural selection for often quite different functions. Unlike adaptations, exaptations are not functionally organized (although they may seem to be); and they accompany adaptations simply because they are incidentally related to them (Gould, 1991; Tooby & Cosmides, 1992). Thus, many human features are by-products or side effects of natural selection rather than its explicit products.

Gould provided a service by pointing out alternatives to a naïve Panglossian adaptationism (i.e., everything is made for the best purpose), but we now have to guard against an equally naïve use of exaptationism (Pinker & Bloom, 1992). Some writers have "run wild" with the exaptation concept, billing it as a "new theory of evolution" (Piattelli-Palmarini, 1989). Gould makes no such claims himself; he has a less grandiose agenda—that of opposing those who posit "genes for" and optimal adaptive utility for every pattern of human behavior that now exists. He is aware that to identify something as an exaptation is not the same as saying that it is not the product of natural selection; it only means that it did not always serve its present purpose. Exaptations—co-optations, seizures, by-products, and side effects—do not arise full blown from nothing; they are still driven by selection. An exaptation may be seized upon and refined by natural selection and become an adaptation in its own right, thus making the adaptation–exaptation argument one that is more semantic than substantive. Pinker and Bloom (1992:459) see very little, if any, difference between an exaptation and what Darwin meant by a "preadaptation." Thus, we should view Gould's concept of exaptation as more of a brake against runaway panadaptationism than as some sort of alternative to adaptationism itself.

GENETICS AND HUMAN BEHAVIOR

Many social scientists' conceptions of genes and genetics probably rely on the dim memory of discussions of Mendel's peas in Biology 101. In this context, genes were presented as immutable and all powerful: If a plant had alleles ttSs, it was going to be short and smooth, no matter what. The baggage of such memories renders it understandable that they should reject the notion that genes influence nonmorphological human traits and characteristics. Unlike the either–or hereditary mechanisms of pea plant matings, the mating of tall and short human beings usually results in offspring of intermediate height. If these offspring were to breed incestuously, they certainly would not produce tall and short children in the classic Mendelian ratio. Human height is an example of *incomplete dominance*, which means that dominant and recessive traits often blend their traits in the phenotype. Many of the traits of interest to behavioral scientists (e.g., intelligence quotient [IQ], altruism, aggression, and so forth) are not discrete single-gene distributions governed by the rules of simple dominance and recessiveness. Rather, such traits are polygenetic (produced by complexes of coordinated genes, each having minor additive effects) traits governed by incomplete dominance. They are also subject to considerable modification by the environment and are continuously distributed in the population in such a way that they describe a normal curve.

Genes differentially affecting human traits, characteristics, and behaviors are facultative; that is, they can have different effects under different environmental conditions and are thus dependent on the environment for the form of their expression.

PLEIOTROPY

Before considering polygenetic effects, I will briefly comment on the concept of *pleiotropy* (literally, "many turnings"). Pleiotropy refers to the multiple effects that a single gene can have on the organism via the action of the enzyme it produces. Although each gene codes only for one protein, every gene is potentially pleiotropic; and each effect may be direct or indirect. By pointing out that while a trait may have genes underlying it, the trait per se may not be adaptive (rather, it may be a side effect of genes coding for something entirely different), pleiotropy highlights the poverty of panselectionism more cogently than does exaptation (Barkow, 1991:29–30).

Pleiotropic effects have been shown to influence behavior in laboratory animals. For instance, the gene for albinism in mice correlates highly with emotionality. Open-field experiments show convincingly that albino mice placed in stressful situations show much lower exploratory behavior and much higher rates of urination and defecation than nonalbino mice and that the relationship is causal. In other words, the single gene that codes for coat color has a pleiotropic effect on emotionality, which, in turn, affects behavior (Plomin, DeFries, & McClearn, 1980:83). Somehow a single recessive gene coding for the synthesis of pigment melanin also influences hormonal and enzymatic processes that lead to hyperactivity of the autonomic nervous system and thus to emotionality.

I am unaware of any studies exploring similar pleiotropic effects among human albinos, although human albinism is known to have a pleiotropic effect on the nervous system (Changeux, 1985:173). However, the pleiotropic process brings to mind early criminological work on somatotyping (the correlating of body type and temperament). After some early enthusiasm, somatotyping was almost universally rejected as a useless idea. Perhaps we would not have seen such cavalier dismissals of data if critics had been aware of pleiotropy; indeed, somatotyping has been resurrected and taken seriously in at least one recent work (Eysenck & Gudjonsson, 1989). Endomorphs (slight build), like albino mice, tend to be temperamentally introverted, while mesomorphs (brawny) tend to be extroverted and overrepresented in criminal and delinquent populations (Eysenck 1977, 1990). Eysenck (1990) has shown that about half of the variance in extroversion is attributable to genetics; so perhaps the observed correlation between body build and behavior is mediated by pleiotropic genetic effects on the autonomic nervous system, the reticular activating system, above-average androgen levels, or a complicated combination of all three.

PARTITIONING GENETIC VARIANCE

Almost all behavior is mediated by many genes interacting with environmental input. The major concern of behavioral or population genetics is to predict or infer the average phenotype of offspring from Mendelian laws. Phenotypes vary, and so do genotypes. Thus, to understand the effects of genes on behavior we have to understand three further concepts: the additive, dominance, and epistatic effects of genes. Because most behavioral scientists are more familiar with statistics than with genetics, I shall couch the following discussion of polygenetic effects in terms of the familiar regression model.

All normally distributed continuous traits have variance (squared deviation from the mean effect). We attempt to explain this variance by determining how much of it can be accounted for by variance in other theoretically meaningful factors. Variance in phenotypical traits is accounted for by genetic and nongenetic variance, with variance accounted for by genetics being further partitioned into additive, dominance, and epistatic variance.

Every gene having influence on a particular trait has some mean or average effect. Under normal conditions, the mean effects of a number of genes (gene dosage) at different chromosomal loci can be summed to obtain the additive effect much as we can sum r^2 values in multiple correlation if there is no "overlap" or shared variance among the predictor variables. Thus, additive genetic effects are allelic effects for a particular trait that are simply summed across the genotype. Additive effects are very important because they are the effects that are transmitted to the offspring, and as such they are relevant to predicting average offspring phenotypes. We can think of the additive genetic effect as the expected value of a trait in much the same way that statisticians refer to the mean as the expected value in a distribution of quantitative scores.

Dominance effects are nonadditive genetic effects. These effects are not transmitted to offspring and are, therefore, not relevant to the prediction of average offspring phenotypes. When we say that these effects are not transmitted to offspring, it is not meant that the alleles are not transmitted. It simply means that the allelic interaction per se is not transmitted. Dominance effects are deviations from the expected value (of a phenotype) predicted by gene dosage that decrease similarity between parental and offspring phenotypes. Dominance effects represent the interaction of alleles at a single homologous locus, with only the dominant allele of a dominant–recessive pair being expressed in the offspring phenotype. We may think of dominance as the standard deviation of the expected value or as the sum of the squared residuals from an ordinary least-squares regression slope predicting phenotype from gene dosage. Genetically, these deviations from the regression line indicate the degree to which the geneotype does not "breed true."

The third source of variation associated with genetic effects is epistasis. Epistatic effects represent the interaction of alleles at a number of chromosomal loci in contrast to interaction at just one locus (dominance). Interaction is conceptualized here as it is in any statistical analysis; that is, alleles at locus A and at locus B may interact in a nonlinear manner to produce a phenotypical trait not predictable from their summed effects. Epistatic interaction effects are generally considered not to be an important source of variation for most behavioral traits.

We may now express phenotypical variance in symbolic form as

$$V_p = V_a + V_d + V_i + V_e$$

where

$$V_p = \text{phenotypical variance}$$

$$V_a = \text{additive genetic variance}$$

$$V_d = \text{dominance variance}$$

$$V_i = \text{epistatic variance}$$

$$V_e = \text{environmental variance}$$

In regression terms, phenotypical variance is expressed as the linear combination of all four sources of variance. Because V_d and V_i usually have quite small effects on many characteristics, behavioral geneticists often reduce the equation to

$$V_p = V_g + V_e$$

where V_g is the total genetic variation.

THE CONCEPT OF HERITABILITY

The preceding discussion of variance leads us into a concept of central importance to behavioral genetics: *heritability*. Heritability is the ratio of genetic variance to total phenotypical variance for a particular trait and is thus a quantification (ranging between 0 and 1) of the extent to which variance in a trait is due to genetic influences. Much of the work in behavioral genetics involves partitioning phenotypical variance in traits into genetic and environmental components and is thus just as important for environmental as for genetic explanations of behavior. Many intellectual, behavioral, and personality traits have been shown to have moderate to strong heritabilities (Buss, 1990; Bouchard, Lykken, McGue, Segal, & Tellegen, 1990).

Heritability is a population parameter describing trait variance in a *population*, not in an individual. For instance, if a heritability coefficient (h^2) for IQ were to be computed at 0.5, meaning that 50 percent of the variance in IQ in a population is attributable to genetics, it would not mean in the case of someone with an IQ of 120 that 60 points is attributable to his or her genes and 60 points to the environment. What is does mean is that an estimated 50 percent of the *difference* (i.e., 20 points) between his or her score and the population mean of 100 is attributable to genetic effects.

Heritability, it must be emphasized, does not place constraints on environmental effects; that is, knowing what percentage of the variance in a trait is genetic does not set limits on creating new environments that could influence the trait (Jencks, 1980). Heritability measures the proportion of variance in traits attributable to *actualized* genetic potential; and whatever the unactualized potential may be, it cannot be inferred from h^2 (Bronfenbrenner & Ceci, 1994:315). However, if some magic potion were able to tap everyone's unactualized cognitive potential such that everyone in the population realized an IQ increment of 10 points, h^2 would not change, since everyone's IQ had increased uniformly; and IQ would still vary as much as it did before. Nor does the decomposition of variance into genetic and environmental effects tell us how much of the trait itself is due to these factors; it only tells us how much of the *variance* in the trait is accounted for by those effects (Plomin, 1989).

The determination of heritability, whether we are interested in the height of sunflowers, the milk output of cows, human IQ and temperament, or any other phenotypical trait of organisms, requires that every phenotype be exposed to identical environments. Any variability among phenotypes can only be attributed to a factor that varies. For example, if we were to take a random sample of thoroughly shuffled genetically heterogeneous sunflower seeds and plant them in identically nourishing environments, phenotypical trait variance among them would be *entirely* attributable to genetics; and h^2 would be 1.0. Because the environment was held constant across phenotypes, it cannot be considered a source of variance. Similarly, if we took a random sample of genetically homogeneous sunflower seeds and planted them in diverse environments, phenotypical trait variance would be 100 percent attributable to environmental conditions; and h^2 would be zero. In this case, genetic material was the constant and, therefore, not a source of variance.

What if we planted heterogeneous genotypes in diverse environments and tried to decompose phenotypic variance into genetic and environmental effects? The task would be much more difficult and is the situation that confronts us when assessing genetic and environmental effects on human traits. Such a situation does not preclude our ability to assess human heritability because we can control genetic variability by the twin-study and adoption-study methods (adoption studies are addressed in Chapter 5). In the twin-study method, behavioral geneticists sort out the genetic and environmental sources of variance by comparing interclass correlations for a trait between monozygotic (MZ) twin pairs and same-sex dizygotic (DZ) twin pairs. The twin-study method takes advantage of the fact that MZ twins are genetically identical; that is, the coefficient of their genetic relationship is 1.0. DZ twins, on average, share half of their genetic inheritance; so their coefficient of genetic relationship is 0.5. If genes are an important source of variation for a trait, then individuals who are genetically similar should be more similar on a measured trait than individuals who are less genetically similar.

Under the assumption of a purely polygenetic model (no environmental effects), theoretically the correlation between a trait and genetic material between two halves of MZ twin pairs should be 1.0, 0.5 for DZ twin pairs, and 0 for unrelated individuals. Departures from the theoretically expected correlations reflect environmental or nongenetic effects plus measurement error. Computation of the coefficient of heritability is accomplished by the simple formula:

$$h^2 = 2(rMZ - rDZ)$$

For example, if the correlations among a sample of MZ and DZ twin pairs are 0.80 and 0.60, respectively, for a particular trait, h^2 would be

$$h^2 = 2(rMZ - rDZ) = 2(.80 - .60) = 2(.20) = .40$$

Thus, 40 percent of the variance on this measured trait is attributable to genetics and 60 percent to the environment and measurement error. As with any other population parameter, h^2 is a point estimate around which must be placed a range of interval estimates.[3]

The proportion of variance in a trait accounted for by the environment can be further broken down into common environmental (CE) and specific environmnental (SE) sources. CE influences are those shared environmental experiences that make people similar to one another; SE influences are those nonshared experiences that make them different from one another. We may estimate CE from our hypothetical data by the following:

$$CE = 2rDZ - rMZ = 1.20 - .80 = .40$$

Thus, genetics and common environmental experiences together account for 80 percent of the variance in the measured trait. The variance accounted for by SE is simple:

$$SE = 1 - (h^2 + CE)$$

which is the same as

$$SE = 1 - rMZ$$

In the present case,

$$SE = 1 - (.40 + .40) = .20$$

There are two types of assessed heritability: broad and narrow. Broad heritability is concerned with all sources of genetic variance (additive, dominance, and epistasis); narrow heritability, on the other hand, is concerned only with additive variance. Because MZ twins share all sources of genetic variability and DZ twins share additive variance but only about one-fourth of the variance due to dominance and very little due to epistasis, to the extent that non-additive genetic variance influences a trait, twin-study methods may inflate heritability estimates (Plomin, Chipuer, & Loehlin, 1990:229). Although most behavioral geneticists tend to discount the importance of nonadditive effects, others insist that the importance of nonadditive genetic effects may vary from trait to trait. Anytime h^2 is greater than the correlation between MZ pairs (the upper limit of h^2), we are dealing with traits with significant nonadditive genetic effects (Plomin, Chipuer, & Loehin, 1990:227).

It is important to realize that the coefficient of heritability is not a constant. Like other population parameters, it changes with the composition of the population and with changes in the environment and only refers to the proportion of variance attributable to genetic effects at a particular time for a particular population. A variety of studies have shown that heritability of human traits is different in different environments and that genetic effects are different (they are expressed or repressed) in different environments (Scarr-Salapatek, 1971; Heath et al., 1985; Goldsmith, 1994). Because variation can only be attributed to sources that vary, it follows that the more environments are equalized (the less variability there is within them), the greater will be the genetic effects and thus the larger h^2 will be. Conversely, the more variable the environment, the lower will be the heritability of any such traits.[4]

In addition to the homogeneity and heterogeneity of environments, heritability varies with environmental quality. More advantageous environments allow for greater genetic expression; more disadvantaged environments depress full expression (Bradley & Caldwell, 1991; Walsh, 1992). Differences in heritabilities on important traits, such as IQ, within different environments could provide sociologists with additional important indices of relative environmental advantage or disadvantage. Because heritability changes, "A relatively unexplored benefit of the concept of heritability is that it can describe changes in the mix of genetics and environmental factors in various populations, times, or developmental stages" (Plomin, DeFries, & McClearn, 1980:225). If sociologists become sensitive to genetic data for no reason other than this, the benefits to the field will be great.

How do we reconcile the tendency of natural selection to move species toward genetic fixity with the genetic variability required by the concept of heritability? The traits fixed by natural selection are shared by all members of a species. We all have noses, so the absence or presence of a nose has zero heritability, although possessing a nose is inherited (it is specified by our DNA as a species characteristic). Heritability is about *variation* in traits, not their presence or absence. Our noses vary in size, shape, and color; but, barring accidents, we all have one. Variation in the presence or absence of a nose reflects environmental factors, not genetic differences; but variability in their size, shape, and color (unless altered by environmental intervention) reflects genetic differences. Likewise, aggression, altruism, intelligence, sexual behavior, and the like are panhuman traits inherited panhumanly. They are uniform designs against which heritable variation in them is measured. Tooby and Cosmides (1990) point out that "genetic" and "heritable" and "inherited" and "heritability" have come to mean different things for geneticists and social scientists and that much confusion in the social sciences results from the failure to distinguish between them.

In addition to what genes are, we can now say what they are not. They are not armies of mysterious homunculi pushing a button here and a button there to determine our behavioral destiny. This is the straw-man image drawn by biophobics and then attacked as untenable. Such an image is easy to demolish (that is why straw men are so useful), but there are kernels of truth there: They are a legion, they are still somewhat mysterious, they do "push buttons," and they do impact behavior, albeit indirectly.

Instead of speaking in strong terms like *determinism* and *destiny*, we need to speak softly of *influence* and *directional bias*. Neonates of all species bring with them genetically programmed preferences for particular patterns of sensory, neural, and motor arrangements with which they will react to the external environment. These preferences impacting networks of connecting nerve circuits will, in turn, influence each person's behavioral pattern somewhat differently. However, the genetic code itself is environment dependent (facultative) in many ways in that the environment may facilitate or suppress these genetic "preferences" to various degrees. There are many plausible routes from genes to behavior, none of which are "predestined" and all of which are regulated by developmentally canalized physiological processes.

To assume that any behavior is a function of *either* heredity *or* environment is to assume that they are mutually exclusive causal agents. We have already seen that geneticists speak of the futility of thinking about genes and environments as alternative explanations for human traits rather than as mutually dependent segments of a feedback loop. Genes may affect some trivial behaviors directly, but nontrivial behavior—the kind that excites social scientists—results from genetic influences mediated by the environment in active and reactive ways. Behavioral geneticists are the first to emphasize that there is "no firm evidence for a single-gene effect that accounts for a detectable amount of variation for any complex behavior" (Plomin, 1989:110).

There is a sense in which all human traits are "environmental" in that they represent evolutionary genetic selection for adaptation in response to environmental contingencies faced by our distant ancestors. Genes are instructions for "survival machines" (individual organisms) for assuring their own survival down through the generations (Dawkins, 1976). Genes that confer some advantage to their carrier organism will help both the carrier and the genes to propagate. Genes are the engines of evolution, selecting those traits that best assure the organism's adaptation to a particular environment. In this sense, genes can be viewed as "selfish" (Dawkins, 1976). The term *selfish* in this context is, of course, pure metaphor. Genes have no machinery of consciousness. They simply organize physiological processes according to chemical blueprints so that they will remain part of the DNA stream of life. Changes in gene frequency reflect the success of their "survival machines" in adapting to environmental challenges affecting survival and reproduction.

GENE–ENVIRONMENT CORRELATION

Gene–environment (GE) interaction and GE correlation are important concepts in behavioral genetics. The concept of GE interaction involves the reasonable assumption that different genotypes will interact with and respond to their environments in different ways. We should not confuse genetic interaction effects (nonadditive effects) with interaction effects in analysis of variance (ANOVA), that is, as a nonlinear combination of genetic and environmental effects. Most developmental traits are main effects, with very little variance ever accounted for by nonadditive effects (Scarr, 1993). In addition to this possible confusion, it has been pointed out that the concept of GE interaction has taken on an "almost mystical aura" and that its most connotative idea, the organism's active transactions with its environment, is better conveyed by the idea of CE correlation (Plomin, DeFries, & McClearn, 1980:360; Scarr, 1993).

Temperament-induced behavior will be used as an example of GE correlation. Temperament is a heritable trait that can be identified very early in a person's life and may be defined as his or her characteristic or habitual mode of emotionally responding to environmental stimuli. Temperamental variability is largely a function of variability in central and peripheral nervous system arousal (Kochanska, 1991). It is a polygenetic trait in which each participating gene with its own biochemical constitution contributes to the particular molecular "trail" traveled to produce one kind of temperament rather than another. Since it is unreasonable for people to seek out environments incompatible with their genetic dispositions, people with genes coding for different temperaments will seek out different kinds of environments when they are able (genes and environments will covary positively).

Geneticists distinguish between passive, reactive, and active GE correlations (Plomin, DeFries, & McClearn, 1980:360–362). Passive GE correlation is imposed on individuals by circumstances outside their control. If a child receives genes coding for a tranquil temperament and is reared in an environment conducive to tranquility, that is, a home in which such behavior is modeled and reinforced, the genotype and the environment in which it operates are positively correlated. Having been provided by its parents with both genes and an environment favorable to the expression of tranquility, tranquility occurs independently (passively) of what the child does or does not do. Negative GE correlation would exist if a temperamentally tranquil child were to be adopted into a noisy, frenetic, and disharmonious family. Plomin and his colleagues limit the pertinent environment in passive GE correlation to that shared only with parents and siblings. As would be expected, passive GE correlation decreases with age as the scope of environmental interaction widens and the person is confronted with a wider variety of other people and a wider variety of behavioral options (Scarr & McCartney, 1983; Scarr, 1992).

Reactive GE correlation is a particularly important concept for social science. Reactive GE correlation refers to the way others (parents, siblings, teachers, peers—in short, anybody)·in the human environment react to the individual on the basis of his or her behavior. Note that reactive GE correlation reverses the direction of the typical social science causal chain which typically sees the child's behavior being shaped only by the way others treat it. This is not substituting one unidirectional causal chain for its opposite. The concept of reactive GE correlation simply avers that the behavior of others toward the child is as much a function of the child's evocative behavior as it is of the interaction style of those who respond to it. Children bring characteristics with them to interpersonal situations that increase of decrease the probability of evoking certain kinds of responses from others. A fussy, bad-tempered, and "difficult" infant will be reacted to with less solicitude than will a bubbly, good-natured infant; and a hyperactive, moody, and mischievous child will be less well thought of by parents, peers, and teachers than one who is pleasant, gregarious, and well behaved.

Some children may present an extremely difficult challenge by their resistance to parental control for even the most patient and loving parents. Such children may be selected out for special attention and, by a variety of strategies of reward and punishment, may be humbled into conformity (negative GE correlation). A child's temperament may sometimes be too strongly formed to be diverted from its normal course, and this could result in many negative consequences.[5] The reactions of others in the form of abuse and punishment may serve to exacerbate a child's already antisocial personality and drive him or her to seek social environments in which such behavior is more accepted, which are usually populated by individuals similarly disposed. Reactive GE correlation, then, serves to magnify differences among phenotypes. This brings us to the concept of active GE correlation.

The environment for active GE correlation is any environment sought out by individuals that is compatible with their genetic dispositions. Our genes, within the range of cultural possibilities and constraints, determine what features of the social world will be salient and rewarding to us and what features will not. Active GE correlation gains more explanatory power as individuals mature and acquire the ability to take greater control of their own lives (assuming an environment allowing for such freedom). Twin studies provide striking evidence of this. Large-scale studies of MZ twins provide us with the insight that the intelligence, personalities, and attitudes of MZ twins are essentially unaffected by whether they were reared together. "On a variety of measures of all kinds of traits and abilities, we consistently find that MZ twins reared apart as singletons, often without knowledge of each other, score just about as similarly as MZ twins reared together" (Bouchard, Lykken, McGue, Segal, & Tellegen, 1990). In other words, MZ twins reared apart construct their environments about as similarly as they would have had they been raised together and considerably more similarly than DZ twins or other siblings raised together.

The power of active GE correlation can be inferred from changing patterns of hertability and correlation coefficients over time. Heritability increases for IQ and certain personality traits from childhood to adulthood because as twins grow up, they grow apart, with DZ twins becoming less similar to one another than MZ twins. Sharing 50 percent of their genes, DZ twins are more likely to construct their adult environments differently from one another than are MZ twins (McCartney, Harris, & Bernieri, 1990). Correlations between both MZ and DZ pairs on many traits will shrink as individual twins gain the ability and the freedom to construct their own environments; but because DZ correlations will shrink further than MZ correlations, heritability will increase.[6] Similarly, a longitudinal study of 181 pairs of genetically unrelated siblings reared together showed a steady decline in the correlation between pairs on IQ, from 0.16 at age 8 to −0.01 at age 18 (Loehlin, Horn, & Willerman, 1989). All of this shows that shared environmental effects are real in childhood, but their influence wanes considerably and sometimes disappears in later life when individuals are freer to construct their environments in ways consistent with their genotypes. The idea of GE correlation (especially reactive and active) should pull us away from whatever vestiges of Dennis Wrong's "oversocialized concept of man" remain in sociology and toward thinking of human beings as active agents participating in the creation of environments who cohere with their genotypes when free to do so.[7]

CONCLUSION

The goal of this brief introduction to genetics is to assure sociologists that genes are real and powerful but also that they have been invested with too much power to influence behavior by those lacking an understanding of what genes are and what they do. Genes are self-replicating molecules coding for proteins, which, in turn, code for hormonal and metabolic physiological processes. They do not code for behavior, but they do code for predispositions such as temperament, conditionability, and intelligence, variations in which provide people with relative advantages or disadvantages in different social situations. Human beings are active explorers of their environment; they change it and mold it just as it changes and molds them. Environmental experiences function to augment genetic predispositions, doing so weakly or strongly at different stages of development and within different social contexts. We cannot allow ourselves to be lulled into the assumption of a constancy in either individuals' constitutions or the social environments they find themselves in. Human beings engage in dynamic transactions with their environments; and in the process, they change both themselves and their environments. Although genes play a role in determining the life course, there is no neat linear cryptography existing by which genes code for certain types of brains, which, in turn, code for different kinds of behavior. But genes do provide directions by which our development and our behavior are guided in ways favored over alternatives.

NOTES

1. In a critical response of Sandra Scarr's presidential address to the Society for Research in Child Development, Diana Baumrind (1993:1313) offers a standard social science argument against genetic explanations: "For psychologists, as for medical researchers, the purpose of identifying undesirable predispositions of individuals should be to devise more health-promoting interventions, not to discourage such attempts on the supposition that these predispositions are genetically based and therefore intractable." Scarr (1993:1351) responds with three statements. First, "We might want to know the scientific truth (about undesirable predispositions) per se, because deceit does not enhance the scientific enterprise." Second, she asks that "if some predisposition were found to be 'genetically based' (presumably genetically variable), would denying the results enhance intervention efforts?" She answers, "Surely not." Third, she exclaims that "genetic does not mean intractable!" Scarr (1993:1351) suggests that social scientists' fears would be allayed greatly if only they would become educated about genetics.

2. The classic example is selection for black coloration of the English peppered moth. At the time of the Industrial Revolution, the black variety of this moth constituted about 1 percent of an otherwise gray population. With the blackening of trees caused by factory pollution, black moths were camouflaged against predators, a survival and reproductive advantage formerly enjoyed by gray moths on gray trees. Over about 100 generations, the black moth constituted almost 100 percent of the peppered moth population in England. With the implementation of strict antipollution rules in the 1960s, gray moths are making a comeback as black moths become more and more the victims of predation (Futuyama & Risch, 1984:159).

3. MZ and DZ twins reared together share common genes and common environments. Consequently, when we subtracted 0.60 from 0.80, substantively we subtracted the variance in the trait for DZ twins due to common genes and common environment from the variance for MZ twins due to common genes and common environment. The only source of variance left after subtraction (except for measurement error) is the greater genetic similarity of MZ twins. Because the coefficient of genetic similarity is 1.0 for MZs and 0.5 for DZs, we are left with a quantity that represents one-half of the genetic variance (the covariance of DZ twins includes only one-half of the genetic influence as compared with the covariance of MZ twins), which is represented by the difference of 0.20 in the example. Thus, the estimate of variance in the trait due to genetics is obtained by twice the difference between the *r*s for MZ and DZ twins.

Some readers may wonder why the correlations are not squared, since h^2 has a "variance explained" interpretation. They are not squared because, as Plomin and Daniels (1987:16) point out, "The issue is not whether we can predict one twin's score from the other twin's score. Rather, the issue is the extent to which the observed variance is due to shared variance—that is, covariance—among the pairs. The correlation itself rather than its square expresses the proportion of total variance that is shared within pairs."

4. For the behavioral geneticist, the "environment" means more than it does for the social scientist, who generally limits it to sociocultural variables such as socioeconomic status (SES), schooling, race, religion, family of rearing, and so on. For the behavioral geneticist, "environment" is synonymous with "nongenetic." Nongenetic influences include prenatal influences (maternal stress, health, and illness), accidents, changes in cytoplasm, and even whether MZ twins in the womb shared or had separate chorions (the membrane surrounding the embryo). Concordance levels for IQ have been found to be higher for MZ twins who shared a chorion than for those who had separate ones (Goodman, 1987:35).

5. In a series of longitudinal studies of middle-class children summarized in Thomas and Chess (1977), it was found that infant temperament fell into four distinct clusters: "easy" (40%), "slow to warm up" (15%), "difficult" (10%), and "other" (35%). Easy infants were characterized by regular sleep and eating habits, positive moods, and were adaptable to novel stimuli and environmental changes. Difficult infants displayed characteristics opposite of these, and slow-to-warm-up infants were intermediate. By age 17, 70 percent of the difficult children and 18 percent of the easy children had developed behavioral disorders. An odds ratio calculated from these data revealed that infants described as "difficult" were 10.63 times more likely to have developed behavioral disorders by age 17 than infants described as "easy." However, the cases not consistent with expectations (the 30 percent of difficult children who did not develop disorders, and the 18 percent of the easy children who did) affirms the reaction range of environmental influence on temperamental dispositions.

Not all temperamentally difficult children are so purely for genetic reasons. Maternal stress, substance abuse, poor nutrition, exposure to toxic agents, or anything else in the environment that can adversely affect central nervous system (CNS) development is a potential source of early problem behavior.

6. For example, if the rs for a trait for MZ and DZ twins at age 10 are 0.75 and 0.50, respectively, h^2 will be 0.50. If the same rs at age 30 are 0.73 and 0.35, respectively, h^2 will be 0.76.

7. Of course, symbolic interactionists also emphasize that people react to situations according to the subjective meanings situations have for them. Active GE correlation, however, moves the proposition away from a mere statement of the obvious to indicate the foundations of those subjective meanings.

Chapter 3

The Brain and Its Environment

All environmental experiences enter the individual through the brain. In turn, the brain codes, organizes, and responds to such environmental input by way of the motor systems and behavior. Behavior is controlled by the brain, and without an understanding of the brain, we have no way of understanding behavior.

—C. Jeffery

The human brain—a walnut-shaped, grapefruit-sized, three-pound mass of gelatinous tissue—is the most immensely complicated, awe-inspiring, and fascinating entity in the universe. "In the human head there are forces within forces within forces, as in no other cubic half-foot of the universe we know," wrote Nobel Prize–winning neurophysiologist Roger Sperry (quoted in Fincher, 1982:23). Within this blob of jelly—which consumes 20 percent of the body's energy while representing only 2 percent of body mass—lie our thoughts, memories, self-concepts, desires, emotions, loves, hates, intelligence, creativity, and the contents of our cultures.

As the executor of all that we do and think, the brain and its processes must be a vital part of the biosociologist's repertoire of knowledge. We can no longer afford to view the brain as a mysterious and foreboding "black box" that can be safely ignored as irrelevant to our work. Although we need not concern ourselves with the minutiae of brain anatomy and physiology any more than with the minutiae of molecular genetics, we should learn neuroscience's basic language so that we understand what they are talking about. In anticipation of major advances in the neurosciences, the National Institute of Mental Health (NIMH) spearheaded the effort, which culminated in President George Bush declaring the 1990s as "the Decade of the Brain"

(Haier, 1990:371). Powerful technologies such as positron emission tomography (PET) and magnetic resonance imaging (MRI), as well as advances in psychopharmacology and psychoendocrinology, are providing new and important insights relevant to many areas of behavioral science. We should be prepared to understand the meaning of these anticipated findings and how they mesh with our theories.

BASIC NEUROANATOMY AND PHYSIOLOGY

The brain may be divided into four principle parts: the brain stem, diencephalon, cerebellum, and the cerebrum.[1] In an evolutionary sense, the most primitive part of the human brain is the brain stem, having evolved some 500 million years ago. The brain stem—also referred to sometimes as the reptilian system because it amounts to just about all the brain a reptile has—consists of the medulla, pons, and midbrain; the lower end of the brain stem is a continuation of the spinal cord. The brain stem controls the survival reflexes such as breathing and heart rate, as well as sleep and consciousness. Part of the brain stem contains a finger-sized network of cells called the reticular activating system (RAS), which also intrudes into the limbic system's thalamus ("inner chamber"). The RAS regulates cortical arousal and various levels of consciousness that underlie sensitivity to the environment. The RAS plays an important role in augmenting or reducing the meaningfulness of incoming sensory information from the environment and may be a very important network for helping us to explain certain aspects of sex-role behavior and deviance.

Attached to the rear of the brain stem at the pons ("bridge") is the cerebellum ("little brain"). The cerebellum is sometimes considered with the brain stem as part of a larger brain mechanism called the hindbrain. It is the motor part of the brain concerned with balance, coordination, and perhaps some memories of simple learned responses (Ornstein & Thompson, 1984). Some neuroscientists believe that the cerebellum plays a role in modulating emotional development, and a lack of optimal development of the nerve pathways between the cerebellum and the limbic system has been implicated with various behavioral pathologies (Prescott, 1975; Restak, 1979).

Wrapped around the brain stem like a protective claw is the limbic ("bordering") system, also called the mammalian system because it is most developed in mammals. The limbic system is also sometimes called the "visceral" or "emotional" brain because, although behavior is a function of the entire nervous system, it controls most of its involuntary and emotional expressions. It is in the limbic system that we experience pleasure and pain, anger and affection, joy and sorrow, rage and docility, sex and aggression, the basic emotions from which all others may be consider epiphenomena. Some neuroscientists like to think of limbic system functions in terms of the "four Fs" of survival: feeding, fighting, fleeing, and, well, reproduction (Ornstein & Thompson, 1984:28).

A key part of the limbic system is the hypothalamus ("under the thalamus"). The hypothalamus is often referred to as the "brain's brain" because it regulates so many things, including internal bodily homeostasis, the emotions, and sexual and nurturing behavior. As the principal intermediary between the nervous system and the endocrine system via its control over the body's master gland, the pituitary, it is involved in nearly all aspects of behavior. It also controls and integrates the autonomic nervous system (ANS), which is of no little importance to understanding many of the behaviors of interest to sociologists.

Forming the bulk of the human brain is the cerebrum, which is divided into two cerebral hemispheres (the "split brain") with their own lateralized allocation of functions. The two halves of the brain work in unison like two lumberjacks on each end of a saw. The left hemisphere specializes in the analytical and verbal skills and is considered more logical and linear in processing information. The right hemisphere is more specialized in processing visual-spatial patterns and is more holistic in that it grasps the fragmentary abstractions processed by the left hemisphere in a more integrated way. Roger Sperry, who won the Nobel Prize for his split-brain research, sees the split brain as "two separate selves—essentially a divided organism, each with its own memory and will—competing for control" (quoted in Fincher, 1982:34). However, information is readily exchanged between the two hemispheres via several commissures, the most important of which is the corpus callosum ("hard" or "thick body").

The surface of the cerebrum is covered by the cerebral cortex ("rind"), an intricately folded layer of nerve cells about one-eighth-inch thick. This folding appears to be nature's way of solving the problem of confining an extremely large cortical surface (the cortex takes up more area of the human brain—about 80 percent—than it does in any other animal) in a cranium that remains small enough to pass through the birth canal (Kolb & Whishaw, 1985:17). The cortex is our vaunted human "gray matter" that receives information from the outside world, analyzes it, makes decisions about it, and sends messages via other brain structures to the right muscles and glands so that we may organize responses to it. It is our large cerebral cortex that sets humanity apart from the rest of the animal kingdom and which makes it possible for us to adapt to and survive in all manner of conditions through the exercise of reason.

The folds of the cerebrum are known as sulci ("furrows"), and the deepest of these furrows divide the two hemispheres into four lobes which are named after the main skull bones that cover them: the frontal, parietal, occipital, and temporal lobes. Although the lobes have functional differences, there is no radical discontinuity of functions between what are essentially convenient anatomical regions. The task of being human is shared among them all, and the labels attached to them simply serve the purpose of trying to map and understand them.

The occipital ("back") lobe is primarily devoted to vision and need not concern us here. The frontal ("front") lobe, the largest of the lobes, is most involved with purposeful behavior by processing sensory information. Part of the frontal lobe, the prefrontal lobe, is richly endowed with neuronal pathways to the limbic system and is thus the brain area that interprets and processes emotion. Paul MacLean (1973) has proposed that the prefrontal area evolved in close relationship to the area of the limbic system involved in maternal care; and it has been termed, somewhat extravagantly, "the organ of love" by French neurophysiologist Paul Chauchard (1968:30).

The parietal ("cavity") lobes provide us with our unified perceptions of the world by integrating information coming to us from our various senses by cross-matching sensory information with abstract symbols (language) representative of the sum of the sensory input surrounding it. The parietal lobes systematize, classify, and consolidate our knowledge and form it into abstract concepts, an ability which, as far as we know, is only possessed by human beings. From the ongoing *active* process of collecting, correlating, analyzing, and categorizing, we not only perceive and come to terms with the world but also develop a sense of self. Inadequate development or damage of the parietal lobes leaves one unable to fully integrate sensory information and symbols, leading to faulty perceptions. As the Gestalt psychologists have shown us, the brain imposes perceptual structure; and, in a certain sense, "reality" at the sensorimotor level is in the brain before it is experienced. As Edelman (1987:7) explains, "One of the fundamental tasks of the nervous system is to carry on adaptive perceptual categorization of an 'unlabeled' world—one in which the macroscopic order and arrangements of objects and events (and even their definition or discrimination) cannot be prefigured for an organism."

The temporal ("temple") lobe is primarily involved in perception, memory, and hearing. While the parietal lobes integrate information, the temporal lobes, especially the hippocampus ("sea horse"), appear to be where these integrations are stored, retrieved, and associated with previous information. This associative process is obviously crucial for learning because we have to assign connotative properties to stimuli in accordance with their significance to us. If we do not associate incoming stimuli with the motivational and affective significance they have for us, behavior would never be modified because all stimuli would be treated as more or less equivalent (Kolb & Whishaw, 1985:405).

Neurons

The brain contains about a trillion cells. About 100 billion of them are the communicating neurons that give rise to all those cerebral things—intelligence, emotion, creativity, memory—that define our humanity (Fischbach, 1992). Each neuron is a separate "individual" with its own particular form and function, but each is also a fully integrated member of a "society" or network of neurons with a particular set of "kinship" connections (Llinas,

1988:vii). Neurons are much like other cells in our bodies, containing a nucleus with DNA material, ribosomes, mitochondria, and many of the other constituents of somatic cells. The "specialness" of brain cells lies in their patterns of connectivity rather than in their molecular nature. One major difference between brain cells and somatic cells, however, is that they lose their mitotic apparatus well before birth and thus their ability to reproduce themselves. There is a very important reason for this that points to the tremendous importance of the environment for human development. Neuronal patterns develop and connect as communications networks as a result of particular experiences and learned behavior patterns. If neurons were to divide and form new cells as body cells do, these patterns of connections—and hence the behaviors and memories they reflect—would be lost (Ornstein & Thompson, 1984:69).

Although the number of communicative neurons does not appreciably change after birth, the brain itself quadruples in size from neonate to adult. Much of this size increase is attributable to the increase in glial cells and myelination (see next paragraph). Another important aspect of brain development is that the neurons in the neonate's brain are largely unorganized and undifferentiated. "From a single collection of immature, undifferentiated cells," writes neuroscientist Ronald Kalil, "emerges an organ so structurally complex that most other natural or human-crafted systems seem simple by comparison" (1989:76). Except for those neuronal connections governing reflexive behavior, the human infant's brain at birth is not ready "wired" to function independently in its environment almost immediately as are the more rigidly programmed brains of lower animals. Most nonhuman neonate mammals are developmentally at the stage that it will take human infants about one year to reach, at which time the infant's brain will be 60 percent of its adult weight.

As nerve cells, neurons are specialized for conducting information from one cell to another. Nerve cells transduce stimuli from the environment into nervous impulses and transmit it via the appropriate networks (pathways) of other cells so that a response may be made. They accomplish this by way of *axons* ("axis") that originate in the cell body and *dendrites* ("tree"), which are branched extensions of the cell. Axons are coated by a sheath composed of a fatty substance called myelin, which is formed by the glial cells using cholesterol as a precursor. Myelin functions to protect the axon from "short-circuiting," much like the insulation around electrical wiring, and also to amplify nerve impulses. There is only one axon per cell, but the number of branching dendrites varies from neuron to neuron. Axons serve as transmitters sending signals to other neurons, and dendrites serve as receivers picking up impulses from neighboring neurons.

A cell passes its information along the axon in the form of electric signals made possible by the exchange of charged atoms (ions) in and out of the cell's permeable membrane. A cell at rest contains negatively charged potassium ions and is thus internally electrically negative with respect to the outside (i.e., it is polarized). A cell that is stimulated by a nerve impulse to a critical point will become depolarized and "fire." Depolarization occurs when tiny gates are opened along the axon's membrane, allowing in a flood of positively charged sodium ions and making the inside of the cell more electrically positive than negative for about 0.001 second. The closing of the gates restores the normal internal negative voltage. The electrical current generated by this rapid ionic exchange will depolarize adjacent areas in a self-reinforcing process of opening and closing new gates all along the axon, alternatively changing the membrane from positive to negative and back again. This brief change of the electrical potential of an axon is called the *action potential.*

Nerve impulses travel down axons like neon lights flicking on and off until they reach terminal points known as synaptic knobs or, more simply, *synapses* ("union"). The nerve-impulse message is changed from electrical to chemical form at the synapse. Synapses are actually microscopic gaps between the axon of one cell and the dendrite of another. Axon and dendrite never actually come into physical contact; they communicate across the synaptic gap chemically. After the message is received at the synapse, it may be again converted to electric impulses to continue its journey to the next cell. A neuron potentially has the capacity to make many thousands of synaptic connections with other neurons, which, in turn, may make as many connections with still other neurons. Each synapse corresponds to a particular brain state, with the number of potential brain states being virtually boundless. Nobel Prize–winning neuroscientist Gerald Edelman estimates that there are about one million billion connections in the cortical sheet, and "If we consider how connections might be variously combined, the number would be hyperastronomical—on the order of 10 followed by millions of zeros" (1992:17). Of course, nowhere near all possible brain states are ever realized because brain states depend on genetic potential meeting experiences. But such huge, almost unimaginable numbers point once again to each individual's uniqueness.

Neurotransmitters

When an electrical impulse arrives at the synaptic knob, it causes tiny synaptic sacs called vesicles to burst open and spill out one or more of a variety of chemicals. These chemical messengers are called *neurotransmitters;* which kind of transmitter is released depends on the function and location of the particular synaptic ending. Neurotransmitters are the "translators" of the message, hence the switch from electrical current to chemistry. The neurotransmitters pour across the synaptic gap and lock onto receptor sites on the dendrite's postsynaptic membrane. Once it has passed on its message, excess amounts of neurotransmitters are either pumped back into the vesicles or destroyed by enzymes.

Information from many different neurons is processed at the postsynaptic receptor sites, some of which are inhibitory (they prevent the "firing" of the receiving cell), and others of which are excitatory (they promote firing and the continuation of the impulse). It is the totality of these messages that makes the neuron democratically "decide" whether the message should be forwarded or canceled. If enough chemical excitation occurs, the message is retranslated into electrical form and is sped along to the next synapse where the whole process is repeated; if not, the message is terminated as unimportant.

The receptor cells, large protein molecules located on the postsynaptic membrane, let in only those transmitter substances that they chemically recognize. Just as codons on mRNA are attached to appropriate anticodons in protein synthesis, neurotransmitters have a particular chemical shape that can only be locked onto by their chemical complements. Receptor-cell functioning is important because more than one kind of transmitter can be present at a synapse and a target cell can respond to a transmitter differently depending on the specific receptor activated. It should be emphasized that while the transmitter substances are the medium by which the message is transmitted, they are not the message per se. What the transmitter "does" depends on the region of the brain where it is being utilized.

There may be hundreds of different neurotransmitters—neuroscientists argue about whether candidates fit a set of specific criteria for defining it as such (see Rogawski & Barker, 1985). We shall be concerned here only with those defined neurotransmitters that indirectly impact social behavior: serotonin (an indoleamine), norepinephrine, and dopamine (monoamines) transmitters synthesized at the axon or axon terminals. Other neurocommunicating substances such as the neuropeptides that have been discovered relatively recently have properties mimicked by psychoactive drugs such as Valium, morphine, and PCP (all drugs work either by mimicking or blocking the effects of natural neurotransmitters). Polypeptides, such as the endorphins and enkephalins, contain longer chains of amino acids than the monoamine transmitters and are synthesized in the cell body (soma) rather than at the axon (Bloom, 1988).

One further chemical substance, monoamine oxidase (MAO), requires mention at this point because it has been implicated in a variety of behavioral traits. It has been pointed out that few topics excite as varied a group of biological and behavioral scientists more than MAO (Singer, 1987). We have seen that excess amounts of neurotransmitters not pumped back into their vesicles are destroyed by enzymes at the synaptic juncture. MAO (there are two varieties: MAO-A and MAO-B) is one such deaminating enzyme that removes a variety of amine neurotransmitters by oxidation (the combining of molecules with oxygen atoms or the loss of hydrogen atoms) after they have performed their excitatory task. If deamination is not sufficiently accomplished, excess neurotransmitters may build up on the axon terminals, hindering the brain's ability to exclude false transmissions. Schizophrenia, for instance, may be thought of as resulting from "false transmissions" received by the schizophrenic that have no environmental referents. The plethora of faulty impulses received by schizophrenics may be the result of excess dopamine, excess dopamine receptors, insufficient MAO (MAO-B in the case of dopamine), or any combination of the three (Meltzer & Zureick, 1987).

The complicated interrelationships between neurotransmitters, hormones, and the MAO regulating them have important implications for many behaviors of interest to sociologists, especially gender and criminal behavior. Ellis (1991), for instance, reviewed forty-four studies in which associations had been found between low MAO activity and various correlates of criminal behavior (e.g., impulsiveness, childhood hyperactivity, learning disabilities, sensation seeking, substance abuse, and extroversion). Ellis also pointed out that the demographic variables generally considered to be the best predictors of delinquent and criminal behavior—age, gender, and race—all evidence wide variation in MAO activity. It is interesting to note that testosterone (T) depresses MAO activity, and that T levels are at their highest and MAO levels at their lowest during the second decade of life, the time when delinquent and criminal activity is most prevalent. A two- to threefold increase in MAO and an approximate tenfold decrease in T is experienced between the ages of 30 and 80 (Weyler, Hsu, & Breakfield, 1990). Women have only about 5 percent of the male level of T and about 15 to 20 percent more MAO than men, and black males have 5 to 10 percent more T and about 10 to 15 percent less MAO than white males (Weyler, Hsu, & Breakfield, 1990; Ellis, 1991; Ellis & Nyborg, 1992).

There is no simple causal relationship between MAO activity and aberrant behavior. Stress-related hormones such as epinephrine (a metabolite of which, norepinepherine, functions as a neurotransmitter) also seem to depress MAO activity (Oxenkrug & McIntyre, 1985). Thus, the path from MAO activity to behavioral activity is a long and twisted one in which the causal direction is not always (if ever) clear (Ellis, 1991:241). However, some promising preliminary gene linkage work has been done in the Netherlands on a mutation in the gene that codes for the MAO-A enzyme and how this mutated gene is linked to violence and aggression (Morell, 1993). The gene is X-linked recessive and results in very low MAO-A levels. Stressful events experienced by low MAO-A individuals have a greater probability of resulting in violent behavior than they would for those with normal levels (all other things being equal) because the abnormal accumulation of neurotransmitters at the synapse keeps the individual in an extended state of arousal.

THE PLASTIC HUMAN BRAIN

The brain is often likened to a buzzing interactive computer network, with organic compounds substituting for silicon chips. The computer is a marvelous tool; but disconnected from its inputs and outputs and from its electrical energy, it becomes useless. The human brain disconnected from its environment would likewise be just a gelatinous mass of tissue. Sensory-deprivation studies show just how important environmental input is to the brain's proper functioning. Many subjects find such experimental conditions unbearable and withdraw within twenty to thirty minutes. Subjects remaining in sensory-deprived conditions for very long suffer hallucinations, disorientation, and become temporarily mentally impaired when asked to perform simple tasks. The brain is still working; but deprived of input, it is a buzz of random synaptic confusion. Very few of us ever experience this kind of deprivation; but varying degrees of it are suffered by jail inmates, the bedridden, the lonely, and the unloved. Sensory deprivation during the active period of dendritic proliferation at infancy is especially deleterious (Kraemer, 1992).

There are nature–nurture arguments in the neurosciences surrounding the issue of brain development, but they are not about naïve either–or dichotomies. They are about the relative contributions to brain development of processes intrinsic to the brain (the genetic blueprint) relative to contributions extrinsic to it, such as nutrition, experiences, hormonal states, and so forth. As one neurobiologist put it, "To what extent does the information needed to build an organism reside in the genome of the fertilized egg, and how much does neural development depend on interaction between the growing organism and its environment?" (Ribchester, 1986:166).

Genes are marvelous entities that carry an immense amount of information. However, they are task specific and few relative to the much larger number of neurons and the staggering number of interneuronal connections. Thus, unlike the "one gene, one enzyme" rule, there cannot be a "one gene, one synapse" rule. Although one-third to one-half of all human genes are probably involved in brain development (Byerley & Mellon, 1989), there are nowhere near enough to cope with the task of guiding these neuronal connections across the neuronal jungle to their proper place. One view, perhaps the dominant one, is that the genes play only a minor, albeit crucial, part in specifying the billions of relationships that will eventually exist among the brain cells of the adult human being (Changeux, 1983; Edelman 1987, 1992).

If the genes alone were responsible for cell connections, all our behavior and the contents of our cultures would be preprogrammed. In the jargon of the neurosciences, our brains would be "hard-wired." The human brain stem and certain other brain structures are hard-wired because they carry out vital basic survival functions that must operate unerringly and consistently. If the cerebral cortex were also hard-wired, we would always do the right thing at the right time as long as we remained more or less in the same sort of environment to which we are adapted, which is all very perfect but all very sterile. The more varied and complex the environment, the more organisms living within them must change and adapt. Human environments are much too varied and much too complex for hard-wired brains, and natural selection takes far too long to incorporate new environmental contingencies into the genome. There is a limit to the amount of DNA that can be stuffed into our cells; and that limit, whatever it is, would freeze us in a genetic destiny if all brain activity were gene coded.[2] Genes have surrendered much of their control over human behavior to a more open, plastic, complex, and *adaptive* system of control that we call the human brain.

The genes, of course, specify basic brain architecture; build the cells; and synthesize the various neurotransmitters, neuropeptides, and enzymes. Let us think of brain development in the form of a construction site analogy. The genes have written a general architectural blueprint, roughed out the basic patterns of neuron connections, erected scaffolding (the physical structure of the brain), and have made the bricks (neurons) and mortar (neurotransmitters, etc.). The eventual form of those parts of the edifice not vital to sheer survival, however, is mainly determined by factors external to the organism. These factors differ from individual to individual: *We and the experiences we encounter will largely determine the patterns of our neuronal connections.* Humans do not passively adjust to nature's requirements. We make our own history but not from cloth of our own making: The human brain is "free to be uniquely human only with the shared mammalian heritage as its foundation" (Gadpaille, 1980:17).[3]

To reiterate, GE transactions are a central feature of brain development, governing cortical thickness, the amount of neurotransmitter chemicals, and the brain's neuronal pathways. Neurophysiologists distinguish between two neurophysiological mechanisms that utilize environmental input to facilitate synaptic proliferation (synaptogenesis)—*experience-expected*, and *experience-dependent* (Bertenthal & Campos, 1987; Greenough, Black, & Wallace, 1987)—or between *developmental* and *experiential* (Edelman 1987, 1992). The experience-expected or developmental mechanisms reflect the phylogenetic specificity of the brain; the experience-dependent or experiential mechanisms reflect its ontogenetic plasticity. The distinction between the two processes may be viewed as roughly analogous to that we made between "inherited" and "heritability" in Chapter 2. We all inherit the brain structure and functions of our species produced by a common pool of genetic material resulting from our phylogenetic history, but there will be variability in brain functioning as genes interact with environments in our individual ontogenies.

Experience-expected processes have evolved as neural preparedness to incorporate environmental information that is vital to an organism and ubiquitous in its environment. As noted in Chapter 2, natural selection moves population traits toward genetic uniformity; the more important the trait to organism survival, the more genetic variability is eliminated (i.e., the less heritable it becomes). In terms of the present context, this means that natural selection has recognized that certain processes—sight, speech, depth perception, mobility, sexual maturation, and so forth—are vital, and has provided for neurophysiological mechanisms designed to take advantage of experiences occurring naturally within the range of environments experienced by the species. These processes are stable because their alternatives failed evolutionary selection tests eons ago. Maturational (developmental) processes will always occur "as expected" in genetically normal individuals experiencing the normal range of human environments (Scarr, 1993).

These processes are so normal that developmental psychologists often interpret the outcome as the simple unfolding of the genetic blueprint—an interpretation called "predetermined epigenesis" by Gottlieb (1983, 1991). Gottlieb and others prefer to think of maturation processes in terms of "probabilistic epigenesis" to emphasize their variability and that they do not take place in an experiential vacuum. Order is imposed on experience by preexperiential rudimentary brain organization because maturational–sensory systems have strong genetic predispositions to occur at certain age junctures, but they can be delayed or accelerated by experience. Experience-expected processes lose their activity-dependent plasticity after relatively brief "critical periods" so that the organism will respond consistently and stereotypically to vital stimuli (Kalil, 1989). These "wired-in" responses render the organism independent of short-term fluctuations in the environment and keep it, as it were, developmentally "on track." In any case, the occurrence of the maturational processes awaits the development of the relevant synaptic wiring patterns in the brain that control them.

Behavioral scientists are more interested in experience-dependent processes, which do not exhibit the relative age dependency of experience-expected processes. Experience-dependent synaptogenesis depends on acquired information unique to the organism's particular environment, "information about the physical characteristics of the surroundings, the social system and the roles of specific individuals" (Greenough, Black, & Wallace, 1987:546). In other words, much of the variability in the wiring patterns of the brains of different individuals will depend on the kinds of physical, social, and cognitive environments they will encounter. The parts of the brain that depend on experience for their wiring patterns maintain their plasticity throughout the life span so that every time we experience or learn something, we shape and reshape the nervous system in ways that could never have been programmed.

A major contender for the primary integrative theory of neuronal development in the neurosciences is Edelman's (1987, 1992) *neural Darwinism*, which posits a selection process among competing cortical modules occurring in somatic time in ways analogous to natural selection in evolutionary time. Neuronal connections are selected for and selected against according to environments experienced by the individual during his or her lifetime; and like biological evolution, order is eventually generated in ways that are lawful but also indeterminate. Just as environmental challenges "select" from the organism's repertoire of genes those that help the organism and its progeny meet them, the brain's repertoire of cortical modules are all candidates for selection or pruning, the decision being made by the input pattern provided by the environment (Smith, 1993).

All cortical modules are not *equal* candidates for selection; GE correlation assures that some modules enjoy a greater probability of selection than others. Further, neuronal development is influenced epigenetically (i.e., by nonlinear genetic dynamics with autonomous organizing properties) so as to make even identical twins reared together different in many ways (Molenaar, Boomsma, & Dolan, 1993). The brain's probabilistic epigenesis has been invoked as an explanation for why nonshared (unique) environment is consistently found to be more powerful in accounting for variation in a wide variety of human traits than is shared (common) environment (Smith, 1993; Molenaar, Boomsma, & Dolan, 1993). Let us explore this process of brain development in the context of topics of great importance to behavioral science.

AFFECTION, ATTACHMENT, SELF-ESTEEM, AND THE BRAIN

Many sociological problems and issues (e.g., crime, drug abuse, poverty, the inability to form intimate interpersonal relationships, violence, and so on) may have their roots traced to early experiences that have left their mark on the neuronal pathways of the brain (Kraemer, 1992). I do not mean to deny or downplay sociocultural factors that are well known to be associated with these phenomena or to assert that neuronal wiring places any absolute limits on their influence. I do suggest that experience-dependent neuronal wiring patterns provide facilitating or inhibiting substrata that may affect how different individuals respond to similar experiences. Sociologists do not deny that characteristics and experiences that individuals bring with them to social networks and situations impact the way those networks are perceived and responded to. Biosociologists simply go one step further to explore the epigenetic rules that underlie the origins of those characteristics and experiences. The position taken here is that the affectual (love) experiences of infancy are a person's most important life experiences and that the self-esteem that emerges from those experiences is a person's most important attribute: "Research findings strongly support the centrality of a loving, dependable relationship for good start in life" (Hamburg, 1993:66).

Although modern behavioral scientists seem loathe to introduce such a "mystical" and "unmeasurable" variable as love into their work, the early giants of our disciplines waxed enthusiastically about it. August Comte saw love as the guiding principle of his positivist philosophy (Coser, 1971), Freud (1961) viewed it as the wellspring of civilization, and Maslow (1954) considered it a human imperative. Even such "macro" social thinkers as Marx and Engels saw love as the taproot of human personality when they wrote,

"Love, which first really teaches man to believe in the objective world out-side himself, which not only makes man an object [in the Meadian sense of 'becoming an object to oneself'], but the object a man" (1956:32). It is in-deed remarkable that such diverse thinkers, operating from quite different metatheoretical assumptions and with such contracting methodologies would arrive at the same conclusions about love (Walsh, 1986).[4] The relationship between early love experiences and social phenomena has been explored by anthropologist Ronald Rohner (1975), who studied it in 101 different cultures over a period of fifteen years. Rohner's studies led him to conclude that the need for love is not "culture bound," as some might suggest, but rather that it is a universal need of all human beings. If we do not receive it, he writes, "pernicious things happen to us" (Rohner, 1975:166); and these pernicious things "have implications permeating throughout both personality and the entire social system" (1975:173). Neurobiologist James Prescott (1975) came to the same conclusion from his study of forty-nine cultures.

The point I am making here is that love is not some ineffable phenomeno-logical mystery woven from cultural romanticism. I wish to locate love in a fully corporeal way in the neuronal lattices of the brain as part of our emo-tional programming. It has been pointed out that the great weight of the de-velopmental neurophysiological literature supports the notion that the lack of the physical manifestations of love during infancy produce "physiological effects that interfere with subsequent physiological maturation and/or normal physiological/behavioral interactions" (Reite, 1987:598). We have powerful neural and neuroendocrine structures that demand the formation of affectual bonds, and these structures are responsive to experience in both enduring and transient ways (Konner, 1982:301). Out of these experiences will emerge our self-evaluations.

Howard Kaplan (1982:139) has described self-esteem as "the dominant motive" in human personality, and William Glasser (1975) asserts that the need to feel worthwhile coupled with the need to love and be loved are the two basic psychological needs that must be fulfilled for healthy functioning. Glasser goes on to describe how these two needs are bound to one another: "Although these two needs are separate, a person who loves and is loved will usually feel that he is a worthwhile person, and one who is worthwhile is usually someone who is loved and can give love in return" (1975:11). A num-ber of studies (e.g., Buri, Kirchner, & Walsh, 1987; Walsh & Balazs, 1990) have supported this vital connection. The concept of experience-dependent neuronal development may elucidate the mechanism through which love and self-esteem are intimately related.

Phenomenologists and symbolic interactionists will look askance at any attempt to locate self-esteem in the physiology of the brain, especially at at-tempts to trace that physiology to the distal experiences of infancy. After all, they have already exorcised the psychoanalytic notion of subconscious de-terminants of behavior having their origin in early childhood. Central to the

nature of self-esteem, they would say, is the principle of reflected appraisals—we see ourselves as others see us. These appraisals are shifting, dynamic,
idiosyncratic, and located primarily in the phenomenology of the moment
(Rosenberg & Kaplan, 1982). Through these shifting reflected appraisals and
social comparisons we arrive at self-evaluation of personal worth, and these
evaluations of ourselves as worthy or unworthy are central to our lives and
greatly influence how we will live them. Further, these processes are "minding" processes that only involve the brain because minding is what the brain does.

Other than their disconnection of the individual from his or her past and
their mind–brain dualism, I have no disagreement with them. I believe that
they properly delineate the process of self-esteem development that flows
from their assumptions of a biologically irrelevant human nature. They view
the formation of self-esteem (and of the more general self-concept) as a purely
incorporeal cognitive process by which rational beings receive and process
verbal and nonverbal information relevant to their self-worth independent of
biological input. Certainly, as we acquire language and cognitive maturity
(both products of a brain maturation that exhibits considerable variability from
person to person), we do arrive at our evaluations via self-talk and introspec-
tion; and we can and do modify our evaluations accordingly. The information we pay attention to, however, and how it is processed and responded to
is rooted in preverbal experiences etched in our brains in response to genetic
and environmental influences. To ignore these rooted predispositions and how
they got there is to misunderstand the nature and origin of self-esteem.

It is not being implied that consciousness, subjectivity, and the human spirit
are nothing but the mechanistic firings of neurons, or that mind is simply an
epiphenomenon of the brain. The giants of neuroscience such as Charles
Sherrington, Wilder Penfield, John Eccles, Roger Sperry, and Gerald Edelman
have repudiated such extreme reductionism after once embracing it (Jones,
1992:187). Roger Sperry (1991:243) views the relationship between conscious thought and its physical and chemical referents as combining "traditional bottom-up [reductionist] with emergent top-down causation in a
'reciprocal' or 'doubly determinate' form of hierarchical control." We know
that by purely mental acts we can control and regulate all sorts of cerebral
and peripheral physiology, making subjectivity "no longer a mere impotent
epiphenomenon of brain activity . . . [but] a powerful impelling force in its
own right" (Sperry, 1991:239). Thus, my purpose in emphasizing the reductionist side of Sperry's "doubly determinate" notion of mind–brain–body causation is simply that it is the side with which sociologists are least familiar.

Learning to Love

Intelligence and adaptability are so crucial to human life that we require a
cerebral cortex much larger relative to body size than is necessary for other
animals. Humans are not developmentally equal to other primates at birth. If

they were, the size of the human head would be too large to pass through the birth canal. We have already seen that some scientists (e.g., Kolb & Whishaw, 1985) view the intricate folding of the cerebral cortex, along with the unfused sutures in the skulls of infants, to be an adaptive mechanism by which the need for cerebral mass and the necessity to pass through the birth canal was accommodated.[5]

Notwithstanding these mechanisms, the human female pelvis is still not as accommodated to the birthing process as are the pelves of other primates; and human females generally have more difficult births (Abitol, 1987). The pelvis of *Australopithecus*, our earliest hominid ancestor, was probably shaped by natural selection more to satisfy upright posture and bipedalism than to allow for increased fetal brain size (Abitol, 1987). Natural selection works on trajectories already in motion; it cannot anticipate future needs and must work with what it has. This conflict between obstetrical and postural requirements probably posed little difficulty until hominids were under strong selection for increased brain size. Hominid cranial capacity doubled between *Australopithecus afarensis* and *Homo erectus* (from a mean of 450 cubic centimeters to a mean of 900 cubic centimeters), placing tremendous reproductive burdens on females (Bromage, 1987). Selection for larger pelves may have been one strategy tried, but pelves large enough to allow the passage of human infants as developmentally advanced as other primate infants may have severely hindered locomotion and placed both mother and infant at the mercy of predators.

The evolutionary mechanism that accommodated the obstetrics–posture conflict was for human infants to be born at earlier and earlier stages of development as cerebral mass increased. The extent to which selection for premature birth has gone can be gauged by comparing the growth trajectories of the human and nonhuman primate fetal brains. The growth trajectory of the human fetal brain is unique. Whereas the fetal brain growth trajectories of other primates decrease at or before birth, the human trajectory continues for approximately one year after birth (Bromage, 1987:270). In other words, human infants experience a continuation of normal primate gestation outside the womb. Developmental scientists call these two gestation periods *uterogestation* (gestation in the womb), and *exterogestation* (gestation after birth). Such a high degree of developmental incompleteness of the brain assures a greater role for the extrauterine environment in human brain development than is true of any other species.

Although interuterine experiences can exert influence on the infant's subsequent development, the experiences it has during the ten months or so after birth are of greater importance. The infant is safe and secure in its sac of amniotic fluid during uterogestation, and one infant's experience during this period is very much like every other's unless the mother is particularly cavalier about her habits during pregnancy. Exterogestation environments are obviously more diverse, but as Montagu (1981:93) points out, the two gestation periods constitute "a continuing symbiotic relationship between mother and child in the exterogestation period . . . designed to endure in an unbroken continuum until the infant's brain weight has more than doubled." Montagu goes on to expand on this by stating that love is the cement of this relationship: "It is, in a very real and not in the least paradoxical sense, even more necessary to love than it is to live, for without love there can be no healthy growth or development, no real life. The neotenous principle for human beings—indeed, the evolutionary imperative—*is to live as if to live and love were one*" (1981:93, emphasis in original).

Closely allied with the concept of exterogestation is the concept of *neoteny*. Neoteny literally means "holding on to youth" and refers to the retention of fetal and juvenile traits of the species, and of related species, in its adult members (Montagu, 1981:9). Newborn chimps, for instance, possess many traits (e.g., rounded skull, flat face, lack of body hair, nonopposable big toe) that they will lose as they mature. Human beings lose far fewer of their fetal and juvenile features (both morphological and behavioral) than other mammals, including—as Montagu suggests previously—the need for love.

Neoteny has many important evolutionary advantages. Because human development is so delayed and prolonged, the developing human is given time to become adaptively affected by its developmental environment to a far greater degree than any other animal. The retention of the growth trends of the infant brain in humans allows for the process of "neural Darwinism" and thus the freedom from genetic control that humans have relative to other animals. As Stephen Jay Gould (1977:9) has remarked, "Neoteny has been a (probably *the*) major determinant of human evolution. Within this 'matrix of retardation,' adaptive features are easily retained. Retardation as a life-history strategy for longer learning and socialization may be far more important in human evolution than any of its morphological consequences."[6]

But developmental retardation and the plasticity associated with it is a double-edged sword. What if infants do not experience Montagu's "continuing symbiotic relationship"? Because we are so plastic, so sensitive to environmental influences, we can be seriously damaged by these experiences. A human infant is not only at the mercy of adults in terms of its physical survival. It can be lovingly cultivated into a decent, caring, and responsible adult; or its development can be distorted horribly. For better or for worse, humans have no hard-wired instincts that can override their experiences and protect their development into well-adjusted adulthood. Thus, applying Montagu's neotenous principle to the infant at the neurophysiological level means that the neonate's plastic brain must be organized for love—a quite literal "wiring" of the neuronal pathways via the process of neuronal selection.

The human infant has perhaps as many as 25-percent more synapses than it will have by the age of 12, thus providing ample choice for selection (Ackerman, 1992:99). As we have seen, synaptogenesis can be viewed in evolutionary "survival of the fittest" terms, with many adaptations (connections) being tried and discarded. In this competition for scarce synaptic space, strength and frequency of experience will determine which connections will survive (are "adaptive") and which will be pruned (Joseph, 1982; Kalil, 1989; Edelman, 1992; Kraemer, 1992). Interneuronal communication becomes habitual the more often the electrochemical synapses governing a particular response are activated, meaning that the "competition is biased in favor of the [neuron] populations that receive the greatest amount of stimulation during early development" (Levine, 1993:52). The process of forming and maintaining new synapses is rather like the establishment of a trail in the wilderness. The more often the trail is trodden, the more distinct it becomes from its surroundings and the more functional it becomes.

Eric Kandel (1983) has demonstrated the process of synaptic habituation in his laboratory. He used four-pound marine snails called *Aplysia Californica* because of the exceptionally large size of their neurons and because their synapses are virtually identical with those of human beings. Kandel subjected his snails to a variety of stimuli and was able to observe and photograph changes at the synapses produced by the stimuli. Kandel's work unequivocally demonstrated how environmental input regulates gene expression in the brain and how it modifies brain function by altering synaptic strength. Such findings strongly suggest that the relationship between biological and environmental processes in the brain is more intimate than was realized up to that time.

From this and similar research, biochemists Lynch and Baudry (1984) developed a biochemical theory of long-term memory. They theorize that an experience with strong emotional content is accompanied by especially strong nerve impulses. The strength and frequency of the impulse results in the neurons involved becoming more sensitive and responsive to similar stimuli in the future in a process Lynch and Baudry call *long-term potentiation* (see also Kandel & Hawkins, 1992). Their work suggests that in the process of long-term potentiation, an enzyme called calpain works on the neuronal membrane to expose additional receptors at the synapse. Membranes are incredibly "bright," and they "remember" via an intricate interplay of voltage-dependent channels what they have experienced (Llinas, 1989). Membrane changes in frequently activated neurons means that they are "primed" to fire with less provocation in future, thus laying down neurological tracks along which information is predisposed to travel. If the information being transmitted is negative (e.g., "You're not worthwhile or lovable," "The world is a cold, harsh, and abusive place"), the long-term potentiation consequences are obvious. Later communications, even if they are positive, will tend to be relayed along the same negative track via well-traveled action potentials as though some mischievous switch operator were stationed at a critical neurological junction ready to derail any train of pleasurable thought or feeling. What we call emotional programming at the neurological level is actually habituated electrochemical messages traveling along well-grooved synaptic pathways.

Liebowitz explains how these brain pathways established in early life in-
trude into our later lives. Although he emphasizes early negative environments
in this passage, the opposite is true for those who have experienced positive
early environments.

If someone grows up in a cruel, neglectful, uncaring or cold family atmosphere, the
chances are that as an adult he or she is going to have a store of painful memories.
What this means is that there will be a series of well-established links between memory
and the displeasure centers. As adults these people will be more prone to depression,
sadness, or pessimism. Anytime an unhappy childhood memory is evoked, the displeasure circuits will be activated. Also, new interactions that touch on any of these
old memories will often cause excessive emotional reactions in people who may not
even be aware of the connections between present and past. (Liebowitz, 1983:45)

Neuronal pathways blazed from the early experiences among experimentally deprived monkeys have been identified via aberrant electrophysiological activity (Restak, 1979:150) and by the viewing of actual dendritic wiring
(Suomi, 1980:10). In a seminal article derived from decades of laboratory
work, Kraemer (1992) reviewed the psychobiological effects of affectual
deprivation and attachment failure among Rhesus monkeys. Among the many
findings were (1) reductions in cortical and cerebellar dendritic branching;
(2) altered electrophysiology in the cerebellar and limbic regions;[7] (3)
disregulation of biogenic amine systems, particularly a reduction in norepinephrine concentrations in cerebrospinal fluid; (4) a neurobiological and
behavioral "supersensitivity" when exposed to pharmacological agents or
novel stimuli that act on biogenic amine systems; (5) changes in brain
cytoarchitecture (the cellular structure); and (6) the failure to organize emotional behavior in response to stressors. In other words, early attachment deprivation may cause permanently altered neurophysiological systems that will
adversely affect the organism's ability to interact adaptively with its world.

Caution should be exercised when extrapolating findings derived from one
species (monkeys) to another (human beings). As Kraemer (1992:526) indicates, whether we can validly make these comparisons is an empirical question. The fact that we share up to 99 percent of our genes with other primate
species (Feder & Park, 1989:145) notwithstanding, because humans possess
brains that are much more plastic than monkey brains, we are *more* likely to
be influenced by early experiences than monkeys are. Our plastic brain in-
ternalizes experience, we remember it, we respond to future experience influenced by it, we stew over it, and we "get even."

We can, of course, recognize the power of the environment in shaping the
human life course without becoming overly alarmist about negative or "dysfunctional" environments. Most people are not "horribly damaged" by most
negative experiences; people are more resilient than that. Deprivation studies such as Kraemer's elucidate certain mechanisms by which normal development may be diverted, but they also show that for diversion to occur among

genetically normal animals the deprivation must be severe. Although severely deprived environments can have a powerfully negative effect on proper development, among genetically normal individuals, cultural-normal behavior will develop within a wide range of "average expectable environments" (Scarr 1992, 1993). Certainly we can make judgments about the relative desirability of developmental environments. Some may be empirically demonstrated to be superior to others, but an extremely wide variety of environments allow for normal (culturally appropriate) human development.

ATTACHMENT STIMULI AND SYNAPTOGENESIS

We have seen that synaptic connections are pruned by disuse, just as a trail can disappear if no longer trodden. Well-trodden pathways laid down during infancy and childhood are more resistant to pruning than pathways laid down later in life, and that is why we cannot discount the affects of very early experience. The strength and durability of early learning in contrast to later learning can be grasped by observing how well very young children can learn two languages simultaneously with very little effort. They can continue to be comfortable with both languages throughout their lives, with neither language being contaminated by the accent of the other. Anyone who has tried to learn a foreign language in adulthood knows how difficult it is and how it is almost impossible to speak it without an accent. Children have this ability because their remarkably absorbent neotenous brains are physiologically more receptive (plastic) than are older brains.

Studies showing fairly robust positive correlatations between intercranial volume and IQ via MRI techniques (Willerman, Schultz, Rutledge, & Bigler, 1991; Andreasen et al., 1993) point to the possible great importance of the early years to the development of intelligence. Head size is greatly influenced by brain growth, which is nearly completed by the age of 6. The greatest period of brain growth occurs by the age of 2, however, by which time the cranial sutures are closed, setting a physical limit on further significant growth. From the results of their study, Andreasen and her colleagues (1993:133) conclude that "one might infer that the factors that influence head and brain growth and intelligence are in operation quite early." Of course, the volume of various brain structures reflect "quantity" and not necessarily "quality." However, such MRI studies add further evidence relative to the importance of the first few years of life to the future of the human organism.

The forging of neuronal pathways requires stimuli, and stimuli for the infant originate in a very limited environment. The more stimuli experienced by the infant, the greater the number, complexity, and speed of the interneuronal connections. The less stimuli experienced, the fewer will be the functional neuronal connections and the weaker they will be (Goldman-Rakic, 1987). Animal studies have repeatedly shown that organisms raised in stimuli-enriched environments develop greater cortical density and generate greater quantities of essential neurotransmitters than organisms raised in less stimulating conditions. Among earlier experiments of this kind, Rosenzweig, Bennett, and Diamond's (1973) series of sixteen experiments conducted over a period of nine years found that rats raised in stimuli-enriched environments had significantly greater cortical weight and significantly greater quantities of a number of neurotransmitters than rats raised in stimuli-impoverished environments. The biophysical brain enrichment of stimuli-enriched rats translated into a greater ability of the enriched rats to perform a number of learning tasks.

Evidence of the same phenomenon among human infants is provided by Rice (1977). Knowing that premature infants are at greater risk for physical, neurological, and social handicaps, as well as at greater risk for parental abuse, Rice explored the effects a daily dose of tactile stimulation would have on these infants. The experimental infants (n = 15) were given a full-body nude massage by their mothers for fifteen minutes four times a day for one month. Following the massage, the infants were rocked and cuddled for an additional five minutes. Infants in the control group (n = 14) were provided with the usual hospital care, with the massages being the only difference in otherwise identical treatment for the two groups.

Although there were no differences between the groups on the variables of interest measured at the onset of the study, comparing them after a period of four months it was found that the experimental infants were significantly superior to the control infants in weight gain; mental development; and, most markedly, in neurological development. Rice also provided evidence that the mothers and infants in the experimental group became more attached to one another than did the mothers and infants in the control group. Plentiful tactile stimuli is thus reflected in neural structure and chemistry and a more secure love bond between mother and infant.

The particular stimuli with which we are concerned are acts of cutaneous stimulation—affectionate touching, kissing, cuddling—tactile assurances for the infant that it is loved and secure. These manifestations of motherly love are not merely mutually satisfying psychological experiences; they are neurophysiologically critical during the sensitive period in which the neural pathways are being laid down. The importance of tactile stimulation to infant development demonstrated by Rice and many other researchers is rather dramatically stated by neurologist Richard Restak (1986:141): "Touch, it turns out, is as necessary to normal infant development as food and oxygen. Mother opens her arms to the infant, snuggles him, and a host of psychobiological processes are brought into harmony. Disrupt this process because the mother cannot or will not caress, touch or otherwise make skin-to-skin contact with the infant and psychobiological processes go askew . . . [and there are] physiological imbalances, behavioral peculiarities, hostilities, suppressed anger and rage."

The effects of tactile stimulation on the structure of the brain can be appreciated in the understanding that the skin is almost an extension of the brain, formed as it is from the same layer of tissue during the embryonic stage of life (Taylor, 1979:136). The intimate connection between the skin and the brain has been attested to by many neuroscientists who find that even light stimuli deprivation during the stage of active cell growth results in reduced neural metabolism, reduced dendritic growth, and the atrophy of neuron-nourishing glial cells. It is, therefore, of the utmost importance that infants be exposed to multiple stimuli, especially loving tactile stimulation, during this critical period. The more stimuli the infant receives, the more its neural machinery is honed and oiled to deal with all kinds of future emotional and intellectual problems.

In addition to its effect on dendritic growth, tactile stimulation also appears to increase the rate of axon myelination. Most of the axons in the human brain are unmyelinated at birth; most of it is laid down during the first two years of life. While myelinogenesis is primarily a function of unfolding gene expression (Campagnoni, 1985), it has been shown experimentally that tactually stimulated animals have significantly greater amounts of the material (cholesterol and the enzyme cholinesterase) necessary for myelin formation than animals who are not (Denenberg, 1981). It is a basic neurophysiological principle that the more frequently the nerve fibers of the brain are used, the more rapidly they become myelinated. The increased myelination results in greater ability to function in the environment, as determined by greater curiosity, problem-solving ability, dominance, and general liveliness among petted animals.

The importance of tactile stimulation is made palpable by the fact that the infant can only experience and express love or its absence through its body. It has none of the cognitive referents stressed by phenomenologists or symbolic interactionists with which to interpret the multitude of emotional states it is experiencing. Physical connectedness to mother has a long evolutionary history cemented by strong physiological and hormonal mechanisms (see Chapter 9). We are programmed to secrete the brain's own opiates (the endorphins) in situations of social comfort. On the other hand, a lack of intimate bodily contact between mother and child has been interpreted as abandonment, since, in a very real sense, the infant can only "think" with its skin. The infant's contact comfort experienced from its mother's sensitive responses during times of duress tells it that everything is OK: "She's there for me." "I'm safe." "All's right in my world." In the terminology of transactional analysis, this is the origin of an "I'm OK, you're OK" life position. Loved infants will know that they are OK because the taproot of "OK-ness" is love. Ashley Montagu (1978:208) summarizes the relationship between tactile stimulation and human development when he writes, "The kind of tactuality experienced during infancy and childhood not only produces the appropriate changes in the brain, but also affects the growth and development of the end-organs in the skin. The tactually deprived individual will suffer from a feedback deficiency between skin and brain that may seriously affect his development as a human being."

GENE–ENVIRONMENT
CORRELATION REVISITED

It has been noted that "the affection dimension of child rearing appears to pull in more correlates with child behavior than any other dimension" (Rowe, 1992:402). The vital importance of love and affection renders my argument that love resides in the brain, and that this "love" framework provides a system for developing a self-esteem framework evolutionarily quite plausible. Of course, there are no "love genes" or "self-esteem genes" at work to organize brain systems for the emergence of either, but there may be genes that organize the human infant to experience its world in such a way as to move it to grasp every opportunity to get as much of both as it can. Success in this endeavor lies largely in the hands of caregivers; but, as we have seen, human infants are not entirely passive recipients of experiences. They engage their caregivers in a reciprocal interchange of behavioral and affective responses that serve to shape the relationship. The active participation of the infant in acquiring and organizing experiences at one stage sets up a neuronal framework for subsequent experience-dependent systems (Black & Greenough, 1986). This participation, of course, depends heavily on the prior capacity of neuronal modules to provide perceptual and associative categorizations (Smith, 1993).

Behavioral genetic studies have demonstrated heritabilities in the 0.20 to 0.60 range for many measures of the family-rearing environment, especially for parental affection (Baker & Daniels, 1990; Plomin & Bergeman, 1991).[8] That is, pairs of individuals with a greater degree of genetic relatedness assess family-rearing variables (e.g., parental warmth and affection) more similarly than do individuals with a lesser degree of genetic relatedness. This will not surprise sociologists—after all, we all know that twins are treated more alike than nontwins—until it is realized we are talking about twins reared apart. That MZ twins reared apart assess the affectual experiences they had with their different parents of rearing more similarly than do siblings reared by the same parents suggests that affectual bonds between parents and children may have as much to do with the temperament and personality of the children as it does with parental child-rearing styles. In other words, reactive GE correlation is particularly strong where it involves parent–child love relationships (as evolutionary theory predicts it should); and these relationships profoundly affect the child throughout its life.

One of the genetically driven ways in which an infant shapes the degree of solicitude from mothers and other caregivers is smiling. In light of the numerous important sequelae of the smile in every culture and across the life course, Konner (1990:90) opines that "it is difficult to believe that natural selection could have left so important a signal to the vagaries of individual learning." A neonate's smile is brain stem generated and is reflexive (nonelicited), indiscriminate, and, as Konner indicates, is probably an evolutionary trait selected to evoke caregiving behavior. The so-called "social smile" is learned and discriminating after the smiling mechanism is transferred to the higher brain regions after some two months of life (Anastasiow, 1986:45). Infants who are temperamentally disposed to smiling provide a strong reinforcer for caregivers to administer to its needs, which, in turn, evokes further smiling behavior (Scarr & McCartney, 1983). This love–smile–love–smile feedback loop provides the infant with its first experience in human relationships and is an example of reactive GE correlation. Because infants with sensitive skin tend to smile more frequently (Freedman, 1974), their participation in the "expected" experience of love may reflect a pleiotropic effect of genes coding for sensitive skin and perhaps even a greater overall sensitivity to environmental stimuli mediated by RAS and ANS functioning.[9]

CONCLUSION

The lessons that the neurosciences have for sociology are many and exciting. Neuroscience stresses that the brain, like the genome, is a system of adaptation that responds to environmental challenges. It is an information processing organ that, to a large degree, "programs" itself in response to the information it receives from the environment in the form of nerve impulses; and it is a dynamic system that has changed in size, form, and function over evolutionary time just as radically as has the human body it operates. I have organized my discussion of the brain in this chapter around two concepts of central importance to the behavioral sciences—love and self-esteem—but there are many other important lessons to be reviewed in later chapters.

However, although the neurosciences have learned an awful lot about the physical and chemical properties of the various units that make up the brain, they still cannot tell us much about their aggregate properties. Out of the complex interactive function of these units emerges a new property (albeit consistent with states of the CNS) we call mind. As far as we know, "minding" is a unique property of humankind; and we are a long way from understanding how the brain's electrochemical processes produce it. Whatever mind is, it emerges from the interface of brain and its environment. We can probe the anatomy and physiology of the brain and discover many wonders; but in any ultimate sense, the brain cannot be understood apart from the environment in which it operates. Neuroscientists are the first to emphasize that we cannot expect answers to moral and ethical questions from analyses of brain structure and physiology and that we cannot eliminate the humanistic concept of rational human beings endowed with rights and responsibilities (Restak, 1992).

Neurobiological theoretician Gerald Edelman (1987:329) insists that his concepts of neural functioning have no place for "genetic determinism. . . . Instead, genetic and developmental factors interact to yield a system of remarkable complexity capable of a remarkable degree of freedom." Thus, sociologists need no more fear a neurodeterminism that neglects input from other areas of behavioral science than they need fear a monocausal genetic determinism. The combination of genes, environments, and the higher-order concept of neuronal selection that flows from them inclines me to have a more humanistic and liberating vision of the human condition than I could ever have if limited to the traditional social science image of human nature as simply a product of culture.

NOTES

1. Other brain structural divisions have been proposed depending on theoretical orientation. Evolutionists like to divide it up according to evolutionary stages—reptilian, paleomammalian, and neomammalian—and some anatomists prefer a forebrain, midbrain, and hindbrain division.

2. Human response plasticity does not mean less genetic involvement than hard-wired response systems. On the contrary, an open-response program requires more genetic information than a closed-response (hard-wired) program (Symons, 1987:127–128). Think of this in terms of the relative sophistication of the wiring programs for a television set and for an interactive video system such as those used by the armed services in their war games. A television is a closed system designed to pick up electronic signals and translate them into pictures. One does not need much information wired in for such a relatively simple task. The television watcher can only "interact" with the set by changing channels or switching it off; he or she cannot change the outcome of the drama being played out on the set. The interactive video system has to have much more information wired into it because, although it is also designed to pick up signals and translate them into pictures, it has to interact with a number of players who can alter the outcome of the drama in ways not easily predictable.

3. The idea that genes alone do not determine neuronal organization can be experimentally tested in the lab. Cloned animals, who are thus genetically identical, can be subjected to different environmental experiences and their neuronal patterns then compared. If genes were solely responsible for synaptogenesis, then axonal branching would be identical in isogenetic animals. Yet it is found that while the genes guide the neuronal architecture in each animal identically, the pattern of axonal branching is usually more variable from one clone to the other than between the left and right sides of the brain of the same individual (Changeux, 1985:207–208).

4. For a comprehensive view of the many putative physical, social, and psychological affects of love deprivation, see Walsh (1991b).

5. It might be more correct to refer to the unfused sutures of infants as an example of an exaptation (co-opted for their current role) rather than as an adaptation (explic-

itly designed by natural selecting for their current role [see Chapter 2]). Birds and animals which emerge from shells rather than birth canals also have unfused sutures.

6. Neoteny may have had even more profound effects on human evolution. Just a few "macromutations of genetic loci involved with developmental timing [leading to a high degree of neoteny]," explain Feder and Park (1989:145), may have been all that it took for protohumans to branch off the evolutionary line we shared with the apes.

7. This finding supports earlier theorizing by neuropsychologist James Prescott (1975), who posited an important link between the cerebellum and the limbic system in developing the ability to love. Prescott proposed that "somatosensory deprivation" (the lack of movement, rocking, cuddling, being whirled around, and so on) resulted in inadequate wiring between the cerebellum and the limbic system and has adverse affects on the infant's later ability to experience love and pleasure. He believed that this inability was a basic cause of many pathological behaviors.

8. Of course, environmental measures contain no DNA; but genetic effects on these measures are the result of covariance with the characteristics of individuals creating those environments (Plomin & Bergeman, 1991).

9. Low MAO (a measurable genetic characteristic) infants have been shown to be fussier, more active, and as having higher-than-normal rates of enuresis and thumb sucking (Ellis, 1991).

Chapter 4

Emotion and the Autonomic and Endocrine Systems

How important are the emotions in society? I would argue that they are quite fundamental. This is especially so if one conceives of emotion as a form of social energy, which can take any state ranging from completely passive inactivity on through strong affectual arousal.

—Randall Collins

If genes and brains are the engines and transmissions of our behavior, the ANS and the endocrine system are its carburetors and gasoline. ANSs, like carburetors, function variably, and the hormones that facilitate behavior vary in their effects and available quantities. As regulators of the engine's output, ANS functioning and hormone levels have major effects on emotion; and emotions have an impact on our behavior every bit as important as that of the intellect, perhaps even more so. "When we have characterized the biology of moods," writes Melvin Konner, "we will have characterized the major forces behind behavior" (1982:104). The acquisition of classical Pavlovian conditioned responses, and perhaps even of the human conscience, may be primarily a matter of ANS functioning (Eysenck, 1977; Mednick, 1979; J. Wilson & Herrnstein, 1985), and variability in sex-based behavior (aggressiveness, altruism, nurturance, visual-spatial and verbal skills, etc.) may depend to a great extent on hormone levels (Ellis, 1986; Udry, 1988; Fishbein, 1992).

ANS and hormonal processes are physiological processes that are of interest to sociologists only insofar as those processes find expression in social behavior. They can only find such expression in their interplay with the environmental stimuli that evoke them. Emotional states rely on social construction for their meaning, and culture has much to do with which stimuli we will perceive as affectively important and whether the impulse will be amplified or reduced. Although the impulses that stimulate the mechanisms of emotion demonstrate variability from culture to culture, the emotions they mediate (e.g., fear, rage, aggression, lust, etc.) are universal and due to a common evolutionary history (McNaughton, 1989; Levenson, Ekman, Heider, & Friesen, 1992). As is the case with almost all phylogenetic characteristics, the range of tolerance (variation in reactivity) for emotional stimuli within cultures is greater than the range between cultures; that is, individual differences also amplify or reduce the emotional impact of social stimuli.

Although there is an increasing interest in ANS and endocrine processes within psychology, there is little within sociology. The subfields of medical sociology and criminology find some interest in emotional processes, and a small "sociology of emotions" section was formed within the ASA in 1987 (Kemper, 1990b). By way of contrast, Randall Collins points out that early sociological theorists such as Durkheim and Weber employed concepts implying strong emotional content; and he himself believes that the importance of emotions in society is "quite fundamental . . . if one conceives of emotion as a form of social energy" (Collins, 1984:385). Many sociological phenomena may arise more from Collins's emotional "social energy" than from rational cognitive processes.

Sociologists of emotion tend to ignore the physiological side of the emotional equation, apparently under the assumption that the physiological mechanisms underlying emotional expression are constant across individuals and, therefore, irrelevant. (An important exception is Theodore Kemper's *Social Structure and Testosterone*, [1990a].) The assumption of equipotentiality in this area is just as wrong as it is for genes and brains. Emotion-driven behavior results from factors involving social structure, the phenomenology of the actor, and his or her physiology, all of which vary and interact in both predictable and ideosyncratic ways. I find it difficult to believe that an adequate sociology of emotional behavior can be developed without considering all three sources of variation. If Averill (1992:805) is correct in his appraisal of emotions as "the glue that holds societies together and sometimes the explosive that tears them asunder," sociology can no longer afford to neglect them.

Sociologists may be inclined to discount emotions because emotions are "irrational" and, therefore, difficult to think about in rational terms. Emotional behavior represents the failure of our vaunted neocortex to control the organism. Sociology is about "socialized" beings; and, as Freud's (1965:80) famous quote, "Where id was, there shall ego be," implies, socialization means divesting ourselves of "primitive" id impulses and substituting rational, cognitive (ego) processes. But there are times when nonrational behavior suits the purposes of natural selection, regardless of the havoc it may cause to the individual or to the group. Barkow (1991:121–123) sees emotions as "limbic-system overrides" of the rational neocortex in the service of natural selection. A moment's reflection on the many reproductive benefits of such emotions as love, jealousy, and anger—emotions no fully rational person would own because the pains, at least in the latter two emotions, are rarely accompanied by pleasure—should convince us of that.[1]

Emotionality is certainly more primitive than rationality. In the absence of well-organized cognitions and language, emotion-driven gestures and behavior patterns are the only ways social animals have of communicating. It is reasonable to speculate that natural selection for the emotions may have started shortly after the emergence of the first eukaryotic cells, perhaps some one billion years ago (Montagu, 1979:92). The selection pressures for the social emotions such as love, nurturance, gregariousness, altruism, and attachment probably increased as human offspring became more and more altricial as a consequence of selection pressures for increased brain size. The extreme degree altriciality and long dependency of human infants render it imperative that rapid social bonds between infant and mother be established and maintained and that adult monogamous sexual pair bonds be formed for at least long enough to form an infant caregiving team. To more fully understand the nature of social bonds, one needs at least an elementary grasp of the nature and role of emotions.

BASIC PRINCIPLES OF ANS FUNCTIONING

One of the primary distinguishing features of living things is their active responsiveness to the environment. Environmental events serve as stimuli which initiate responses from the organism via internal communication systems. There are two intimately related systems of internal communication in humans and other animals: the nervous system and the endocrine system. The nervous system consists of two parts: the central nervous system and the peripheral nervous system. The CNS—the spinal cord and the brain—is discussed in Chapter 3. All other parts of the nervous system not contained in the brain and spinal column constitute the peripheral nervous system.

Peripheral nervous system processes connect the CNS with receptors, muscles, and glands which are classified as either afferent (sensory) or efferent (motor) systems. The afferent system's nerve cells pick up information from receptors in the periphery of the body (as well as receptors that monitor the organism's internal environment) and convey it to the CNS, where it is processed and conveyed to the efferent system's motor cells. The efferent system is subdivided into the somatic (body) nervous system and the autonomic nervous system. The ANS conveys impulses from the CNS to areas not under conscious control, such as the heart and the glands, which are collectively referred to as the viscera.

Physiologists and psychologists formerly believed that the ANS functioned autonomously of the CNS (hence its name) and that it, unlike the CNS, was not open to learning or conditioning. We now know that it does not function independently of the CNS but that it is regulated by various brain structures (e.g., the hypothalamus via the cerebral cortex) and, as a consequence, is conditionable to some extent. The CNS–ANS distinction is another one of those artificial anatomical divisions made only for the purpose of convenience of study. Recent PET studies have shown that glucose metabolism rates vary in different brain areas, depending on the emotion being experienced (Gottschalk, 1990), pointing to the interplay of thought (CNS activity) and feeling (CNS plus ANS–hormonal activity).

The ANS itself is divided into two branches—the sympathetic (SNS) and parasympathetic (PNS)—which are antagonists in that they serve two different but complementary biological systems. The PNS serves the vegetative functions of the body; it conserves energy, is essentially inhibitory, and reflects the organism's functions during times of relaxation. The SNS serves the activation functions of the body; it is excitatory, mobilizes the body for action, and reflects the organism's functions during times of excitement and stress. SNS and PNS functions are analogous to the arousal and inhibition functions of the RAS and brain stem–spinal cord systems of the CNS, respectively. The SNS activates the body, and the RAS activates the brain.

The SNS is often referred to as the adrenergic system because it activates the same transmitter substances or their metabolites with analogous functions in the brain. The most familiar of these substances are epinephrine (adrenaline), which is associated with fear and anxiety, and norepinephrine (noradrenaline), which is associeted with anger. The PNS is referred to as a cholinergic (e.g., acetylcholine) system for the same reason. It operates as a counterbalance to return the body to a chemical balance when the emergency situation has passed. Although the SNS is a motor system with its primary effects being on muscles, in concert with the integrated functions of the CNS and endocrine system, it is considered an important regulator of our emotional life, guiding our pleasurable arousal and our avoidance of pain.

The catecholamines released from the adrenal glands in response to SNS activation contribute to the "feeling" component of emotions, but they do not constitute the emotion felt per se (i.e., they invest the emotion with visceral feeling, but they do not determine the emotion). Although there is evidence that under certain circumstances some emotion processes can operate independently of cognition (Izard, 1992), emotions usually arise from cerebral interpretations of environmental events; and they are produced by the hypothalamus and other limbic structures, not the ANS. Thus, emotions depend on perceptions of environmental stimuli and the meanings we invest in them more than on perceptions of visceral arousal, although proprioceptions can modify them. The artificial administration of catecholamines under laboratory conditions, while producing "feelings" (i.e., visceral arousal), do not usually result in emotions that subjects can identify (McNaughton, 1989:51–66).

THE ANS AND CONSCIENCE

Ever since human groups first established rules, people have been tempted to violate them. Many have done so, and many have been prevented from doing so by fear of punishment or by the bite of conscience. Violation of the constraints imposed on us by our conscience generates varying feelings of guilt, stress, and anxiety. We acquire this thing we call conscience by internalizing the moral proscriptions and prescriptions of our social groups in an ongoing process of socialization. I use the term *acquire* rather than *learn*, a term connotative of rational calculation, because I believe with Wilson and Herrnstein (1985:217) that "conscience differs from calculation and is a powerful force in its own right."

This is not to say that many aspects of the conscience are not derived from operant contingencies or deep reflection upon general moral principles. It means rather that these later-developed "higher reaches" of conscience develop on a substratum of self-reward based on ANS reactions to stimuli experienced early in life. Indeed, the affective component of conscience is observed as early as eighteen months, long before the child is able to reflect cognitively on its behavior as morally right or wrong (Kochanska, 1991). Commenting on the role of the ANS in the development of conscience, Trasler (1987:12–13) writes, "There are . . . good grounds for arguing that the essentials of conscience are laid down in the early years of dependent childhood, so that the later development of conscience consists in the elaboration and refinement of its cognitive superstructure, whereas the affective mechanism on which it is based, which provide its motivational mainspring, remain largely unchanged."

Trasler's "essentials of conscience" are derived from the "gut-level" principles of classical conditioning. Children must learn which behaviors are acceptable and which are not. Closely supervised children soon discover that unacceptable behavior is often followed by some form of parental reprimand. If John is reprimanded for sticking pins in the cat, the reprimand he receives will result in a variety of emotions mediated by his ANS such as fear, anger, hurt, and anxiety. Which emotions he experiences and the degree to which they affect him will depend on the severity of the reprimand and on his temperament (Kochanska, 1991). Assuming John is adequately responsive to his parent's discipline style, he will eventually name the punished behaviors as "naughty," "wicked," or "bad." This naming helps him to generalize his behavior so that in the future he will not stick pins in his sister either. If he refrains from such transgressions in the future, it is not because he has calculated the cost–benefit ratio involved but rather because his internal emotional response system will not allow it. How well John learns his lessons will not depend so much on his cognitive skills as it will on the amount of anxiety produced by his contemplation of unacceptable behavior, and this will be partially a function of the reactivity of his ANS.

The hypothesized physiological mechanisms by which children learn, or fail to learn, the moral contents of their culture should be of considerable interest to sociologists. Such learning (or failure to learn) is not a simple function of the input of socializing agents; rather, it is a function of those inputs interacting with the capacities and propensities children bring to the process, such as intelligence and the reactivity of their ANSs (GE interaction). Mednick (1979:50–51) offers a theory based on ANS responsiveness of how children learn to inhibit aggression, a theory which could be applied to many other learning situations. Succinctly put:

1. A child contemplates aggressive action.
2. Because of previous punishment, he suffers fear.
3. He inhibits the aggressive response.
4. His fear begins to dissipate, to be reduced.

Mednick further explains that this sequence of psychophysiological events requires a censuring agent, which can be the individual's own conscience or some outside agent, and an ANS that responds quickly, both in terms of generating the fear response and in terms of quickly returning to equilibrium. An individual who inhibits the contemplated aggression (perhaps by using verbal skills in self-talk) is reinforced by the reduction of ANS upheaval as it switches from the "fight or flight" reaction of the SNS to the PNS, which acts to restore visceral homeostasis. The fast recovery of the ANS reinforces the individual's aggression-inhibiting behavior and constitutes a pattern of self-reward in the form of fear reduction, "the most powerful, naturally occurring reinforcement that psychologists have discovered" (Mednick, 1979:50).

An individual whose ANS is relatively unresponsive to fear is less likely to inhibit the aggressive action because the contemplated aggression does not evoke fear and anxiety. Since fear and anxiety are not evoked, no reward can be forthcoming from its reduction. It is instructive to note that the cognitive experiencing of sanctions and the possible fear and anxiety they may provoke is a left-hemisphere (verbal) brain function (Buikhuisen, 1989:187), the area that is relatively nonresponsive in serious delinquents (Andrew, 1977; Ellis, 1990b; Walsh, 1991a). If such an individual does experience fear, slow recovery does not provide the aggression-inhibiting reinforcement that individuals with fast-reacting ANSs experience. People differ in their readiness to be conditioned to internalize rules—to develop a conscience—because of differential ANS reactivity, and this differential reactivity is often manifested in differential levels of norm-violating behavior (Eysenck, 1977; J. Wilson & Herrnstein, 1985; McNaughton, 1989; Kochanska, 1991).

This general line of thinking has been supported in a number of studies. Among a sample of children, Kagan, Reznick, and Snidman (1987) found that the behaviorally inhibited had significantly higher levels of the stress hormone cortisol than behaviorally uninhibited children based on both home and laboratory measures. Raine, Venables, and Williams (1990) found that measures of ANS and RAS underarousal (resting heart rate, skin conductance, and electroencephalographic activity) at age 15 correctly classified 74.7 percent of their subjects as "criminals" or "noncriminals" at the age of 24. Although they did not discount the role of social factors, their study failed to show that measured social factors mediated the relationship between ANS–RAS underarousal and criminal behavior. Summing up the literature on crime and ANS functioning, Mednick and Finello (1983:8) state that across a wide variety of studies and national settings, "The antisocial individual consistently evidences a relatively unresponsive ANS."

Serotonin, Impulsiveness, and Antisocial Behavior

The preceding discussion linking violence to ANS hyporeactivity may seem quite puzzling. Aggressive and violent behavior requires the powerful *arousal* of the sympathetic "action" branch of the ANS, so it is difficult to understand why individuals with hyporeactive ANSs are more violent than those with ANSs that are hyperreactive. Focusing on violent psychopaths, Mawson and Mawson (1977) have developed a neuropharmacological theory involving fluctuations in the relative dominance of two neurotransmitters systems: the andrenergic and cholinergic systems. The andrenergic (norepinephrine- and dopamine-based) system is responsible for sympathetic ANS arousal and behavioral activation, and the cholinergic (acetylcholine- and serotonin-based) system is responsible for parasympathetic ANS activation and behavioral inhibition. The Mawsons focus on the character of the oscillations of these systems and provide evidence suggesting that violent individuals are *both* hypo- and hyperarousable, depending on the situation. They are hypoarousable to relatively mild stimuli but hyperarousable when confronted with physical challenges and threats. While oscillations between adrenergic and cholinergic activation are physiologically normal and necessary, the rate and magnitude of the violent psychopath's oscillations may be much greater than normal.

A number of animal studies support the notion that serotonin modulates violence and generally inhibits behavioral responses to emotional stimuli (van Praag et al., 1987; Spoont, 1992). Similar findings among humans are reported by Virkkunen, DeJong, Barkto, Goodwin, and Linnoila (1989), who found that low serotonergic activity (measured by cerebrospinal levels of 5-HIAA, a metabolite of serotonin) significantly differentiated recidivist from nonrecidivist violent offenders and compulsive fire setters. Overall, research has supported the hypothesis that low CNS serotonin turnover is correlated with low impulse control (Virkkunen & Linnoila, 1990).

The concept of impulse control has received attention from mainstream criminology of late. Two of its most esteemed practitioners—Michael Gottfredson and Travis Hirschi (1990)—have developed a general theory of crime based on the concept of self-control in which they posit that poor self-control, more than any other stable individual difference, defines crime proneness. Weak self-control (impulsiveness, lack of constraint) is closely associated with negative emotionality, which is the tendency to experience aversive affective states such as anger, anxiety, and irritability more readily than positive emotionality (Caspi, Moffitt, Silva, Stouthamer-Loeber, Krueger, & Schmutte, 1994:187). Scores on the negative emotionality and constraint scales of the Multidimensional Personality Questionnaire (MPQ) are strongly related (rs ranging from 0.51 to 0.91) to self-reported and officially recorded criminality and are found across "countries, genders, races, and methods" (Caspi, Moffitt, Silva, Stouthamer-Loeber, Krueger, & Schmutte, 1994:163).

Emotionality (negative-positive) and constraint (control–dyscontrol), as measured by the MPQ, have been found to have heritability coefficients of about 0.50 to 0.60 (Tellegen, Lykken, Bouchard, Wilcox, Segal, & Rich, 1988; McGue, Bacon, & Lykken, 1993). Explorations of neurobiological mechanisms underlying individual differences on emotionality and constraint have emphasized the role of serotonin. Serotonin modulates negative emotional reactivity and promotes feelings of well-being and sleepiness by constraining dopamine-based signals (Spoont, 1992). Because serotonin constrains dopamine-based signals, it also blocks responsiveness to gonadal hormones and the behavior they facilitate (O'Connor & Fischette, 1987). Alcohol rapidly raises serotonin turnover and depletion rates, which allows for gonadal hormone responsiveness, which, in turn, may account for the aggressive and libidinous behavior of many chronic drinkers (Fishbein & Pease, 1990).

Negative emotionality and impulsive behavior are also traits associated with rearing in an abusive and discordant family environment (Caspi, Moffitt, Silva, Stouthamer-Loeber, Krueger, & Schmutte, 1994). Children growing up in such harsh environments will have experienced enough theatening events evoking negative emotionality that it may become a stable part of their response patterns. In other words, during the formative years of these children, threats to personal safety may have been so rooted in their everyday reality that a perceptual bias (well-habituated synaptic pathways) may now exist so that even mundane events sometimes evoke anger, irritability, aggression, and anxiety in their various combinations. This observation brings us back to the role of the early environment and its possible effect on the organism's typical neurohormonal status.

CONDITIONING THE ANS

The role of the ANS in the development of conscience and norm-violating behavior may not excite many sociologists unless it is tied in with the more general process of socialization. What might be going on in the family home that might lead to differential functioning of the ANS? The Mawsons conclude their article by writing, "Neither the present theory nor the low-arousal theory explains what is, perhaps, the major distinguishing characteristic of the psychopath: namely, his lack of affect and the inability to form close, personal relationships" (Mawson & Mawson, 1977:65). Picking up the thread we left in Chapter 3, a child's early attachment experiences may lead to both a lack of later attachment experiences and ANS functioning such as the Mawsons describe (Flaherty & Richman, 1986).

While the mechanisms underlying ANS functioning are primarily hereditary, the ANS is remarkably open to both operant and classical conditioning (McNaughton, 1989). One such mechanism that may permanently alter the way the ANS functions is frequent and protracted stress experienced during childhood. Hans Selye (1956, 1970) has examined the process of ANS conditioning in detail, focusing on the consequences of repeated exposure to environmental stressors of both a physical and psychological nature. He has termed his general theoretical model the *general adaptation syndrome* (GAS). Selye posits that the ANS and endocrine systems react to stressors in three general stages. The first—the *alarm reaction* stage—is an immediate and short-lived reaction initiated by hypothalamic stimulation of the SNS. The alarm stage mobilizes the body's resources for immediate activity by stimulating the adrenal and other endocrine glands to pour out large quantities of the "fight or flight" hormones that lead to greatly increased alertness and vigor. The heart beats faster, oxygen and other nutrients rush to the brain, blood surges to the muscles, and other "housekeeping" tasks are temporarily shut down. If the stressor lasts long enough or is repeated frequently, the second—or *resistance*—stage is reached in which there is elevation of some hormonal secretions, one of which (cortisol) suppresses the immune system if the stress is chronic. If this stage is successful in overcoming the stressor(s), the body "de-stresses" those parts under primary stress, and a general decrement of arousal is achieved. If this latter process is unsuccessful in returning the body's internal system to equilibrium, the organism may enter the third— or *exhaustion*—stage. Experiencing this stage may result in death or a marked change in the organism's physiochemical system (e.g., suppressed immunity, lower digestive rate, and emphasis on catabolic processes).

The process of physiochemical adjustment to constant stressful arousal has been demonstrated in laboratories. Most of us successfully navigate the resistance stage; and as a consequence, our ANS may become tougher (less reactive). The repeated cascade of chemical changes wrought by exposure to stressors is hardly good for our somatic or psychological health, so the body has to adapt. Solomon (1980) has shown that repeated stressful stimuli, in the form of electric shocks administered to laboratory animals, has a steadily decreasing effect on autonomic responses as the body succumbs to the accumulating effects of chronic stress. Over a period of time, the administration of negative stimuli has little or no effect on an animal's ANS, indicating that it has accepted the stimuli as "normal" and nothing to be particularly fearful about.[2]

Such evidence may provide clues as to why many abused children have been shown to possess ANSs similarly unreactive to fear and anxiety. Frequent exposure to cruel, brutal, and loveless environments may dampen ANS responses and thus make individuals who have been exposed to such environments more likely to engage in "fearless" antisocial behavior themselves and, furthermore, even to enjoy it. Buikhuisen (1982:214) suggests that this is indeed the case: "After some time he [the abused child] feels rejected and no longer loved by his parents. The continuous stress he is experiencing makes it necessary to look for defense mechanisms. To avoid being hurt, he develops a kind of flat emotionality, a so-called indifference with its physiological pendant: low reactivity of the autonomic nervous system."

Empirical evidence linking ANS functioning to negative childhood experiences and to delinquency is provided by Wadsworth (1976). He found that slow pulse rates among 5,362 young boys were predictive of later violent and sexual delinquent behavior. Boys with slow pulse rates were also shown to have been victims of childhood emotional stress at a significantly higher rate than boys with normal pulse rates. Other studies have confirmed these findings. Farrington (1987) found that convicted violent youths had significantly lower pulse rates than a control group of nonoffenders, and Venables (1987) found that "antisocial" youths had a significantly lower pulse rate mean than "prosocial" youths. Wadsworth (1976:246) makes the connection between ANS reactivity and childhood stress as follows: "Certainly from the published work it would be reasonable to speculate that children who in early life lived in surroundings of stress and emotional disturbances are more likely to develop some kind of mechanism for handling the effects of stress, and this may be reflected in later autonomic reactions to stressful stimuli."

There have been a number of animal experiments that help us to understand and link the line of thought presented by Wadsworth (1976) to the Mawson and Mawson (1977) theory of ANS lability. It has been shown that the stress-responsive adrenal cortices of rats unstressed during infancy weighed more than the cortices of rats subjected to stress during infancy. This suggested to Konner (1982:392) that the cortices of stressed rats had been "toughened" and would help to explain why stressed rats remained relatively calm when faced with fearful situations in adulthood.[3] However, Levine, Halmeyer, Karas, and Denenberg (1967) have shown that rats subjected to stresses during infancy are not uniformly unresponsive to stress. Rats stressed during infancy were shown to secrete less of the stress hormone corticosterone when mildly stressed as adults; but when confronted with severe stress they secreted significantly *more* corticosterone. Early stresses and emotional deprivation may, therefore, produce an ANS that is both hyporeactive to mild stressors and hyperreactive to severe stressors. Applying this to humans, we may speculate that a person with a highly labile ANS, because of his or her relative lack of fear, may be ready to put himself or herself in a potentially violent situation and, once there, may be more ready to respond aggressively.

More recent work on socially deprived rhesus monkeys supports this thesis at the neurotransmitter level. Kraemer's (1992) review of the literature reveals that maternal deprivation leads to a reduction in amine system output but also to a greater sensitivity of postsynaptic receptor systems. Amine supersensitivity is elicited by novel stimuli or pharmacological agents, such as stimulant drugs, that act to increase secretion of dopamine and norepinephrine. Kraemer (1992:500) points out that with the introduction of threatening stimuli or the administration of amphetamines, maternally deprived monkeys "become lethally aggressive and have inordinate increases in CSF [cerebrospinal fluid] and NE [norepinephrine] at dose levels that have little effect on the aggressive behavior or CSF NE of socially reared monkeys."

The responsibility for failure of socialization should not all be placed at the parental doorstep. Children are born with varying degrees of resistance to socialization, perhaps largely because of variation in ANS reactivity; and sometimes this resistance is too strong for parents to cope with. Even two children born to the same parents may differ radically on conditionability, an observation that led Zuckerman (1987:42) to state that "all parents are environmentalists until they have their second child." A first child may be temperamentally "sweet" and easy going, one who responds to parental affection with good behavior and affection of its own. A second child may be temperamentally difficult, withdrawn, moody, prone to temper tantrums, and react to affectual overtures with relative indifference.[4]

Punishment for misdeeds may be responded to by children adaptively or maladaptively, which will shape subsequent parental behavior in different directions. Parental responses to "difficult" and "easy" children present the children with different child-rearing environments (reactive GE correlation), which are, to some extent, the creations of the children themselves. Observations such as these have been responsible for behavioral geneticists (and some psychologists and sociologists) moving away from attributing nongenetic components of personality and behavioral differences to shared environments and toward the effects of nonshared environments (Plomin & Daniels, 1987).[5]

THE ENDOCRINE SYSTEM

The nervous system activates the body via the electrical stimulation of neurons; the endocrine system activates it by releasing hormones (they may be proteins, amines, or steroids) directly into the bloodstream. Working in unison with the ANS, the endocrine system's seven ductless glands secrete hormones to control the automatic functions of the body. Two of these glands—the pituitary and the pineal—are located in the brain, and the other five—thyroid, parathyroids, adrenals, pancreas, and gonads—are located in the body cavity.

Hormones, like neurotransmitters, are chemical messengers synthesized by genes that excite, stimulate, and set into motion chemical changes at target cells or organs to speed up or slow down biological processes. Hormone action can be very specific, affecting only one target; or it can be very general, speeding up or slowing down the entire body. When hormones have completed their tasks, they are inactivated by the target tissue or excreted in the urine. The nervous system (both the CNS and ANS) and endocrine system are interactive, with nerve impulses stimulating or inhibiting the release of hormones and hormones stimulating or inhibiting the flow of nerve impulses.

If genetics is the bête noire of social scientists engaged in studying learning, crime, and social class, endocrinology can be said to occupy a similar status with feminist and sex-role sociologists. Much of their animosity probably results from the view that behavior is a function of competing biological *or* psychosocial variables, a view exemplified by statements such as "No single hormonal state is a good predictor of any form of social behavior" (Andersen, 1988:57). Andersen is correct, but I wonder if she has ever heard anyone assert that hormonal states in isolation from an environmental context can predict social behavior. Such statements may arise from the old notion that the endocrine system is a closed one in which hormones transduce other hormones without involving the central nervous system (Rossi, 1977:10).

It has long been known, however, that the CNS's hypothalamus is in control of the pituitary (the master endocrine gland), that the pituitary controls both the autonomic and endocrine systems, and that hormones can act as neurotransmitters. The various biological systems are intimately related to each other and to the psychosocial world of the organism. It has been shown that the immune system's macrophages and lymphocytes have receptors for neuropeptides and can secrete them (Adler & Cohen, 1985). Since the brain can apparently communicate with the immune system and vice versa, it is hardly farfetched to assume that the way we think can affect our emotional states and that our emotional states can affect the way we think. Indeed, it is now often assumed that psychosocial effects are are among the most powerful determinants of immune system reactions (Kennedy, Glasser, & Kiecolt-Glasser, 1990; Cacioppo & Bernston, 1992).

Although some social scientists will never be convinced, psychoneuroendocrinologists insist that hormones, especially the sex hormones, play a powerful role in explaining our emotions, moods, and behavior. But they are well aware that the biological and social worlds overlap, that biological influence is not immutable, and that even such manifestly "biological" processes such as aging, health and illness, and reproduction are influenced by culture (Gottschalk, 1990). "In fact," writes Alice Rossi, "contemporary endocrinologists and primatologists are just as likely to study the influence of social and psychological factors upon hormone secretion as they are to trace the influence of hormones upon behavior" (1977:10). It can only be hoped that mainstream social scientists will drop the remnants of sterile nature–nurture thinking and become equally sophisticated in viewing human nature as a perpetual interaction of both.

The hormones of greatest interest to behavioral scientists are the powerful gonadal steroids, or sex hormones. The three major types of sex hormones are the "male" androgens and the "female" estrogens and progestins. Testosterone, the major androgen, is an anabolic steroid that promotes tissue growth and many other physiologically enhancing processes that make for an active and strenuous life (Khan & Cataio, 1984). Estradiol is the major estrogen, and progesterone the major progestin. Estrogen and progesterone promote the formation of fat and prepare the body for childbearing (Khan & Cataio, 1984). Both sexes secrete all three kinds of the major sex hormones, hence the qualifying quotation marks around "male" and "female." The ovaries and the adrenal glands secrete about 50 percent each of the androgens (primarily as precursors of estradiol) present in females. Males have between ten and fifteen times more testosterone than females, with 95 percent of it produced by the testes.

The steroid hormones represent different stages of biosynthesis rather than being strictly distinct substances. Using cholesterol as their major precursor, the testes and the ovaries, as well as the adrenal cortex, convert it into the steroid hormones. Both the testes and the ovaries secrete male and female hormones, sex differentiation being a function of the secretion patterns and the amount and availability of these hormones at various stages of sexual development (Khan & Cataio, 1984:15). The hormones produce varying levels of mood and behavioral activation, but their activating capacity depends on their free availability. Only those molecules (about 10%) not bound to SHBG, a large protein molecule that cannot pass through cell membranes, are available for biologic activity. Prior to puberty, males and females have about the same levels of SHBG; but by the end of puberty, males have only about half their former level. Thus, although men have about ten to fifteen times the concentration of total testosterone that women have, they have about twenty to thirty times more free (activating) testosterone (Udry, 1990; Buchanan, Eccles, & Becker, 1993).

The links between hormones and behavior are more complicated than naïve accounts imply, which lead some theorists either to discount their influence altogether or to misunderstand them seriously. Andersen (1988:56) does both when she correctly notes that postmenopausal women have lower levels of the "female" hormones estradiol and progesterone than males of the same age but then goes on to say, "Because there is no empirical evidence that older men are more feminine than older women, we must doubt the conclusion that hormonal differences explain differences in the behavior of the sexes."

Andersen's "conclusion," while based on a true premise, is a poor syllogism. First, the modifier "sex" in "sex hormones" loses its descriptive power after the reproductive phase of the human life span is over; nature is only interested in maximizing sex differences during this period. Second, the missing minor premise of her syllogism is that hormonal influence on sex-typed behavior is not a simple matter of their absolute levels but rather of their ratios; how, where, and if they act on the brain; and the hormone/SHBG ratio. Steroid hormones function in the brain as regulators of the genes that control the production of the various neurotransmitters in male and female brains in structurally different areas that are differentially sensitive to them (Khan & Cataio, 1984; Nyborg, 1984; Udry, 1990). The excitatory potential of neuronal receptor sites, as well as the number of receptor sites available, depends to a great extent on their exposure to specific hormones during the secondary stage of sexual development in utero.

Anne Moir and David Jessel (1991:9) have remarked that "there has seldom been a greater divide between what intelligent, enlightened opinion presumes—that men and women have the same brain—and what science knows—that they do not." There would be fewer erroneous syllogisms if "intelligent, enlightened opinion" knew what science knows—that the human brain, like the human body, is intrinsically female (this is true of all mammalian species). Unless induced by testicular androgens between the sixth and eighth week of gestation (the "androgen bath"), all mammalian brains will develop along feminine lines (Goodman, 1987). The effects of androgens and their metabolites first sensitize the male brain to the effects of androgens and later activates it to engage in male-typical behavior. Because femaleness is the intrinsic human form, no analogous trigger mechanism has been posited for the development of femaleness. Thus, hormones act on the brain to affect behavior in two ways: First, they have organizational effects on the brain in utero; second, they have activational effects, particularly at puberty and thereafter, which may or may not be dependent on prior organizational effects (Buchanan, Eccles, & Becker, 1993).

Once the brain is "sexed," the hypothalamus organizes hormone-secretion patterns in different ways; that is, sex hormones interact differently in male and female brains in areas sensitized in utero to be receptive to them. Both the estrogens and androgens act on the limbic system, the brain's emotional center, in areas that are structurally different in males and females. Testosterone is transformed in the adult brain into sex-specific variations—estradiol in females (but also sometimes in males), dihydrotestosterone (DHT) in males. Estradiol promotes nurturing behavior in females by lowering the threshold for firing the nerve fibers in the media preoptic hypothalamic area (Konner, 1982:318). Testosterone, on the other hand, lowers the firing threshold of the amygdala, the area of the brain most associated with violence and aggression (Konner, 1982:117; Gubernick, Sengelaub, & Kurz, 1993). Among rodents and other mammals, the male preoptic area responds to testosterone but not to estradiol; and the female preoptic area does not respond to testosterone (McEwen, 1981:1307).

Administering testosterone to animals of either sex increases fighting, while administering estradiol reduces it. Castration (removing the gonadal source of testosterone production) makes males less aggressive, and administering estrogen (neutralizing the effects of testosterone) is fairly successful in treating aggressive sex criminals (Emory, Cole, & Meyer, 1992). Although I do not wish to invest hormones with morality, the various hormones do influence our moods in ways that may be considered "good" or "bad." There is an abundance of literature indicating that estradiol and progesterone increases nurturing behavior and that testosterone diminishes nurturing behavior in both sexes (Terkell & Rosenblatt, 1972; LeVay, 1993). Females taking progestogen-dominant contraception pills report strong feelings of nurturance and affiliation and feel irritable and hostile when progesterone levels are low (Asso, 1983:64). The treatment of sex offenders by antiandrogen agents such as medroxyprogesterone acetate (DepoProvera) often results in reduction of hostile feelings and a general calming and sedation effect, along with a dampening of the libido (Emory, Cole, & Meyer, 1992). Thus, hormones participate in the way we feel and act and may do so rather strongly for some people at certain times.

PREMENSTRUAL TENSION SYNDROME
AND FEMALE VIOLENCE

Ellis and Austin (1971:395) conclude their study of female violence by writing, "In the case of the woman who kills her husband, lover, child . . . this study suggests that it is important to ask: What was her menstrual condition at the time of the event?" The emotional ups and downs accompanying the various phases of the menstrual cycle has received much attention over the years. An early study (Cooke, 1945) found that 84 percent of all reported violent crimes committed by women were committed during what is known as the paramenstruum period (four days prior to onset and four days into the menstrual period). Over a number of similar studies, it is estimated that about 62 percent of violent crimes committed by women are committed during this period (Taylor, 1984). If the monthly hormonal cycle had no effect on female violence, we would expect such acts to be evenly distributed throughout the cycle, not highly concentrated at this one eight-day period.

These studies have been criticized on methodological and interpretive grounds. A study designed to accommodate the various criticisms was conducted by d'Orban and Dalton (1980). Using a refined methodology, they did find a smaller percentage of violent crimes committed by women during the paramenstruum. However, the percentage (44%) was still significantly in excess of the expected rate of 29 percent ($p < 0.02$). They were also able to dismiss the various social learning alternative explanations posited by various critics. Nevertheless, they do not propose that homonal changes "cause" violence among women unalloyed by experience. They argue that the paramenstruum acts as a triggering factor probably only for "a group of women who are also prone to unstable and aggressive behaviour at other times" (d'Orban & Dalton, 1980:358).

Although the great majority of women manage to deal with the mild mood swings associated with the monthly cycle, a small number experience deep mood changes that they have difficulty dealing with. Such women are said to suffer from premenstrual tension syndrome (PMS). Although there are a number of theories about the causes of PMS, the most usual is the progesterone-deficiency theory. Hormonal assays of progesterone do appear to indicate consistently that women with PMS have lower levels than non-PMS women, and the administration of progesterone alleviates the symptoms of PMS for most women (Trunnell, Turner, & Keye, 1988).

Many studies have found that upwards of 75 percent of menstruating women report mood shifts during the menstrual cycle (see Thompson [1988] for a review). Positive moods are reported around ovulation, when estrogen peaks; and negative moods are reported during the paramenstruum period. During the paramenstruum period, progesterone levels drop almost to zero; estradiol levels drop to 50 percent of midcycle baseline measures; and testosterone remains relatively high at 82 percent of baseline (Utain, 1980:32). Recalling the putative "feeling" affects of these substances, we might speculate with Glen Wilson (1983:36) that the male-like violence sometimes expressed by women who suffer extreme PMS is a function of these women being chemically more "male-like" at this time. Possible support for this view is the review of the literature on the physiological fluctuations accompanying the menstrual cycle by Barfield (1976:71–73). Some of these studies report premenstrual increases in metabolic rate and visual–spatial sensitivity and decreases in sensitivity to touch, sound, and smell. A more recent study (Kimura & Hampton, 1988) among 150 premenopausal women found that the average discrepancy in male–female spatial ability was halved when estrogen was at its lowest. The abilities that increase among premenstrual women are those in which males normally excel, and those that decrease are areas in which females normally excel.

The regulation of the menstrual cycle involves complex interactions between neurotransmitters, pituitary gonadotropins, and the ovarian steroids. Since all women experience some degree of mood change over the cycle, it has been suggested that those who suffer extreme symptomology be considered to be suffering from "premenstrual dysphoric disorder" rather than the more common PMS (Haskett, 1987). Haskett cautions that the state of our knowledge about the pathophysiology of this disorder is poorly known and that researchers can do little more than speculate about the mechanisms relating this disorder to female violence at present. It is plain, however, that we cannot correlate hormonal and mood swings while disregarding whatever else is occurring in women's lives at the same time.

Environmental Influences on Hormonal Secretion

Hormones do not "cause" behavior unalloyed by social experience. Taking the putative causal influence of testosterone on aggression as an example, in a review of eighteen studies using various kinds of samples and various definitions of aggression, Rubin (1987) found only one study in which testosterone level was related to aggression as "strongly positive." Five studies showed a "weakly positive" relationship, six were "moderately positive," and six showed no relationship. The absence of any negative studies, however, indicates that aggressive behavior does not fluctuate randomly around testosterone levels. One large-scale study divided a sample of 4,462 men into normal and high (upper 10%) levels of testosterone (Dabbs & Morris, 1990). High-testosterone men were shown to be a higher risk for a number of antisocial acts, having risk ratios ranging from 1.3:1 for number of sex partners to 2.1:1 for hard drug usage. When risk ratios were computed within low and high SES (split at the median), the risk ratios for normal- and high-testosterone males increased slightly among low SES males. Risk ratios became smaller among high SES males, with one exception: They remained in the predicted direction. This study provides us with two lessons regarding the correlation of testosterone with antisocial behavior: (1) Strong effects of testosterone on male behavior appear to occur mainly at extreme levels, and (2) even at those extreme levels, its effects are mediated by sociocultural variables.

The thermostatic interaction of the CNS and the endocrine system (the brain is both crucial to the release of hormones and a target for their effects) supports this. Absent activating environmental input, the level of circulating hormones is not appreciably altered because when hormones are present in sufficient quantities to meet the organism's present needs, the hormones themselves inhibit further production. When the organism is presented with environmental challenges, hormone-releasing peptides trigger the release of additional hormones to meet them (Whybrow, 1984). The hormonal feedback loop illustrates one of the many ways that environmental stimuli regulate gene expression. Hormones circulating in the blood reach into the nucleus of the target cell to activate the DNA to produce more hormones whenever environmental challange calls for their production (Gottlieb, 1991:5).

Rose, Holaday, and Bernstein (1971) have dramatically demonstrated the responsiveness of testosterone levels to environmental experience. They took a number of male rhesus monkeys and placed them individually into colonies consisting of thirteen or more female monkeys. In every instance, the lone male assumed dominance and settled into a blissful existence, which included frequent copulation with all females. After several weeks of this, testosterone assays were taken; and it was found, compared to baseline levels, that each male's level of circulating testosterone showed an approximate fourfold increase. The experimental monkeys were then removed from the all-female colonies and placed individually into different colonies of all-male monkeys in which dominance hierarchies were already established. The intruder monkeys were immediately set upon by the others and quickly subjugated. After thirty minutes of this treatment, each monkey was removed from its respective colony; and testosterone levels were again assayed. It was found that in every case the testosterone levels banked from their experience in the female colonies had declined precipitously. Apparently, testosterone increases to meet demand (frequent copulations) and declines when submissiveness is deemed the path of least resistance.

The relationship between testosterone levels and dominance is not limited to nonhuman subjects. Ehrenkranz, Bliss, and Sheard (1974) found that socially dominant and aggressive prison inmates had significantly higher testosterone levels than did a control group of prisoners identified as nonaggressive and nondominant (see Kemper [1990a] for a review of numerous such studies). Most studies finding moderate to strong correlations between testosterone and violence have focused on actual behavior, while studies finding weak to nonexistent relationships have focused on psychological tests (Gove, 1985). An exception to this is Schalling's study (1987) of a group of Swedish delinquents. She found that testosterone levels were associated with various measures of aggression (physical, verbal, and preference for physical sports), as well as extroversion. Correlations were particularly strong among youths who had reached pubertal maturity, a period during which males experience a ten- to twentyfold increase in testosterone and a halving of SHBG (Udry, 1990). The correlations for overall aggression, preference for physical sports, extroversion, and monotony avoidance were 0.56, 0.61, 0.48, and 0.50, respectively.

Further evidence of the role of testosterone in violence and aggression comes from studies of aging and castration. Increasing age brings with it a gradual decline in testosterone levels (most noticeably, but still very gradually, after 50 years of age) and an increase in the deaminating enzme MAO, as well as a dramatic decline in aggressive and other antisocial behaviors (Rushton, Fulker, Neale, Nias, & Eysenck, 1986; Balazs, 1992). In a review of the European literature on the therapeutic castration of rapists, Bradford (1990) found recidivism rates ranging from 0 to 7.4 percent over a twenty-five-year follow-up period. The large number of rapists (2,055) studied, the long follow-up time, and the contrast with recidivism rates among noncastrated American rapists followed for minimal periods (reported to be around 40 percent [Heim & Hursch, 1979]) renders this a powerful argument for the involvement of testosterone in sexual offending and for a biosocial theory of rape (Ellis, 1989). This does not mean that castration eliminates sexual behavior, only that it decreases its frequency and assertiveness. In rare instances, sexual responsiveness may not significantly decline for years after castration (Thompson, 1988:56), which supports the position that hormones facilitate, not "cause" behavior.

Researchers exploring the link between aggression and testosterone are careful to emphasize that the direction of facilitation is not clear. Experience may have a greater effect on testosterone production (and on the production of other hormones) than endogenous hormonal production has on behavior (Kemper, 1990a). It is probable that high testosterone levels function as an additional risk factor for individuals predisposed by social and psychological factors to be violent. Certainly youths inhabiting violent and disadvantaged environments have many occasions to react aggressively, and hormonal levels will increase to meet the environmental challenge. Successful aggression may then lead to even higher levels of testosterone and to a greater risk of further violence. The synergistic nature of biological–environmental interaction is perhaps nowhere more evident than in the ups and downs of the gonadal steroid hormones. We may conclude, as did one expert in the field of the chemistry of violence, that "overall there are fairly consistent data indicating that vertebrate male aggression is organized by the early influence of androgens [on the developing brain] and is triggered post pubertally by androgens" (Thiessen, 1976:75).

SEX DIFFERENCES IN EMOTIONALISM

An emotion is a person's subjective awareness and feeling accompanying physiological changes, the affective aspect of consciousness. Emotionalism is the tendency to invest experience with more feeling than rationality. The tendency toward emotionalism may be considered good or bad depending on the emotion being expressed (e.g., nurturance versus anger). Given the putative emotional affects of the various "male" and "female" sex hormones, we should not be surprised to find that males tend to exhibit negative emotions to a greater degree than females, and vice versa (Miller, 1988; Ellis, 1990b; Heller, 1990). Rushton, Fulker, Neale, Nias, and Eysenck (1986) conducted a behavioral genetic study of various emotions among 573 twin pairs and found heritability coefficients for most emotions near 0.5. They also found strong age and sex differences in emotionality, with females and older people being more altruistic, nurturant, and empathetic, and males and younger people being more aggressive and dominant. They implicated hormones as largely responsible for these differences: "Larger amounts of gonadal hormone such as testosterone predisposes toward aggressiveness, which in turn decreases empathy. This would explain the negative relationship between aggression and altruism, as well as the age and sex difference, for testosterone production is known to decrease with age and to differentiate the sexes in the predicted direction" (Rushton, Fulker, Neale, Nias, & Eysenck, 1986:1197).

The role of social factors (i.e., sex and age differences), although difficult to disentangle from genetic–hormonal factors, cannot be ignored. Role expectations change with age: There is less antisocial peer pressure, a greater psychosocial maturity, an increase in conservatism, and more reasonable ambitions (Balazs, 1992:227). Most of the nongenetic variance in the afore-mentioned study by Rushton and his colleagues (1986) was attributed to the twins' specific environment, however, with negligible variance in either aggression or altruism being accounted for by shared environment.

Because emotion is a neuroendocrine process, sex differences in brain structure and function should also provide clues to sex differences in emotional behavior. One area of the brain of importance to emotional behavior is the RAS. As was briefly noted in Chapter 3, the RAS is a component of the CNS that monitors and adjusts the level of arousal of higher brain centers to the ongoing level of sensory information from the environment. It functions as a stimuli "filter" so that the higher brain centers will consciously attend only to those stimuli that are meaningful to the organism. It is assumed that there is an "optimal" level of sensory arousal for all individuals, but what that optimum is varies from person to person (Thompson, 1988:26). Some people have RASs that augment or exaggerate the meaningfulness of incoming stimuli; others have levels of RAS arousal that lead them to reduce or diminish it. Using various psychological and physiological indices of cortical arousal, it has been found that females have a greater tendency to be augmenters and males have a greater tendency to be reducers (Zuckerman, Buchsbaum, & Murphy, 1980; Martineau, Tanguay, Garreau, Roux, & Lelord, 1984). The greater sensitivity of females to sound, touch, taste, and smell, as well as their greater sensitivity to the emotional content of stimuli, may be at least partially explained by their higher level of RAS arousal (Walsh & Walsh, 1993).

Ellis and Coontz (1990) review evidence from a variety of sources that organizational effects of androgens circulating prenatally make for a decrement in male RAS arousal relative to that of the female. Included in this evidence is the significantly greater death rate of male infants from sudden infant death syndrome (SIDS) or crib death, which may be a function of cessation of RAS control over respiratory and cardiac functioning during sleep, although the exact etiology of SIDS is still unknown. Another indicator of male low RAS arousal relative to that of the female included in Ellis and Coontz's review is that males have been found to have hyperactivity rates up to ten times greater than those of females. The hyperactive child is chronically bored with a stimuli level most individuals would find appropriate. Chronic boredom leads the hyperactive child to seek unacceptable novel sensations impulsively, which gets him or her into frequent trouble. High levels of sensation seeking are significantly associated with elevated androgen levels among both males and females, as well as with low levels of MAO (Zuckerman, Buchsbaum, & Murphy, 1980; Daitzman & Zuckerman, 1980; Zuckerman, 1990). The apparent inability of psychopaths to experience normal emotional states such as anxiety, fear, empathy, and love may be seen as the tandem hyporeactivity of their autonomic and reticular activating systems to environmental stimuli (Ellis, 1987b).

Hemisphericity and Emotions

There is also a growing body of evidence that the two hemispheres of the brain play different roles in our emotional behavior. It appears that the right hemisphere is more involved in responding to emotional stimuli, especially negative stimuli, than is the left hemisphere (Miller, 1988; Davidson, 1992). Electroencephalographic (EEG) studies have shown that the joy experienced by infants being approached by their mothers is associated with left-hemisphere activation and that displeasure at being separated from mother is associated with right hemisphere activation (Fox & Davidson, 1987). Further evidence comes from studies of brain-injured patients. Although the two hemispheres are in intimate communication, some researchers believe that they may exert a kind of "inhibitory control" over one another, functioning as a kind of hemispheric check-and-balance system. When an injury to one side occurs, this reciprocal control is disturbed, which allows for the emotional biases of the other to dominate. Injury to the left hemisphere often results in depression as the right hemisphere predominates, and injury to the right hemisphere often results in indifference or euphoria (Miller, 1988).

We know that male brains are more lateralized (more task specific) than female brains, that the cortical rind of the right hemisphere is thicker in males, and that the cortical rind of the left hemisphere is thicker in females. Indications are that the slight retardation of neurological development of the left side of the male brain (which allows the right side to assert itself a bit more) is caused by the level of androgens circulating during the process of diverting the male brain from its default female development (Marx 1982, 1983; Gerschwind, 1984; Diamond, 1984). The less rigid hemispheric division of labor among females may allow them to experience the emotional life in more comprehensive ways. Research indicates that males only recognize the emotional content of a visual message when it is transmitted to the right-brain hemisphere (i.e., when it is presented to the left eye). Women recognize the emotional content regardless of which side of the brain it was transmitted to (Moir & Jessel, 1991:46).[6]

A brain structure that may partake in the greater "holism" of stimuli processing in the female brain is the splenium, the posterior portion of the corpus collosum. Female splenia have been found to be significantly larger than male splenia, containing perhaps a few hundred thousand more connecting axons (de Lacoste-Utamsing & Holloway, 1982). While cautious in their interpretation of this finding, the implication is that the more fibers contained in the splenium, the greater is the capacity for interhemispheric information transfer. These findings remain controversial, however, because of the failure of some attempts to replicate them (Kimura, 1992).

Women's ability to "get to the heart" of emotional stimuli faster and more efficiently than men allows them to experience emotion in ways considered more psychologically healthy than it is experienced by men. Psychoneuroendocrinologist Paul Pearsall (1987) believes that the more brain-lateralized male tends to be more "self-oriented," while the more integrated female brain tends to be more "other" and "us oriented." He goes on to write that the "whole brain orientation is more in tune with the principles of healthy living in our world and for our world" (1987:33).[7] From a sociological point of view, Miller (1984:1) sees male development of self as entailing a process of separating, of becoming "one's own man," and the female process as more "encompassing," and "closer to the elementary necessities from which our dominant culture has become unnecessarily removed" (1984:5). Whether we work from a biological or a sociological position, we arrive at the same conclusion: Females are generally more affiliative, nurturing, empathetic, and altruistic than males; and males are generally more prone to anger, dominance, and aggression. The qualifier "generally" emphasizes that we are talking about trait distributions with mean values differing by sex but which also contain significant overlap, more so on some traits than on others. I do not wish to create caricatures of "Man, the beastly destroyer" and "Woman, the loving creator." There are certainly many sensitive, caring, and pacifist men and many insensitive, uncaring, and aggressive women.

CONCLUSION

As emphasized in previous chapters, human beings and their social organizations are not determined by biological fiat. We saw that genes are units of potential that are differentially expressed or repressed in different environments and that our brains are, in a very real sense, "programmed" by our environments and how we react to them (although our genes bias our reactions in one direction or the other). It is not farfetched to say, then, that our genes and brains are in some meaningful sense environmentally "determined." If this is true of genes and brains, it is even more true of the physiological foundations of emotional behavior. Emotional expression is a function of environmental events, our expectations related to those events derived from experiencing similar events, and the neurohormonal propensities individuals bring with them to the situation. Although I have emphasized the reductionist side of the hormone–environment relationship, perhaps in no other area is the biological and social mix more intertwined than in the area of emotion.

NOTES

1. Barkow's position is an echo of Desiderius Erasmus's posited in his famous book, *The Praise of Folly*, published in 1511. Erasmus posited the notion that the human race owes its existence to folly, the definition of which included emotions, impulses, and instincts. Note the agreement with Barkow in Will Durant's (1957:277) account of Erasmus's book: "The whole human race . . . owes its existence to folly, for what is so absurd as the male's polymorphous pursuit of the female, his feverish idealization

of her flesh, his goatish passion for copulation? . . . If men and women paused to reason, all would be lost."

2. Studies show that chronic stress that is predictable in time or duration, and over which the individual has a sense of control, has less physiological and psychological effect than unpredictable chronic stress over which the individual has no control (Thompson, 1988:52; McNaughton, 1989:59).

3. Many researchers would suggest that this "toughening" indicates increased demand for glucocorticoids due to chronic stress, resulting in adrenal hypertrophy. Indeed, before the development of sensitive hormone assays, adrenal weights were used as a measure of stress (Alfred Dufty, personal communication, 1993).

4. Differences in temperament are observed in infants only days, weeks, and months old. Significant mean differences are found among infants of different racial groups, with white infants falling rather consistently between black and Asian infants on many traits. Asian infants are more adaptable, quiet, stoic, and serene, while black infants are more active, noisy, and difficult to console (Freedman, 1984).

5. The concepts of GE correlation and nonshared environment are related in that differences between family members who share a common environment are the products of the "microenvironments" unique to each family member: "Microenvironments are largely the construction of individual family members in the ways they evoke responses from others, actively select or ignore opportunities, and construct their own experiences" (Scarr, 1992:14). The effects of nonshared environments often work to make siblings no more alike in terms of personality than any two same-sex individuals chosen at random from the general population.

6. Brain injuries to one hemisphere are less likely to be permanently disruptive of brain processes in females than in males because any information associated with the specific injured area can be more readily transferred to the other hemisphere. It is consistently found that female stroke victims, for instance, recover more readily from the ravages than do male victims (Witelson, 1976).

7. Some readers may find Pearsall's "healthy living" statement troubling in the sense that he may appear to be rewriting our biological history. Male and female brains evolved in response to the pressures of natural selection and sexual selection, and thus it makes little biological sense to call either "healthy" or "unhealthy" with respect to one another. The traits that Pearsall (and Miller) consider less than healthy, such as aggression and dominance, were useful in our ancestral environments in that they favored individuals possessing them at higher levels by allowing them to better survive and reproduce. Hence, in this strictly evolutionary sense, these male traits are every bit as "healthy" as evolved female traits, even though our value orientations may lead us to favor female traits. However, the fact that these male traits were valuable in our ancestral environments does not mean that they are necessarily beneficial in their manifestations in our current environments. Adaptations may have many "side effects" that gainsay *culturally* healthy living. For instance, human rape has been considered a maladaptive ("unhealthy") side effect of the more general adaptive ("healthy") male reproductive strategy (Ellis, 1989; Thornhill & Thornhill, 1992).

Chapter 5

Intelligence and Society

> Constitutional differences in personality are recognized in differences in the processing of sensory information, in intelligence, temperament, and motivation. These constitutional features of persons interact with lessons learned. . . . Questions can be asked about how one learns and about what one learns.
>
> —Gwynn Nettler

If there is one proposition with which all sociologists would agree, it is that the human neonate has no preprogrammed values, attitudes, or beliefs and that these mental abstractions, the behaviors associated with them, and a million other things must be learned in social interaction. Human learning requires cognition, and cognition makes use of symbols—letters, words, pictures, formulas, and so on—that stand for the physical aspects of our environment and the relationships among them. Sociologists and anthropologists are interested in *what* we learn (the contents of our cultures), and psychologists are interested in *how* we learn (the associative methods humans use to acquire adaptive knowledge). The differential *ability* or *capacity* to learn—to make efficient use of symbols—is studied by psychologists and behavioral geneticists, but mainstream behavioral scientists have rarely considered this aspect of learning when exploring the whats and hows of becoming social beings.

Almost everyone learns the basic requirements of social participation, but the rewards of a modern complex society go to those with the ability to assimilate a culture forever in flux and forever moving in the direction of broadening scope and deepening complexity. To the extent that this is true, the issue of differential ability (differential intelligence) becomes more and more socially relevant: "Intelligence has a profound effect on the structure of society, not necessarily because it is the most highly valued of individual differences—although conceivably it is—but rather because it may have the widest and most stable distribution among all the traits that are valuable in industrialized nations" (Gottfredson, 1986:406).[1]

The term *intelligence* has aquired something of a bad name among social scientists (consider the brouhaha following the publication of Herrnstein and Murray's *The Bell Curve* [1994]). Intelligence as operationalized by IQ tests is at the center of tension between two sets of imbedded American values: merit and equality. Merit stresses individuality and differences; equality stresses fairness and similarity. Confronted with a wide range of within- and between-group IQ scores, those who hold for merit will attribute it to variability in individual capacity; those who hold for equality will attribute it to environmental variability. The issue could not remain at an impasse for long because, although saturated with ideological fanaticism, it was amenable to scrutiny by those holding the firm conviction that science is self-correcting. If there are meaningful measured differences in capacity to learn, surely it is better to confront them rather than to continue to deny they exist. Only when we are able to correctly identify sources of variation can we hope to identify agents of change correctly.

The position taken here is one increasingly accepted in the behavioral sciences; that is, differences in cognitive ability are significantly and substantially associated with genetic variability. The ever-increasing evidence of substantial genetic influence on intelligence led Plomin and Neiderhiser (1991:369) to ask, "Would any scientist today dispute this conclusion, which created such a furor in the 1970's?" There are some who would. Brand (1987:768) calls them "flat-Earthists," an impolite and not altogether fair characterization but more civilized than the verbal and even physical attacks visited upon hereditarians in the 1970s by environmentalists.

Although general intelligence may now be psychology's principal theoretical construct, "on par with the gene for geneticists, social class for the sociologists, and the ion for chemists" (Brand, 1987:767), there is still a vast amount of literature seeking to come to grips with its definition. Intelligence is easier to recognize (and to measure) than to define. The root word of intelligence is *intelligo*, which means "to select among." Etymologically, then, intelligence implies the ability to select from among a variety of elements (whatever they may be) and analyze, synthesize, and arrange them in such a way as to provide satisfactory—and sometimes novel—solutions to problems the elements may pose. Nevertheless, any nominal definition of intelligence is wide open to criticism, as are all verbal definitions of meaningful concepts such as love, truth, and justice. We argue over verbal definitions of important concepts because they encompass a multitude of subconcepts. They would hardly be important if they did not. Most definitions, however, do contain elements about which there is general consensus: "Love is the recognition of special value in the loved one." "Truth is speaking in a manner consistent with the facts." "Justice consists of impartial adjustments of conflicting claims." These are grossly simplified definitions, but they serve as prolegomena to more critical extensions.

This is not the place to review the voluminous literature debating the "essence" of intelligence, but we do need a definition from which to proceed. Although a head count of experts is no guarantee of accuracy and truth, it does provide an authoritative place to begin. A survey of 1,020 Ph.D.s identified as experts in developmental and educational psychology, educational sociology, and behavioral genetics was conducted by Snyderman and Rothman (1988:56), who asked them to check all behavioral descriptions that they considered to be important elements of intelligence. Responses were placed into three categories: (1) those for which there was virtual unanimity—"abstract thinking or reasoning," checked by 99.3 percent of the respondents, "problem-solving ability" (97.7 percent), and "capacity to acquire knowledge" (96 percent); (2) those checked by the majority (e.g., "memory" [80.5 percent], "adaptation to one's environment" [77.2 percent], and "mental speed" [71.7 percent]); and (3) those rarely checked (e.g., "achievement motivation" [18.9 percent] and "goal directedness" [24 percent]).

Taken as a whole, the listed elements provide a basis for formulating a definition which would differ little from the general substance of that offered by David Wechsler, who defined it as "The aggregate or global capacity of the individual to act purposefully, to think rationally, and to deal effectively with his environment. It is aggregate or global because it is composed of elements or abilities (features) which, although not entirely independent, are qualitatively differentiable" (quoted in Matarazzo, 1976:79).

By emphasizing "aggregate or global" capacity, Wechsler is recognizing that different mental tests measure different cognitive abilities or "intelligences" but also that there is a factor common to them all—a positive manifold uniting the various abstracting functions that may be fairly specific to a given specialized cognitive task. Psychometricians call this common factor *Spearman's g*, which, operationally, is the principal component derived from factor analysis of a variety of mental tests. Spearman's g ("g" for "general" intelligence) is the only independent factor common to all "intelligences" as they are operationalized by various cognitive tests. Factor loadings (i.e., the correlation between a test and a factor) on g across a number of mental tests are mostly in the range of 0.40 to 0.90 (Jensen, 1992); thus, there is no measure of human learning ability that is independent of g. Since psychometricians of all ideological persuasions apparently agree that g conforms to what both they and laypersons mean when they speak of intelligence (Sternberg, 1983), when I speak of intelligence, the concept I have in mind is Spearman's g.

Intelligence is thus a complex web of intellectual behavior that is both general (global) and specific to the various situations requiring cognitive evaluation of incoming information. Information comes in a variety of academic, moral, ethical, technical, and other sundry forms, often presenting us with problems requiring satisfactory resolution through the exercise of reason. Because intelligence is intellectual *behavior*, it can be measured, albeit imperfectly; and these measures can be correlated with other measured behaviors to determine how intelligence influences them.

Some theorists reject the idea that IQ tests measure intelligence, suggesting instead that IQ be thought of as "a broad set of verbal and problem-solving skills which are better labeled academic aptitudes or scholastic readiness" (Simons, 1978:269). Simons fails to appreciate that "intelligence" is an umbrella label that professionals and laypersons alike readily recognize as appropriately encompassing the bundle of intellectual skills he enumerates. The litmus test of IQ testing is empirical—how well it predicts outcomes—and not universal agreement on the appropriateness of the label.

I use the terms *intelligence* and *IQ* interchangeably with the knowledge that IQ is an operational definition of intelligence. IQ tests no more capture the "essence" of the concept of intelligence than scores on an alienation scale capture the essence of alienation, or numbers on a spectrophotometer reflecting the color intensity of chemically altered sugar capture the essence of sweetness. I do not subscribe to the position that the operationalization of a concept *is* the concept, but it is only by operationalizing concepts that we can make reliable predictions from concept to concept, and often we cannot know very much about a concept apart from the way we measure it.

Intellectual behavior is phenotypical behavior, the outcome of genotypes interacting with all sorts of physical and social stimuli. Genes influence intelligence but do not determine it in any completely prescribed way. Rather, genes place constraints on the extent to which one's intellectual behavior is responsive to environmental stimuli and on the extent to which that behavior can be shaped by that stimuli. Because the major defining characteristic of human beings is the cognitive ability to plan, execute, monitor, and evaluate what we are doing, intelligence may be seen as a "master" behavior directing and guiding most other forms of human activity.

IQ AND TEST BIAS

Although the prestigious National Acadamy of Sciences, after extensive study of the matter, concluded that IQ tests are *not* biased (Seligman, 1992:155), there are a number of academics, unaware of mainstream opinion on this matter, who still believe that they are. Debates about whether a measuring instrument is biased are usually addressed in terms of reliability and validity. IQ tests are designed to predict individual performance on intellectual tasks such as those enumerated by the professionals surveyed by Snyderman and Rothman (1988). The more reliable and valid a measuring instrument is, the more accurate our predictions based on the trait the instrument purports to measure will be. Reliability coefficients for IQ tests typically range between 0.94 and 0.97 (Anastasi, 1976:251), truly exceptional figures when compared to reliability coefficients of other social and behavioral science constructs.

Reliability is a necessary but not sufficient requisite for a useful instrument. It must also be valid. There are various methods of determining validity, but we limit the discussion to criterion-related (predictive) validity, a type that comes closer than any other to what is normally meant by "valid" (Zeller & Carmines, 1980:79). A validity coefficient is usually expressed as a correlation coefficient between performance on a test and some criterion performance such as scholastic success, occupational status, and income level.[2]

For many critics of IQ tests, the only "evidence" required to level charges of bias is that they reveal substantial group differences, rendering them ipso facto biased. This is sheer nonsense. To say that a test is biased for or against a particular group is to say that it predicts accurately for one group but not for another. If, for instance, IQ scores accurately predicted task performance for whites but not for blacks, the test from which the scores were derived would have to be considered biased. Technically speaking, with both the predictor variable (IQ) and the criterion variable (task performance) standardized, a test is biased if the regression slopes are significantly different across tested groups.

Three articles in the same issue of *Sociology of Education* (Guterman, 1979; Gordon & Rudert, 1979; Eckland, 1979), came to the same conclusion: IQ tests are not biased against blacks or lower-SES individuals (see also Gottfredson, 1986; Humphreys, 1986; Locurto, 1991). In Gordon and Rudert's analysis of individual test items, although black and lower-SES children missed more items, the *rank ordering* of relative item difficulty was almost identical for both races and across social classes. In fact, item difficulty levels correlate between 0.95 and 0.98 between black and white subjects (Snyderman & Rothman, 1988:113). Scores on IQ tests predicted educational attainment equally for all subjects tested and was substantially more powerful a predictor than either SES or race. In other words, black children with high IQs show evidence of greater educational attainment than white middle-class children with low IQs. The predictive equality of IQ tests for all races was further demonstrated in a British study correlating IQ scores with scores on standardized reading and mathematics tests for white, black, Indian, and Pakistani children which found almost identical correlations (the low to mid-0.70s) among all four populations (Mackintosh, 1986).

Although some still refuse to believe that IQ tests are unbiased, the psychometric literature provides no evidence that they are. Studies of reliability, predictive validity, factor structure, race-by-item interaction, and so forth uniformly point to a lack of bias. We must learn to live with these findings and to incorporate them into our thinking rather than condemn them or deny their existence. Studies have shown that taller men entering the business world are more likely to be hired than shorter men, to receive higher average starting salaries, and to enjoy better promotion prospects (Ellis, 1992:279). These findings strike me as eminently unfair, but they certainly do not lead me to question the reliability or validity of yardsticks. Some people are tall, some are short, and some people score higher on IQ tests than others. To blame the instruments that measure these differences for the differences is much like shooting the bathroom scale for its unflattering reminder that one is overweight. IQ scores, like height and weight, are the result of environmental circumstances interacting with genetic endowment, not of the instruments that reveal the unpleasant truths. As African-American economist Thomas Sowell (1983:145) opined, "To condemn a test for revealing consequential differences is to condemn those who are disadvantaged to remain handicapped by undiagnosed and misdiagnosed problems."[3]

When most sociologists speak of IQ test bias, they do not mean that the tests are biased in terms of the reliability and validity of the tests, although they sometimes confuse these technical aspects with what they really mean. What is most often meant by test bias is that lower-SES and black children are less likely to have the kinds of intellectual experiences that prepare them for some kinds of items found on IQ tests. Here we have to distinguish between *crystallized* and *fluid* intelligence. Crystallized intelligence is heavily dependent on culture and acquired knowledge ("Who wrote *Pride and Prejudice*?" "What is the capital of Latvia?"); fluid intelligence is much less so. Most items on modern tests rely minimally on acquired snippets of knowledge; rather, they rely heavily on Spearman's *g*—the ability to analyze in novel ways, to synthesize, and to recognize relationships between the various elements of a problem (Eysenck & Kamin, 1981:20). This does not mean that we can develop "culture-free" tests in any absolute sense. By definition, any test requiring the use of mental faculties depends on skills and knowledge developed and accumulated in a culture. Yet paradoxically, many lower-SES and black children appear to be more deficient on tests designed specifically to compensate for cultural deprivation than on "culturally loaded" tests (Steelman & Doby, 1983; Jensen, 1985).

Certain critics of IQ tests maintain that the tests are biased because they do not take into account the motivation of the test takers (Simons, 1978). It cannot be denied that, to some unknown extent, motivation to do well influences performance on any test and that, to some (also unknown) extent, IQ tests measure motivation (recall that motivation was not considered a particularly important element of IQ by Snyderman and Rothman's sample of experts). However, most studies attempting to determine if black–white differences in test-taking motivation exist have been null (Herrnstein & Murray, 1994:284). Most damaging to the motivation argument are results from the various digit-span subtests of IQ scales. The digit-span tests consists of a series of numbers given orally by the examiner which subjects are to repeat both forward and backward. Backward repetition is more mentally demanding and has about twice the *g* loading of forward repetition. The black–white difference is about twice as great for backward than for forward repetition. If differential motivation explains the black–white difference, how is it that "motivation" fluctuates consistently with the *g* loading of the two parts of the same subtest such that black subjects suddenly become doubly unmotivated when repeating digits backwards? (See Jensen [1980] and Herrnstein & Murray [1994] for a review of the motivation issue.)

Tests have been designed that measure one's knowledge of the content of black culture, such as the Dove Counterbalance General Intelligence Test (the "Chitling Test") to "prove" that IQ tests are biased. Blacks score higher than whites on such tests, and this constitutes evidence for critics that standard IQ tests measure nothing but the cultural content of white middle-class society in the same way that the Chitling Test measures the content of the black culture. However, the idea behind these tests is naïve and misleading; there is no body of evidence showing that they successfully predict performance on any important criterion for blacks or whites (Kaplan, 1985:473). The Chitling Test, and others like it, merely measure knowledge of the peculiarities and idiosyncrasies of a particular subculture (crystallized intelligence). Unlike standard IQ tests, they do not measure the ability to reason, evaluate, synthesize, or any of the other cognitive abilities that are needed to be successful in the larger culture.

Those who continue to maintain that IQ tests merely measure the content of white middle-class American culture in the same way that the Chitling Test measures knowledge of the African-American subculture will have to explain why the Japanese, *using translations of American tests*, typically show a mean IQ of 107, which is 7 points higher than the American white mean and 22 points higher than the American black mean (Rushton, 1990a:316). Even mainland Chinese peasants, again using translations of American tests, show a mean IQ of 101 (Seligman, 1992:122).

Nettler (1982:97) summarizes the issue of cultural bias by stating that it is irrelevant "because one gets similar results from so-called 'culture-free' tests" and, more important, "because the skills measured by mental tests are those which have general applicability for the guidance of lives around the world." Similarly, Brody (1985:382) summarizes a large number of studies designed to explore test bias in relation to black–white differences by writing, "It is quite clear that black–white differences in intelligence are not a function of type of items or tests. As far as is known, it is pervasive and exists on virtually all measures that are generally assumed to be measures of general intelligence" (see Humphreys [1988] for a broad review). Further, blacks do relatively worse on nonverbal tests (the manipulation of symbols and objects) than on verbal tests than do whites: "If cultural bias is to creep into a test, it presumably has a better opportunity to do so through language than through abstract symbols, yet blacks do better on language tests [than on nonverbal tests]" (Snyderman & Rothman, 1988:114). Indeed, the more culturally infused the test, subtest, or item, the lower the black–white gap; the more culture free (emphasizing abstract reasoning) the test, subtest, or item, the greater the black–white gap (Seligman, 1992:154). This pattern could not be more damaging to the "cultural bias" explanation for black–white differences in IQ.

The mean difference between white and black IQ found across numerous studies is about fifteen points, and adjusted for SES it is about twelve points (Synderman & Rothman, 1988:106). This difference is found in all nations of the world having black and white populations (see Lynn [1978] for a review of international studies) and has been resistant to change since large-scale IQ testing began in the United States about seventy years ago, despite all kinds of attempts at remedial intervention (Gottfredson, 1986:403). This does not imply the conclusion that blacks are *innately* less intelligent than whites, that is, that the difference between the mean IQ scores of blacks and whites are attributable to genetic differences between the races. The full range of IQ scores is present in the black population, with about 16 percent of blacks scoring above the white mean. It is possible, even if 100 percent of the variance in IQ *within* each racial population is attributable to genetics, that the *difference* between the two populations could be attributable to environmental variability. Phenotypic behavior is the result of genotypes interacting with environments in ways known and unknown. Until such time as both races experience identical environments in a color-blind society, we can say nothing definitive about the origins of black–white differences in measured intelligence.[4]

GENES AND INTELLIGENCE

Whatever intelligence is, it involves complex interneuronal communication. Nerve impulses require the participation of many proteins, enzymes, and neurotransmitters, all of which are synthesized by genes at neuronal nuclei or at axonal sites. There is wide individual variability in the amount, concentration, and metabolism of the substances that drive nerve impulses; and this variability is under appreciable genetic control (see, in general, Zomzely-Neurath & Walker [1985]). Variability in any or all of these physiological factors will be reflected in variability in information-processing ability, that is, the speed and accuracy of nerve impulse activity. Nerve impulse activity is measured by evoked potentials (a train of slow, large waves recorded electrically from the scalp) and nerve-conduction velocity (the speed with which electrical impulses are transmitted). Rather large correlation (some as high as 0.83) have been reported between averaged evoked potential and nerve-conduction velocity measures and scores on standard IQ tests (see Vernon [1991] for a review). These more direct measures of the construct "intelligence" in the form of neurological efficiency constitute independent evidence for the usefulness of indirect measures (IQ tests) by virtue of their strong correlations with them (criterion-related validity).

Other neurophysiological mechanisms correlating highly with IQ include cerebral glucose metabolism (CGM). These mechanisms are measured by PET scans, which reveal neural metabolic functioning as the brain takes up positron-emitting glucose isotopes (fluoro-2-deoxyglucose) intravenously administered. As the energy supplied by the glucose is metabolized, the computer reveals colorized biochemical "maps" of the brain, identifying the parts activated while engaged in some task. Cortical absolute metabolic rates (CAMR) at various brain-slice scan levels have been correlated with scores on Raven's Advanced Progressive Matrixes (RAPM), a nonverbal test of abstract reasoning. Correlations ranging between –0.44 and –0.84, depending on brain-slice level and hemisphere, and an overall whole-slice mean of –0.75, have been found (Haier et al., 1988:208). Similar patterns of correlations are reported by Parks and his colleagues (1988) between CAMR and scores on verbal fluency tests. The pattern of negative correlations means that subjects scoring high on standardized "paper and pencil" tests of intellectual functioning expend less cerebral energy when performing intellectual tasks, as measured by CGM rates, than lower-scoring subjects. Otherwise stated, high-IQ subjects possess brains that are speedier, more accurate, and more "energy efficient" than low-IQ subjects (see Matarazzo [1992] for a review).

Modest significant correlations (ranging from 0.26 to 0.56) have also been found between IQ and the volume of a variety of brain structures, such as the cerebrum, temporal lobes, cerebellum, and the hippocampi, using MRI (Willerman, Schultz, Rutledge, & Bigler, 1991; Andreasen et al., 1993; Wickett, Vernon, & Lee, 1994). Earlier studies of brain size and IQ relied on crude measures such as the head perimeter. MRI techniques create three-dimensional models, not only of gross cranial volume but also of specific brain structures. While correlations between sheer volume of brain structures and IQ are neither as large or as readily interpretable as PET studies of neural efficiency and IQ, they do point to covariation of physical structures and intellectual functioning.

Advances in neuro-imaging technology occurred in the same decade that saw the advent of recombinant DNA technology and the beginning of the Human Genome Project. The fortuitous concomitance of these advances has paved the way for molecular genetics to get into the intelligence picture (McGue, 1989). Molecular genetics looks for DNA markers that account for proportions of variation for the trait(s) in question. Molecular geneticists do not expect to discover a single "intelligence gene," but they may uncover a number of genes that account for small additive amounts of variation and for genes that may have pleiotropic affects on intelligence: "We need to find many tiny needles in the haystack" (Plomin, 1990:187). More than 100 recessive genes, which include decreased intelligence among their effects, have been identified in human beings. However, because these effects are rare and only effect homozygous individuals, they only account for a minuscule proportion of the variance in population intelligence (Plomin, 1990:185).

Some interesting preliminary molecular genetic work has been done comparing allelic frequencies at a variety of loci between high- and low-IQ children. Plomin and his colleagues (1994) found five two-allele DNA markers out of the forty-six examined to differentiate the two IQ groups significantly. Although very large IQ gaps were necessary (high IQ mean = 142, low IQ mean = 59) to locate significant differences, larger samples should be able to discover allelic loci that significantly differentiate between samples of less extreme IQ differences. This is exciting research; but as the first attempt to actually locate IQ enhancing and IQ depressing alleles, too much should not be made of it too soon.

THE HERITABILITY OF IQ

Claims of genetic transmission of intelligence rest today more on heritability studies than on relatively new neurophysiological and molecular genetics studies. If IQ tests do not measure some innate characteristic, then it would be both logically and empirically impossible to obtain heritability coefficients significantly greater than zero. In a summary of 111 IQ heritability studies conducted between 1963 and 1980, Bouchard and McGue (1981) reported weighted average correlations between IQ scores of pairs of individuals with a variety of familial relationships. The pattern of these correlations is consistent with that which would be predicted on the basis of broad polygenetic inheritance of intelligence: The greater the degree of genetic relatedness between pairs, the higher the correlation between their IQs. A similar but smaller effect is seen for increasing similarities in environment. Figure 5.1 shows the observed pattern of correlations for selected pairings, as well as the pattern predicted from a strict polygenetic (no environmental effect) theory of broad inheritance of IQ.

MZ twins reared together showed the highest average correlation (0.86), followed by MZ twins reared apart (0.72). A strict theory of polygenetic inheritance would predict a correlation of 1.00 in both cases, since MZ twins are genetically identical. The difference between the two correlations provides a rough estimate of shared environmental affects. Because MZ twins reared together share identical genes *and* the same family environment, the lack of a perfect correlation (taking measurement error into consideration) indicates that the term *environment* means more than simply sharing the same parents and the same home. Individuals obviously experience environmental influences specific to themselves that influence IQ. Similarly, a strictly genetic theory of IQ would predict a zero correlation between adopted child and parent, when in fact the average weighted correlation is 0.19. The departure of these correlations from those predicted by a strictly genetic position, as well as the differences in IQ between twins reared together and twins reared apart, underscore the contribution of family environmental differences—as well as differences specific to the individual—to IQ levels.

Figure 5.1
Weighted Average Correlations between Pairs of Individuals of Different
Degrees of Genetic Relatedness and Correlations Expected from Strict
Polygenetic Theory

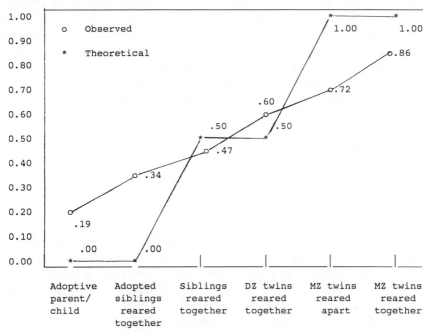

Source: Adapted from Bouchard and McGue (1981:1057).

The Bouchard and McGue study is cited in some sociology textbooks but not always accurately. John Macionis's (1989:124) annotated instructor's edition of *Sociology*, for instance, states that while there is evidence for a genetic component in IQ, "The correlation of IQ scores for unrelated individuals reared together is twice as high as that of identical twins reared apart." The pattern of correlation Macionis reports enabled him to conclude that nurture is more important than nature in determining intelligence. Since Bouchard and McGue report a correlation for unrelated individuals reared together of 0.34 and one of 0.72 for identical twins reared apart, let us give Macionis the benefit of the doubt and suppose that his misrepresentation of the data was the result of numerical myopia caused by an overly enthusiastic attempt to be politically correct.

Bouchard and McGue (1981:1056) point out that the magnitude of the correlations as well as the pattern of biological relationship–IQ correlations "would be difficult to explain on the basis of any strictly environmental hypothesis." In other words, the fact that IQ scores across 111 studies are most similar among genetically identical twins and least similar among genetically unrelated persons provides strong support for the position that the abilities measured by IQ tests are genetically influenced. Commenting on this study, Rowe and Osgood (1984:537) opine that "although individual studies can be faulted on one ground or another, the overall pattern of results is so regular that to ignore genetic factors requires either outlandish assumptions or a very selective reading of the literature."

The computed heritability coefficient from the Bouchard and McGue data is obtained by using the weighted averaged correlations for MZ pairs reared together (0.86) and DZ pairs reared together (r = 0.60), yielding an estimate of 0.52 (see Chapter 2). If the coefficient is corrected for measurement error, we attain a maximum h^2 estimate of 0.60, a value that matches to the mean "reasonable estimate" of Snyderman and Rothman's (1988:95) experts.[5]

Just as heritability estimates vary among different populations at different times, they also differ among the various tests of cognitive ability. The Swedish Adoption–Twin Study of Aging (Pedersen, Plomin, & McClearn, 1994) found a healthy 0.77 correlation between the *g* loadings of cognitive tests and their heritabilities. In essence, this means the more a test taps *g*, the stronger the genetic influence on people's performance on them. Earlier studies showed that factor loadings on *g* are lowest for measures of crystallized intelligence and highest for measures of fluid intelligence. The IPAT Culture Fair and the Raven matrixes load 0.75 and 0.71, respectively, on *g*, while arithmetic reasoning and spelling load 0.46 and 0.20, respectively (Cattell, 1985).

HERITABILITY IN DIFFERENT ENVIRONMENTS: THE STICKY ISSUE OF BLACK–WHITE IQ DIFFERENCES

Let us now reconsider the black–white difference in mean IQ. As we have seen, the strict determination of heritability requires that all elements of the population possessing a given trait be exposed to absolutely identical environments. Consider our "seeds-in-a-barrel" thought experiments in Chapter 2. Let us this time take two random samples from a population of genetically heterogeneous seeds and call one sample "white" and the other "black" and plant each of them in two separate environments (this example is adapted from Lewontin [1982:132–133]). Both samples are planted in completely homogeneous environments, but the "black" seeds receive only half the care and nutrients of the "white" seeds. Thus, both environments are homogeneous within themselves but heterogeneous with respect to one another. When phenotypical traits are measured some time later, we find the variability expected from genetic diversity within both samples; but we also find that the "white" phenotypes are significantly more robust with respect to the measured traits than the "black" phenotypes.

Because the genetic material is variable and the environment is constant, heritabilities for the phenotypical trait being measured will be 1.0 in both samples. With heritabilities at unity, we would be correct to attribute 100 percent of the variance in measured traits within both samples to genes but absolutely wrong if we attributed mean *differences* between the two samples in the traits to genes also. The *within-sample* variance is entirely accounted for by genetics, but the *between-sample* variability is entirely a function of the different environmental conditions in which the samples were grown.[6]

Although adequate to make the intended point, the foregoing example should not be taken too literally when extrapolated to cover human populations. Blacks and whites are certainly not the products of "random samples" of genetic material, and we certainly cannot manipulate environments to the extent that we did in the thought experiment. We can only imprecisely achieve such environmental "control" via statistical adjustment when dealing with the complexities of the human environment. Thus, we will never encounter situations in which we can attribute all of the within- or between-group variance to one source or the other. The only thing we can reasonably say is that the average environment for the average black person is more IQ depressing than is the average environment for the average white person.

We can underline the previous conclusion if we find that heritabilities differ across various kinds of environments. We know that genes are protein molecules of *potential* that are more or less realized in a given environment, with certain environments allowing for the full expression of a given trait and others serving to suppress the trait. Thus, we should observe low heritability in the most disadvantaged environments, high heritability in advantaged environments, and moderate heritability in environments falling in between. Variables that serve to suppress the full expression of gene-based traits such as IQ are low birth weight, lack of prenatal and neonatal medical care, deficient tactile stimulation during periods of active neuronal growth, malnutrition, abusive parenting, maternal drug use during pregnancy, and a stimuli-deprived home life. Although not limited to lower-SES and black families, these deficiencies are more prevalent among those groups (Bouchard & Segal, 1985).

Using a median split on SES, Scarr-Salapatek (1971) divided a sample of 992 black and white MZ and DZ twin pairs into "advantaged" and "disadvantaged" groups. Consistent with behavioral genetic theory, she found greater phenotypic variability in IQ among higher-SES children of both races: "One can see that the percentage of total variance attributable to genetic sources was always higher in the advantaged groups of both races" (1971:223). She found heritability coefficients for verbal intelligence of 0.343

and 0.723 among low- and high-SES black children, respectively. Combining both groups, she calculated h^2 to be 0.522, a figure consistent with the coefficient calculated from the Bouchard and McGue (1981) data and one that also suggests that black and white heritabilities are identical. A later study by Fischbein (1980) among white twins produced almost identical results, with heritabilities of 0.30 and 0.78 in low- and high-SES groups, respectively. Both studies provide evidence that human heritability for IQ is high in advantaged environments and low in disadvantaged environments.

It is also reasonable to assume that *environmental* variation will be greater among disadvantaged groups than among advantaged groups; that is, the range of negative events experienced in disadvantaged environments is probably greater than in the comfortable "standard" experiences of higher-SES groups. If the experiences of higher-SES groups are more homogeneous, it follows statistically that there is less environmental variance within them and h^2 will be greater. Conversely, greater IQ-depressing environmental variability within lower-SES groups leads to a decrease in the heritability coefficient. In other words, change the environment and the genetic contribution to phenotypical IQ variability changes.

It follows from this that we may expect an increase in the heritability of IQ if the environment becomes more favorable for its development across all social groups. The fear has been expressed that environmental equality (to the extent that it can be achieved) raises the specter of a meritocracy and a permanent underclass based on IQ (Herrnstein, 1973). Although Herrnstein was unfairly pilloried for expressing this paradoxical notion, it is entirely consistent with the principles of genetics. For example, a Norwegian study of 8,389 twin pairs found that the heritability of educational attainment has increased dramatically with the equalization of educational opportunities (decreasing environmental variability) in Norway (Heath et al., 1985). Family background accounted for 47 percent of the variance in educational attainment among individuals born before 1940; but for males born between 1940 and 1961, it accounted for only 8 to 10 percent, with genetic factors accounting for 67 to 74 percent of the variance. If we wish to increase the proportion of variance in IQ and its various correlates that are attributable to the environment, then we must increase social inequality, something hardly anyone is willing to advocate.

Similar findings of increasing genetic influence on educational attainment, occupational status, and IQ with increasingly egalitarian conditions were reported by Tambs, Sundet, Magnus, and Berg (1989). Thus, the closer we come to optimizing the environment for everyone, the more we differentiate people by their genes. Herrnstein's corollary to this is that sooner or later people will sort themselves into classes based mainly on merit, which he associated primarily with IQ, leaving those with the lowest IQs locked into a permanent underclass. There is evidence that this may have occurred to some extent in the black community as affirmative-action programs skim high-IQ blacks from it, leaving others behind in terrible ghetto conditions (Loury, 1987). To the extent that the observed bifurcation of the black community is a function of division by IQ, we can expect the continuation of high levels of crime and delinquency within that community. Such is the paradox of affirmative-action and other "special favors" programs aimed at ameliorating the plight of blacks. "Improving the environment" must go beyond civil rights–type programs to encompass those factors that most impact on IQ in a society that is becoming increasingly based on merit.

People of conscience instinctively recoil at the prospect of a division of society into Huxleyesque "alphas" and "betas," regardless of the criteria used for doing so. Such an unconscionable prospect is by no means inevitable. Because genes appear to account for more of the variance in IQ than environment, it does not mean that the genetic contribution is more important than the environmental contribution. Hydrogen contributes twice as much as oxygen to rain, and the length of the garden on which it falls may contribute twice as much to the garden's area as its width. Heredity and environment are to intelligence as hydrogen and oxygen are to rain, and length and width are to area. None of these pairings "contribute" anything in isolation from the wholes they constitute: IQ, rain, or area. Jencks (1980) has demonstrated rather elegantly that nongenetic variation $(1 - h^2)$ does not provide a measure of the upper limit of the possible explanatory power of environmental variables nor on the effects of creating new and better environments. Regardless of what the reaction range for IQ might be in existing environments, the issue is whether low-IQ children have been deprived of the environmental stimulants for optimal intellectual development for their geneotype.

REGRESSION TO THE MEAN AND ASSORTIVE MATING

Regression to the mean and an apparent decline in assortive mating are phenomena opperating to some extent to prevent social bifurcation on the basis of IQ. Although the genetic shuffling of meiosis assures a great deal of variability in the traits being passed from parents to offspring, we know that bright parents give birth to bright children and that dull parents give birth to dull children. However, children of exceptionally high-IQ parents, despite all the environmental advantages afforded them, are usually less bright than their parents, although they remain brighter than average. Conversely, children of low-IQ parents, despite all the disadvantages this entails, are usually brighter than their parents, although still below normal. This phenomenon is known as regression to the mean (of the population) and is most pronounced at parental IQ extremes. On average, children of the brightest parents regress downward the most, and children of the dullest parents regress upward the most.

Regression to the mean is common for a number of polygenetic traits and is generally viewed as a statistical artifact arising from imperfect correlations (in this case, between mid-parent IQ and offspring IQ) due to factors that may affect one set of scores but not the other (Locurto, 1991:94). To the extent that it reflects some underlying biological phenomenon, it may operate in the following way: Extremely bright parents and extremely dull parents are, respectively, the recipients of a larger than average number of IQ-enhancing or IQ-depressing alleles. Since parents pass on a random half of there genes and not their entire genotype, the odds are greatly against their offspring receiving the same large number of enhancing or depresssing alleles for the phenotypic trait. The larger the difference between mid-parent IQ and the population mean, the less the odds are, and thus the greater the offspring regression. The laws of genetics (the principles of segregation and recombination) work against the hardening of populations into castelike systems of social stratification: "Regression mixes up the social classes, ensures social mobility, and favors meritocracy" (Eysenck & Kamin, 1981:64).

Assortive mating is a process that tends to maintain social classes. To the geneticist, assortive mating means the tendency of genetically similar men and women (as that similarity manifests itself in similar phenotypes) to marry. For the sociologist, assortive mating means homogamy: the likeness or similarity of married couples as they relate to such variables as race, class, ethnicity, education, and religion. Homogamous norms are strong, especially for race and religion (Eshleman, 1988). The "birds of a feather" theory of attraction is strongly supported by positive correlations between spouses for physical traits ranging between 0.10 and 0.40 and for intellectual traits ranging between 0.30 and 0.73 (Ehrman & Parsons, 1976:157–158). Assortive mating for intelligence increases intellectual differences between families; decreased assortive mating should lessen the difference.

Random mating reduces the frequency of phenotypes at both extremes of the IQ distribution because of the decreased probability of extreme parental phenotypes mating (Scarr & Carter-Saltzman, 1986:818). Although random mating is never likely to occur, extreme assortive mating conditions exist only in caste systems. Open societies in which individuals from diverse backgrounds are thrown together in educational, occupational, and recreational situations will reduce, but by no means eliminate, assortive mating. Eshleman (1988) reviews literature showing a steady decline in homogamous marriages within a number of social structural dimensions. For those of us who believe the data indicate that fluid intelligence is largely gene driven but who also have a commitment to social equality, this is good news.

ENVIRONMENTAL INFLUENCES ON INTELLIGENCE

Heritability notwithstanding, intelligence is a malleable trait. The range of that malleability is a controversial issue; and how the preponderance of evidence is judged is of great importance "because the social implications are profound, involving basic propositions concerning universal education, general social structure, and, perhaps, democracy itself" (Ramey, 1992:239). The data must be allowed to speak for themselves, but the profound implications attending this issue strongly imply that we should tread lightly and demand evidence "beyond all reasonable doubt" rather than a simple "preponderance" before making statements that policymakers may interpret as definitive. It should be made clear that the malleability of intelligence per se is not in question; the issue is rather one of the *reactive range* of IQ provided by intervention—of how much can we raise IQ. Our operating assumption must continue to be that intervention in the lives of children at risk for low IQ is worthwhile, both substantively and morally.

Curiously, the best and most solid evidence for environmental influence on intelligence comes from genetic research: "The findings of greatest social significance to emerge from human behavioral genetic research to date involve nurture, not nature" (Plomin & Daniels, 1987:1). Since any human phenotypic trait is the result of genes interacting with environments, and since the best modern estimates of the percentage of IQ variance attributable to genetics are between 50 and 60 percent, it follows that between 40 and 50 percent of the variance (and perhaps more in certain environments) has to be attributed to environmental factors minus measurement error. Yet no researcher has been able to empirically account for such a proportion: "No specific environmental influences nor combination of them [have been found to] account for as much as 10 percent of the variance in IQ" (Plomin & DeFries, 1980:22).

Absent heritability studies, environmentalist researchers (assuming that their best efforts had accounted for 10 percent of the variance in IQ) would have to conclude that the remaining 90 percent of the variance *had* to be accounted for by genetics because there are only two gross sources of variation in any trait: the environment and genes. The low percentage of variation empirically accounted for by environmental variables is probably more a function of our inability to nail them down rather than an underestimation of genetic effects. As Fincher (1982:72) points out, "The environmental contributions to intelligence—nutrition, loving care and attention and intellectual stimulation—have been harder [than the genetic contribution] to prove scientifically."

It is far more difficult to get a firm grasp on environmental influences than on genetic influences because the variables we refer to when we speak of the "environment" encompass the multitude we subsume under the physical, psychological, and social worlds. Not only are they legion; they interact and permutate in myriad ways, and many have transactional effects. Any attempt to account for them all would be an impossible task requiring constant monitoring of children's environmental experiences from the moment of conception and would necessarily entail a major intrusion into the lives of their families. Even if such close scrutiny were possible and desirable, and even if it did not contaminate the study by influencing parental behavior, we would still not obtain an adequate accounting of environmental influence.

Such an accounting would require experimental groups of MZ and DZ twins to be exposed to different environments beyond their common prenatal and perinatal experiences. They would have to be separated at birth and raised in quite different environments, that is, different racial and SES households and a variety of family constellations (biological versus step-families, birth order, cross-sex sibship, etc.). Given the rarity of such occasions occurring naturally, as well as the thicket of environmental influences to be constantly monitored, it is probably true that we will never be able to account empirically for the percentage of variance in IQ that genetic research informs us is attributable to the environment. We can, however, explore environmental influences on IQ by examining how certain environments lead to increases or decreases in intellectual functioning.

Increases in IQ have been demonstrated in a variety of studies, many of which have been severely criticized for extravagant claims and poor research designs (Flynn, 1984; Longstreth, 1981; Locurto, 1990). One such study is the Milwaukee Project (Strickland, 1971) which concentrated its efforts on black infants of forty mothers with IQs typically in the low seventies. After dividing the infants into experimental and control groups, the project team launched into a comprehensive program of intervention in the lives of the experimental group. Teachers visited the home for several hours each day, exposing the infants to a wide range of stimuli and instructing the mothers on proper infant-care techniques. When the children were older, they were picked up and taken to educational centers, where they received individual attention from specially trained teachers.

The reported results of this treatment were gratifying. The average IQ of the experimental group at forty-two months was thirty-three points higher than that of the control group; and at sixty-three months, the mean IQ of the experimental group was 124, compared to the control group mean of 94. Other researchers found these results to be too good to be true. Clarke and Clarke (1976) indicate that the mean IQ scores of the experimental group had faded to 106 shortly after the children entered regular schools, and at ages 12 to 14 it had further fallen to 100 (Flynn, 1984). This is typical of the so-called "fading effect" often found among Head Start children who initially tend to show rather large IQ gains which largely reflect such things as "test-wiseness" and crystallized intelligence and not true gains in intellectual ability (Brody, 1985:366).

Despite the fading effect, something is happening when we see an experimental group significantly outscore a matched control group, even if the difference was twelve points rather than the initial unrealistic claim of thirty-three points. An IQ of 100 is a long way from the children's predicted average score of 70 based on their mothers' average (Flynn, 1984:40), but the thirty-point difference (100 versus 70) between predicted and observed averages cannot all be attributed to the experiment. Given the low average IQ of the mothers, regression toward the mean would have had a fairly large effect regardless of intervention, as it did for the control group. Regression toward the mean would have placed the predicted score IQ of these children, without intervention, at around the black population mean of 85. Nevertheless, environmental intervention did stretch their potential beyond the level these children would have attained had they not experienced environmental enrichment.

As we have seen, one of the major bones of contention among IQ researchers is whether racial differences in IQ are genetic in origin or can be traced to environmental circumstances. One interesting study not involving experimental manipulation was conducted by Jensen (1977), who tested the so-called "cumulative deficit hypothesis," that is, the hypothesis that an increasing decrement in IQ scores relative to population norms is found among children in deprived environments. Jensen compared IQ scores of 1,300 black and white children living in a low-SES region of rural Georgia with the IQ scores of black and white children in Berkeley, California. He found that IQ scores decreased among the rural Georgian black children an average of 1.42 points per year between the ages of 6 and 16 years for an overall decrement of 15 points. There was no corresponding decrement for either the Georgian white children or the Berkeley black children.

Jensen attempted to rescue partially his genetic hypothesis for black–white IQ differences by citing studies showing that California blacks have a larger admixture of Caucasian ancestry than do Georgian blacks. But like the scientist he undoubtedly is, he let the data speak for themselves in concluding that "the present results on Georgia blacks, when viewed in connection with the contrasting results for California blacks, would seem to favor an environmental interpretation of the progressive IQ decrement. If the progressive IQ decrement were a genetic racial effect, it would have shown up in the California blacks as well" (Jensen, 1977:190).

Jensen's claim that California blacks may have a greater admixture of white genes than Georgia blacks, and that this white "blood" may account for the higher IQs of California blacks, is not supported by the evidence. Scarr, Pakstis, Katz, and Barker (1977) used blood group and serum-protein markers to estimate the degree of European and African ancestry among 181 pairs of black twins. Previous testing has shown that American blacks have an average of about 80-percent African and 20-percent European ancestry, with a range of African ancestry between 40 and 95 percent. Scarr and her colleagues found that higher degrees of European ancestry did not result in higher IQs in their sample.

ADOPTION STUDIES

Adoption studies, although consistently finding that genes account for more IQ variance than the environment, do tend to show that being raised in an environment more advantageous than that which could be provided by biological parents of adoptees can increase IQ. Adoption studies thus demonstrate both the genetics and the malleability of IQ. The Bouchard and McGue

(1981) data show that the average weighted correlation between adopted parents and adopted children (0.19) is not significantly different from that found between adopted children and their biological mothers (0.22). Both these correlations are, however, significantly different from the 0.42 found between biological parent and children, a difference that once again underscores the synergistic effect of genes and environment.

Most adoptions involve higher-than-average-SES couples adopting children from lower-than-average-SES backgrounds. If IQ were highly malleable, then adopted children should "reach the average intellectual levels provided by their adoptive families" (Locurto, 1990:277). Locurto provides evidence from the eight most cited adoption studies to show that while IQ is malleable, it is less so than an environment-emphasizing interpretation might suggest. He provides unweighted mean IQ levels from these studies for adopted children (106), adoptive parents (116), biological children of adoptive parents (114), and comparison children from the same SES category as the adoptive parents (113). This pattern of means shows that although adopted children, on average, achieved IQ scores above the population mean of 100, they failed to reach the average of those within the SES strata into which they were adopted.

Locurto (1990:278) points out that these studies tell us nothing about malleability per se absent knowledge of what the IQs of these children would have been had they not been adopted. Selective placement is a function of adoptive parents' choices, as well as agency matching attempts. Children or infants who may appear unhealthy, lethargic, or to have symptoms of retardation may be excluded from consideration (Locurto, 1990:278). This screening process may be part of the reason that samples of adoptees tend to have mean IQs six to ten points greater than the population mean. It is, of course, impossible to know what IQ would have been in the absence of adoption, but it is possible to estimate it by comparing the IQs of adopted children with those of biological siblings who were not adopted. Dumaret (1985) was able to do this by comparing IQs of thirty-three French adoptees (M = 109.2) with the IQs of twenty-two half-siblings raised by the biological mothers of both (M = 93.0), and with twenty half-siblings taken into the care of social services (M = 80.8). This pattern of means shows that the adopted children had a mean IQ advantage over their "stay at home" half-siblings of sixteen points, and one of almost twenty-nine points over their "in care" half-siblings (Dumaret, 1985:562).

The interpretation of these findings is not unambiguous. The comparison children were *half-siblings* (same mothers, different fathers), so genetic differences cannot be discounted. Neither can we discount selectivity on the part of adoptive parents or the possibility that charactaristics associated with the IQ of the "in care" children evoked reactions from mothers that led to the children being taken into care. Nevertheless, if only half of the IQ difference shown in this study was the result of environmental intervention, we have cause for optimism. Certainly, the adopted children will have been given a better start in life than their less fortunate half-siblings.

One further study merits mention because of its unique design and because it has generated enthusiastic comment from prominent researchers more prone to genetic interpretations (McGue, 1989). This French cross-fostering study by Capron and Duyme (1989) is unique in that it compared adoptive parent–adopted child pairs from both extremes of SES. At the high-SES parental extreme were senior executives and professionals, and at the low extreme were small farmworkers and "diverse-unskilled." All children were relinquished at birth, and the mean age of testing was 14 years. Unfortunately, because of the extreme rarity of low-SES parents adopting high-SES children (only 1 in 600 cases in this study), the study was limited by sample size. Nevertheless, the results were remarkable and should certainly generate many attempted replications. The pattern of means found is presented in Table 5.1.

The marginals show that children born to high-SES parents, regardless of SES of adoptive parents, have higher IQs (M = 113.55) than children born to low-SES parents (M = 98.0) and that children adopted by high-SES parents, regardless of SES of biological parents, have higher IQs (M = 111.6) than children adopted by low-SES parents (M = 99.95). Despite limited degrees of freedom, both these effects are statistically significant. The difference of 12.10 IQ points between children of low-SES biological parents adopted by high- and low-SES parents is also significant (1-tail). The cases that fall on the main diagonal of the table constitute examples of positive GE correlation. The difference of 27.2 points between children both born to and adopted by high-SES parents (M = 119.6) and children both born to and adopted by low-SES parents (M = 92.4) points out the synergistic effects of heredity and environment.

Consider the secondary diagonal of the table containing instances in which GE correlation is negative. Children born to low-SES parents adopted by high-

Table 5.1
Mean IQ of Adopted Children at Extreme SES Levels

Biological Parents' SES	Adoptive Parents' SES		
	High	Low	Marginals
High	119.6 (n=10)	107.5 (n=8)	113.55 (n=18)
Low	103.6 (n=10)	92.4 (n=10)	98.00 (n=20)
Marginals	111.6	99.95	

Source: Adapted from Capron and Duyme (1989:553).

SES parents show a lower mean IQ (103.6) than children born to high-SES parents adopted by low-SES parents (107.5), despite an average of fourteen years' exposure to high- and low-SES environments, respectively. This points to the limits of incremental malleability of IQ and to the resistance to IQ decrement within the normal range of human environments (Locurto, 1990:289). Thus, although this study once again shows stronger effects for genetics, it provides unequivocal evidence for environmental effects, the reaction range for IQ of which appears to be about an average of twelve points.

OTHER ENVIRONMENTAL INFLUENCES

The greatest period of malleability is during early infancy and childhood, the period of greatest plasticity and absorbency of the brain. One adoption study found a significant correlation of –0.36 between age at adoption and IQ (Scarr & Weinberg, 1976). As Wolman (1985:865) writes, "In one area, intelligence and mental health are closely related—namely, in early childhood deprivation." He cites various authors unanimous in their belief that if children are not loved and accepted, they will develop inadequate self-love, inadequate self-esteem, inadequate cognitive skills, and hostile attitudes toward other people. For instance, Watters and Stinnett's (1971:91) review of the literature concludes, "Consensus existed among the studies reviewed that academic achievement, leadership, and creative thinking of children was positively related to warm, accepting, understanding, and autonomy-granting parent–child relationships."

If positive conditions such as those just enumerated have positive effects, it follows that negative conditions, such as physical and emotional abuse, can have the opposite effect on intellectual development. Hoffman-Plotkin and Twentyman (1984) report a mean IQ difference of twenty IQ points between abused and nonabused preschool children, and Salzinger, Kaplan, Pelcovitz, Samit, and Kreiger (1984) found that three times as many (27% versus 9%) abused and neglected children than nonabused and nonneglected children were two years below grade level in verbal ability and that eleven times as many (33% versus 3%) were behind to the same extent in math ability.

The difficulty in evaluating such studies is that the parents of abused and neglected children provided them with genes as well as with their environment. If low-IQ parents are more likely to abuse and neglect their children than higher-IQ parents, then genetics confounds the relationship between children's abuse and their IQs. This observation is also true of parents of children who are successful in academics, leadership, and creativity (passive GE correlation). However, if CNS damage results from abuse, we can attribute much of the observed intellectual deficiency to the abuse. Elmer's (1977) study of abused children found that 30 percent of them had CNS damage and that 57 percent had IQ scores of 80 or less.

Malnourishment is yet another factor contributing to low IQ. If temporary malnourishment occurs in adulthood, no brain damage results because the body will take nourishment from other organs to satisfy the voracious appetite of the brain; but a protein-deficient diet has terrible consequences for infants. Protein is essential for axonal myelination; and adequate myelination is necessary to minimize neuronal fatigue, maximize conduction velocity, and to maximize the rate of neuronal firing (Konner, 1982:163). The infant brain is low in myelin at birth, with the vast proportion being laid down in the first two years of life, and not fully established until the age of 4. The lethargic and apathetic behaviors characteristic of individuals from diseases of malnutrition, such as pellagra and kwashiorkor, can be traced in many instances to myelin deficiency. Apart from retarded myelination, a number of studies have shown that severe malnutrition during infancy is related to a number of other adverse neurochemical consequences (Bouchard & Segal, 1985:403).

These studies lead us to suspect that the lower mean IQ of children from poverty-stricken homes may be attributable to some extent to protein-deficient diets during their early years. One study found that school children who were malnourished during their first two years of life had a mean full-scale IQ 8.27 points less than a comparison group of children who had been adequately nourished (Hertzig, Birch, Richardson, & Tizard, 1972). However, genetics may again confound such findings if the children's malnourishment was at least partially a function of parental behavior. In addition, malnutrition must be quite severe to have significant effect on IQ; and it rarely occurs to this extent in modern industrialized nations.

IQ AND SUCCESS

I began this chapter by stressing the importance of intelligence to "success," which in the United States generally means occupational success. Summarizing eleven meta-analyses of hundreds of studies relevant to this issue, Gottfredson (1987:510) makes the following points:

1. Intelligence tests predict performance in training and on the job in all kinds of work.

2. Job performance is more correlated with test performance in higher-level (more complex) jobs than in lower-level ones.

3. The relation of tested intelligence to job performance is linear, meaning that there is no threshold above which higher levels of intelligence are not associated with higher mean levels of job performance.

4. It is almost entirely the g factor in psychometric tests that accounts for their validity for predicting job performance.

5. The predictive validity of intelligence tests remains largely the same, but that of experience fades among workers with higher mean levels of experience.

6. Intelligence tests predict job performance even after controlling for differences in job knowledge.

7. Intelligence tests predict job performance equally well for blacks and whites, whether performance is measured objectively or subjectively.

Gottfredson (1987:512) indicates that these findings are very socially un-settling, given the goal of racial parity in employment, particularly at higher levels. Contrary to those who would maintain what she calls "a discreet si-lence" about such matters, Gottfredson (1987:512) feels that social justice demands an ongoing "dialogue on the social consequences of black–white differences in *g* under alternative social policies." Similarly, writing of the many negative correlates of cognitive deficits (crime, drugs, illegitimacy, welfare dependency) in an increasingly intelligence-grounded society, Humphreys (1986:432) stated, "I believe that we have a social problem that is at least the equivalent of the AIDS epidemic, but there is a good deal more constructive action being taken about the latter."

Gottfredson's (1987) and Humphreys's (1986) concerns are, of course, a major concern of Herrnstein and Murray's "notorious" *The Bell Curve* (1994), although they were not pilloried for expressing them the way Herrnstein and Murray were. Very little fuss is made if politically incorrect statements are kept safely tucked away in obscure scholarly journals, where occuptional psychologists and sociologists have been trumpeting *The Bell Curve*'s mes-sage for quite some time.[7]

Although cognitive ability usually accounts for only a small to middling proportion of the variance in any one area of social concern, when a variety of social and economic outcomes and behaviors are considered, cognitive ability accounts for a number of significant differences. The larger the IQ gap, the larger the outcome difference. A particulary informative study is the Na-tional Longitudinal Survey of Labor Market Experience of Youth (NLSY), conducted by the National Opinion Research Council since 1979. A national probability sample of over 12,000 youths ages 14 to 22 in 1979, the NLSY seeks to gather detailed information about the occupational, educational, fam-ily, and social histories of these youths. Herrnstein and Murray (1994) uti-lized data from this sample collected in 1989, when the participants were between 24 and 32 years of age. They compared life outcomes for subjects in the bottom (IQ of 87 and below) and top (IQ of 113 and above) 20 percent on IQ and found substantial differences between groups relating to risks for dropping out of school, poverty, long-term unemployment, chronic welfare dependency, bearing children out of wedlock, having a criminal record, and so on. The results are too numerous to recount in detail, but the basic lesson is clear: IQ is an important attribute in modern society and is becoming more and more so.

CONCLUSION

The emphasis on learned behavior in sociology makes it important that we pay attention to differential capacities to learn, a capacity that is substantially genetic in origin. The study of the effects of the environment on behavior and development cannot be properly understood without understanding genetic factors. Indeed, as indicated in Chapter 3, it is quite probable that many "environmental" measures themselves, such as SES, level of nurturing, number of books in the home, and so forth, are mediated by genetics (Plomin & Bergeman, 1991). Individual and group differences in IQ have such far-reaching social, political, educational, and economic consequences that one wonders why so many sociologists seem to want to ignore them. Surely the time has come for us to acknowledge the role of intelligence—the "master" human trait—in so many of the problems studied by sociologists.

The importance of fluid intelligence in modern society is beyond doubt, but we should not discount the value of crystallized intelligence. Success in modern society requires motivation, inspiration, perspiration, and mastery of a body of acquired (crystallized) knowledge as well as fluid intelligence. Neuroscience tells us that routinely stretching our minds develops new synapses and neural networks and channels to increase the efficiency of information processing. Nobel Prize–winning geneticist John Watson, for instance, revealed on a 1974 CBS television program called "The IQ Myth," that his measured IQ was 110, which is on the border between "average" and "bright average." A distribution of 146 science faculty members of prestigious Cambridge University revealed almost as many members with IQs in the "bright-average" range as in the "superior" range (Eysenck & Kamin, 1981:31).

Thus, "genius," whatever it is, requires more than fluid intelligence. In addition to the g factor, perhaps we should also be looking at what Itzkoff (1987:161) calls the P (for "postponement") factor, which he describes as "the ability to concentrate, focus, plan, persevere, and above all to postpone the momentary gratifications with which life tempts us, all for the sake of the long-term goal." Itzkoff's P is probably just as necessary as Spearman's g for the achievment of success in an open society (although I suspect that if P is ever properly defined and adequately measured, it will be rather strongly positively correlated with g). Clearly, "success" in modern society relies on more than IQ alone; and we should do what we can to assure all get an equal shot at it via social policies that take into account, not hide from, the fact of individual and group differences in IQ.[8] What these policies might be is beyond the scope of this work (see Zigler & Seitz [1986]); my present concern is only that sociologists become more conversant with the "other side" of the learning equation that has been so sadly neglected.

NOTES

1. The IQs of Nazi war criminals tested by the Allies before going to trial remind us not to confuse intelligence with worth. Herman Göring, Franz von Papen, and Albert Speer all tested at or above the ninety-seventh percentile, with scores of 138, 134, and 128, respectively. Richard Nixon, not exactly the most revered of American presidents, scored 143 on his high school IQ test; John Kennedy, who bested Nixon in the 1960 campaign debate, tested at 119 (Seligman, 1992:34).

2. These criteria constitute the sociologist's usual measures of SES, and many might argue that IQ is measuring social class and thus SES determines IQ. However, 60 percent of Snyderman and Rothman's (1988:66) panel of experts felt that IQ is an important (but not the most important) determinant of social class rather than the other way around; only 3 percent felt it was not important at all as a determinant of social class. It might be useful to report that as a group this panel was politically "slightly left of center" (Snyderman & Rothman, 1988:133).

3. Sowell's argument is exemplified by a curious case in California. Under a 1979 Federal Court ruling in *Larry P. v. Wilson Riles,* the schools in California may not administer IQ tests to blacks, although nonblacks may be tested. This ruling was supposed to protect black children from the "inherent bias" in IQ testing. Mrs. Mary Amaya, a black California mother whose son had been recommended for remedial course work without the benefit of IQ testing, sued the state school system for her son's right to be tested. Prior to the Federal Court ruling, an older son of Mrs. Amaya had been likewise recommended for remedial work; but the recommendation was overridden on the basis of an IQ test. Mrs. Amaya hoped that her younger son would also be rescued from misassignment by the results of an IQ test. Commenting on the court ruling, W. B. Allen (1988:369) of the U.S. Commission on Civil Rights opines that this "supposed shield for disadvantaged youths and adults has become a strong rod to punish or prohibit ambition."

Worse yet, as Sowell emphasized, a problem not diagnosed is a problem not addressed. In response to the Amaya case, the Federal Court overruled itself in 1992 and ruled that blacks may be IQ tested but only for the purpose of avoiding remedial classes, not placement into them (Seligman, 1992:197). Now we are in the curious position of being allowed to diagnose the problem but forbidden to apply any treatment that may be indicated.

4. The only method now known that would allow us to make definitive genetic inferences regarding population differences in IQ would be to cross-mate random samples of individuals from those populations and then to cross-foster the offspring. Since this is hardly likely to happen, and barring the development of esoteric methods sometime in the future, all arguments about black–white intellectual differences at present merely support or fail to support one side or the other. However, 45 percent of Snyderman and Rothman's (1988:128) sample of experts believe the black–white gap to be partially genetic, 15 percent thought it was entirely environmental, 1 percent said it was entirely genetic, and the remainder indicated that the data were insufficient for them to offer a reasonable opinion.

5. We may estimate h^2 from a variety of kinship correlations. For instance, the difference between the correlations of MZ twins reared together (0.86) and unrelated siblings reared together (0.34) is 0.52. This value represents h^2. We do not double the difference as before because there is no genetic variance to be accounted for among unrelated siblings reared together; so once common environments are eliminated by subtraction, we are left with 100 percent of the difference between the correlations attributable only to genetics (see Chapter 2, note 3). Because estimates from some kinship correlations tend to overestimate h^2 and others tend to underestimate it, it is preferable to estimate h^2 by calculating all possible estimates, with the mean h^2 yielding the most accurate overall estimate.

6. It might be worth thinking about the issue of "biased" measures again in the context of this example. Although the designers of such an experiment would know that

the "black" seeds had not been given the same opportunity as the "white" seeds to develop phenotypically, they certainly would not blame the instruments they use to measure various traits of interest for the differences they reveal; nor would they expect criticism of their work in the form of charges of instrument bias. Like IQ tests, these instruments measure only what is there; they say nothing about how it got there.

7. The December 13, 1994, issue of the *Wall Street Journal* contained a statement signed by fifty-two research scientists who work primarily in the area of intelligence indicating that the material in *The Bell Curve* is "mainstream" expert opinion and, for the most part, entirely noncontroversial.

8. An entire issue of the *Journal of Vocational Behavior*, edited by N. Betz (1988), was devoted to the question of intelligence in employment and of the social consequences of the increased complexity of intellectual demands. Even if academics ignore the role of IQ, we can be sure that employers do not. Even bureaucrats in the former Soviet Union accepted hereditarian interpretations of IQ for practical purposes (Eysenck, 1982).

Chapter 6

Sexual Dimorphism and Sex-Role Behavior

If any human society—larger or small, simple or complex, based on the most rudimentary hunting and fishing, or on the whole elaborate interchange of manufactured products—is to survive, it must have a pattern of social life that comes to terms with the differences between the sexes.
—Margaret Mead

Sex roles, the expectations surrounding them, and the ideological and ethical issues on their periphery, are important sociological topics. Although it has been called a "clearly indefensible hypothesis" (Goldberg, 1991:4), it is safe to say that most sociologists still believe sex differences in behavioral traits and characteristics are quite trivial and mostly the consequence of social conditioning. Other scientists accept the notion of nontrivial differences between the sexes as axiomatic and mostly biological in origin (Rossi 1977, 1984; Symons 1979, 1987; Ellis, 1986; Moir & Jessel, 1991).

The attitude of some mainstream social scientists to the mounting evidence of sexual dimorphism is analogous to the religious response to Darwinism in the nineteenth century: "Let us hope that it is not true; if it is, let us hope that it not be generally known." Some even use their positions as reviewers to try to prevent such information from becoming "generally known." Jo Durden-Smith and Diane de Simone (1983:20) related how one researcher's proposal for a book dealing with sex and the brain was dismissed by a reviewer with the words, "This book ought not be done." This was not a reflection of the reviewer's assessment of the researcher's scholarship but of his or her opinion that to explore the biological bases of sex differences is "sexist" and "antihumanist." Sex difference researchers categorically reject such labeling as silly and unduly constraining of the scientific endeavor to uncover the biological bases of such differences.[1] The use of pejorative labels to intimidate those in serious scientific pursuit of knowledge is particularly galling in this area, for many of its most outstanding researchers are women (e.g., Alice Rossi, Carol Jacklin, June Reinisch, Sandra Scarr, Diana Fishbein, Eleanor Maccoby, Marian Diamond, Margo Wilson, Helen Fisher).

In light of the strong sociological opposition to the biology of sex differences, it was gratifying to read Alice Rossi's presidential address to the ASA published in the *American Sociological Review*. Berating her sociological colleagues for ignoring the biological sciences, she wrote the following:

Gender differentiation is not simply a function of socialization, capitalist production, or patriarchy. It is grounded in a sex dimorphism that serves the fundamental purpose of reproducing the species. Hence, sociological units of analysis such as roles, groups, networks, and classes divert attention from the fact that the subjects of our work are male and female animals with genes, glands, bones and flesh occupying an ecological niche of a particular kind in a tiny fragment of time. And human sexual dimorphism emerged from a long prehistory of mammalian and primate evolution. Theories that neglect these characteristics of sex and gender carry a high risk of eventual irrelevance against the mounting evidence of sexual dimorphism from the biological and neurosciences. (Rossi, 1984:1)

Rossi is pointing out that basic gender differences have arisen out of the fundamentally different reproductive roles males and females play that have been fine tuned by eons of evolutionary pressure. She was also pointing out that sociologists must integrate the hard data from the more basic sciences into their own theories if they and their theories are to attain credibility within the broader scientific community. A similar point is made by Ellis (1986:537), who, after an extensive review of the neurohormonal literature, concluded that "social scientists in the future should avoid attributing sex differences in human behavior to training and social expectations until they have first given careful attention to neurohormonal factors."

INTERSEX ANOMALIES: WHAT THEY CAN TELL US ABOUT NORMAL SEX-BASED BEHAVIOR

Species mutants serve biologists to clarify the species norm (Ribchester, 1986:184), and brain-damaged patients provide neurophysiologists with a wealth of information about the organization of the normal cognitive system (Shallis, 1991). A number of scientists have suggested that the study of human intersex anomalies can likewise provide behavioral scientists with important clues to the biological substrates of sex-typical behavior (Rossi, 1984; Mosley & Stan, 1984; Money, Schwartz, & Lewis, 1985; Ellis & Ames, 1987; Tallal, 1991). The behavior patterns of males who are insensitive to androgens or of females who get too much androgen may tell us a great deal about the role of androgens on the behavior of hormonally normal men and women. The behavior of individuals with extra or missing chromosomes may tell us much about how genes and the processes they control influence our behavior. Although these "experiments of nature" are extreme deviations from the norm, like deviant case studies in other fields of inquiry, they help us to define what the norm might be.

Until the present century, a hermaphrodite was defined as a person who possessed to varying degrees the genitalia of both sexes; but simple anatomical definitions no longer suffice. The new terminology defines the true hermaphrodite (*hermaphroditus verus*) as an individual who possesses both ovarian and testicular tissue in the form of one ovary and one testicle, gonads composed of both kinds of tissue (ovotestis), or any combination of these. Individuals with matched gonads (two testes or two ovaries) but whose external sexual appearance is ambiguous, are now classified as pseudohermaphrodites, of which there are several varieties.

All mammals are intrinsically female: It is not the presence of two X chromosomes that makes a female; it is the absence of the Y chromosome. Otherwise put, maleness is induced (the male is "defeminized"), whereas femaleness is not. Sometimes there are infants born with several X chromosomes; and although the X chromosome carries far more genetic information than the Y, no matter how many X "units" of femaleness are present, the presence of a single Y results in the male pattern of sexual differentiation.

In the normal course of embryonic and fetal development, certain events occur that differentiate humans along sexual dimorphic lines. Ever since the Y chromosome was shown to be male determining, geneticists have been trying to narrow down the male-determining location further. The search finally turned up a single-copy gene called the SRY, or "sex-determining region of the Y" (McLaren, 1990). All females have all the material needed to make a male except this one gene, and all males would be females absent this single gene. These chromosome-driven changes constitute primary sexual differentiation. At about five months, testicular androgens (DHT) cause the penis and scrotal sac to develop; without androgens, the vagina, clitoris, and labia develop. Hormonal effects on sexual dimorphism represent secondary sexual differentiation.

The human brain is also "sexed" dimorphically by the action of fetal testosterone (T) and its by-products, DHT and estradiol, as they interact with the hypothalamus and the limbic system between the fourth and seventh month of fetal life. The complicated nature of neuroandrogenic processes is emphasized by findings indicating that it is the "female" hormone estradiol (a metabolite of T) that masculinizes XY brain tissue. Thus, while estradiol has a masculinizing effect on the brain, at least during the period of neuronal sex differentiation, it has feminizing effects outside the brain (Khan & Cataio, 1984; Ellis, 1986).

The diversion of the male form from its intrinsic female form by hormonal processes has profound implications for sex differences throughout the life span. It is by no means the entire story; but it does bias males and females in different directions, coloring their perceptions and making them differentially sensitive and receptive to social input. This position has been strongly stated by Nyborg (1984:501) in his "hormonal general covariance model," which "assigns to sex hormones the ultimate biochemical responsibility for producing not only gender-related differences in sensory modality priorities, but also in interests, cognitive style, gender role differences, physical energy expenditure, androgenization of muscles and fat distribution, and in other gender-related somatic characteristics. All these traits would depend on whether or not sex hormones were present at the right place, and at the right time, and in the right amount."

Brain masculinization is not an all-or-nothing process; rather, it is one that describes a continuum on which there may be significant male–female overlap. The female fetus is protected from the diverting effects of androgen, but this protection is by no means complete. Female children of mothers who were given progestin (a synthetic androgenic compound) to prevent miscarriage display significantly more malelike characteristics than either female children of mothers given prenatal estrogen or female children not exposed to synthetic fetal steroids (Reinisch 1977, 1981). Small amounts of testosterone and its metabolites may even have a more diverting effect on the female brain than a similar amount would have on a male brain at certain critical times (Udry & Talbert, 1988). However, once prenatal androgens have sensitized receptors in the male brain to their effects, later—especially at puberty—they activate the brain to engage in male-typical behavior.

Hormone-induced brain sex differences are particularly striking in areas of the hypothalamus. Ever since it was discovered that male rats have a three- to sevenfold greater volume of neurons than female rats in a control region of the medial preoptic area (Arnold & Gorski, 1984), neuroscientists have speculated about similar sex differences in neural circuitry among humans. Motivated by this fascinating possibility, Swaab and Fliers (1985) found the volume of the nucleus in the preoptic area of the hypothalamus to be an average of 2.5 times larger in human males than in human females and to contain an average of 2.2 times as many cells, and LeVay (1991) found a cluster of cells in the interstitial nucleus of the anterior hypothalamus to be twice as large in males as in females. These areas play a crucial role in the initiation of sexual and maternal behavior. If we want to come to grips with sex differences, we must understand that "sex differences in masculine and feminine behaviors appear to be dependent upon differences in neural organization laid down during early development" (Ader, 1983:260).

Unlike the external genitals, the internal reproductive structures do not develop from the same unisex organs. In this sense all embryos are hermaphroditic, possessing both male Wolffian and female Mullerian ducts. At about three months, androgens from the male testes cause the Wolffian structures to develop into the male internal sex organs—vas deferens, seminal vesicles, and ejaculatory duct. The fetal testes also secrete Mullerian inhibiting substance (MIS), which causes the Mullerian structures to atrophy. Without androgens, the Wolffian structure degenerates; and without MIS, the Mullerian structures will develop into the female internal sex organs—uterus, Fallopian tubes, and the vagina.

With all the genetic and hormonal events occurring at the embryonic and fetal stages of life, it is inevitable that nature will make mistakes occasionally, mistakes that offer us rare opportunities to approach long-standing questions from a fresh angle. One such issue is the origin of the huge gap in male–female rates of deviant behavior of all kinds. Despite the ubiquity of such findings, environmentalists have not been able to render a plausible account of them. If we conceptualize sex–gender as a neurohormonal continuum rather than as a dichotomy, and if we then identify discrete locations along this continuum and examine deviant behavior among individuals found at these locations, perhaps we will arrive at a more biologically informed answer to male–female differences in general.

Turner's Syndrome

At the feminine extreme of the sex–gender continuum are *Turner's syndrome* (TS) females. TS females are generally karyotype X0, indicating the absence of the second sex chromosome, although a structurally abnormal second X may be present. TS females are sterile and lack secondary sexual characteristics, and some bear a number of physical stigmata such as webbed neck and extremely short stature. Lacking normal functioning ovaries, TS females are deficient in sex hormones; and they evidence many of the deficits in right-hemisphere brain functioning that one would expect from prenatally androgen-absent or androgen-deficient individuals. TS females have a mean verbal IQ (VIQ) significantly greater than their mean performance IQ (PIQ), sometimes by as many as thirty points (Plomin, DeFries, & McClearn, 1980:164). This cognitive imbalance probably reflects the absence of brain defeminization (the rightward switch), which occurs in genetically and cytogenetically normal individuals of both sexes to varying degrees (Money, 1993).

TS females may be expected to be exaggeratedly feminine, and they are. There are both positive and negative aspects of exaggerated femininity, as there are of exaggerated masculinity. But whereas the negative aspects of femininity (e.g., passivity) usually only affect the individual herself, negative aspects of masculinity (e.g., aggression) spill over to negatively affect others also. TS females are consistently found to be very coy, nurturing, passive, submissive, "phlegmatic, compliant, equable, and accepting" (Downey, Ehrhardt, Gruen, Bell, & Morishima, 1989:192). Whatever one's view of the desirability of such characteristics, they are not associated with antisocial behavior. The lowest mean score on neuroticism of any group reported in the literature (11.62), versus the American norm of 20.66, has been reported for

TS females (Baekgaard, Nyborg, & Nielsen, 1978). The only study located assessing any form of antisocial behavior among TS subjects found that one of twenty-three TS women had a lifetime history of alcoholism or drug abuse compared with eight of a matched group of constitutionally short-stature women (Downey, Ehrhardt, Gruen, Bell, & Morishima, 1989).

Androgen-Insensitivity Syndrome

The importance of the androgens in masculinization is dramatically shown by the *congenital adrenal hyperplasia* (CAH) and *androgen-insensitivity* (AIS) syndromes. AIS is an X-linked recessive syndrome in which receptor sites that normally bind androgens are partially or fully inoperative. If the receptors are completely inoperative, AIS represents a complete degree of deandrogenization and results in XY genotypical males developing as phenotypical females. AIS individuals have androgen-producing testes (undescended); but since androgen receptors are insensitive to its effects, the internal male sex structures (Wolffian structures) do not develop. Since the testes secrete normal male amounts of MIS, causing the internal female sex organs (Mullerian structures) to atrophy, AIS individuals have neither male nor female internal sex organs. Because the external genitalia are unambiguously female, AIS is rarely diagnosed until puberty, when concern over failure to menstruate materializes. Apart from being about three inches taller than the average XX female, having little or no body hair, and having a short vagina, AIS persons whose androgen receptors are fully inoperative are totally female in external physical appearance.

AIS males, unresponsive to the masculinizing effects of androgens on the brain, conform to typical behavioral patterns of normal women—and, as with TS females, exaggeratedly so (Money, Schwartz, & Lewis, 1985). Also like TS females, AIS males, in spite of their Y chromosome, show poor spatial ability, which reinforces the importance of androgens to spatial ability. As expected from this, AIS individuals have superior VIQ relative to PIQ (Hoyenga & Hoyenga, 1979), a trait often considered a marker of prosocial behavior (Walsh, 1992). There is an unfortunate dearth of studies on the behavior of the AIS person, however. Only three studies are listed in the *Psychological Abstracts* for the period encompassing 1987 to 1993, and all three were interested in AIS and homosexuality. ("Homosexuality" in this case is gauged with respect to hormonal and genital status, not chromosomal or gonadal status.)

A rare condition known as *5 alpha-reductase deficiency* offers further insight into role of androgens on sexual identity. The enzyme 5 alpha-reductase (5αR) is necessary for the synthesis of DHT, which is required to masculinize the external genitals but not the internal reproductive system or the brain. Thirty-eight 5αR individuals from a certain region in the Dominican Republic were studied by Imperato-McGinley, Peterson, Gautier, and Sturla (1979).

Eighteen 5αR subjects appeared at birth to be unambiguous females and were raised as such. At puberty, the final (tertiary) stage of sexual differentiation, they underwent a physical transformation to maleness, including growth of the penis and descent of the testes. All but one of these males were able to make the social and psychological transition to the male role with relative ease despite twelve years of female socialization. This suggested to Imperato-McGinley and her colleagues that while DHT is necessary for the promotion of the external male genitals at birth, testosterone makes for a relatively normal masculine puberty. It also suggests that testosterone has a prenatal masculinizing effect on the brain despite the absence of DHT and that this prenatal effect is crucial in the formation of male gender identity. Imperato-McGinley and her colleagues (1979:1236) concluded from this study that "it appears that the extent of androgen (i.e., testosterone) exposure of the brain in utero, during the early postnatal period and at puberty has more effect in determining male-gender identity than does sex of rearing."

Studies of 5αR have been challenged by those favoring a socialization model of gender identity–role who assert that the ease or difficulty of making the gender transition may depend to a large extent on the cultural emphasis placed on gender roles. A study of five 5αR-deficient males raised as females in a highly sex-segregated culture (the Sambia of New Guinea) found that these individuals had more difficulty making the gender switch than their Dominican counterparts (Herdt & Davidson, 1988). Others have challenged Imperato-McGinley and her colleagues' interpretation as theoretically flawed: "Let us assume first that DHT is an organizing principle in prenatal human males. If so, the 5α-reductase deficient males should not be able to assume a male gender identity (or gender role) in adulthood" (Feder, 1984:176). Unfortunately for this argument, the role of DHT is to masculinize the external male genitalia, not to serve as an organizing principle of gender identity. Another critic (Hoult, 1984:142) writes that 5αR had become common enough in the two villages studied to lead villagers to expect some children to change sex at puberty. Thus, 5αR children may have been raised as "sort of girls" who were "expected to turn into full-fledged males when they reach puberty." However, Imperato-McGinley and her colleagues' (1979) description of socialization practices in these villages provides no evidence for this. Further, knowing that a certain percentage of children will have the deficiency does not mean that villagers know a priori which children actually have it.

Congenital Adrenal Hyperplasia

CAH is an autosomal recessive trait that, via one of a number of possible enzymatic defects (most commonly, 21-hydroxylase deficiency), prevents the synthesizing of cortisol from androgen by the adrenal cortices. Instead of cortisol, androstenedione—from which testosterone is metabolized—is secreted, resulting in precocious sexual development in males and variable degrees of masculinization of the genitalia and brains of females (Khan & Cataio, 1984:14). CAH is the most common cause of genital ambiguity among females, with infants showing varying degrees of clitoral enlargement and fusion of the labia. Because the androgen stimulus arrives too late to switch on the Wolffian ducts, virilization involves only the external reproductive organs. If CAH females are treated with cortisol and have any reproductive organ defects surgically corrected, they are able to function reproductively. If CAH is untreated, there may be further masculinization of the external sex organs at puberty.

CAH females are studied more frequently than AIS females, probably because they come to the attention of medical authorities sooner and thus can be tracked. CAH females engage in more male-typical behavior and possess more male-typical traits than normal females, for example, tomboyism (Berenbaum & Hines, 1992); slightly better visual–spatial than verbal skills (Nass & Baker, 1991b); lower maternal interests; less interest in marriage; a greater interest in careers (Dittman, Kappes, Kappes, & Borger, 1991); and a greater probability of homosexuality (Money, Schwartz, & Lewis, 1985; Meyer-Bahlburg, 1990–1991). Although no studies assessing the criminal behavior of CAH women are available, because they score higher than hormonally normal women on characteristics positively associated with crime (a liking for rough-and-tumble play, PIQ > VIQ discrepancy, and experimental sexual behavior) and lower on characteristics negatively associated with crime (maternal interest, commitments to relationships), we have reason to believe that they may be somewhat overrepresented in criminal populations relative to their number in the general population.

Klinefelter's Syndrome

Klinefelter's syndrome (KS) males have two or more X chromosomes and one or more Y chromosomes, the XXY pattern being the most common. KS males tend to be born to older mothers, and the syndrome appears to be the result of a fault in cell division in the ova. Although KS males have smaller-than-normal genitalia, they are capable of erection and satisfactory intercourse. They tend to be taller than normal males, to develop relatively well-formed breasts at puberty, to have about half the male postpubertal amount of testosterone, a low level of sexual activity, and difficulty forming pair-bonded relationships with either sex (Money, 1986; Wu, Bancroft, Davidson, & Nicol, 1982; Schiavi, Theilgaard, Owen, & White, 1988).

Understandably, KS males often have sexual identity problems and are significantly more likely than XY males to be homosexual, bisexual, transvestites, transsexuals, and inmates in prisons and mental hospitals (Hoyenga & Hoyenga, 1979:35). However, a recent study found that XXY males are no more likely to be found in prisons that XY males when IQ and SES are controlled for (Mandoki, Sumner, Hoffman, & Riconda, 1991). Because KS individuals tend to be passive, indecisive, and to evidence pronounced antiaggressiveness (Theilgaard, 1983), their crimes are almost always nonviolent or of a sexual nature. Although most KS subjects are of normal intelligence, mental retardation rates are significantly above expectations. When mental retardation is present among KS subjects, it is usually a function of both VIQ and PIQ deficits in contrast to TS and XYY subjects, where the deficits tend to be sex-typical, that is, mostly PIQ for TS subjects and mostly VIQ for YY subjects (Money, 1986:75).

The XYY Syndrome

No syndrome has generated more attention in behavioral cytogenetics than the XYY syndrome. Early accounts of XYY males labeled the condition *Jacob's criminal syndrome*, but this label was later dropped (Woodward, 1992). The XYY male is not a "supermale," nor is he a homicidal maniac. He is, however, significantly more likely than XY males to evidence pathological exaggeration of male-typical behavioral traits. Normal XY males are often accused of being insensitive to feelings and incapable of making commitments; and in this sense, XYY males are quintessentially male (Money, 1986:81). XYY males are significantly more likely than XY males to be impulsive, enuretic, short-tempered, to have a PIQ > VIQ intellectual profile, and to show atypical brain-wave patterns (Hoyenga & Hoyenga, 1979:38; Schiavi, Theilgaard, Owen, & White, 1988). Psychometric testing has shown that XYY males had lower levels of emotional stability, less mature self-concepts, and lower tolerance for inappropriate responses than a matched group of XY males (Noel & Revil, 1974).

Plasma testosterone concentrations of XYY men are usually found to be significantly higher than in matched samples of XY men, but testosterone levels do not appear to distinguish between XYY men who had and who had not committed a violent offense (Schiavi, Theilgaard, Owen, & White, 1988). Although most XYY males lead fairly normal lives, a large Danish sample found that XYY males are imprisoned or in psychiatric hospitals at rates exceeding their incidence in the general population (1.24 per 1,000) by 7.0 and 2.6 times, respectively (Nielsen & Christensen, 1974). Although there have been studies in which the rate of XYY males found in prisons did not significantly exceed the rate of XYY males in the general population, a survey of thirty-five studies of XYY males in institutions led Hook (1973:143) to conclude that "there is no question that the prevalence rate of XYYs is markedly increased over baseline." Another study of males at the top 16 percent of the height distribution (XYY males tend to be taller than XY males) found XYY males to be most criminal (Witkin et al., 1976).

Figure 6.1 presents a hypothetical scattergram summarizing the present argument in which "deviance" is predicted from masculinity–androgen levels across the gender continuum. *Deviance* is broadly defined to include all

Figure 6.1
Hypothetical Scattergram Relating Masculinity–Androgen Level (Designated by Karyotype) to Deviance

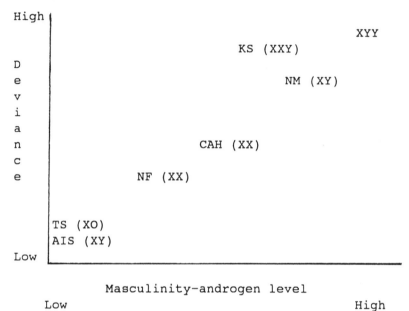

Source: From Walsh (1995).

Key: TS = Turner's syndrome; AIS = androgen-insensitivity syndrome; NF = normal female; KS = Klinefelter's syndrome; CAH = congenital adrenal hyperplasia; NM = normal male.

socially nonconforming behaviors ranging from the most minor sins and peccadilloes to the gravest of crimes. As we have seen, TS and AIS individuals are the least masculine in terms of androgen levels and are the most socially conforming of all groups of individuals on the continuum. XX females have higher androgen levels and higher levels of deviance than TS or AIS individuals; but as a group, they are still very much at the lower end on both. CAH females have both higher androgen levels and higher deviance levels than XX females, although lower levels on both than normal males.

Were it not for the existence of KS males, the relationship between masculinity–androgen level would be strictly monotonic. KS males have significantly less testosterone than XY males, although significantly more than XX females, and have a greater level of (mostly sexual) deviance than both XX females and XY males. Their below-average intelligence and sex-role ambiguity may have more to do with their deviance than hormone levels. If sexual deviance were omitted from consideration, KS males may fall below

XY males on average levels of deviant behavior. Finally, XYY males have higher androgen levels, evidence many more traits consistent with psychopathy, and exhibit higher levels of behavioral deviance than XY males.

Although we cannot discount the effects of social learning on the differential probability of deviance between men and women, neither can we ignore that what is learned is learned in the context of passive GE correlation (Scarr & McCartney, 1983). Males and females receive both genes and socialization experiences conducive to the development of masculine and feminine roles and behaviors, respectively. Only in rare instances are they exposed to sex-role socialization experiences that run against the grain of their genotypes. Male socialization produces male-typical behavior because it is usually consistent with propensities males bring with them to the socialization experience; female socialization produces female-typical behavior for the same reason.

It would appear that females are biologically protected from deviating too far from the central tendency of behavioral propriety in any given culture in the same way they are biologically protected from the physiological ravages of X-linked recessive diseases. Just as a homologous X chromosome protects women physically via allelic and mosaic control, female hormonal-secretion patterns and a lesser degree of hemispheric laterality probably protects them from many behavioral pathologies. Sensation seeking, impulsivity, aggression, dominance, and a propensity toward greater visual–spatial skills relative to verbal skills are overwhelmingly male traits; they are all androgen facilitated; and they are all traits linked to behavioral nonconformity of all kinds.

As indicated in Chapter 4, the facilitative influence of testosterone does not appear strong enough to account for significant variance in antisocial behavior when it is assayed within the normal male range; and quite a large difference is required to detect significant behavioral differences (Dabbs & Morris, 1990). However, the normal male range is a severely restricted one in a much larger distribution of testosterone levels, that is, the full range of adult human beings. The intersex syndromes reflect extreme differences ranging from either complete absence or complete insensitivity to testosterone (TS, AIS) to the upper level of the normal male range where most XYY males are located.

Although the rarity of pseudohermaphroditism renders the evidence sparse, it is both consistent and convincing: Crime, deviance, and nonconformity of all kinds increase as we move from extreme femininity to extreme masculinity (as defined by androgen levels). While environmentalists may continue to insist that male–female differences in socially disapproved behavior of the form male > female is explicable in terms of sex-role socialization, it would require extraordinary sophistry to similarly explain the XYY > KS > XY > CAH > XX > AIS = TS pattern. Mainstream social science has no theory capable of making sense of this pattern, but an understanding of the behavioral organizing effects of gonadal steroids circulating in the developing fetal brain renders it intelligible.

True Hermaphroditism

True hermaphroditism—*hermaphroditus verus*—may also provide valuable insights into why XY males and XX females differ along so many behavioral dimensions. The majority (about 70%) of true hermaphrodites have karyotypes indistinguishable from those of the XY male or XX female. Since both karyotypes have ovarian and testicular tissue, they offer rare proof that ovarian tissue can develop absent a second X chromosome (in the case of XYs) and that testicular tissue can develop absent a Y chromosome (in the case of XXs). Most true hermaphrodites (about 57%) are XX, and approximately 80 percent of these have internal female organs capable of sexual functioning and with some potential for fertility (Luks, Hansbrough, Klotz, Kottmeier, & Tolete-Valcek, 1988).

A classification scheme for the external genitalia of true hermaphrodites has been proposed by Luks and his colleagues (1988) based on the degree of male or female genital appearance. These classes range from class I (clitoris normal or slightly enlarged) to class VI (penis normal to small) and are distributed in an approximate normal curve.

Although it appears that we have come full circle by again using external genital appearance to assign sex of rearing, doing so has practical consequences. *The degree of virilization of the genitalia provides indication of the extent of brain masculinization: The more masculinized the genital features, the more likely the brain has been organized along male lines; the more feminine the genital features, the less brain masculinization has taken place.* Anatomy is not destiny, but to deny any concordance at all between sex-specific physical differences and sex-specific behavioral differences is contrary to the evidence. Luks and his colleagues are medical doctors indifferent to the grinding of ideological axes among the warring "biological" and "environmental" camps of social science. Their only motive is a concern with the practical issue of raising children in a manner consistent with the degree of brain virilization.

If gender were nothing more than a social creation, then the status of a person's genitalia indicates nothing, least of all, the degree of masculinization of the brain. A case study reported by Money and Ehrhardt (1972) has long been hailed by environmentalists as providing strong support for the extreme malleability of gender (Durden-Smith & de Simone, 1983:103). The study reports the case of one of a pair of male identical twins whose penis was accidentally mutilated during circumcision who subsequently underwent further surgery and hormone treatment to feminize his appearance. The child was then raised as a female.

Because this child was one of a pair of monozygotic twins, "she" provided an extraordinary opportunity to examine the effects of nature and nurture on gender identity. Money and Ehrhardt (1972) wrote glowingly of how feminine she was relative to her genetically identical brother, thus highlighting the effects of learning and modeling. However, when the pubescent surges of testosterone arrived at her masculinized brain, the story changed. The British Broadcasting Company (BBC) decided to do a follow-up story on her, and a number of psychiatrists who had examined her were interviewed. It turned out that this unfortunate child had developed a number of psychological problems and was decidedly unhappy with her assigned gender, leading one psychiatrist to seriously doubt whether she could ever make the adjustment as a woman. When Money found out about this, he withdrew his support from the BBC project and refused to be interviewed (Durden-Smith & de Simone, 1983:109). Money (1986:235) now rejects the notion of gender neutrality at birth: "Clearly, the brain holds the secrets of the etiology of gender identity differentiation."

This study is an example of how "supporting" studies become part of the lore of the sociological literature, from which no amount of contrary evidence is apparently sufficient to remove them. It is quoted approvingly in Macionis's (1989) introductory sociology textbook despite his awareness of the contrary evidence (also see Andersen [1988:51–52]). The contrary evidence is provided by Macionis himself in the instructor's annotated version where he quotes Milton Diamond as writing, "It is regrettable that so much of a theoretical and philosophical superstructure has been built on the supposed results of a single, uncontrolled and unconfirmed case" (quoted in Macionis, 1989:316). By placing this information in the instructor's version but not the student's version, Macionis is assisting the instructor to perpetuate the myth of gender neutrality at birth if he or she is so inclined.

Gender and Culture: Mead's Work

Behavioral and temperamental differences between the sexes, although overlapping, are universal (Symons, 1979; Brown, 1991). Andersen (1988:55) disputes this by stating that this assertion is "a fact that simply does not stand up to the cross-cultural evidence." She cites Margaret Mead's *Sex and Temperament in Three Primitive Societies* (1935) as her sole source of "cross-cultural evidence." Mead's book, which has become an icon for the environmentalist, is an ethnographic study of the Arapesh, Tchambuli, and Mundugumor peoples of New Guinea. The cultural practices of these three tribes as they relate to sex roles are purported to provide evidence for the extreme malleability of gender. Mead reported that the Arapesh are a gentle people who believe the feminine temperament to be ideal for both sexes, and that the Mundugumor consider the masculine temperament to be proper for both sexes. Strangest of all were the Tchambuli (or Chambri) who favored femininity (as Westerners would define it) for males and masculinity for females. No wonder Mead's work was received so favorably by cultural determinists—culture can make what it will of us.

Mead's work is cited approvingly in almost all introductory sociology textbooks to perpetuate the notion that culture alone determines masculinity and femininity, a position that Mead herself later took pains to deny (Mead, 1949).

"Mead's research is therefore strong support for the conclusion that gender is a variable creation of society," writes Macionis (1989:317); and Farley (1990:152–153) characterizes Tchambuli society as "female-dominant" and cites Mead's work to dispute the notion that males are intrinsically more aggressive than females. Criticism of Mead's research in the anthropological literature has been virtually ignored in the feminist and sociological literature, despite the fact it has been coming in since the 1930s (Brown, 1991:20–23). Rushton (1990b:120–121) concludes from the sum of this criticism that Mead's ideological fight against biological universals renders her work more dubious than Cyril Burt's work on IQ, the dubiety of which rarely fails to make the textbooks.[2]

It turns out that sex-based behavioral expectations within these three tribes were not all that different from the expectations of other cultures throughout the world. Fortune's (1939) study of the Arapesh pointed out that they did not expect the two sexes to have the same temperament and that warfare was a well-developed art among these "gentle" people. Mundugumor women were considerably more masculine in their behavior than Western women but far less so than their menfolk, who thoroughly dominated them. Deborah Gewertz's (1981) fieldwork among the Tchambuli showed that it is clearly a male-dominant society; any female dominance existing among the Tchambuli being limited to women's matters. A recent book documents the "twisted histories" and "altered contexts" of these people that have so long served to perpetuate environmentalist myths regarding masculinity and femininity (Gewertz & Errington, 1991).

In light of the reams of cross-cultural and historical evidence pointing to the opposite conclusion, it is remarkable that Mead's work, based on her subjective interpretation of three very small and exotic cultures, should have been so readily accepted. Mead's work may be considered a "deviant-case" study that was not, and the continued citation of her work to "prove" the extreme malleability of gender is either an example of the intrusion of ideology into science or a sad commentary on the nature of interdisciplinary communication. Culture can and does mold masculine and feminine characteristics in many diverse ways, but the biasing framework supporting these characteristics is plainly biological, and Mead's later works appear to support this (see this chapter's epigraph). She even traced these differences to "sex differentiated reproductive strategies" (Mead, 1949:160), a concept that, while fully consistent with biological science, tends to raise the hackles of radical feminists.[3]

Gender and Culture: Spiro's Work

Perhaps the most devastating blow to come from the social sciences to the notion of cultural primacy in the determination of gender identity comes from studies of Israel's 240 kibbutzim (Spiro 1975, 1980). The kibbutzim movement, heavily influenced by the Marxism of Russian immigrants, was founded in 1910 and has proven to be remarkably successful in many ways. It contributes a disproportionately large number of its members to the political, military, professional, and creative classes of Israeli society and about 12 percent to its gross national product (GNP), despite constituting only about 9 percent of its population (Spiro, 1980:4). The kibbutzim movement is a natural cultural experiment, the scope and size of which could never be duplicated by scientists. The purpose of the movement was to strip its members of all vestiges of "bourgeois culture" and to emancipate women from their socioeconomic, intellectual, and sexual shackles. Boys and girls were raised collectively. They were taught the same lessons by teachers of both sexes; given equal responsibilities; and shared the same toys, games, living quarters, and even the same toilets, dressing rooms, and showers. This sex-neutral environment was supposed to result in androgynous beings devoid of observable differences in nurturance, role preferences, empathy, aggression, sexuality, and so on. The movement proudly proclaimed it had achieved this goal in 1950, forty years after its founding (Spiro, 1980:6).

Melford Spiro, a self-described cultural determinist, studied the Kiryat Yedidim kibbutz in 1951 and again in 1975 to evaluate these revolutionary claims. As one who believed in the cultural relativism of human nature, he thought that he was setting out merely to discover and document the dimension of the changes effected by the movement, taking it for granted that he would find them. However, what he actually found forced on him what he describes as "a kind of Copernican revolution on my own thinking" (1980:106). "As a cultural determinist," he wrote, "my aim in studying personality development in 1951 was to observe the influence of culture on human nature or, more accurately, to discover how a new culture produces a new human nature. In 1975 I found (against my own intentions) that I was observing the influence of human nature on culture" (1980:106).

Spiro found a counterrevolutionary feminization of the Sabra (kibbutzim-born and -reared) women. Despite the exhortations of their ideologically committed mothers and grandmothers, Sabra women fought for formal marriage vows; for greater contact with their children; for separate male–female toilets, showers, and living arrangements prior to marriage; for modesty of dress in the company of men; and for possession of "bourgeois" means of enhancing female charms. Even in an earlier work, Spiro (1975) found that the activities and fantasy lives of young children varied significantly between the sexes despite adult role models striving assiduously to eliminate those differences. As a reluctant apostate, Spiro could not fully bring himself to impose a biosocial interpretation on his data, preferring to write that his data supported the notion that "sexually appropriate role modeling is a function of precultural differences between the sexes" (1980:107). Yet what could "precultural" differences mean other than biological differences?

It should be emphasized that the reversion to femininity and familism was in response to female, not male, disatisfaction (van den Berghe, 1979:74;

Leibowitz, 1978:152). As such, Moir and Jessel (1991:148) view the refeminization of the Sabra women as "a reassertion by women themselves of their fundamental, innate biogrammar against a system, which, like most Utopias, has been created by men." Lesser-Blumberg (1983:136), on the other hand, argued that women never really had a chance because they were "integrated into 'male' economic and political roles, but there was no systematic attempt to integrate kibbutz men into 'female' roles." Lesser-Blumberg's is a rather patronizing view of Sabra women, as radical feminist's views of "traditional" women tend to be (see Jagger and Rothenberg [1984] for a variety of such views). Moir and Jessel's (1991:148) view of the refeminization of the Sabra is consistent with the concept of active CE correlation when they write, "It is far more likely, and more respectful of their dignity, to say these women know their own minds and act accordingly."

To the extent that male and female minds are "set" along sexually dimorphic lines by the action of fetal hormones, the more interesting question is not the conformity of the Sabra women to their inner nature but rather its disavowal by the pioneer kibbutzim women. There is a major and very powerful difference between Sabra women and their grandmothers: The kibbutzim pioneers were self-selected; their granddaughters were not. The decision to leave traditional living patterns behind in favor of an untested communitarian system implies powerful ideological commitment. The level of commitment would become somewhat diluted among their daughters and more so among their granddaughters. The more distant kibbutzim women became from the initial motivation, the freer they became from its ideological commitment to sexual neutrality, and the freer they became to behave in ways compatible with their female genotypes.

SEXUAL DIMORPHISM AND SEX ROLES

The dominant sociological position is that sex roles are primarily the result of socialization in a patriarchal society. Let us agree that all known societies have been patriarchies and that this has had many negative consequences for men as well as for women. To acknowledge this is not to condone it; all societies would most likely be kinder and gentler places if they were less male dominated (Konner, 1982; Walsh, 1991b). Two sociologists, Goldberg (1974) and Kemper (1990a), however, view patriarchy and dominance as consequences of testosterone levels and, therefore, inevitable (asserted in the case of Goldberg, implied in the case of Kemper). Kemper is more optimistic because he recognizes the mutually influencing feedback nature of testosterone and social dominance. He feels that if women are afforded more opportunities to enter male roles and occupations, they will secrete more testosterone, which, in turn, will further their ability to succeed in these roles.

Although Kemper's argument sounds simplistic, it has been found that professional and managerial women have higher testosterone levels than women in clerical and service work (Purifoy & Koopmans, 1980). Cross-sectional studies leave the causal ordering unknown (e.g., do females with more testosterone gravitate to more competetive jobs, or do such jobs have the effect of generating more testosterone in women holding them?); but even if the "male" role leads to more testosterone, since females lack testes, one wonders where it is to come from.

Notwithstanding this point, an emphasis on the role of hormones in female occupational success is not warranted. In the first place, it implies a causal rather than facilitative role for testosterone; and second, it implies that to be occupationally successful women have to become more aggressive, competitive, and domineering. Women can be just as successful, perhaps more so, if they bring their emotional sensitivity and greater caring to the workplace. Degler (1991:138) points out, in contrast to the assertive–oppositional stance of many modern feminists, that this was the position of early twentieth-century feminists. Even in the "macho" world of police work, women do equally as well as men but in different ways. Although they may be less aggressively active than men in making arrests and issuing tickets, they are better able to calm a tense situation; engage less in conduct unbecoming an officer; and are viewed by the public as more competent, pleasant, and respectful (Walker, 1992:338).

Women are not biologically precluded from occupations that are stereotypically male, and men are not biologically precluded from occupations that are stereotypically female. This is not to say, however, that there are not biological differences that move men and women to choose occupations that are compatible with those differences. The concept of active GE correlation informs us that when people are afforded the opportunity to do so, they will seek activities compatible with their geneotypes. While this does not mean that the underpinnings of the sexual division of labor is rigidly determined by genes, it does mean that it has biological roots. To deny this is to hold a view of human beings as being passive recipients of their environments. These biological roots are, of course, grounded in reproduction. Responding to environmental challenges related to their separate reproductive roles, evolutionary pressures created mechanisms in men and women that increased the reproductive success of each. One such mechanism which may explain the tendencies of modern men and women to seek different roles is sexual dimorphism of the brain.

Across a wide variety of studies and types of tests utilized, males have been shown to be superior to females in visual–spatial abilities; and females have been shown to be superior to males in verbal abilities (Durden-Smith & de Simone, 1983; Johnson & Meade, 1987; Maccoby, 1988). Reliable sex differences in visual–spatial ability show up as early as 7 years of age, increase at puberty (indicating gonadal hormonal influence), and continue throughout the life span (Linn & Petersen, 1986). Likewise, females show a marked superiority to males in verbal abilities throughout the life span; and verbal disabilities such as stuttering and dyslexia are four to ten times more likely to appear in males than in females (Sutaria, 1985; Witelson, 1987). EEG studies are able to discriminate between males and females with 90-percent accuracy based on brain-wave patterns when they are performing spatial and verbal tasks (Flor-Henry, Koles, & Reddon, 1985).

These differences arise from brain sexual dimorphism reflecting the effects of fetal androgens, not sex-role socialization. As indicated earlier, fetal androgens slightly retard the development of the verbal left hemisphere of males, thus allowing the visual–spatial right hemisphere to assert itself a bit more relative to the left. Not subjected to the same androgen-induced diverting experience (with the exceptions and overlap previously noted), female brains typically maintain a superior verbal left hemisphere and more interhemispheric scatter. Androgen-deprived TS females show even greater diffusion of brain organization than XX females (Kimura, 1985), and they do so poorly on visual–spatial tasks that they are said to suffer from "space–form blindness" (Hoyenga & Hoyenga, 1979:32).

Male and female brains have been forged by evolutionary eons based on the different roles the sexes have played. Man's evolutionary history as a hunter and fighter exerted pressure for the selection of muscular and bone strength greater than that of women, a metabolism and vascular system more geared to an active lifestyle, and a brain attuned to the visual–spatial aspects of his environment (Mosley & Stan, 1984; Geary, 1989). Females were more diverse in the tasks they had to perform and were thus subjected to different and less specialized evolutionary selection processes that did not lead to the favoring of one brain hemisphere over the other. Women's diverse roles as nurturers, caregivers, comforters, and peacekeepers provided pressure for the selection of social skills such as language and greater emotional sensitivity (Mellen, 1981; Mosley & Stan, 1984; Ellis, 1989). From evidence provided by sex-differentiated chimpanzee behavior, Fisher (1992:199) concludes that "some of the modern differences between the genders preceded our descent onto the grasslands of Africa."

As society becomes more open and less bound by stereotypes regarding "proper" male and female roles, we should see more robust GE correlations, that is, a greater propensity for males and females to enter occupations consistent with their abilities and proclivities. Changes in female consciousness, equal opportunity laws, affirmative action, and other social forces have paved the way for female entry into many high-paying occupations from which custom formerly largely precluded them (Kemper, 1990a:120). Women have been moving into high-status occupations such as law and medicine at an ever-increasing rate. A National Science Board (NSB) study found that the percentage of women among doctoral-level scientists increased from 7 percent to 14.4 percent from 1971 to 1987 (1987:223).

Yet, women have been less inclined to move into areas most dependent on visual–spatial skills than into areas most dependent on language and nurturing skills. In 1985, female Ph.D.s constituted 2.3 percent of the total Ph.D.s in engineering, arguably the field most dependent on visual–spatial skills. On the other hand, 32.1 percent of the Ph.D.s in psychology, arguably the most "verbal" and people-oriented scientific field, were female. If gender had no effect on occupational choice, the percentage of women in both fields would not be significantly different from the percentage of total female Ph.D.s (14.4%) in all sciences. What we observe, however, is that females are underrepresented among Ph.D. engineers by a factor of 6.3 and overrepresented among Ph.D. psychologists by a factor of 2.23. I calculated a Yule's Q of 0.948 from the NSB data. A 94.8-percent reduction in error predicting Ph.D. field (engineering versus psychology) from gender would be difficult to interpret in purely environmental terms.

Further indicative of male visual–spatial superiority is a study of over 10,000 mathematically gifted children (McLoughlin, 1990). This study found that the higher the cutoff point on math scores, the greater the ratio of boys to girls (at a score of 420 or more, there were 1.5 boys to every girl; at 700 or more, the ratio was 13:1). The typical argument raised against such evidence is that females are not encouraged as much as males to take math in school. McLoughlin (1990:59) writes that this argument does not wash because at every elementary and high school level, girls actually get better than average math grades than boys. This does not contradict the assertion of male superiority in visual–spatial skills because such skills are not involved in solving math problems until one reaches the higher levels of mathematical skills. The fact that girls get better than average grades but boys do better at the higher skill levels means that many boys also score well below girls in math. This is a reflection of the often-noted greater variability among males for all kinds of traits and skills; that is, there are more males at both distribution extremes than females (Hoyenga & Hoyenga, 1979; Mosley & Stan, 1984; G. Wilson, 1987).

Overlap in visual–spatial abilities in men and women was illustrated in a series of computerized visual–spatial tasks demonstrating an overall male superiority, with performance being mediated by MAO levels (Klinteberg, Levander, Oreland, Asberg, & Schalling, 1987). Consistent with expectations, male subjects had lower MAO levels than females (MAO and testosterone are inversely related). Low-MAO females did significantly better on these tasks than high-MAO females, particularly on tasks involving left-side presented (and, therefore, right-hemisphere processed) stimuli. Low-MAO females even did better than high-MAO males, although they did significantly less well than low-MAO males. It has also been found that the difference between males and females on spatial tasks is halved when estrogen is at its lowest peak of the hormonal cycle, a period in which testosterone can assert itself more readily (Kimura & Hampton, 1988).[4]

The overrepresentation of women among Ph.D. psychologists relative to the total number of Ph.D.s, as well as in other nurturing, social, and relationship ("helping") fields, point to female abilities and proclivities in those areas. Language is women's special skill. They learn it earlier and use it more efficiently than males; they have lower rates of language disabilities; and they consistently outscore males on the language sections of the scholastic aptitude test (SAT), the graduate record examination (GRE), and professional school entrance exams (Hoyenga & Hoyenga, 1979:238). Experiments tracing blood flow through the cortex during language tests have shown that there is a tight fit between brain areas in the left frontal lobe involved in processing language and the motor areas required for its expression (tongue, jaw, etc.) in males. For females the fit is much looser, with blood flow observed across both hemispheres. Neuropsychologist Cecille Naylor exclaimed that it is almost as though women's brains are "ablaze" when processing language and that they bring "additional imaging functions" and a "richer, more expanded emotional component into play" (cited in Phillips, 1990:46). Of course, just as there is significant overlap between the sexes in visual–spatial skills, there is significant overlap in language skills.

Commenting on data similar to the NSB's from Britain and Israel, Moir and Jessel (1991:154) conclude that "the minds of men and women are different. . . . Ultimately boys and men live in a world of things and space, girls and women live in a world of people and relationships." From a different data source, Gaylin (1986:192) writes, "Biological and genetic research suggests that women have been handed a primary drive for attachment while men have been oriented toward work and mastery." High-status occupations are not high status because they are male dominated; they are male dominated because they are high status. The physiological factors that spur their drive for Gaylin's "mastery" also direct them into areas in which dominance, status, and financial rewards are greatest (Ellis, 1989). All too often men have been willing to submerge their emotional and affectual needs in this pursuit, thus doing themselves and their wives and children an egregious injury. Likewise, women have sacrificed their career goals in order to pursue that which males have sacrificed. Both sexes make their choices driven by their biological urges augmented by social expectations.[5] The goals that men and women strive for are rooted in biology; the social sin is to take these "primary drives" and assign gender exclusivity to them.

WHY SEXUAL DIMORPHISM?

If we accept the evidence that males and females are "programmed" differently and that these programs move men and women into different roles and occupations compatible with them, we have to ask ourselves, "To what purpose?" On the whole, men benefit socially from their greater aggressiveness, dominance, and need for achievement. They occupy more positions of power, they earn more money, and they generally achieve greater success in attaining positions of respect and prestige in all areas of human endeavor. The reverse of this is males pay a high price in that they greatly exceed females in rates of physical, neurological, intellectual, behavioral, and characterological disorders of all kinds (Montagu, 1974; Hoyenga & Hoyenga, 1979; Khan & Catiao, 1984; Mosley & Stan, 1984; G. Wilson, 1987; Walsh & Walsh, 1993). The male biological legacy is such that males are more likely than females to be located at both distributional extremes of many traits and characteristics (showing greater variability but not necessarily greater range). From a strictly biological point of view, greater male variability renders males both the "advantaged" and the "disadvantaged" sex; and the greater "conservatism" of female biology places more females than males at the distributional centers, being neither as advantaged nor as disadvantaged as males at the extremes.

Sexual dimorphism exists because our male and female ancestors faced sex-specific environmental challenges involving reproduction, which led to the selection of sex-specific propensities. I examine the process of sexual selection more fully in Chapter 7; at present, I wish to examine an even more fundamental basis for sexual dimorphism as outlined by Mosley and Stan (1984). Mosley and Stan argue that females are more reproductively valuable to the species than males, and thus the species can ill-afford to reduce its number of females. Sexual dimorphism provides a mechanism by which genetic risk to females is minimized by reducing the probability of the expression of X-linked recessive genes. Recessive genes present on one X chromosome, which may be advantageous, disadvantageous, or neutral, are moderated by homologous genes on the other. Genetic conservatism is advantageous to the individual female but gainsays the genetic variability needed for the species to adapt to changing environments (on a species, not individual level). On the other hand, lacking an homologous "backup" X chromosome, males are exposed to both the advantages and disadvantages of recessive gene expression and, therefore, show greater variability than females on many human traits and characteristics.[6] This constitutes a risk for individual males as well as a possible payoff, but an advantage for the species. As Mosley and Stan put it:

In the male the X chromosome is subjected to the extraction of maximum genetic expression. In the female, however, both mosaicism and allelic control lead to an attenuation of the expression for the genes situated on and interacting with those on the X chromosome. Over generations a balance has been established between the conservation of genetic potential via the female and expression of genetic potential by the male. By altering the balance of the effect of new variation away from the equality of risk in the two sexes [moving it on to the male and away from the more reproductively valuable female], the human is equipped with a unique mechanism for coping with the challenge of survival, i.e., human sexual dimorphism. (1984:178)

Because females are demonstrably victimized by male social dominance, it is acknowledged that to posit any evolutionary "purpose" behind sexual dimorphism may be misconstrued as a justification of that victimization. But Mosley and Stan give equal weight to the male and female contribution to species survival, which is, after all, nature's only "grand design." Females function as defenders, preserving that which is valuable to the species; males function as a kind of genetic "laboratory" with which nature can experiment and occasionally introduce some advantageous alleles. In this view, both functions are necessary; but neither is superior or inferior to the other. However, it is not "the species" that bears the brunt of social discrimination. Individuals do, and reproduction of the species may be irrelevant to individual women fighting sex-segregationist male attitudes and discrimination.

CONCLUSION

As Alice Rossi (1977, 1984) has long argued, recognition of the evolutionary and neurohormonal basis of sexual dimorphism must be an important item on the agenda of sex-role sociologists. Sex-role sociologists can no longer refuse the valuable insights offered to them by the biological and neurosciences. There is nothing inimical to social justice for women in the recognition that sex differences exist and that they are grounded in the fundamental purpose of reproduction. Biological explanations of sex differences no more inherently lend their support to either social justice or social injustice than do environmentalist theories. If social practices are to be justified, they must be justified by ethical and moral principles, not biology. Biology may lead men and women to opt for different occupational roles, but male prejudice often leads them to devalue the roles that most women prefer. Prejudice and male dominance cannot be justified on any moral grounds nor on the basis of the evidence of sexual dimorphism. If some women, for whatever reason, have preferences that are not typically female, then prejudice should not deny them their preference when their biology clearly has not.

There are always ill-willed characters who will jump on anything that will give their prejudices an easier ride; but the fault is with the rider, not the vehicle. The truth of a scientific assertion must be judged solely on the available evidence for or against it, not on whether it can possibly be used for negative ends. Surely it is better to acknowledge and welcome our complementary sex differences than to continue to deny their existence—a denial that sometimes leads scientist and layperson alike to view sociology as something of an eccentric discipline devoted to either asserting or denying the obvious. Let us offer our sex-related abilities and characteristics to one another in a spirit of humanism, equality, and mutual respect.

NOTES

1. Many early twentieth-century feminists emphasized and gloried in differences between the sexes (Degler, 1991:123–125). Carol Tavris (1992:58–60) sees modern feminists divided into those who see no significant personality differences between the sexes that are attributable to biology and those who recognize and celebrate women's special (and superior) qualities.

2. Two recent books (Joynson, 1989; Fletcher, 1991) argue cogently that Burt's fraud was nonexistent and that he was railroaded by Marxists dedicated to destroying his hereditarian claims. Neither book allays all doubt, but the major arguments alleging Burt's delinquencies are persuasively countered.

3. Alice Rossi is among the many social scientists who once held purely cultural notions of human behavior but who now find such notions untenable. Although, like Margaret Mead, she has never deviated from her commitment to many of the goals of feminism, she is first and foremost a scientist whose thinking is driven by data, not ideology. Her analysis of the social interchangeability of the sexes published in *Daedalus* in 1964 marked her as a traditional social scientist. Thirteen years later, in the same forum, she found her previous biology-free position "wanting" and corrected it (Rossi, 1977:2).

4. Also relating to the relationship between testosterone and MAO, it has been found that low MAO has been linked to PMS (Hallman, Oreland, Edman, & Schalling, 1987).

5. Margaret Mead (1949) has pointed out that the male need for achievement is observed in every society. She points out that femaleness is defined automatically in the act of childbearing but maleness has to be defined, redefined, and proved. This relentless seeking of achievement is seen as a search for the self and its worth.

6. Take a sex-linked trait for which there are two alleles at a locus with the recessive variant having a frequency of 0.10 in the population. Because males only receive one X chromosome, the probability of a given male showing the variant trait is exactly equal to the frequency of the variant allele in the population (i.e., 0.10). For the female phenotype to manifest the variant trait, she would have to receive homologous alleles from maternal and paternal X chromosomes. With a population frequency of 0.10, the probability of a given female showing the trait is thus 0.10×0.10, or 0.01.

Chapter 7

Human Sexuality and Evolution

> Bear in mind that some day all our provisional formulations in psychology will have to be based on an organic foundation. . . . It will then probably be seen that it is special chemical substances and processes which achieve the effects of sexuality.
>
> —Sigmund Freud

Underlying the human species' great cultural diversity is our common humanity, our human nature. Perhaps no other species-specific behavior is more predictable across cultures and across time than are patterns of human sexuality (Symons 1979, 1992; Buss, 1989; Ellis, 1992; Wilson & Daly, 1992). It is recognized that there are many different patterns of sexual behavior reflecting different cultural conditions and which, therefore, require cultural or proximate explanations. However, I wish to emphasize the more fundamental and distal phylogenetic causes underlying the superficially different patterns anthropologists observe, while again emphasizing that distal and proximate explanations are no more conflicting explanations than phylogeny and ontogeny are conflicting processes.

All human beings share the same evolutionary history and, therefore, share common mechanisms in our genes and brains that direct the desire to reproduce. Culture is a human adaptation that allows humanity to adapt quickly to changing environments, including those changes we ourselves produce. But let us not forget that culture does not proceed in a biological vacuum. Current patterns of behavior are always informed by our evolutionary history. An understanding of this history provides a framework for an enhanced understanding of the currently pressing social problems of marriage and divorce, sexual violence, illegitimacy, crime rates, and the spread of sexually transmitted diseases (STDs).

SEXUAL SELECTION, PARENTAL INVESTMENT, AND r/K SELECTION

The scope of sexual activity (strength of desire, frequency of copulation, number of partners, and so forth) varies considerably from person to person due to a complicated mixture of neurohormonal, psychological, and socio-cultural factors; but the underlying basis for much of this variability is a special type of natural selection called *sexual selection*. Charles Darwin proposed the theory of sexual selection to complete his theory of evolution, noting that while natural selection accounted for differences *between* species, it did not account for the often profound male–female differences *within* species. Sexual selection involves competition for reproductive partners and favors characteristics that lead to success, even though those characteristics may not be favored overall by natural selection. Sexual selection, like natural selection, causes changes in the relative frequency of alleles in populations in response to environmental challenges but in response to sex-specific mating challenges rather than general sex-neutral challenges.[1]

There are two primary paths by which sexual selection proceeds: intrasexual selection and epigamic or mate-choice selection. Although both sexes engage in both processes, intrasexual selection is primarily male competition for access to females; and epigamic selection is more a female domain. The more sexual selection operates on a species (the more competition there is for mates), the more sexual dimorphism will be selected for. In species where intrasexual selection is paramount, there are large differences between males and females in size, strength, and aggression; in species where epigamic selection is stressed, males are more striking in their appearance than females. Sex characteristics that provided advantages in maximizing reproductive fitness gradually become standard sex-differentiated features of a species (Degler, 1991:25).

In a truly seminal paper, Trivers (1972) extended Darwin's sexual selection theory by adding the concept of *parental investment*. Parental investment is the investment of resources in gestating, feeding, and guarding offspring (Trivers, 1972:139). Female investment is enormous in terms of physiological energy and time investment, but the only *necessary* male investment is time spent copulating. It is generally accepted today that it is this difference in relative parental investment that controls the operation of sexual selection. If we begin with the requirements imposed by physiology, we must note the periodicity of the female reproductive pattern in which women typically shed only one of a finite number of ova each month. In order to reproduce, she requires a fertile egg, the proper uterine environment, sexual receptivity, and a healthy partner. If the male reproductive pattern were also periodic, sperm shedding, sexual receptivity, and the aggressive impulses necessary to fend off competitors would have to be synchronized with the female's. Such a synchronicity would be very difficult to achieve, and many precious ova would be wasted. The biologically efficient strategy required that males constantly produce fertile sperm and be constantly able and willing to shed them. This difference in gamete production and shedding may be considered the beginning of a long chain of events leading to many features of sexual dimorphism, both physical and psychological (Naftolin, 1981).

Endowed with cheap and plentiful sperm, males were free to spread their genes as far as their aggression and charm would take them. The more females a given male could mate with, the greater his reproductive fitness. Females were generally better reproductively served by sexual restrictiveness. While unrestricted females could attract numerous males to vie for the privilege of fertilizing their eggs, offspring survival—not simple fertilization—is the goal of the female reproductive strategy. In most Pleistocene environments, a monogamous sentiment would be more likely to assure reproductive fitness through the care and protection provided by a mate who could be relatively sure of his paternity. In short, males had little to lose and much to gain by attempting to mate with as many females as possible; but females who did not mate with the right kind of male, one who showed evidence of his willingness and ableness to support her and offspring, risked reproductive failure.

Sexual restrictiveness in the animal kingdom is not so much linked to femaleness per se as it is to degree of parental investment. Although females of most species overwhelmingly invest more in parenting than males, in avian species in which female investment is limited to laying eggs (which males then brood and care for after hatching), sex roles are strongly reversed (Trivers, 1972:143). Females fight one another over access to males, and they are bigger and more aggressive than males. Thus, as both sexual selection and parental investment theories predict, the sex that invests most in parenting is the more discriminating and passive one, and the sex that must compete intrasexually for partners is stronger and more aggressive than the sex engaged in epigamic selection. Among a variety of species, equality of parental investment and lower levels of sexual selection pressure is associated with monogamy (Trivers, 1972; Clutton-Brock, 1991; Krebs & Davies, 1993).

A third evolutionary concept useful in explaining sex differences in sexual behavior is *r/K selection* theory (Lancaster, 1985). This theory originated in the mathematics of population biology and refers to a continuum of reproductive strategies among animal species. The r and K strategies have evolved as reproductive strategies for different species populations in their typical habitats in response to environmental contingencies. A population will reproduce exponentially at species-specific rates if not prevented from doing so by the limited resources available in the environment (food, water, space). Species eventually evolved specific mechanisms that provide for the best chance of producing offspring that will survive and produce progeny of their own in the habitats they occupy (Gould & Gould, 1988).

The extreme r reproductive strategy ("r" stands for the intrinsic rate of population growth) is characterized by maximum egg production and no parental care. It is a strategy opted for by species inhabiting areas of abundant resources and is typical of fish, whose extreme fertility ensures genetic continuity even though the vast majority of offspring will perish before they are able to reproduce. The K strategy ("K" stands for the carrying capacity of the environment) opts for quality over quantity. It is the strategy of animals in environments in which the population is close to carrying capacity and is the strategy followed by mammals. The K strategy is characterized by the production of a few and relatively infrequent offspring who are extensively nurtured to minimize infant mortality. There is r/K variation within the various classes of mammals, with apes, for instance, being more K selected than cats. Reproductively, r-selected species expend more energy in mating efforts than in parental care; in K-selected species, the reverse is true. These general strategies covary with many physiological and behavioral features that function to maintain the evolved strategy.

If these traits differ between species, might they differ within species and between sexes? It has been alleged that this is so, with females being more K selected than males (Horn & Rubenstein, 1984; Ellis, 1989; Rushton & Bogaert, 1989). Because human males and females are of the same species and, therefore, share a common history of natural selection, any variability between the sexes on r/K traits would have to be a function of sexual selection; and any within-species racial differences would have to be a function of evolution in semi-isolated groups (to the extent that genes are the prime movers of intraspecies variability in reproductive strategies).

Although there is some opposition to applying r/K selection theory to within-species issues (Shields, 1992), it was initially formulated to account for just these differences (Chisholm, 1993:18) and is a convenient way to think about sex-differentiated behavior because it provides a number of quantifiable indices of it (Smith, 1987). If reproductive strategies differ between sexes, we should find that males exhibit r-selected traits to a greater degree than females (e.g., lower parental investment, shorter gestation period, greater prenatal and neonatal mortality, higher fertility potential, higher gamete production, sexual promiscuity, unstable pair bonding, and shorter life expectancy). However, it must be stressed again that when we speak of r- or K-selected traits as *behavioral* traits, we are talking about facultative strategies, not genetically fixed ones. Different human populations might employ different reproductive strategies at different times depending on the vicissitudes of their environment, as might the two sexes (Lovejoy, 1981; Mealey, 1990).

The three interrelated concepts—sexual selection, parental investment, and r/K strategies—provide us with a strong theoretical framework for interpreting and understanding modern sexual behavior. Although hypotheses derived from these theories are falsifiable in the best Popperian tradition, decades of testing across cultures and across species have failed to do so. The reproductive strategies followed by our ancestors have left their mark in the DNA of modern men and women such that "it is almost impossible to visualize circumstances in which selection would have failed to produce divergent male and female sexualities" (Symons, 1987:125). Neuroanatomist Roger Gorski (1990:74) agrees: "Sex differences are ubiquitous. The entire process of reproduction and the whole brain are geared toward survival of the species."

ENVIRONMENTALLY CONTINGENT STRATEGIES

Perhaps the most important environmental factor affecting sexual behavior in both sexes within a variety of species is the sex ratio—the number of females per hundred males. Where there are significantly more males than females, monogamy is the norm; where there are more females, "monogamy is rare or nonexistent" (Trivers, 1972:151; Krebs & Davies, 1993:226–233). The human species is no exception to this rule. As with everything governed by the laws of supply and demand, scarcity determines value and abundance implies devaluation. When there is a significantly greater number of one sex of marriageable age than of the other, the sex with the fewer members becomes a scarce resource and holds the power in dating and mating relationships. If there were no differences in the mating strategies of men and women, scarcity would mean that, although the members of the more numerous sex would have to try harder to land a mate, the essential moral nature of the mating environment would not change. However, mating strategies of men and women are very different; so in times when sex ratios are significantly skewed, mating environments are considerably altered.

Guttentag and Secord's (1983) seminal work on the sex ratio question surveyed the historical and sociological literature on cultures ranging from ancient Greece to modern America and found in all cases that when males or females are freer to choose their behavior (because the sex ratio favors them), they will behave in ways compatible with their innate inclinations. When the sex ratio does not favor them, males and females must compromise their natural mating strategies and conform more to the strategy of the sex favored by the sex ratio or risk being mateless. Changes in the social and moral climate can be anticipated when the sex ratio is appreciably skewed. When sex ratios are low (indicating a surplus of marriageable-age women), we can expect weaker commitments of men toward women, more illegitimate births, increased sexual promiscuity (and an increase in the STDs that come with it), greater misogyny, greater female depression, and an increase in women's liberationist sentiment as women become more conscious of the negative aspects of a low sex ratio (Guttentag & Secord, 1983:174; for similar analyses, see Gilder, 1976; Heer & Grossband-Shechtman, 1981; and Pedersen, 1991). These hypothesized consequences of a low sex ratio create a social ambiance (pornography, obscene musical lyrics, destigmatization of out-of-wedlock births, etc.) that is conducive to promiscuity in its own right.

Guttentag and Secord showed that, because of immigration and "frontier blazing," every U.S. census up to 1970 showed a significant excess of males, although deviations from the general pattern occurred at various times and in different areas of the country. Such a sex ratio is obviously female favoring, and it helped to shape American values as they relate to marriage and the family. Under such a sex ratio, men had to offer what women wanted because if they did not, there were many others who would. Women were prized and respected, marriage was an attractive and permanent prospect, sexual intimacy was an expression of love, and adultery was morally unacceptable and legally punishable. Promiscuity was both difficult to achieve and nonadaptive for most males under these conditions. As Buss (1990:11) explains, "The adaptive payoff of a given trait for each sex decreases as the members of that sex become more numerous."

In the 1960 census, there were still 111 men of marriageable age for every 100 women; but the 1970 census showed that the sex ratio has become male favoring with only 78 white men of that age for every 100 white women. Things were even worse in the black community, with a sex ratio of 73 men for every 100 women. With this dramatic change in the sex ratio, men gained the upper hand; and they used it with a vengeance. A licentious and misogynistic environment ensued in which men, now following *their* natural inclinations, flitted from bed to bed and resisted romantic involvement as long as possible.[2] Women now had to compromise their inclinations and conform to the male strategy or risk being left out in the cold. On the whole, women did respond to this male-favoring environment; but many found it to be distasteful. Many women conforming to the male strategy report that it left them feeling used, dissatisfied, dirty, and degraded (Doudna & McBride, 1981; G. Wilson, 1983). Jean Elshtain (1991:183) quotes one formerly conforming woman as saying that the sexual revolution induced women to "act like predatory men. I'm sick of it."[3]

Because the sex ratio among blacks is larger than among whites, it might be more instructive to examine its impact on that population. Illegitimate birth is the most palpable indicator of the rate of nonmarital sexual activity. Estimates of illegitimacy in black inner-city areas range from 60 to 70 percent (Taylor, 1992). Illegitimacy is not simply an issue of sexual morality. It is known that illegitimate children are particularly at risk for abuse and neglect, lower levels of intellectual functioning, delinquency, and many other forms of social pathology (West & Farrington, 1977; Wilson & Herrnstein, 1985; Leyton, 1986; W. Wilson, 1987; J. Wilson, 1991; Walsh, 1992). Guttentag and Secord (1983:219) correlated black sex ratios and illegitimacy rates state by state and found a highly significant correlation of –0.87 (the lower the sex ratio, the greater the proportion of illegitimate births). The correlation for whites was much smaller at –0.27.

This does not mean that black women are "naturally" more promiscuous than white women. Data from slave plantations (where there were typically many more men than women) indicate that female slaves were quite "prudish," and that illegitimate births fathered by black males were comparatively rare (Guttentag & Secord, 1983:223). Further evidence is found by comparing black illegitimacy in states having different black sex ratios. In New York state, where there were 86 black males for every 100 black females in 1980, about 50 percent of black families were headed by a single female. In the same year in North Dakota, where there were 160 black males for every 100 black females, only 2.9 percent of black families were headed by a women, which is less than one-fifth of the 1980 national white average of 17 percent (Guttentag & Secord, 1983:221). Messner and Sampson's (1991) multiple-regression analysis of 171 American cities found that the percentage of female-headed households in the black community is highest in cities with low sex ratios and lowest in cities with high sex ratios ($\beta = -0.60$).[4]

International evidence from 117 countries provides further support for the sex ratio hypothesis (South & Trent, 1988). South and Trent found support for seven of eight hypotheses they tested; and the more consistent with evolutionary theory the hypothesis was, the more strongly it was supported. Averaged across all countries, the correlation between the sex ratio and illegitimacy was -0.28, which became -0.74 controlling for an index of national socioeconomic development and "data quality" (a variable based on the United Nation's evaluation of the relative reliability of a country's demographic data).

These data, combined with Guttentag and Secord's historical analysis, provide compelling arguments for sex differences in reproductive strategies. Yet the authors of these studies found it difficult to account for the totality of their findings. Guttentag and Secord (1983) limit their discussion of possible biological underpinnings to less than two pages. South and Trent (1988:1112) failed to consider biology at all, preferring to flounder all over the place looking for explanations they admit are difficult to envision. Yet the data are elegantly consistent with evolutionary theory; and when viewed from the theory's powerful logic, they become compelling. Evolutionary theory locates us in the web of natural life and tells us that we are as influenced by the sex ratio as other species are, perhaps more so.

SEXUALITY AND DEVELOPMENTAL VARIABLES

That men and women alter their sexual tactics and strategies in response to environmental contingencies is precisely what evolutionary theory predicts. The tactics individuals employ in pursuit of goals depend on environmental conditions confronting them at the time they are pursuing those goals. How organisms deal with environmental contingencies is at the heart of evolutionary theory, and the compromise factor is but one example of what Crawford and Anderson (1989) call "concurrently contingent strategies." Humans have evolved innate neural learning mechanisms that adaptively organize their experiences (memories, perceptions, and other conscious and subconscious cognitions) in a variety of environments that help to determine their current behavioral choices in response to proprioceptive and environmental stimuli.

Concurrently contingent strategies reflect adaptations which may be positive or negative with respect to the more general reproductive strategy favored by one sex or the other. As we have seen, the more important traits are for the organism, the more natural selection moves toward eliminating genetic variability in them. Selection tends to favor heavily whatever species are already doing, as long as it continues to be adaptive, and to conserve that behavior as long as selective environments remain relatively constant. Assuming that this was generally so, orthoselection would continue to favor promiscuity in males and restrictiveness in females (i.e., additive genetic variance for traits related to reproductive success would be removed over time). However, overspecialization may lead to dead-end adaptation; and there certainly is a point at which male promiscuity and female reticence is maladaptive.

Nevertheless, most males in female-favoring environments still prefer unrestrained sexuality; and most females in male-favoring environments still prefer love and commitment first. In extremely high sex ratio environments, such as the old American west, every town had its share of bordellos. Similarly, despite the "sexual revolution," the male-favoring sex ratio, and the availability of contraceptives, women are still more sexually discerning than men. We see this male–female "tension" in reports of dating behavior. Crooks and Baur (1983:422) view dating as a "contest between the young man and woman, he trying to proceed as far as possible and she attempting to go only as far as 'respectable.' " Hunt (1974:132) also views dating as something of a sexual skirmish, with males trying to get what they can and females giving as little as they can decently give in recompense for the attention lavished on them. The better "he 'made out,' the higher was his status among his fellows, while the less she gave in, the more desirable she was deemed."

Although this last point underlines the double standard feminists have been fighting for a long time, evidence that it is still alive and well is provided by a variety of sources. A meta-analysis of 177 studies showed that females still endorse the double standard more strongly than males and that, after masturbation frequency, attitudes toward casual sex is the largest sex difference found in the literature, with an effect size of 0.81 (Oliver & Hyde, 1993).

Males also subscribe to a different set of expectations for themselves and for women. Sheldon Cholst (1990:140), a human relationship psychiatrist, writes that "many males feel that females who have sexual activity too early are not good marriage partners and may lose respect or not think too highly of them." This clinical insight was supported by a 1990 national survey of 815 American males that found that 67 percent expressed a dislike for women who bestowed their sexual favors too early in the relationship (cited in Walsh, 1991b:226). Other recent studies (Williams & Jacoby, 1989; Gangestad & Simpson, 1990) find that males are more committed to, more easily fall in love with, and find more suitable as marriage partners females who demonstrate a pattern of sexual restrictiveness. This male ambivalence (the desire for sex paired with contempt for the giver) appears to be ubiquitous and is probably connected to the "whore–Madonna" image of women many men hold.[5]

Some theorists view the whore–Madonna image as one of a variety of male strategies having their origins in selection for the avoidance of cuckoldry (van den Berghe, 1979; Buss, 1989; Barkow, 1991). They view this bipolar image as an evolved cognitive algorithm that motivates males to abandon "easy" women and to invest their resources in women whose sexual reticence offers cues to future fidelity. Males enhance paternal certainty by preferring and committing to "females who are 'virginal' or at least lack a reputation for having many sexual partners. The more the male is likely to invest in the female's offspring, the more selection will favor his being concerned with her behaviour" (Barkow, 1991:61). Ancestral males who were unable to discriminate, or who ignored the behavior of prospective long-term mates, ran not only the risk of assisting the survival of some other male's genes (i.e., of becoming a cuckold) but also the risk of having their own culled from the gene pool. Males adept at making such discriminations were reasonably assured that their resources were invested in their own reproductive success, while at the same time perhaps playing the cuckoo with the resources of less perceptive males. Of course, just how particular males can be about the women they invest their resources in depends more on what they have to offer in return than on their perceptual abilities.

The male ability to detect a "whore" relies on female behavior as well as the power of male perception, for there has to be something for them to perceive. Helen Fisher (1992:94) views the behaviors described by the whore–Madonna dichotomy as two alternative evolutionary strategies females have used to acquire male resources. A uniform strategy may have been useful for male reproductive success; but females, faced with greater reproductive complexities, may have been at a disadvantage if confined to a single strategy. What if the environmental situation was such that women committed to sexual restraint could not acquire male resources to allow them to reproduce but less restricted women were able to garner at least temporary male investment? "Sexual coyness," argues Pedersen (1991:280) "would appear a 'risky' endeavour for women in periods of male scarcity and abundant alternative partners for males." Under such environmental conditions, a sexually unrestricted woman would have an evolutionary advantage over her more restrained sisters. An unrestrained strategy allegedly increases a female's chances of mating with a "quality" (high-status) male willing to copulate with her but not to commit to her, thus producing "quality" offspring, especially "sexy sons" (Belsky, Steinberg, & Draper, 1991; Wilson & Daly, 1992).[6] (For critiques of this argument, see Hinde [1991] and Maccoby [1991].) Thus, two alternative strategies are possible; and although sexual restrictiveness may be the general female strategy, some women may be more disposed to the alternative strategy, and others will conform to it under certain circumstances, such as during a male-favoring sex ratio period.

If Fisher is correct in assuming that females are genetically "prepared" to follow either reproductive strategy, we would like to know the more proximate conditions under which one of the alternatives may come to be favored over the other. These conditions may be demographic (the sex ratio), neurohormonal (see the next section), or developmental. A number of theorists (Draper & Harpending, 1982; Gangestad & Simpson, 1990; Barkow, 1991; Belsky, Steinberg, & Draper, 1991) have tied the choice to "sensitive" developmental periods of early childhood that "set" the reproductive strategy the sexually mature woman will follow. In other words, sexual strategies among both sexes vary facultatively with expectations about parental investment (Cashdan, 1993).

Although this argument does not make references to neural mechanisms, it is similar to the one made in Chapter 3 regarding synaptic habituation based on early experiences with strong emotional content. It is also reminiscent of the r/K theory in that the identified strategy-determining factor is the relative predictability or unpredictability of the early attachment environment. The basic argument is that children who grow up in unpredictable and negative families (e.g., divorce, desertion, lack of parental attachment, and so on) learn that close relationships are undependable and ephemeral and thus find monogamous commitment to be psychologically untenable. Conversely, children who grow up in predictable and positive environments learn that close relationships are viable and choose the committed monogamous strategy as sexually mature adults. Needless to say, neither strategy is consciously "chosen" but rather flows from differential expectations of stability and instability of interpersonal relationships based on experience. The importance of reproduction strongly suggests that we have evolved programs during our developmental years to make us particularly sensitive to cues relevant to later reproductive success (Smith, 1987; Crawford & Anderson, 1989).

The relationship between attachment experiences and instability of early environments and sexual promiscuity is amply supported in the literature (Draper & Harpending, 1982; Frost & Chapman, 1987; Belsky, Streinberg, & Draper, 1991; Cherlin et al., 1991). From a psychoanalytic viewpoint, Halleck (1971:141) sees female promiscuity arising from inadequate parental nurturance, the lack of which leads them to seek sex to satisfy their love needs with a "desperate intensity," and "the price for affection is usually sexual intercourse." Walsh (in press) found correlations between parental attachment and number of coital partners for males and females to be -0.448 and -0.453, respectively (the poorer the attachment, the greater the number of reported sexual partners). Thus, the reproductive strategy followed in maturity is at least partially contingent upon developmental experiences in which individuals learn lessons about the dependability of interpersonal bonds.

INDIVIDUAL DIFFERENCES
AND SEXUAL BEHAVIOR

Up to this point, I have been concentrating on generalized processes and conditions to explain variation in sexual behavior; but we cannot ignore the fact that these environmentally contingent alternative strategies are expressed by males and females whose neural mechanisms for processing environmental stimuli are, on average, different. Males whose brains have been incompletely defeminized, or females whose brains have been masculinized to some extent, may not conform to "average" level of sexual behavior evidenced by their gender, regardless of developmental experiences. For instance, high masculinity scores on the Bem Sex-Role Inventory have been found to correlate positively with testosterone levels, extroversion, sensation seeking, and a large number of sexual partners for both genders; high scores on femininity are negatively related to these variables (Daitzman & Zuckerman, 1980; Udry, 1988).

Testosterone is the hormonal mediator of sexual arousal for both sexes; and as Nyborg and Boeggild (1989:29) explain, testosterone switches females off their "safety first approach and onto a more masculine approach" to sexual behavior. Elevated testosterone may have a greater influence on female than on male sexuality because, among androgen-normal males, there are "ceiling effects" beyond which additional testosterone has no activating influence (Ellis, 1986; Udry, 1988). Supportive of this (to the extent that masculinity–femininity scores on the Bem inventory function as proxies for testosterone levels), Walsh (1993) found maculinity to be more strongly correlated with sexual "game playing" among heterosexual females ($r = 0.40$) than among heterosexual males ($r = 0.24$), and femininity to be negatively related to sexual game playing among males ($r = -0.49$) but not related at all among females ($r = 0.02$).

Given the strong relationship between attachment and self-esteem, the effect of self-esteem on sexual activity should be of some significance. Because males usually initiate such activity, and behavior that carries with it the possibility of rejection requires a certain amount of self-esteem to initiate, self-esteem should have a greater influence on male than on female sexual activity. Barkow (1991:186–192) writes that male self-esteem has replaced dominance based on agonism as the basis for sexual success (the replacement of raw, aggressive intrasex competition with human symbolic prestige). Since "mate quality" is not amenable to direct measurement by prospective partners, they must assess it in a number of indirect ways. Male self-esteem is symbolic of the ability (if not necessarily the willingness) to invest in offspring, making high self-esteem males prime targets for female choice. We should be clear that Barkow is emphasizing the ability of male self-esteem to attract females to males, not as an aid to males seeking sexual favors from females, although the two aspects are, of course, fairly synonymous.

This makes good evolutionary sense and has been supported empirically by Kenrick, Sadalla, Groth, and Trost (1990), who asked a sample of males and females to consider the criteria for involvement in (1) a single date, (2) sexual relations, (3) steady dating, and (4) marriage. They found that a partner's status (a composite of nine subvariables) was consistently ranked significantly higher for females than for males ($p < 0.001$) across all relationship categories and increasing in importance with the intimacy of the relationship. These researchers also assessed fifteen other nonstatus criteria for becoming involved and found that physical attractiveness (for marriage) was the only variable for which males exhibited a greater "choosiness" than females.

Barkow (1991) and Kenrick, Sadalla, Groth, and Trost (1990) were primarily interested in providing evidence for evolutionary theory and its concern for parental investment and reproductive success. I am presently more interested in connecting these concepts with current sexual behavior and its psychosexual referents. Neither frequency of copulation nor the number of partners involved is identical to reproductive success, and reproduction is rarely the conscious motive for copulation. In fact, we often take great pains to subvert nature's reproductive goal. Thus, "number of partners" is an imperfect indicator of reproductive success, which is something requiring multigenerational studies to assess accurately. Nevertheless, the mechanism by which reproductive success may be achieved is so pleasurable that we utilize it on numerous occasions without the slightest recognition of its ultimate purpose. Natural selection has shaped us to seek the *means* of reproduction rather than reproduction per se. In our ancestral environments, the lack of adequate contraception assured a much tighter fit between means and ends than we now observe. Thus, frequency of copulation and number of sexual partners would have been good indicators of reproductive success in environments of evolutionary adaptation.

The relationship between self-esteem and number of coital partners among males across studies and across measures of self-esteem is uniformly positive. Among females the relationship is equivocal; some studies find it to be positive, some find it negative, and some find no relationship (reviewed in Walsh, 1991c). One recent study (Walsh, 1993) found that women's evaluation of their own physical attractiveness (a proxy for self-esteem?) was the most powerful predictor of number of partners in a ten-variable regression. The less attractive women considered themselves to be, the more sexual partners they tended to have had. Among males the relationship was positive. This illustrates a well-known principle of human behavior in all areas of activity: The less you have to offer (or believe you have to offer), the more you must compromise.

Men's self-esteem tends to flow from their success or failure in the activities they pursue, and women's from their success or failure in interpersonal relationships. Two recent studies utilizing two different samples illustrate this. Each study asked men and women to complete the Rosenberg self-esteem scale. One study (Walsh & Balazs, 1990) assessed the amount of love subjects perceived themselves to be getting from their circle of friends, relatives, and acquaintances; the other (Walsh, 1991c) asked about the number of sexual partners subjects had experienced. The first study divided the sample by gender and love level (low, medium, and high). Females perceiving themselves as being recipients of a low level of love had the lowest self-esteem mean (M = 31.4), and those perceiving themselves as recipients of a high level of love had the highest self-esteem score (M = 42.9). The amount of love males perceived themselves as getting did not significantly affect their self-esteem. In the second study, it was males who had both the lowest (M = 36.3) and the highest (M = 41.5) self-esteem scores, depending on their sexual experience, with male virgins having the lowest score and sexually experienced males having the highest score. Sexual experience (virgin versus nonvirgin) had no significant affect on female self-esteem.

HOMOSEXUALITY

I now pick up the "deviant case" thread left in Chapter 6, and the compromise factor developed earlier in this chapter, to explore what homosexuality can tell us about heterosexuality. Glen Wilson (1987:98) comments on the importance of one in understanding the other in writing that homosexuals are of "great theoretical interest because they provide an opportunity to look at the way in which men and women behave sexually when they have no need to compromise with the different proclivities of the opposite sex." Similarly, Whitam (1987:176) states, "The study of variant sexuality has important implications not only for the origins of variant sexuality—a question interesting in its own right—but for the origins of nonvariant sexuality as well." These views express the biosociological position that the sexes are necessarily different by nature and that in many cases, social learning minimizes rather than maximizes those differences (Ellis, 1986; G. Wilson; 1987; Rushton & Bogaert, 1989; Walsh, 1991b). With the great veil of compromise lifted, we may look into the faces of men and women and more easily discern their raw sexual natures.

Ever since the Kinsey reports of 1948 and 1953, sexual orientation has been considered a continuous rather than a discrete trait. The Kinsey homosexual rating scale ranges from 0 (exclusively heterosexual) to 6 (exclusively homosexual), with all other ratings indicative of varying degrees of bisexuality (Kinsey, Pomeroy, & Martin, 1948:638). Kinsey, Pomeroy, Martin, and Gebhard (1953) found that between 18 and 42 percent of 5,000 men and 11 to 20 percent of 5,500 females studied had had at least one homosexual encounter. They also found that about 10 percent of the males and approximately 4 percent of the females were exclusively or almost exclusively homosexual (ratings 5 and 6 on the Kinsey scale). The 10-percent prevalance rate for male homosexuality is widely cited by gay organizations, but it is generally considered to be a huge exaggeration (Bailey & Pillard, 1991). Kinsey recruited his sample through friendship networks, and it was by no means a probability sample. Fay, Turner, Klassen, and Gagnon's (1989) 1970 and 1988 national probability samples of males produced an estimate for the prevalence of exclusive male homosexuality of 3.3 percent.

Nevertheless, it is clear that we must differentiate between occasional homosexual *behavior* as secondary homosexuality and the possession of a homosexual *identity* as primary homosexuality. Most people who admit engaging in homosexual behavior at some time in their lives experienced it in atypical situations (boarding schools, when drunk, etc.), and do not consider themselves homosexual. Their homosexuality may be considered situational or "deprivation" homosexuality engaged in to satisfy immediate sexual urges in the absence or unavailability of the preferred sex. We may view such behavior as a simple deviation from the basic sexual aim, which is preferentially directed toward opposite-sex encounters when they are available. We may thus account for episodic homosexuality in terms of situational contexts and socially learned behavior.

However, learning is not a viable explanation for the origin of primary homosexuality, that is, those individuals for whom homosexuality is as natural and normal as heterosexuality is for heterosexuals and who have always had an exclusive sexual attraction for members of their own sex. Most sociological theories of homosexuality overlook the distinction between primary homosexuality and occasional homosexual behavior, thus giving the impression that when the social context of the latter is elucidated, it also serves as an adequate explanation of the former.

Coleman and Cressey (1987:316–318) offer a typical social learning explanation that conflates the distinction. They feel that although homosexuality is socially condemned, society actually unwittingly encourages it by allowing same-sex youths to sleep and shower together while forbidding opposite-sex youths to do the same. These arrangements may lead to reinforcing sex play and, as a consequence, to self-labeling as a homosexual. They also say that sex-role differences and the pressures of mate selection makes same-sex associations more rewarding and less embarrassing than opposite-sex association; and this, too, may lead certain people to become homosexuals.

Learning theories of homosexuality basically assert that one's first pleasurable orgasmic experience is crucial to future sexual orientation. If the first experience is homosexual and rewarding, homosexuality is reinforced and the foundations are set for a homosexual identity. Stoller and Herdt's (1985) study of the Sambia of New Guinea provides strong evidence for dismissing this notion. Sambian males are required to indulge in exclusive homoerotic behavior from the ages of 7 to 10 until heterosexual marriage in the late teens to early twenties (sperm ingestion is considered crucial to masculine development). Young males frequently fellate older males and are told about the "horrors" of female fluids. With the passing of the culturally required homosexual phase of their lives, men make the change to heterosexual erotic behavior, doing so with much enthusiasm, seeking as much as they can both within and outside the bonds of marriage, and despite the belief that heterosexual orgasm depletes their manhood (sperm) more than homosexual orgasm. As Stoller and Herdt (1985:401) point out, "Even the terrors of female fluids cannot halt their heterosexual tension." There are those who remain preferentially attracted to their own sex, but they constitute the proportion of primary homosexuals to be expected in any culture.

From a biosocial point of view, the fact that the overwhelming majority of Sambian males embrace heterosexuality when allowed to, despite years of homoerotic conditioning, points to why claims that isolated social experiences can divert something as fundamental to our beings as sexual orientation border on the incredulous. If someone is receptive to a homosexual approach, it is because he or she is probably predisposed to the behavior which the situation facilitated. To the extent that social situations allow for the exercise of choice, they inform us only of the social conditions in which inclinations may flourish or be suppressed. People make choices, and the choices they make are correlated with the inner preferences they bring with them to situations. The issue here is not whether a person will sometimes turn to same-sex relations in the absence of the opposite sex; for the answer to this revolves around such variables as situation, conditioned moral scruples, willingness to experiment with alternative sexuality, and the strength of one's sex drive. Rather, the issue is "For which sex does the individual have an abiding preference, given equal availability of both?"

As for Coleman and Cressey's second point, few would dispute that on the whole most people prefer same-sex associations for most activities; but many an individual has risked much more than embarrassment in the pursuit of sexual goals. Only embarrassment of neurotic proportions would seem to have the power to divert one's sexual aim and that away from all sexual encounters, not just heterosexual encounters.

Bell, Weinberg, and Hammersmith (1981) conducted a large-scale sociological study of 979 homosexual and 477 heterosexual men and women to explore other social–psychological theories of homosexual etiology, particularly those centered around parent–child relationships. They found that parental attitudes and behavior were not significant in the development of sexual orientation and that the often-cited anxious maternal solicitude and paternal coldness and hostility are more responses evoked by a child's disappointingly gender-discordant behavior rather than the cause of it (reactive GE correlation). Simon LeVay, an unabashed homosexual and major researcher in the biology of homosexuality, said in an interview with Gelman (1992:49), "My point would be that gays are extremely different when they're young and as a result they can develop hostile relationships with their fathers. It's just a big mistake to think it's the other way around and the relationships as causative."

The same can be said of poor peer relationships and labeling effects. Not all homosexuals exhibit childhood gender nonconformity; and among those who do, there is wide variability (Bailey & Pillard, 1991). The conclusion of

Bell, Weinberg, and Hammersmith (1981:190–191) augments LeVay's when they write, "Homosexuality is as deeply ingrained as heterosexuality, so the differences in behaviors or social experiences of prehomosexual boys and girls and their preheterosexual counterparts reflect or express, rather than cause, the eventual homosexual preference." Bell, Weinberg, and Hammersmith (1981:212) go on to say that "There is a growing body of opinion that posits biological factors as the primary basis for sexual attraction."

When we hear the term *biology*, we tend to think in terms of genetics. Early studies of the heritability of homosexuality (e.g., Kallmann, 1952) have been largely dismissed for extravagant claims of 100-percent concordance for homosexuality for MZ twins, the use of convenience samples, the use of opposite-sex DZ twins, and for ambiguous zygosity (Futuyama & Risch, 1984). A recent study of 115 twins and 46 adoptive brothers (Bailey & Pillard, 1991) found a more modest concordance of 52 percent for MZ twins and 22 percent for DZ twins. Depending on the specific assumptions made (primarily assumptions about the prevalence rate for homosexuality in the general population), these figures yielded heritability coefficients ranging from 0.31 (under the assumption of a 10-percent prevalence) to 0.74 (the assumption of a 4-percent prevalence). Thus, there seems to be at least a moderate to strong genetic component to homosexuality. This conclusion would be stronger if it were based on twins reared apart to eliminate variance due to shared environment, although as we have seen, much recent research has tended to discount the effects of shared environment in the development of many traits (Plomin & Daniels, 1987).

Heritabilities, as gross estimates of variability attributable to genes, are merely the first step in establishing a possible genetic influence on any behavioral syndrome. More definitive evidence must come from DNA-linkage studies of extended families in which the trait appears to be genetically segregating. Hammer, Hu, Magnuson, Hu, and Pattatucci (1993) used such a pedigree strategy with 114 families and found an absence of paternal-line transmission of the trait, as well as a paucity of female homosexuals. This suggested that any gene or genes for homosexuality would be found on the X chromosome. The researchers then searched the X chromosome at various loci for markers that homosexual brothers might have in common and found that thirty-three out of forty such pairs shared a fragment of the X chromosome called Xq28. Although the probability of this occurring by chance is about 0.005, the seven discordant pairs of brothers indicates that the gene (or genes) at this location constitute(s) neither a necessary or sufficient cause of homosexuality.

The next step in the analysis of the role of genes in homosexuality is to further fine map the identified loci to discover the specific gene or genes (there are several hundred at the Xq28 site), then where and when it is expressed and the pathways it follows to affect sexual orientation. The genes at this location are likely to exert their influence in interaction with many other genes at other locations, perhaps in pleiotropic ways via hormonal affects on the brain. "Homosexual genes" are perhaps part of the evolutionary "grand design" to maintain genetic variability via the occasional expression of recessive genes. The absence of paternal transmission strongly suggests the role of recessive genes.

Since adaptation through natural selection is about reproductive fitness, and since homosexuals presumably reproduce less frequently than heterosexuals, the existence of homosexuality has been something of a challenge for evolutionary theorists. Possible advantages have been explored in the context of the "heterozygous advantage" hypothesis (Hutchinson, 1959) and the "kin selection" hypothesis (E. Wilson, 1978c). These explanations have been reviewed and supported by Ruse (1982) and reviewed and disputed by Futuyama and Risch (1984). However, these debates have taken place within a panselectionist conceptual framework in which every trait has to "somehow" be adaptive. We have seen that traits can be "genetic" without being adaptive (selected for); that is, they may be pleiotropic effects, and pleiotropic effects may at times defeat natural selection (Barkow, 1991:31).

Perhaps the most striking feature of homosexuality is that it is far more prevalent in males than in females worldwide (Ellis & Ames, 1987; Goodman, 1987; G. Wilson, 1987; Bailey, Pillard, Neile, & Agyei, 1993). If homosexuality is largely a result of an X-linked recessive gene as Hammer, Hu, Magnuson, Hu, and Pattatucci's (1993) recent work suggests, we should not be surprised. Because the hypothesized "gay genes" are located on the X chromosome, females are afforded the protection of their homologous X. This speculation, of course, assumes that the genetic pathways to homosexuality are similar in both sexes, which they may not be.

This male excess is part of an overall pattern of male overrepresentation in all kinds of sexual variance. Apart from masochism (occurring about twenty times more often in males), sexual paraphilias occur almost exclusively among males (G. Wilson, 1983; Flor-Henry 1980, 1987; American Psychiatric Association, 1987). Developmentally, more things "go wrong" with males; and the usual explanation for this is the diversion of the male brain from its intrinsic female state, a process carrying risks of malfunction at many stages. Mistakes at any point of the switching process may lead to an incompletely masculinized brain or, perhaps more correct, an incompletely defeminized brain.[7] Female brains are not subjected to a modification process; thus, there is less opportunity for things to go wrong. This suggests that "homosexual" genes may not be distinct genes "for" but rather "heterosexual" genes, the hormonal and enzymatic products of which were not fully successful in their fetal diversionary task. In this view, homosexuality is a by-product—a secondary phenomenon—of normal heterosexual development. This is both more parsimonious and empirically supportable than sociobiological explanations that require a direct link between homosexuality and specific genes transmitted according to laws of natural selection.

Much of the pioneering work on the prenatal origins of primary male homosexuality has been done by German endocrinologist Günter Dörner (1976) and Dörner, Rohde, Stahl, Krell, and Masius (1975). The basic reasoning of their work is that if homosexuals have brains that are insufficiently defeminized, they should mimic, to varying degrees, the female response pattern to luteinizing hormone (LH) in response to intravenous estrogen administration. Ovulation is triggered in postpubescent females by natural surges of estrogen. Estrogen, produced by the ovaries, first actuates the secretion of a neurohormone called luteinizing hormone–releasing hormone (LHRH) from the pituitary gland. LHRH stimulates the release of LH, which then stimulates the ovaries to ovulate and further estrogen secretion in an ongoing cycle that endocrinologists call a *positive feedback response*. When administered intravenous estrogen, many (not all) primary homosexuals show varying degrees of the female response as LH levels rise, as though trying to stimulate a phantom ovary. Heterosexual males and bisexuals show no such response. Other studies supportive of Dörner's hypothesis include Boyar and Aiman (1982) and Gladue, Green, and Hellman (1984). (For a failure to replicate, see Goodman, Anderson, Bullock, Sheffield, Lynch, & Butt [1985].) Whether the LH-positive response is an appropriate index of homosexuality remains open to further research.

Because sex-specific behavior is mediated by hypothalamic organization, the next logical step was to look for the same kind of differences in hypothalamic structures of gay and straight men that are known to exist between heterosexual men and women. Recent autopsy research by LeVay (1991) found that a cluster of neurons in the third interstitial nucleus of the anterior hypothalamus (INAH 3) was, on average, twice as large in heterosexual male cadavers as in gay male cadavers. The INAH 3 is the "business end" of the hypothalamus as far as sex goes, and this size difference between gay and straight men is about the same difference that exists between straight men and women. This is an infant area of research, so much more of it must be forthcoming before any definitive statements can be made. Up to this time there have been no analogous studies of lesbian brains (do they have INAH 3s the same size as straight males?). Would neuroimagining techniques with live subjects produce the same results? What about the possibility that a gay lifestyle might produce hypothalamic differences rather than the other way around? Nevertheless, the convergence of multiple lines of inquiry—genetics, endocrinology, neuroanatomy, anthropology, and even sociology—leads to an increasing confidence in the proposition that primary homosexuality is biological in origin.

LESBIANISM

The biology of lesbianism has been much less extensively researched, perhaps because there are fewer lesbians than gays, or perhaps because lesbianism is not associated with the variety of other paraphilias associated with male homosexuality (Flor-Henry, 1987). However, Bell, Weinberg, and Hammer-smith (1981) were able to discount a variety of social learning hypotheses regarding the etiology of lesbianism. They found, as was the case with male homosexuals, that lesbians enjoyed less positive relationships with their mothers (1981:121) and their fathers (1981:128) than heterosexual women but that both effects disappeared in path analysis. As was also the case among male homosexuals, lesbians reported significantly greater degrees of gender-nonconforming behavior during childhood. Sixty-two percent of the lesbians described themselves as having been "very masculine" when growing up; only 10 percent of the heterosexual women described themselves this way (1981:149). Reactive GE correlation may again be invoked to explain paren-tal responses toward their female offspring.

A recent study designed to estimate the heritability of lesbianism found concordance rates of 48 percent for MZ twins and 16 percent for DZ twins (Bailey, Pillard, Neile, & Agyei, 1993). Under various assumptions of popu-lation prevalence, these concordance rates yield heritability coefficients rang-ing from 0.27 to 0.76. These coefficients are close to those calculated by Bailey and Pillard (1991) for male homosexuals, although lesbian sample sizes were smaller (seventy-one MZ and thirty-four DZ twin pairs). Thus, we have further evidence of nonzero heritability for sexual orientation. However, a concordance rate of about 50 percent for both male and female MZ twins draws attention to the environment as well as to genes. When MZ twins dif-fer in any respect, including sexual orientation, it can only be the result of relevant environmental differences. Discovering what those relevant differ-ences are is an exciting challenge for social scientists.

Hormonal studies are more difficult to carry out with females than with males because of such variables as the use of contraceptive steroids and the fluctuation of the steroid hormones during the menstrual cycle (Meyer-Bahlburg, 1979). However, the role of fetal androgens in the development of lesbianism cannot be discounted; and certainly many androgen-dependent measures are associated with lesbianism. Among a sample of 241 lesbians, Wilson-Perkins (1981) found that lesbians have narrower hips, larger arm and leg girth, less subcutaneous fat, and more muscle than heterosexual women. She also divided her sample into groups based on psychosexual identifica-tion (passive, intermediate, and dominant) and found that the dominant les-bians were significantly taller, fatter, and more muscular than the other two groups. LaTorre and Wendenburg (1983) found lesbians to score significantly higher than heterosexual women on psychosexual masculinity, a trait signifi-cantly related to testosterone levels (Zuckerman, Buchsbaum, & Murphy, 1980).

Because they represent the high and low extremes of androgen secretion in females, perhaps the most productive method of evaluating the effects of fetal androgens on homoerotic behavior is to examine differences in such behavior between CAH women and AIS women. As explained in Chapter 6, CAH individuals suffer an enzymatic defect that results in overproduction of fetal androgens from the adrenals; and AIS individuals are XY genotypes with an autosomal recessive defect that prevents the binding or utilization of androgens in cell nuclei. Money, Schwartz, and Lewis (1984) compared thirty CAH women and fifteen AIS women (augmented by twelve Meyer-Rokitansky-Kuster syndrome [MRKS] individuals, the XX counterpart of XY AIS) on self-reported sexual identity. Among the CAH women, only 40 percent identified themselves as heterosexual; 23 percent defined themselves as noncommittal; 20 percent as bisexual; and 17 percent as homosexual. The corresponding percentages among the AIS/MRKS individuals were 93 percent, 0 percent, 7 percent, and 0 percent, respectively. These differences were statistically significant ($\chi^2 = 18.5$, $p < 0.01$, $c = 0.495$). Although based on a small sample, this and other similar studies (e.g., Ehrhardt, Evers, & Money, 1968), combined with findings that males with CAH have a virtual 0-percent likelihood of becoming homosexual (Money & Lewis, 1982) and with findings that ovariohysterectomized and high androgen-dosed CAH women appear to be completely homosexual, provide strong evidence for the effects of fetal hormones on female sexual orientation (Money, Schwartz, & Lewis, 1984).

The gay community appears to be split on whether it is "good" or "bad" to posit biological causes for homosexuality, and there are those who find research in this area to be tainted by personal and cultural prejudices (Ricketts, 1984). Ricketts (1984:67) argues that biological theories, if proven correct, would lift the burden of guilt from parents and accord homosexuals "natural minority status" which could gain gays civil-rights protections. Indeed, Dörner's research defining homosexuality as a biological trait rather than a deviant choice was instrumental in leading the former East German government to legalize it (Murray, 1987). The view of homosexuality as born rather than bred appears to increase tolerance in individuals as well as in governments. Studies in the United States, Sweden, and the Philippines found that people who believe homosexuals are "born that way" are significantly more tolerant of them than people who believe that homosexuality is "learned" or is "a choice" (Ernulf, Innala, & Whitam, 1989). This finding is interesting in light of the many claims that positing biological causes of deviant behavior leads to greater levels of intolerance and prejudice.

WHAT HOMOSEXUALITY CAN TELL US
ABOUT HETEROSEXUALITY

Perhaps more interesting from the sociological point of view than the origins of homosexuality is what it might tell us about heterosexuality. As indicated earlier, biosociologists dispute the notion that sex-role socialization maximizes sex differences, especially in the area of sexuality. Whatever the biological mechanisms are that divert individuals from heterosexuality, they apparently affect only the *targets* of sexual desire, not the *strength* of sexual desire or how often it is expressed. The targets of gays are the targets of heterosexual women, but they are far from female-like in the manner in which they pursue them. Likewise, the sexual activities of lesbians do not take on male characteristics. Indeed, gays and lesbians conform more to the mating strategies of their biological sex than do straight men and women because they are free of the necessity to compromise with an alien strategy (Symons, 1979; Rushton & Bogaert, 1989; Bailey, Gaulinn, Agyei, & Gladue, 1994).

Men, whether gay or straight, are objectifiers. Men possess brains for processing visual material to a greater degree than women, and women possess brains designed more to process the emotional content of stimuli than men. We see this at the very earliest stages of life. Male infants respond more than females to what is visually exciting in their environments, and they respond positively equally to human faces and mechanical objects; female infants generally respond positively only to human faces (cited in Durden-Smith & de Simone, 1983:60). When male schoolchildren are asked to draw pictures, they tend to draw objects, such as cars and trucks; but girls tend to draw people. The evidence suggests that males are born "objectifiers" and that this inborn propensity is carried over into their sexual relationships.

The male preference for visual excitement and impersonal sex maintains thriving pornography and prostitution industries; the female preference for romance keeps legions of romantic novelists in business. "Things" that can produce sexual excitement—rubber, leather, underwear, enema hoses, and other paraphilias—are almost exclusively male "loves" (Money, 1980). It is unfortunately true that women are often treated like these objects by many men who view them as aesthetically pleasing and utilitarian, meaning they look good and can be used to satisfy sexual urges. Treating sex partners or potential sex partners as "objects" without minds or emotions is perhaps the major complaint that dating women have about men in general (Elshtain, 1991).

This male propensity reaches an extreme in the absence of a need to compromise with the opposite sex. Gays do not have to play games; they need not wine and dine or falsely proclaim love, fidelity, or anything else in order to secure sex partners. Both actors know exactly what the other is looking for, and they can get right down to it with typical male speed. Studies of the gay subculture (at least those preceding the AIDS crisis) suggest that gays (and bisexuals) cruising the bathhouses and "tea rooms" were not looking for a man but were looking for a penis (a "thing"), the ultimate in objectification of a sex partner (Humphreys, 1970). An analysis of the gay "personals" from a variety of gay publications showed that both the buying and selling point focused on the penis (size, shape, circumcision status) in at least one-third of the advertisements (Strange, 1980:74).

Of course, homosexuals can and do engage in committed love relationships with one another, but many find fidelity to be quite difficult. One study of 943 bonded homosexual couples found that 79 percent of the respondents admitted at least one instance of infidelity in the previous year (Blumstein & Schwartz, 1991). I want to emphasize that none of this points to the "moral superiority" of heterosexual males. Gay males are first of all men, and they follow the strategy most men would follow were they not constrained by the strategies of the opposite sex. If bathhouses and tea rooms existed offering quick, easy, free, and impersonal sex with females, many straight males would doubtless behave in the same manner. Indeed, one recent study found that heterosexual males expressed greater interest in uncommitted sex than did gay males, although the authors caution that this finding should be viewed in light of the reality of greater actual opportunities enjoyed by gay males (Bailey, Gaulinn, Agyei, & Gladue, 1994).

Lesbians are likewise unconstrained by the necessity to compromise with a strategy different from that of their own sex. Studies spanning twenty years have shown that their female strategy is miles apart from the male strategy in that they seek intimacy rather than casual sex. Gagnon and Simon (1973) found that, like most other women, lesbians rejected promiscuity and stressed the importance of romance and a stable home life. Hedblom (1972:34–35) states, "The lesbian prided herself on the chastity of the lesbian group. . . . It was not unusual for lesbians to remain true to one woman." Thio (1979:209–210) writes that lesbians "tend to see their homosexuality in a nonsexual way. . . . When lesbians fall in love with one another, they simply want to respond to each other as women." Whitam's (1987) study of lesbians in three cultures (Brazil, Philippines, and the United States) emphasized the monogamous and nongenital nature of lesbian relationships. In the Bailey, Gaulinn, Agyei, & Gladue (1994) study mentioned earlier, the ordering of interest in uncommitted sex was lesbians < heterosexual females < gay males < heterosexual males.

Other theorists stress the contrasts between gays and lesbians: "Gay men remain distinctly male as regards the exploratory nature of their libido and their concern with the youth and physical attributes of their partners. Lesbians retain their feminine concern with the emotional aspects of their relationships" (G. Wilson, 1987:99). As distinguished from male homosexuality, which he describes as "sexually oriented and promiscuous," Gaylin (1986:199) writes that "lesbianism, with its emphasis on caring and attachment, tends to minimize the sexual role. It tends to be extraordinarily devoted and monogamous, with warm and tender attachments prevailing over sexual needs." Rushton and Bogaert (1989) write of the promiscuity, detached manner, and emphasis on youthful attractiveness of gays, and of the long-term, stable, and monogamous relationships of lesbians. Even in female prisons, in stark contrast with male prisons, coerced sexuality is extremely rare. Female inmates tend to form close emotional relationships, get "married," and form "families." In women's prisons, "Much of what has been described as homosexuality does not even include a sexual relationship. Rather, the women involved receive the affection and attention they need in a dyad with sexual connotations" (Pollock-Byrne, 1990:144).

We can quantify these general impressions by looking at the number of sexual partners that gays, lesbians, and heterosexual men and women have been reported to have experienced. In doing so, we find the following ordering (from highest to lowest): gay men > straight men > straight women > lesbians. From a variety of studies, G. Wilson (1983:203) estimates that gay men may have as many as 1,000 partners over a lifetime; straight males, 10; straight women, 5; and lesbians, 3. One study asking men and women how many sex partners they would like to have over a series of time intervals ranging from one month to a lifetime found that males would like an average of about eighteen partners over a lifetime and that females would like an average of three or four (Buss & Schmitt, 1993). These figures accord with findings from a national probability sample which found men to have a lifetime average of 12.3 and females to have a lifetime average of 3.2 (Smith, 1991). Sexual preference was not addressed in this study, and numbers of partners differed by age category. Individuals (men and women combined) in their sexual prime during more sexually restrictive times had fewer partners (M = 3.51) than those in their prime during the years of the male-favoring "sexual revolution" (M = 9.71), which again points to the facultative nature of human sexuality.

Because each unique sexual partner for a male necessarily means a unique partner for a female, it has been asserted that any claims of significant male–female differences, although frequently reported, should be treated with suspicion (Phillis & Gromko, 1985). Mathematically, this logic is unassailable. Were we to conduct a census of the American adult population on this subject, and assuming honest answers, male and female means would have to be identical. However, this does not mean that the *typical* female is as sexually active as the typical male. While it is possible that females underreport and males exaggerate, Ellis (1989–1990:28) offers what I believe to be a better explanation when he states, "Extremely active females (e.g., prostitutes, 'nymphomaniacs') are not fairly represented in colleges where most surveys are conducted" (see also Symons [1979:214]).

There is a small number of women who are every bit as promiscuous as the most promiscuous males. Hypersexual females have a significant advantage over their male counterparts in that they are in a position similar to that of gay males; that is, they enjoy easy access to willing sexual partners. Hypersexual heterosexual males, because they must compromise with females—the great majority of whom are not predisposed to casual sex—must work harder for their "successes." Because the mean is sensitive to extreme cases, hypersexual females may have more effect on the female mean than hypersexual males will have on the male mean.

Rather than simply examining means to resolve this issue, we might also examine modes and medians (invariably lower for females than males) to show that atypically sexually active females contribute more to the female mean than atypically active males do to the male mean. However, the rarely reported coefficient of skewness is a better indicator. Two recent studies utilizing different samples reported coefficients of skewness for the number of sex partners distribution for males and females. The first study (Walsh, 1992) reported coefficients of 1.64 and 2.43 for males and females, respectively; and the second (Walsh, submitted) reported coefficients of 0.298 and 1.345, respectively. The respective coefficients of skewness indicate that atypically sexually active females pull the female mean further toward the tail of a positively skewed distribution than do atypically active males.

The same gay > straight > lesbian ordering is seen in comparisons of frequency of sexual activity within the boundaries of a bonded relationship. Blumstein and Schwartz (1991:182) found among couples living together for two years that 67 percent of the gay couples, 45 percent of the straight couples, and 33 percent of the lesbian couples had sex three or more times per week. The corresponding figures for couples together between two and ten years were 32 percent, 27 percent, and 7 percent. This study also cast some doubt on the alleged greater monogamy of lesbian women in comparison to heterosexual women. It was reported that 19 percent of the lesbians and 9 percent of the married women reported at least one nonmonogamous instance in the previous year. However, the comparison of lesbians and married women is not altogether valid given the social and moral restrictions on adultery surrounding the legal institution of marriage.

Interesting sex differences relating to the willingness of males and females to engage in "deviant" sexuality were found in the Bell, Weinberg, and Hammersmith (1981) study. Among their interviewees, 20 percent of the 293 lesbians and 0 percent of the heterosexual women had experienced homosexual oral–genital contact before age 19 (1981:168). By way of contrast, 72 percent of the 686 homosexual males and 15 percent of the hetersexual males had experienced homosexual oral–genital contact by age 19 (1981:100).[8] The proportion of heterosexual men who had experienced homosexual oral sex before age 19 was not statistically different from the proportion of lesbian women who had (z = 1.66, n.s.). This, placed alongside the total absence of heterosexual women who had experienced it, is a striking testimony to the strength and experimental nature of the male sex drive.

Bell, Weinberg, and Hammersmith (1981) provide no comparison figures for involvement in opposite-sex oral–genital contact; but we may obtain such figures from Roche's (1986) study among heterosexual dating couples in college. In a dating situation with no particular affection involved, 10 percent of the males and 2 percent of the females had experienced oral sex. In a monogamous love-centered dating relationship, the respective figures were 79 percent and 59 percent. It would appear that, to the extent that the two samples are comparable, heterosexual women more readily engage in oral–genital sex than homosexual women. Unfortunately, unlike Roche (1986), Bell, Weinberg, and Hammersmith (1981) provide no information on the contextual nature of the relationship (casual versus love-centered) in which their lesbian subjects experienced oral sex.

We might invoke differential socialization to explain male–female differences in sexuality that are exaggerated among gays and lesbians, although van den Berghe (1979:65) argues this would be "really stretching the cultural argument to the breaking point." Males do receive subtle and not-so-subtle messages telling them that it is "manly" to play the field, and females are the recipients of messages telling them it is "unladylike" to do the same. This would not explain why gays and lesbians ignore socialization messages regarding appropriate sexual targets (and even creating countercultures for themselves) while at the same time overly conforming to messages regarding levels of sexual activity. Biosociologists acknowledge that gender-specific messages are sent, but they also insist that they are received by males and females who are biologically receptive to them (active GE correlation).

It is indeed ironic that it is the sexually "deviant" males and females who best conform to our social image of what "real men" and "nice girls" should be in terms of the number of sexual partners they have experienced. These differences point strongly to sex-differentiated preferences and to the compromise factor. Gays and lesbians do not have to compromise with the strategies of the opposite sex, so they engage in the behavior that is typical of their sex—gay or straight. As Rushton and Bogaert (1989:1218) put it, "When the necessities of compromise required by the presence of the opposite sex are removed, males and females are freer to construct their behavior most compatible with their genotypes." Straight males and females, on the other hand, are confronted with the compromise factor and thus become more alike in their mating behavior.[9]

CONCLUSION

This chapter has examined human sexuality from a biosociological perspective, stressing the interplay of ultimate (evolutionary), distal (hormonal, psychological, developmental), and proximate (socioecological) factors producing variability in human sexual behavior. The theories, concepts, and perspectives discussed have been presented to underscore once again the point that biosociology is about the interplay of nature and nurture in determining behavior. Sexuality probably illustrates this interplay more than any other area of human activity. Sexual selection, parental investment, and r/K theories point unequivocally to major differences between males and females in sexual motivation and why they exist. Any theories involving sex–gender roles, in whatever context, must take these differences into consideration if they are to be credible.

It must be stressed again, however, that human sexual behavior is facultative. Although sexual behavior is strongly biased in male or female directions, there are no monolithic "optimum" strategies for either sex; sexual behavior is gender *related*, not gender *specific*. Certain socioecological conditions—such as a badly skewed sex ratio—render it necessary for most members of the sex not favored by the ratio to compromise with the sexual strategy of the sex that is favored. Failure to do so among our distant ancestors would prob-

ably have meant reproductive failure. As with other forms of patterned behavior, our sexual behavior is the result of an incredibly complicated series
of adaptations to ecological challenges faced by our distant ancestors and by
ourselves.

NOTES

1. It is often noted that many sex-specific traits have no apparent adaptive value
and may even be maladaptive in a survival sense. The existence of such traits is at
odds with the otherwise impeccable logic of natural selection. The usual example given
of such traits is the lush plumage on male peacocks which place their possessors in
greater danger than their less elaborately adorned conspecifics. We note that it is the
most decorate animals of some species, if they survive the dangers posed by their
adornments, who produce the most offspring. Thus, Darwin reasoned that many sex-
specific traits arose not from survival imperatives but from reproductive imperatives
(of course, a trait that enables an organism to survive is only useful in an evolutionary
sense insofar as it aids the organism's reproductive success). Evolutionary vectors
sometimes conflict, and the intersection of the survival vector (maximizing safety of
the individual in its environment) and the reproduction vector (maximizing genetic
survival) is one such conflict.

2. The mid- to late 1960s saw the confluence of a number of factors that led to the
low sex ratio. First, there was a large cohort of women born during the baby-boom
years being matched with males from a smaller cohort due to age differences between
males and females in typical marriages. Second, there were far more males than females away from home in the armed forces, other overseas occupations, and in prisons. Third, there are least twice as many homosexual males than homosexual females.
Last, more males die in every age category from homicides, suicides, accidents, and
a wide variety of diseases.

3. Guttentag and Secord (1983) provide a wealth of historical data from many societies and epochs revealing the consistency of their thesis across time and place. Of
medieval Europe they write, "As expected from the low sex ratios, the prevailing ethos
was sexual libertarianism. . . . Sexual cynicism rather than the ideal of committed love
predominated" (1983:69). On the other hand, in countries with high sex ratios (more
men than women) such as France and Spain, the same period saw the rise of "courtly
love," romance, modesty, and sexual restraint (1983:71–73).

4. Data from as far back as the 1930s show strong correlations in the low to mid-
0.80s between the sex ratio and the prevalence of marriage for black women. The
greater the male excess, the more likely women were to marry (Cox, 1940). More
recent data from 270 SMSAs produced essentially the same results. Where females
hold the dyadic power (more men than women), they are more likely to marry; where
males hold the dyadic power, they are less likely to marry (Fossett & Kiecolt, 1993).

5. Broude and Greene's (1977) analysis of the sexual attitudes of 116 cultures found
that none of them was more lenient toward female sexuality than toward male sexuality, although 13 of these cultures (11.2%) were equally tolerant of male and female
nonmarital and extramarital sexuality. It has been noted that even French Revolutionary law, which went to great extremes to abolish all forms of sexual discrimination,
retained it in its differential attitude toward female and male adultery, arguing that the

former is more destructive of the family via the possibilities of cuckoldry and male violence (Wilson & Daly, 1992:311).

6. There is some empirical evidence supporting the "sexy son" hypothesis, which asserts that promiscuous females who mate with high-status males are more likely to have sons than daughters. Gangestad and Simpson (1990:85) looked at the offspring sex ratio as a function of mother's occupation and found that "members of occupations associated with higher Extraversion and Lack of Constraint [e.g., acting and marketing and sales] had relatively more sons than daughters as compared with members of occupations associated with low Extraversion and low Lack of Constraint" (F = 13.79, p < 0.001).

7. It is instructive to differentiate between *masculinization* and *defeminization* here. Masculinization refers to the induction of traits that are well developed in males and weakly developed in females. Defeminization refers to the inhibition of traits normally found in females and weakly developed in males. The importance of this is that exposure (or lack of exposure) to prenatal androgens may change certain behavioral sets while leaving others intact. In the case of male homosexuals, the targets of their sexual desire may have been changed by insufficient defeminization in certain brain areas without this having any consequences for the strength of their sexual desire. For instance, hypothalamic structures may have maintained their intrinsic feminine form while at the same time responding to male levels of testosterone.

8. Comparing gays and lesbians who had and who had not experienced heterosexual oral sex before age 19, I calculated a chi-square of 230.9, with p < 0.00001 and Yule's Q = 0.828. The odds ratio indicates that gays were 10.65 times more likely to have had oral sex by age 19 than were lesbians.

9. A nonsexual example of this is found in the self-reported delinquency study of Caspi, Lynam, Moffitt, and Silva (1993), who found that (controlling for SES and many other demographic variables) girls in mixed-sex schools reported more than twice the number of antisocial acts than did girls in all-girl schools.

Chapter 8

The Nature and Nurture of Criminality

> We [sociology] are the only branch of social science that has, for the most part, failed recognize openly the possible influence of nature on human behavior, and nowhere is this more evident than in our studies of crime.
>
> —Lawrence Cohen

Wilson and Herrnstein (1985) open their masterly *Crime and Human Nature* by informing us that their goal is to understand human nature. They explain that while they could have chosen a variety of human behaviors in their effort to illuminate it, they chose crime "because crime, more dramatically than other forms of behavior, exposes the connection between individual dispositions and the social order" (1985:20).

Wilson and Herrnstein chose to emphasize variability in the propensity to commit antisocial acts among individuals rather than sociocultural processes, as I do. We must, therefore, first distinguish between the concepts of crime and criminality. A crime is a legalistic label placed on socially disapproved behavior and is thus a property of the sociocultural order. Crime—its definition, spread, concentration, and prevalence—is rightly the domain of traditional sociological criminology. The spectacular 300-percent increase in Hungarian crime since the demise of communism documented by Gonczol (1993), and roughly similar figures reported for the former Soviet Union (Dashkov, 1992) and for China (Wang, 1994) reflect social, political, and economic phenomena. They have little to do with individual differences, except perhaps to say that dramatic social change generated anomie, which acted as a "releaser" of criminal behavior among those for whom the threshold for it was low (Durkheim, 1951:208).[1]

Criminality belongs to a more inclusive kind of criminology that is cognizant of the role of biology, psychology, and sociology (Jeffery, 1993; Moffitt, 1993). Criminality is a property of individuals, a defect of personhood among those who seek their own selfish interests regardless of the cost to others (Wilson & Herrnstein, 1985:23). Most individuals are capable of committing a crime under some circumstances, and many of us have done so, but few wake up in the morning thinking about how to take advantage of every opportunity that comes along or even how to manufacture such opportunities. Criminality, like every other human trait, is continuously distributed, not a defect that one either does or does not have, and is itself an amalgam of other continuously distributed traits.[2]

There has been a long tradition of heated opposition to locating the source of socially proscribed behavior within individuals. "Crime is defined," not discovered, runs a well-known argument. Crimes have no "essence," only perceptions; and as such we cannot apply positivist science to discovering why people commit acts which have no inherent meaning and which may be defined away tomorrow. This argument is considered particularly cogent when the cause is alleged to be "in the genes": "Those who claim they have found a gene for criminality must explain how any gene knows what is a crime, why, when and where. They will also have to abolish the concept of guilt, for the born criminal can hardly be more responsible for his supposed criminality than for the color of his eyes" (Senger, 1993:6).

The poverty of this typical social science concept of the influence of genes on behavior aside, Senger's argument conflates the distinction between crime and criminality, as well as the distinction between universally condemned crimes (*mala in se*) and culturally or time-dependent crimes (*mala prohibita*). Senger is correct: There are no "crime genes"; but there are genes which, via any number of neurohormonal routs, lead to particular traits and characteristics that may increase the probability of criminal behavior in some environments. The legal status of an act is fairly irrelevant to individuals possessing such traits. It is the willingness to violate social and moral rules and to largely discount the consequences to others and to oneself—more so than the content of the behavior involved—that most accurately defines criminality. This willingness denotes poor self-control, poor ability to internalize moral norms, relative freedom from fear, and a low level of empathy.

This propensity, whatever its source, in no fashion can be construed as absolving the actor from responsibility for his or her actions. Indeed, it is mainstream social science which most strongly supports the tradition of blaming everyone and everything for crime except those who commit it. "Whenever we find a high rate of delinquency," wrote MacIver (1960:123) over thirty years ago, "we can be sure that the root trouble lies not in the youths themselves, but in the social and environmental conditions to which their families have been exposed." Among modern exculpators, Farley (1990:217) warns, "If we could convince ourselves that inner-city violence was the product of 'bad genes'. . . we could then attribute such violence to the natural deficiencies of the poor rather than to their poverty in the midst of plenty. In short, we could blame the poor themselves for their violence."

Farley implies that the "true" cause of violence ("poverty in the midst of plenty") has been uncovered and that this one factor is both a necessary and sufficient cause. This being so, it is futile and stupid to look further, especially if one is looking within a "discredited" theoretical framework. According to this view, violent individuals are financially rather than morally bankrupt and would be respectable members of the bourgeoisie if only they could legally obtain more of the "plenty" they are in the midst of. We falsely attribute blame for violence to those who commit it, according to this view, because relative deprivation causes violence in a completely prescribed way. "The environment" is everything; the individual is nothing. Thus, McIver's delinquents and Farley's thugs are innocent pawns of their environments.

The opposite view is that subcultures and neighborhoods provide settings that impinge on widely varying individual thresholds for crossing the line that separates lawful from unlawful behavior. Why individual thresholds vary widely in similar settings is at least as interesting as why some settings breach more individual thresholds than other settings. Large cohort studies from Philadelphia of boys born in 1945 (Wolfgang, Figlio, & Sellin, 1972) and in 1958 (Tracy, Wolfgang, & Figlio, 1990) have shown that while about one-third of young boys in our large urban environments may get caught up in the jaws of the criminal justice system before reaching adulthood, a very small proportion of them commit a highly disproportionate number of offenses. In the 1945 study, 6 percent of the cohort (18% of the subset of delinquents) committed 71 percent of all the homicides committed by the cohort, 73 percent of the rapes, 82 percent of the robberies, and 69 percent of the aggravated assaults. In the 1958 study, 7.5 percent of the cohort (23% of the subset of delinquents) accounted for 61 percent of the homicides, 75 percent of the rapes, 73 percent of the robberies, and 65 percent of the aggravated assaults (Tracy, Wolfgang, & Figlio, 1990:279–280). The existence of a relatively small percentage of chronic offenders who commit a vastly disproportionate amount of crimes, consistently found in cohort samples in the United States and elsewhere, calls out for a biosocial criminology attuned to individual differences.

Over the past decade, new criminological theories have tended to downplay structural explanations of criminality. Wilson and Herrnstein's (1985) *net advantage* theory and Gottfredson and Hirschi's (1990) *self-control* theory are examples of the new focus on the individual. Even Robert Agnew's (1992) *general strain* theory adds characteristics such as temperament, intelligence, and self-esteem to attempt to explain why some people choose positive strategies in dealing with sociocultural strain, while others choose negative ones. These theories have in common the idea that all criminal behavior is sufficiently similar to make a general theory of criminality possible and stress *cognition.* In their various forms, these neoclassical theories focus on the ability to learn social mores and to control hedonistic impulses; the tendency to take pride in the approbation of others and to shrink from their opprobrium; an appreciation of the rights, feelings, and needs of others; the ability to consider the remote as well as the immediate consequences of contemplated actions; and the ability to take advantage of educational and occupational opportunities.

IQ AND CRIMINALITY

It was once virtually taken as a given that "feeblemindedness" was a major cause of crime and delinquency (Vold & Bernard, 1986:67). From the 1930s to about the mid-1970s, mainstream criminologists reversed their thinking and insisted that IQ bore no significant relationship to crime and delinquency; and some even considered it taboo to even think that there is (Sagarin, 1980). With the publication of Hirschi and Hindelang's (1977) influential "revisionist" paper on IQ, we witnessed a resurgence of interest in the relationship, although it may have operated as a "silent partner in standard sociological explanations" (Herrnstein, 1980:48) all along.[3] Recent reviews of the IQ–crime relationship have characterized it as ubiquitous and robust (Stattin & Klackenberg-Larsson, 1993; Lynam, Moffitt, & Stouthamer-Loeber, 1993).

Although most criminals and delinquents fall within the "normal" range of IQ (between 90 and 110), they are overrepresented in the "dull normal" (79 to 89) category (Walsh, 1991a:87–88; West, 1982:38). Even so, overrepresentation per se does not demonstrate a necessary relationship between IQ and antisocial behavior; perhaps only the stupid and the foolish get caught. This so-called "differential detection hypothesis" has long been a thorn in the side of the IQ–crime and delinquency relationship, and it certainly has intuitive appeal. However, upon reviewing available literature, Hirschi and Hindelang (1977:583) concluded that "the differential ability to avoid detection and the differential official reaction on the basis of IQ arguments are not supported by available evidence."

Moffitt and Silva (1988) provided support for Hirschi and Hindelang's assertion in an elegantly designed study. Based on a New Zealand birth cohort (all boys born during the year encompassing April 1, 1972 and March 31, 1973), they compared IQ means of three groups of juveniles: (A) self-reported delinquents who had been officially defined as such, (B) self-reported delinquents who were not known to the police, and (C) a self-reported nondelinquent group. Self reports were checked against official police records in order to code the juveniles into one of the three groups. The mean IQ scores of groups A and B (the two delinquent groups) did not differ significantly from one another, meaning, at least in New Zealand, that undetected delinquents are no brighter than their peers who were known to the police. Both the detected and the undetected delinquents, however, had significantly lower IQ means than their nondelinquent peers. Moffitt and Silva's findings are clear: Both detected and undetected delinquents have significantly lower IQs than nondelinquents, and the mean IQs of detected and undetected delinquents do not differ significantly.

The ever-growing importance of intelligence in complex societies bodes ill for a significant proportion of the working-age population and for society as a whole. Well-paying jobs requiring little or no special training or education are disappearing from the American scene at a rapid pace. As Linda Gottfredson's meta-analysis discussed in Chapter 5 pointed out, job performance becomes more highly correlated with g as jobs become more complex. Even jobs that once demanded little more than a high school diploma may now demand at least some college. Status inflation means that the young must spend more time preparing to enter the job market; and the longer the preparation becomes, the less attractive the proposition becomes for those with limited time horizons. Similarly, the more difficult the intellectual demands of the work place become, the more frustrated those who cannot meet them will be. Because of the profound changes in the American occupational structure, it is reasonable to speculate that the negative IQ–crime relationship will grow stronger in the coming years.

INTELLECTUAL IMBALANCE

Many studies exploring the relationship between IQ and crime and delinquency view IQ as a unitary phenomenon in that *full-scale* IQ is correlated with various measures of crime and delinquency. Such a strategy may obscure as much about the IQ–delinquency relationship as it reveals. Full-scale IQ (FIQ) on the Wechsler tests is a composite of two subtests—performance IQ and verbal IQ—with a person's FIQ being the mean of the VIQ and PIQ subtest scores. The average correlation between scores on the subtests is 0.783 (Anastasi, 1976:253), a healthy correlation that attests to a considerable overlap of intellectual domains but not one that justifies treating the subtests as equivalent (by averaging their scores) for all research purposes. The relative independence of the two subscales is revealed by PET studies showing that the neurological processes involved when working on VIQ and PIQ items are lateralized to opposite sides of the brain (Chase, Fedio, Foster, Brooks, Di Chiro, & Mansi, 1984; Duara et al., 1984). VIQ-related thinking is associated with glucose metabolism in the left hemisphere, and PIQ-related thinking is associated with glucose metabolism in the right hemisphere.

The importance of these observations rests in the long-noted tendency for offenders to show a greater deficit in VIQ than in PIQ relative to general population norms. Combining two subscales—one of which almost uniformly shows a significant offender deficit, and the other which rarely shows a significant offender deficit—renders FIQ means of offenders and nonoffenders somewhat more equal than they would otherwise be (Herrnstein, 1989:3). Such a strategy, of course, leads to the underestimation of the effects of cognitive variables on the propensity to violate the law.[4]

The Wechsler IQ tests have been so constructed that the majority of individuals obtain approximately the same scores on both the verbal and performance scales, indicating roughly similar levels of brain hemispheric efficiency. However, a certain proportion of the population evidence an asymmetry of cognitive efficiency that is signaled by a significant discrepancy between scores on the two IQ subscales. Based on normative samples, a significant discrepancy (either V > P or P > V) requires a difference of twelve points at the 0.05 level of statistical significance, and fifteen points at the 0.01 level (Kaufman, 1976). Researchers have been particularly interested in the P > V imbalance profile since David Wechsler's (1958:176) comment that "the most outstanding feature of the sociopath's test profile is the systematic high score on the performance as opposed to the verbal part of the [Wechsler IQ] scale."

Based on a normative sample of 1,100 boys, and using twelve or more points to define a significant discrepancy, Kaufman (1976) reported the profile percentages shown in Table 8.1. Significant departures from these normative expectations are found among offender populations. Among studies reporting category percentages shown in Table 8.1, we see that the P > V category is overrepresented and the V > P category is underrepresented.

The pattern revealed by these studies indicates that although V > P and P > V boys are about equally represented in the general population, P > V boys are found approximately four times more often than V > P boys in delinquent populations. The Barnett, Zimmer, and McCormack (1989) study, showing less than 1 percent of the prison inmates with a V > P profile, is particularly interesting. It suggests that as offenders become older, their cognitive styles further sort them into pro- and antisocial categories, with a V > P profile being a particularly good predictor of nonoffending behavior. Summarizing decades of research on intellectual imbalance, Miller (1987:120) concludes that "this PIQ > VIQ relationship (with crime and delinquency) was found across studies, despite variations in age, sex, race, setting, and form of Wechsler scale administered, as well as differences in criteria for delinquency."[5]

Why poor verbal skills matched with relatively normal performance skills increase the propensity to engage in criminal behavior is open to conjecture. Joseph's (1982) neuropsychological theory of language acquisition may offer some insights. We know from brain-imaging studies that PIQ test items heavily involve the motor areas of the cortex. Motor areas of the brain mature earlier than other areas, which allows for rapidity of response to stimuli without involving areas specializing in cognition. As the infant brain matures, there is increasing communication between the cognitive and motor areas and a concomitant slowing down of responses while the left brain processes and interprets stimuli before initiating motor behavior. This "interpretive" process

Table 8.1
Percentages of Male Delinquents and Criminals in Each P/V Category—Tests of Significance (Goodness-of-Fit Chi-Square) Based on Comparisons with Normative Expectations

	V > P	V = P	P > V	N	χ^{2*}	V**
Kaufman (1976) (expected percentages)	18.0	66.0	16.0			
Andrew (1977)	10.8	55.6	33.8	74	17.3	0.48
Tarter, Hegedus, Winsten, & Alterman (1985)	7.9	63.3	28.7	101	16.2	0.40
Walsh, Petee, & Beyer (1987)	11.3	51.6	37.1	256	85.5	0.58
Barnett, Zimmer, & McCormack (1989)***	0.9	75.0	26.1	1792	498.7	0.53
Walsh (1991a)	7.2	57.3	35.5	513	160.8	0.56
Cornell & Wilson (1992)	5.0	60.0	35.0	149	46.8	0.56

*All chi-square values significant at < .001; **V = Cramer's V; ***The Barnett, Zimmer, and McCormack figures based on adult prison inmates; all other studies involve juvenile delinquents.

is initially post hoc; but with the acquisition of language, the socialized child is eventually able to *foresee* its response before reacting rather than interpreting action after the fact. Very much like Freud's "Where id was, there shall ego be," Joseph's theory sees an ever-increasing engagement of cognition in the processing; organization; and, when needed, inhibition of motor impulses.[6]

The efficiency with which cognition performs its interpretive and inhibitory tasks varies considerably from person to person. Because PIQ (0.405) is less heritable than VIQ (0.632) (Vandenberg & Volger, 1985:43) and because PIQ subscales load lower Spearman's *g* than the VIQ subscales (Jensen & Faulstich, 1988), the cognitive skills reflected in PIQ may be more subject to environmental influences than VIQ.

This line of thought suggests that as many criminals grow older, they retain their childhood priorities for instant pleasure and self-gratification without having developed the "self-talk" necessary to generate a sense of discipline, responsibility, and empathy. A young child processing information in a way similar to that expected from the immature infant brain produces only an obnoxious playground "brat;" but similar brain processing in juveniles or adults produces delinquents and criminals who steal, assault, rob, rape, and murder. The cognitive *processes* of the immature child and the delinquent or criminal are the same (the failure to cognitively modulate inappropriate motor impulses); but the *content* of those cognitions becomes much more threatening as the person becomes older, stronger, and more ambitious in the pursuit of self-gratification.

The common-sense notion that intellectual maturity is a necessary, although not sufficient, precondition for moral maturity is supported by a number of studies. The interpersonal-maturity (I-level) system is often used to classify juvenile delinquents (Andrew, 1980). The I-level system proposes that cognitive and personality integration follows a sequential pattern in normal human development and sets up seven levels from the most basic (I-level 1) to the ideal (I-level 7). Delinquents generally fall into levels 2 through 5, with level 5 so rarely found among delinquents that only levels 2 through 4 are usually used to assess them (Austin, 1981:187). Consistent with the neurological-deficit hypothesis of cognitive immaturity, I-level studies show a significant superiority of the motor skills of the right-brain hemisphere over the "self-talk" skills of the left-brain hemisphere. June Andrew (1974), a pioneer in intellectual imbalance research, conducted a study of 122 juvenile probationers in which she found that I-level 4 probationers (the most mature) had a mean P > V discrepancy of 4.41 points, I-level 3 probationers had a mean discrepancy of 7.33 points, and the I-level 2s had a mean of 17.78.

INTELLECTUAL IMBALANCE AND THE AUTONOMIC NERVOUS SYSTEM

As we have seen, ANS hypoactivity is a fairly reliable predictor of antisocial activity because it signals difficulty in learning the conditioned responses that are the precursors of conscience. A hypoactive ANS may be related to elevated PIQ scores because most of the tests on the PIQ subtest are tests of short-term memory, and short-term memory is more affected by anxiety than is long-term memory (Frank, 1983:74). Individuals who are relatively unaffected by anxiety should score well on PIQ relative to their scores on VIQ. The possible neurological process by which anxiety intrudes on short-term memory has been stated by Keiser (1976:306): "An interference hypothesis might suggest that when affective processes are generally underreactive there will be less distortion of immediate memory traces within the same anatomical structures, for example, the hippocampal circuits that are thought to play a role in short-term memory systems." The lack of anxiety and fear reflected in sluggish ANS arousal in many situations, a lack which often characterizes psychopathic behavior, may also account for a tendency to score within the normal range on PIQ tests while typically scoring below average on VIQ tests.

Another mechanism which may help to account for the elevated PIQ scores relative to VIQ scores is DeLozier's (1982:98) concept of "frozen watchfulness." DeLozier suggests that an abused child's efforts to avoid punishment favor development of the visual–spatial skills of the brain's right hemisphere. If frequently abused children are to avoid as much punishment as possible, they must become sensitive to environmental cues that punishment is imminent. "Becoming sensitive" to anything means that one's neural networks have been sensitized in the struggle for synaptic space by responding with greater frequency and intensity to those stimuli that have the greatest importance for the organism (Edelman's "neural Darwinism"). Thus, some abused children may develop exceptional (relatively speaking) visual–spatial skills, which are reflected in a P > V profile. The frequent interpretation of verbal and visual cues as threatening may explain the abused child's tendency to respond to verbal as well as nonverbal stimuli in aggressive and violent ways as the child grows older.

Because heritability coefficients for IQ vary greatly across different socioeconomic groups, we cannot suppose that the cognitive processes discussed here have similar explanatory power across all environments (Buikhuisen, Bontekoe, Plas-Koenhoff, & Van Buuren, 1984). The genetic contribution to phenotypical traits depends to various extents on how well environments allow for their expression. The impact of P > V on antisocial behavior may well depend on if we are looking at it in advantaged or disadvantaged environments. The more advantageous the environment (the less genetically restrictive), the more biological variables should impact antisocial behavior; the more disadvantageous (genetically restrictive) the environment, the less the impact of biological variables relative to social variables.

Contrasting the relative effects of P > V and abuse and neglect on violent delinquency in homogeneous–advantaged (HA) and homogeneous–disadvantaged (HD) environments, Walsh (1992) found that P > V was more powerful in explaining delinquency in the HA group and abuse and neglect more important in the HD group. When each variable was used as a control for the other, P > V could not account for any significant variance in violent delinquency after abuse and neglect had accounted for all that it could (0.258 percent) in the HD group; and abuse and neglect could not account for any significant variance in violent delinquency after P > V had accounted for all that it could (0.495 percent) in the HA group.

Further supportive of the "different environment, different explanation" contention is Venables's (1987) study of British schoolchildren. This study found significant negative correlations between teachers' ratings (−0.31) and self-ratings (−0.37) of antisociality and tonic heart among high-SES children but nonsignificant correlations among low-SES children (−0.03 and −0.10, respectively). The negative correlations indicate that low tonic heart rate (an indicator of hypoactive ANS activity) is associated with higher rates of misbehavior in both groups but also that its effect is much diminished in disadvantaged environments. Both of these studies are consistent with the principles of behavioral genetics, and they illustrate the need to always consider both environmental and genetic influences on human behavior of all kinds.[7]

THE MAJOR DEMOGRAPHIC CORRELATES
OF CRIME

There is universal agreement among modern criminologists that the strongest and most consistent demographic correlates of criminality across time and place are age, gender, and race (Wilson & Herrnstein, 1985; Vold & Bernard, 1986; Eysenck & Gudjonsson, 1989; Gottfredson & Hirschi, 1990). In terms of mean rates, adolescents and young adults commit more crimes than older adults; males commit more crimes than females; and blacks commit more crimes than other races. The discussion of age and gender effects is necessarily brief because most of the explanatory arguments have been made in previous chapters in other contexts.

Age

Regardless of how we divide ourselves into the various demographic categories of social science, we have all been young; and most of us will get old. Perhaps this is why age is one of the few "individual differences" variables about which one can write without fear of being called something nasty. Criminology has a history of healthy skepticism about official arrest data as they pertain to gender and race, often claiming that offense rates reflect bias in the criminal justice system rather than actual gender or racial differences in offending. No such claims are made about the reality of age differences in rates of offending.

Gottfredson and Hirschi (1990:125–130) produce a series of graphs of age-graded offending rates, ranging from England and Wales in 1842–1844 to New York state in 1979, that so mirror one another as to suggest that the phenomenon these distributions reflect is almost a law of nature. There is a tremendous surge of antisocial behavior in the young in the second decade of life (i.e., the teenage years) which peaks at age 16 and thereafter steadily and rather quickly declines. Any explanation for this phenomenon must be able to account both for its rapid onset and its steady rate of desistance and must keep before it the fact that most juvenile delinquents do not become adult criminals (Boucher, 1985; Moffitt, 1993).

Because "in criminology biology connotes fixation, immutability, or even destiny" (Gottfredson & Hirschi, 1990:135), many criminologists view the phenomenon of age-graded crime rates as particularly damaging to any theory positing biological causes. These causes, whatever they may be, are alleged to create individuals destined to commit crime; so when they do what they were designed to do less and less frequently, the poverty of "biologizing" is revealed. What "really" explains dramatic age-related crime distributions according to many criminologists are the situations people find themselves in, not stable characteristics of individuals. The sharp rise in crime is explained by older children transferring their allegiance from parents to peers ("bad company") and their sudden discovery of various reinforcers such as money, chemical substances, sex, and peer-group status that are usually only obtainable for them in "satisfying" quantities through illegal or immoral means. What explains decreasing frequency in antisocial behavior as youths enter adulthood is that most of these reinforcers may now be obtained legitimately and more safely from marriage and employment, which reflects a return to an allegiance to responsible behavior. In this view, the age effect is not really an effect at all. It is simply that certain ages are correlated with certain events; and these events, not age per se, account for age-graded crime rates.

Situation theorists talk about increases and decreases in delinquency and crime; and by pointing to social situations associated with its rise and fall, they believe that they have rendered individual explanations impotent. Despite the appeal of their argument, it has been found that the age effect survives and remains robust across studies controlling for a host of demographic and situational variables, which indicates that none of the various correlates of age predict crime as well as age itself (Wilson & Herrnstein, 1985:145). These findings suggest that the "situation" theory of age-graded crime merely describes a process of social maturation that almost everyone experiences.

Gottfredson and Hirschi (1990:136–141) point out that situational theorists confuse crime (which changes dramatically with age) with criminality, which is a fairly stable characteristic predisposing individuals to involve themselves differentially in the various situations that are alleged to account for the age effect (e.g., delinquent peer groups, dropping out of school, employment, marriage, responsible parenting). If people largely self-select the situations they are in (and adolescence marks the period when active GE correlation becomes an important factor in explaining behavior), then situation variables are contaminated by individual characteristics and cannot be offered as an argument against "individual differences" explanations of crime. Those who stress individual differences agree that while there is an undeniable shift away from conventional institutions during adolescence on the part of almost all youths, some began the shift earlier, shift further, find it more to their liking, and do not intend reversing: "Individual differences in the likelihood of crime tend to persist across the life course; there is no drastic reshuffling of the criminal and noncriminal populations based on unpredictable, situational events" (Gottfredson & Hirschi, 1990:141).

We still have to explain the general shift in prevalence with age. As we have seen, no set of demographic or situational variables have been shown to explain away the age effect in sociological models of crime and delinquency. This was found to be the case in a sociological model tested by Udry (1990) in which age remained the strongest predictor of "problem behavior" (self-reported delinquency). However, in a biosocial model that included testosterone (T) and SHBG levels, age dropped out of the regression equation. Udry (1990:7) explained that "the age effect on problem behavior is shown to be a spurious consequence of the causal relationship between age and testosterone." When age is included in sociological models of delinquency, it is probably serving as a proxy for the T/SHBG ratio.

The hormonal surges of puberty may well explain the rapid onset of antisocial behavior, but the almost-as-rapid decrease in antisocial behavior starting in the mid- to late teens does not correspond with a similar decrease in T levels. Thus, the age effect (both onset and desistance) requires more than an examination of T levels. It is reasonable to suppose that the age effect is a function of two biosocial processes on opposite trajectories, one of which holds temporary sway. During this time, the young find themselves at the confluence of a number of physical, social, and psychological changes with which they are often not well equipped to deal. Increasing neuropsychological maturation temporarily runs up against the countervailing pubertal surges of T and, among males, the halving of SHBG levels. These changes, especially in males, bring rapid increases in body size and strength, as well as a general increase in novelty-seeking behavior mediated by neurotransmitter activity, which is regulated at the pharmacological level by these same steroid hormones (Udry, 1990; Zuckerman, 1990).

The view that adolescence is a period in which physical desires and abilities outrun neuropsychological maturity is supported by several studies showing generally that the earlier the onset of puberty, the greater the level of problem behavior. Children who enter puberty significantly earlier than their age peers must confront their "raging hormones" with a brain that in all likelihood is no more mature than their age peers (Buchanan, Eccles, & Becker, 1993). Early-maturing boys throw significantly more temper tantrums at pubertal onset than do late-maturing boys at pubertal onset (Buchanan, Eccles, & Becker, 1993), and early-maturing girls have been shown to engage in a number of problem behaviors significantly more frequently and intensely than late-maturing girls (Magnusson, 1988; Simons & Blyth, 1988; Caspi, Lynam, Moffitt, & Silva, 1993). Consistent with the conflicting trajectory hypothesis, a panel study of 100 boys found that T levels predicted future problem behavior only for early-pubertal-onset boys (Drigotas & Udry, 1993).

Exacerbating the effects of the gap between puberty and brain maturity is the gap between puberty and the age when socially responsible roles are typically available to modern youth. A male entering puberty at age 12 today may not achieve a responsible social role (a full-time job, marriage, fatherhood) until he is about 22—a ten-year gap. Fifty years ago his grandfather would have entered puberty about two years later and would have been responsibly employed perhaps only months afterward. The widening gap between an ever-earlier average age of pubertal onset and the ever-lengthening time required to prepare for socially responsible adult roles renders understandable the self-report data indicating that almost every teenager in recent years has engaged in some form of delinquent behavior (Moffitt, 1993).

It has always been necessary for the young to cut the apron strings and assert their independence. The only trouble is that they do many antisocial things along the way. Most adults will probably acknowledge that they often acted stupidly, irresponsibly, and immorally as teenagers and by doing so revealed that, again to paraphrase Freud, "where id was, now ego is." Valuing education, obtaining employment, and settling into relationships are as much effects of evolving mental maturity as they are causes of it. Most young people learn to tame the hormonal chariot they are riding; delinquents who graduate to adult criminal careers never quite got the hang of it. "The adolescent who is antisocial at an early age and continues this behavior well into adulthood," writes Jeffery (1993:494), "is *biologically* different from the adolescent offender who stops at age 18–21." Jeffery (1977, 1990) has been arguing this for a long time, and it is becoming increasingly more difficult to ignore his point.

Gender

The most dramatic and stable of all the demographic correlates of crime is gender. At all times and in all places, males are far more criminally involved than females; and the more serious the crime, the larger the male/female ratio. In the United States in 1992, males committed 90.3 percent of the homicides, 98.7 percent of the rapes, 91.5 percent of the robberies, and 85.2 percent of the aggravated assaults (Federal Bureau of Investigation, 1993:234). The closest females came to matching the male rate for any index crime was larceny/theft, for which females constituted 32.1 percent of the arrests. Although it is true that female crime rates have increased substantially over the last two decades, the male–female gap, especially for violent crimes, remains as wide as ever (Fishbein, 1992).

The size and stability of the male/female ratio has posed serious difficulties for sociological criminologists. The widespread insistence on human equipotentiality suggests (since causal candidates can only be sought among factors that vary) that there could be cultural conditions under which male/female crime prevalence ratios might be equal, or even under which female rates might be higher. No such conditions have ever been discovered. Across the range of environments males and females experience together, males are always the more antisocial sex. A review of seventy-seven studies examining the sex–criminality relationship revealed not even one null relationship (Ellis, 1987a). Some may argue that although the environment may be held constant across the sexes in some senses (e.g., similar neighborhoods, families, SES, schooling), in other respects the environments they experience are sex specific. For instance, parents generally supervise females more closely than males, and this close supervision prevents females from committing offenses at the same rate as males (Farrington, 1988:74). However, Gottfredson and Hirschi's (1990:147–149) review of this issue points out that controlling for "supervision level" has no impact on the strength of the relationship: Males commit more antisocial acts across all levels of supervision.

Male–female differences in antisocial propensities are addressed in Chapters 6 and 7 in terms of neurohormonal differences and require no further comment here. The power of neurohormonal differences is not only evident in sex-based prevalence rates but also in the fact that when female criminality occurs, it typically occurs at higher levels of provocation, that is, females who become delinquent or criminal have usually suffered more environmental disabilities than males who do so. Gwynn Nettler (1982:138) put it well: "Environments—good or bad, and whichever facet of them is considered—affect males, the less viable of the sexes more strongly than they do females, the more durable segment of the species."

Examples abound: Cloninger, Reich, and Guze (1975:20) found that there existed "many kinds of more frequent disruptive home experiences in female sociopaths compared with male sociopaths." Henggeler, Edwards, and Borduin (1987:206) found that "there was more mother–adolescent conflict/hostility and a trend for more parental conflict/hostility in families of female delinquents than in the families of male delinquents." Widom (1989:265) found that abuse and neglect affected the future likelihood of violent offending for males but not for females. Finally, Walsh (1991a:144–145) found that female delinquents, although less frequently and seriously involved in delinquency than male delinquents, were more deprived on all indices of deprivation.

Race

Liberal African-American sociologist William Julius Wilson (1987:22) points out that liberal social scientists have tended to either ignore issues attending "the tangle of pathology in the inner city," or to address them in "circumspect ways." Of course, it is not only liberals who shy away from dealing forthrightly with matters of race. We all know that there is a most disagreeable tendency to label those who do as racists, as if such name-calling actually adds something of substance to what is supposedly a scientific discourse. It is a label that has been applied across such a range of imagined sins by those who favor ad hominem arguments over reasoned discourse that it has lost any stable meaning.[8]

The black/white ratio for delinquency prevalence is roughly the same as the male/female odds ratio for delinquency, that is, about 4:1 (Gordon, 1987; LaFree, Drass, & O'Day, 1992). Although constituting only about 12 percent of the U.S. population, the percentages of blacks arrested for each of the eight index crimes in 1992 were as follows (Federal Bureau of Investigation, 1993:235):

Murder	55.1%
Rape	42.8%
Robbery	60.9%
Aggravated assault	38.8%
Burglary	30.4%
Larcency and theft	31.4%
Motor vehicle theft	39.4%
Arson	21.9%

Blacks are also overrepresented by a factor of about 2.5 in white-collar crimes such as forgery, fraud, and embezzlement (Federal Bureau of Investigation, 1993:235) and are only underrepresented in crimes requiring high-status occupations for their commission. Black crime excess has been consistently in evidence as long as such statistics have been collected (Flowers, 1988:83). In addition, it has been estimated that 50 percent of all black males will be arrested sometime in their lives and that 25 percent of the black males in this country are currently under some form of criminal justice supervision (Whitman, 1993:212). Given such data, race obviously cannot be ignored in any discussion of crime and criminality, regardless of the political "sensitivity" of the issue. As LaFree and Russell (1993:273) put it, "All roads in American criminology eventually lead to issues of race."

The standard answer to figures such as these is that the criminal justice system is racist and discriminatory and that these figures reflect systemic biases rather than the actuality of large black–white differences in criminality. Yet studies comparing official arrest data from the Federal Bureau of Investigation's (FBI's) Uniform Crime Reports (UCRs) with National Crime Survey (NCS) data find that they accord extremely well (W. Wilson, 1987:32; Flowers, 1988:51). For example, about 60 percent of robbery victims describe their assailants as black, and about 60 percent of the suspects arrested for robbery are black (Hindelang, 1979; Wilbanks, 1987). The consensus among criminologists who research the question is that the black/white ratio in arrests is primarily (perhaps entirely) due to the racial differences in crime participation (Blumstein & Cohen, 1987).

Researchers may no longer be able to demonstrate antiblack bias in the arrest and processing of black suspects, but surely we should be able to demonstrate some sort of structural explanation for the black crime problem. Certainly, blacks have had heavy crosses to bear in this country, heavier than those of other races and ethnic groups (Greenberg & Schneider, 1994). Racism, as reflected in fewer educational and economic opportunities for blacks, has often been cited as the prime mover behind black crime rates. However, an analysis of U.S. national crime, education, and labor statistics from 1957 through 1988 found that black crime rates rose even as black income and educational attainment rose (LaFree, Drass, & O'Day, 1992). Similar increases in white income and educational attainment, as the various legitimate opportunity structure theories predict, led to a decrease in white crime rates. Thus, opportunity structure variables have had opposite effects on the black and white populations. The expansion of black crime rates during the thirty-year period of black political, legal, economic, and educational gain renders it difficult to maintain the simplistic notion that white racism is the cause of black crime.

LaFree, Drass, and O'Day (1992:178) suggest that increased education among blacks may have led to stronger *perceptions* of blocked opportunities than actually existed, giving rise to a sense of injustice. These perceptions, and the sense of injustice they generate, may then lead to increased black involvement in illegal activities.[9] There may be something in this argument, and certainly racism and the objective disadvantages that accompany it are not dead in this country. But effects should be proportionate to their causes; so the question is, "Are the undeniable disabilities suffered by previous generations of blacks, due to structural barriers to full participation in American life, adequate to account for the current high level of black crime?" Flowers, a sociologist who favors many "traditional" sociological explanations, provides an answer with which I concur:

Although it would be naive to suggest that slavery, racism, deprivation, and related factors American blacks have uniquely endured have not had at least some negative effect on behavior within this group, the fault of the theory is that it cannot adequately explain why blacks would be affected more by their victimization and injustice than other ethnic minorities, such as American Indians and Chinese-Americans, whose history in this country has also been one of considerable hardship. (1988:92)

Crime rate comparisons between blacks and other minority groups in the United States have consistently found that Asian-Americans have far lower crime rates than both European- and African-Americans (Wilson & Herrnstein, 1985:459–461; Flowers, 1988:190; Gottfredson & Hirschi, 1990:150).[10] Asians constituted 2.9 percent of the American population in 1990 (Bureau of the Census, 1993), yet they were arrested for only 0.8 percent of all violent crimes and 1.3 percent of all property crimes in 1992 (Federal Bureau of Investigation, 1993:235). British data reveal a similar pattern of black > white > Asian crime rates (Rutter & Giller, 1984:159). As in the United States, violent crimes account for most of the black crime surplus in Britain (which has no history of black slavery within its borders). An examination of violent crime rates of eighty-eight countries also found the black > white >Asian pattern (Rushton, 1990). It would seem from the available data, both between and within nations, that the offending pattern by race is consistently black > white > Asian. As Eysenck and Gudjonsson (1989:139) emphasized after reviewing the data, "No societies were found for which this pattern has not been reported."

RACE AND CRIME: EXPLANATIONS

The role of science is to go beyond simple description to attempt explanations. Explanations, of course, can be value laden. We may choose to emphasize the effects of social aggregates on individual behavior, or we may choose to emphasize the characteristics of individuals who selectively aggregate. On the other hand, we may behave like scientists and design studies that pit alternative explanations against one another to see which of them emerges from the wash the cleanest.

The rural–urban difference is one of the most important correlates of crime explored by criminologists. As villages grow into towns and towns into cities, interpersonal ties become less intimate; friendships become transitory; secondary groups take the place of primary groups; normative consensus breaks down to various degrees; and the anonymity of it all allows us to indulge in any deviant activities for which we may have an urge. At the extremes of this process, social control mechanisms tend to break down to intolerable degrees; and delinquent gangs replace the family, school, and church as role models and sources of fulfillment of the needs for affiliation and approval among the young.

Few criminologists seriously doubt that the impersonality and anonymity of the city are conducive to crime and that the city slum contains everything to excess that is negative and criminogenic about urbanism. Do the slum conditions at the city core "cause" crime, or is the correlation explained away by a variable that "causes" both, namely, the characteristics of individuals living there? Although it borders on anathema to suggest that people may be more responsible for the kind of environment they live in than the environment being responsible for the kind of people it produces (Kornhauser, 1978:104), some researchers have suggested that the relationship between urbanism and crime is confounded by race (Gordon, 1976; Laub, 1983; Sampson, 1985; Byrne, 1986; Chilton, 1986). These studies used a variety of methods to test the relative strength of a range of demographic characteristics in accounting for crime rates when pitted against the race variable.

One of the most basic questions is, "Does the black–white difference in crime rates exist because blacks tend to live disproportionately in cities (thus making race more important than place), or is it primarily a function of the fact that a greater proportion of blacks live in large cities (thus making place more important than race)?" Using different methodologies and data sources, all studies came to the same conclusion: that race is more important than place in accounting for crime rates and that once race is controlled for, city size is relatively unimportant above about 10,000 to 20,000 inhabitants. As cities get larger, social restraints become weaker and antisocial tendencies may be stimulated and released; but after a certain level or "threshold" of anonymity is reached, further increases in size do not appreciably affect the probability of antisocial acts (Gordon, 1976:257).

Laub (1983) examined "serious personal" crime rates among blacks and whites in urban and rural areas and found that both races had higher rates of offending in urban than in rural areas, with urban/rural ratios of 2.06 and 1.81 for blacks and whites, respectively. Thus, standardizing by race still left an independent rural–urban effect. The race effect was much larger, however, with the black rate in urban areas 4.23 times greater than the white rate and 3.71 greater in rural areas. Laub (1983:193) concludes that "race appears to be a key variable in accounting for variation in urban and rural crime rates as well as crime rates across various place size categories."

Byrne's (1986) sample of 910 U.S. cities found that the best predictor of robbery rates was the percentage of black residents ($\beta = 0.46$); the independent effect of city size was much weaker at 0.16. These standardized betas were obtained controlling for a host of city characteristics, such as density and housing type, and population compositional variables, such as income and education. Sampson's (1985) study of homicide rates in the fifty-five largest U.S. cities found that "percentage black" ($\beta = 0.55$) had more than twice the explanatory power of other variables in the regression such as population size, poverty, racial income inequality, and unemployment. Finally, Chilton's (1986) study of the 125 largest SMSAs controlled for a wide variety of variables in a number of different regression models. In all cases, the percentage of black residents emerged as the best predictor of murder ($\beta = 0.55$) and assault ($\beta = 0.22$) rates, although population size was a better predictor of rape (0.17) and robbery (0.62).

None of these studies made serious attempts to posit mechanisms that might explain the black–white difference other than to speculate that it may be due to a combination of motivational (racism, poverty, etc.) and releaser (lack of social bonds) factors (Laub, 1983) or "subculture of violence" (Byrne, 1986). Gordon (1976), however, did try to determine why the fourfold difference in crime rates exists and posited that the difference in black–white delinquency rates is a function of black–white IQ differences. Using Hirschi's (1969) data relating scores on the highly *g*-loaded Differential Aptitude Test (DAT) to official delinquency rates, Gordon reasoned that if structural variables (particularly discrimination) were important in explaining black–white differences in delinquency prevalence, then the DAT would be irrelevant; and the rates of delinquency for each race within each DAT category would fluctuate randomly.

However, this was not the case. Percentages of black youths with a police record in each of four DAT categories (from low to high) were 47, 34, 23, and 0; and the corresponding percentages of white youths with a police record were 43, 26, 20, and 6. Prevalence rates thus fluctuate systematically and similarly within DAT categories for both races, meaning that the intellectual abilities tapped by the DAT predict delinquency equally well for blacks and whites. The only factor that could explain the 4:1 ratio in delinquency prevalence for Gordon was the observation that blacks fall into the lower DAT categories about four times more often than whites. He sums up his discrimination-versus-IQ argument by noting that the essence of discrimination models is that all members of the oppressed group are arbitrarily treated alike, without regard to their individual differences. The IQ model, however, works as well as it does precisely because it takes full account of individual differences along the IQ dimension. Ingenious ad hoc assumptions would have to be introduced into the discrimination model to account for the fact that an unfair discriminatory process is as sensitive to IQ as [the data show]. (Gordon, 1976:264–265)

Gordon (1987) expanded his thesis in a later paper contrasting SES and IQ in his race–IQ–delinquency model. He asserted that the only factor that can viably explain the black–white difference in crime and delinquency prevalence is the black–white difference in IQ. In a tightly argued sixty-six-page paper, and using over thirty data sets, Gordon tested various delinquency models by pitting IQ against alleged structural explanations of the black–white rates of delinquency, such as SES and schooling. None of the parameters substituted for IQ produced a better fit, and Gordon concluded that the substituted parameters are simply manifestations of the higher-order abstraction we call intelligence. Gordon also points out that numerous studies have shown that the black IQ mean is about one standard deviation below the white mean and that black delinquency prevalence rates are approximately one standard deviation above white rates. He calls this fit between black–white differences in IQ and in delinquency–crime prevalence rates *IQ commensurability* (1986:35). (A similar argument could be made for the lower Asian delinquency and crime rates relative to those of whites given the Asian > white > black pattern of IQ means.)

Gordon uses IQ differences between races to explain differing rates of delinquency. In doing so, he neither asserts that the black–white IQ gap is the result of genetics or that the greater delinquency proneness of blacks is the result of any other characteristic alleged to be both innate and criminogenic. In asserting that his IQ-commensurability theory explains *between*-race prevalence, he is not denying that variables other than IQ may be more important in explaining crime–delinquency proneness *within* races. Given the greater range of environmental disabilities suffered by blacks, I suspect that IQ does a better job of predicting delinquency among whites than among blacks. I also suspect that family variables (to be discussed in Chapter 9) are at least as powerful as IQ in explaining between-race prevalence rates in crime and delinquency.

r/K THEORY AND CRIMINALITY

More controversial than the hypothesis that race differences in IQ account for race differences in crime rates is the assertion that racial populations aggregate at different points along the intraspecies r/K continuum such that Asians are more K-selected than whites, who are more K-selected than blacks (Ellis 1987a, 1989, 1990; Rushton 1988a, 1988b, 1990a; Lynn, 1990; Whitney, 1990). As indicated in Chapter 7, the r/K continuum is a component of an ecological theory representing the range of bioenergetic reproductive strategies that exist between species and probably within species. Recall that K-selection emphasizes parental effort and care and r-selection emphasizes mating effort and that these strategies covary with many heritable traits help-ful in the maintenance of the utilized strategy (Rushton, 1988a).

At the very least, the r/K concept is a heuristic device for characterizing patterns and traits having to do with reproduction in different environments. Because reproductive strategies carry with them a lot of baggage related posi-tively (e.g., aggression) or negatively (e.g., altruism) to criminal behavior, it was inevitable that some criminologists would become intrigued with it. Lee Ellis (1987a) appears to have been the first to apply r/K selection theory to the problem of criminality. Ellis showed that traits used to identify r-selec-tion were more typical of criminals than of noncriminals and that traits used to identify K-selection were more typical of noncriminals than of criminals. His review of hundreds of studies revealed that persons with serious delin-quent-criminal histories appeared to have the following six r-selected traits to a greater extent than persons in the general population: (1) shorter gesta-tion periods, (2) earlier onset of sexual activity, (3) greater sexual activity (or at least a preference for such) outside bonded relationships, (4) less stable bonding, (5) lower parental investment (high rates of abuse, neglect, and aban-donment of offspring), and (6) shorter life expectancy.

If criminals have been found to be higher on traits used to define r-selec-tion, and the black > white > Asian pattern of crime prevalence is consistently found, does it necessarily imply a black > white > Asian gradient on r-selec-tion? An examination of this question requires that evidence be collected on as many indicators of r- and K-selection as possible and then to rank-order the three populations by their mean scores on those indicators. Rushton sub-sumes at least twenty-six different traits under five higher-order concepts—intelligence, maturation rate, personality and temperament, reproductive efforts, and social organization. Included are traits in which socialization is heavily involved—such as achievement, sexuality, and social organization—and traits such as morphology, speed of physical maturation, and gamete pro-duction, in which social variables are involved minimally, if at all (Rushton, 1990a:316–317). If racial differences are random with respect to r/K indica-tors, then most research results will be null; and the remainder will be about equally split between negative and positive results. Reviews of the literature by both Ellis and Rushton have shown this has not been the case across the hundreds of studies that have examined these traits and characteristics in a variety of contexts and for a variety of purposes. There have been null results, but most have been positive and only one (body size [K-selection favors larger bodies]) has been negative—that is, Asian < white < black (Rushton, 1990).

The population differences on these indicators are not large, and there is considerable overlap, but they are demonstrably there. The r/K theorists have woven a network of meaning joining these diverse phenomena and their cor-relates that both orders the empirical data in ways consistent with gene-based evolutionary theory and makes assertions about origins of and predictions about behavior. The fact that scientists have long admired theories able to incorporate previously unrelated phenomena into a coherent explanatory scheme notwithstanding, many find Rushton's writings to be extremely objectionable; and he has many critics (e.g., Zuckerman & Brody, 1988; Leslie, 1990; Roberts & Gabor, 1990). His critics have attacked him on many grounds, including, of course, leveling charges of racism.[11] Substantive criticism generally centers around problems such as research design, definitions of race, the validity of various measures, and the applicability of r/K theory to within-species differences. These issues are much too involved to address here, but they have provided a very lively literature for those who enjoy intellectual warfare.

The real crux of the matter is the consistent black > white > Asian ordering on r-selected traits. None of the critics of this evolutionary line of thinking have supplied aggregate data indicating otherwise; so unless all measures of the relevant traits utilized in many hundreds of studies are hopelessly invalid, critics will have to come up with theories of their own to explain the observed gradient. Unless or until this occurs, it is incumbent on criminologists at least to view this theory as a useful heuristic and see where it takes them.

The argument is much like the race–IQ argument in more ways than one. We have seen that few scholars today deny that most of the variance *within* racial populations is attributable to genetics, but most decline to attribute the *between-group* variance solely to genetics. On the other hand, between-species differences on r/K traits must necessarily be due overwhelmingly to between-species genetic differences; but within-species differences on r/K traits may be more a function of environmentally contingent factors (Cunningham & Barbaree, 1991; Chisholm, 1993:18). Rushton (1991:126) is fully open to this, characterizing his model as a "mixed evolutionary/environmental" one that "fits the data better than any currently available purely genetic or purely environmental alternative." Elsewhere he writes, "Although genes provide the initial set point, environmental factors move individuals up or down the continuum of reproductive strategies" (1994:42).

The Sex Ratio and Crime

One of the major environmentally contingent factors is probably the sex ratio. As we have seen, the sex ratio influences mating strategies in a variety of species, including ours. When there is a significant excess of males, we see the emergence of mating tactics that behavioral ecologists characterize as the K strategy; and when there is a significant excess of females, the r strategy is likely to emerge. It was also noted that the sex ratio in the black community is particularly low and has been for decades; thus, it is not surprising that the r strategy might characterize that population more than it does populations with more balanced sex ratios.

This argument is consistent with the proposition that genes affect behavior facultatively and that r and K strategies within species are ecologically determined alternatives that have never been considered mutually exclusive

(Lovejoy, 1981; Barkow, 1991). The question begged here is whether environments of evolutionary adaptation might have differed sufficiently among the races to make them differentially responsive to roughly similar environments today as Rushton (1990b), Lynn (1990), and Whitney (1990) suggest. Interestingly, low sex ratios (more females than males) also appear to follow the black > white > Asian gradient, as do levels of gonadotropins in females (James, 1987; Lynn, 1990; Sieff, 1990), a factor that appears to be partially responsible for skewing the sex ratio in the direction of excess female births in the black population (James 1986, 1987).

The route from the sex ratio to crime and criminality is a meandering one. Because gender is the major individual-level predictor of crime and delinquency, at the macro level we should expect that populations with large numbers of crime-prone males relative to females should evidence higher rates of crime than populations with large numbers of females relative to males (Messner & Sampson, 1991). Messner and Sampson (1991:696) comment that it is paradoxical that research on this assumption has been conspicuously null and posit that the sex ratio might be related to a variable mediating the sex ratio–crime rate relationship in one direction and to another in the opposite direction.

In one direction, a high sex ratio means more males and thus more individuals at high risk for crime. But a high sex ratio is also associated with family stability and lower rates of illegitimacy because in a high sex ratio situation females hold the dyadic power and thus largely dictate that mating environment. A low sex ratio, on the other hand, means fewer males available to commit crimes, but it also signals a licentious environment in which males are reluctant to commit to one woman. This situation leads to high rates of illegitimacy and divorce, in short, to family disruption. Family disruption affects crime rates in many ways, most particular, to "unsupervised teenage peer groups" (Messner & Sampson, 1991:697). These two macro-level risk factors (fewer males, implying low crime levels, and a low sex ratio, signaling family disruption), Messner and Sampson hypothesize, cancel each other out.

Messner and Sampson tested their hypothesis separately for blacks and whites based on data from 171 cities in the United States with populations greater than 100,000. They first examined the effect of the sex ratio on the percentage of female-headed households in multiple regression models for blacks and whites. In the black model, the sex ratio was by far the most powerful of the eight predictors included in the model ($\beta = -0.60$); and in the white model (a population with a less skewed sex ratio) it was the third most powerful predictor (-0.29), behind per-capita income and welfare availability (Messner & Sampson, 1991:704). These results indicate that cities with low sex ratios are characterized by high rates of female-headed households and that cities characterized by high sex ratios are characterized by low rates of female-headed households.

Messner and Sampson then regressed nine variables, including percentage of female-headed housholds, on murder and robbery rates separately for blacks and whites. Percentage of female-headed households was the second most powerful predictor of murder rate ($\beta = 0.43$) behind region (non-West/West, $\beta = 0.51$) in the black model and second to population size (0.39) in the white model. Similar results were reported for robbery rates (Messner & Sampson, 1991:706–707). These results suggest that the sex ratio may be one of the most powerful indirect predictors of crime rates available to criminologists. A low ratio leads to the dominance of the male r strategy over the female K strategy and to all the negative consequences that dominance implies.

Testosterone and the r Strategy

This still leaves us with the task of identifying possible biological mechanisms that are facilitative of reproductive effort and which, as "side effects," are also facilitative of criminal activity in some environments. Aggression is a trait which was very useful for males in the pursuit of mating opportunities in our ancestral environments and perhaps still is in some modern environments. Aggressiveness, in conjunction with other traits such as low self-control, is conducive to violence (Buikhuisen, 1987; Huesmann, Eron, & Yarmel, 1988; Kandel et al., 1988); and testosterone is the great facilitator of aggression.

Lynn (1990:1203) considers testosterone levels to be the primary biochemical mechanism that "might underlie the racial differences which Rushton has documented." Indexing prostatic cancer (which is positively related to testosterone) as his measure, Lynn examined age-standardized rates of the disease among the three races residing in a number of American cities. He found that blacks had about twice the rate of whites, who had about twice the rate of Asians. In another study, Rose, Bernstein, Judd, Hanisch, Pike, and Henderson (1986) directly assayed testosterone levels among 100 college males and found that blacks had 19 percent more than whites. A more representative study (Ellis & Nyborg, 1992) assayed a sample of over 4,000 males and found blacks to have 3.3 percent more testosterone than whites but also that a small number (34) of Asian/Pacific Islanders had the highest level of all. However, Native Americans (n = 49), who are also considered "Mongoloids," had the lowest testosterone level. Unfortunately, neither study considered testosterone/SHBG ratios. Despite a degree of ambiguity, then, testosterone levels appear to follow the black > white > Asian gradient predicted by r/K theory.[12]

There is no doubt that the use of r/K selection theory to explain racial differences in crime has potential for misuse; and as such, those who favor it must bear the burden of supplying more and better support for it. As with the concept of the atom among physicists 100 years or so ago, criminologists might be arguing for a long time whether r/K theory represents something "real" for them or whether it is merely a useful idea enabling them to order diverse data. It may well turn out to be neither, but we will never know if critics concentrate on its unpalatability and fail to concentrate on its substance, particularly its ability to account for the overall pattern of correlated variables.

Even one of Rushton's critics (Lynn, 1989:5) admits that "it would take a variety of environmental factors to explain all of the racial differences [that r/K theory] parsimoniously accounts for." Another critic (Mealey, 1990:387) arrives at a conclusion that I endorse when she writes, "All in all, I find the pattern that Rushton presents interesting and worth pursuing."

I also agree with many of Rushton's critics that racists may find his theory congenial and misuse it for their own ends. Misuse of knowledge should be opposed when and where it is misused, but knowledge should not be denied the light of day or pushed back under the rug once exposed because it may be abused. As Vila (1994:329) remarked, "Findings can only be used for racist or eugenic ends only if we allow perpetuation of the ignorance that underpins these arguments." Population variation on numerous traits exists regardless of whether we "discover" and attempt to explain it. To oppose research because racists might misuse it is to give them the power of censorship, and to desist from such research because of possible adverse personal consequences is to default timidly to ideologues.

Not to address the problem of black crime forthrightly is to do a great disservice to the black community, for the great majority of victims of black crime are other blacks. To try to hide or excuse the problem is to feed the tendency among many whites to judge all blacks by the standards of their least-worthy members. Decent blacks resent such an unjust characterization, and rightly so. Most blacks do not commit crimes; nor do they, unlike many white criminologists, support excuses for those who do. In many ways, the black community, on average, may be more conservative than the white community in their attitudes toward criminals, both in terms of punitiveness and in terms of their dismissal of exculpatory rhetoric (Kemp, 1994).

CONCLUSION

This chapter has explored individual differences as they apply to crime (among which categories of people is it most likely to occur, and at what age) and to criminality (what characteristics are most likely to lead individuals within those categories to commit criminal acts). The biosocial approach is particularly useful in differentiating between what Moffitt (1993) calls *adolescent-limited* and *life-course persistent* offenders. Life-course persistent offenders, although a small minority of all offenders, commit the majority of serious street crimes, as well as much of the lower-level white-collar crime. We need to understand the criminality of these offenders at multiple levels and not continue to limit the analysis to social structural variables, which has contributed little to this endeavor. It is time to approach the problem from a different angle—one that locates the causes of criminality within those who commit the crimes.

Perhaps a biosocial model of criminality will fare no better than traditional criminology in terms of providing direction for policymakers. Such provisions are not the reason that science is usually done; intellectual curiosity is reason enough. The biosocial approach goes beyond the macro approaches of the past that targeted "strain," "peer groups," "racism," "social class," "urbanism," "subcultures," and so forth to try to determine the mechanisms by which these alleged causes produce their effects. However, just as I believe that any examination of criminality that does not include neurohormonal factors is inherently incomplete, any examination of neurohormonal factors that ignores environmental factors is likewise incomplete. In this "decade of the brain," and with genetic knowledge increasing almost exponentially, criminologists have an unprecedented opportunity to join other scientists in rigorous biosocial analyses of the causes of criminality. If criminologists pass up the opportunity, the torch will be passed to other disciplines; the study of crime is too important to remain mired in premodern science.

NOTES

1. Durkheim (1982:106) was careful to distinguish between social facts and biological and psychological facts, and between crime and criminality: "From the fact that crime is a phenomenon of normal sociology, it does not follow that the criminal is an individual normally constituted from the biological and psychological points of view."

2. Gottfredson and Hirschi (1990:88) eschew the concept of criminality because "It suggests that people differ to the extent to which they are compelled to crime." The concept of criminality suggests no such thing to me, nor probably to the majority of criminologists. Nevertheless, Gottfredson and Hirschi (1990:88) wish to substitute the concept of self-control because this concept "suggests that people differ in which they are restrained from criminal act." Surely "criminality," stripped of the compulsive properties Gottfredson and Hirschi have imbued it with, more fully and accurately describes the phenomenon of frequent law breaking than does "self-control," although low self-control is a very large component of criminality.

3. Differential IQ also helps us to understand the underlying mechanisms of one of criminology's most revered theories. Rowe and Osgood (1984) showed that many of the principles of differentially association theory were underpinned by differential IQ. They found a correlation of 0.51 between self-reported delinquency and association with delinquent peers among 265 pairs of twins. This respectable correlation should not surprise—the concept of active CE correlation informs us that people tend to do what they enjoy in the company of the like-minded. Rowe and Osgood's data allowed them to decompose the correlation into genetic (61%), common environment (23%), and specific environment (16%) components. The genetic component centered around IQ: "When twin partners have different IQs, they can be expected to have dissimilar rates of delinquency and dissimilar degrees of association with delinquent peers" (1984:537). This selective aggregation process, however, may not apply in environments of greater population density where "good" and "bad" kids occupy the same streets and buildings. In such environments, companion choice is a luxury unavailable to most children (Stark, 1987:896).

4. Another problem of the same general sort exists when pooling IQ scores of childhood-onset delinquents with adolescence-onset offenders (Moffitt, 1993:629). Comparing adolescent-onset and childhood-onset delinquents with nondelinquents on

IQ, Moffitt found one-point and seventeen-point mean deficits, respectively. Similarly, Stattin and Klackenberg-Larsson's (1993:372) longitudinal study of children in which IQs were assessed every two or three years found that nonoffenders and sporadic offenders did not differ significantly on IQ but that nonoffenders and frequent offenders did.

5. The "active ingredient" in P > V discrepancy appears to be elevated PIQ scores rather than significantly depressed VIQ scores. Determination of the active ingredient is usually made by dividing samples at the median of the P > V distribution and then conducting t-tests on VIQ and PIQ. Although the "high" P > V group VIQ mean will probably be significantly lower than the "low" P > V group VIQ mean, the difference between the two groups on PIQ more strongly distinguishes them.

6. Abnormal levels of androgens (or unusual sensitivity to them) during fetal life may delay development of the left hemisphere, thus leading to cerebral imbalance made manifest by a P > V profile. Cerebral profiles of the various cytogenetic intersex anomalies appear to support this contention (Tallal, 1991).

7. Both these studies point to problems inherent in relying on additive models, that is, the assumption that predictor variables have constant effects across all groups. Few multivariate studies evidence any effort to check for interaction effects, most simply reporting "main effects." This may sometimes result in serious distortions of the data by hiding important and interesting interaction effects.

8. There is a disturbing tendency to tar with the same racist brush everyone from rabid Ku Klux Klan (KKK) members to researchers reporting findings unfavorable to races other than their own. Robert Hughes (1993:19–20) writes that you can be called racist "for saying the simple truth that the Rev. Al Sharpton hoaxed New York with the entirely concocted abuse of the black teenager Tawana Brawley by imaginary white goons; or for having doubts about the efficacy of welfare; or, in some minds, merely by virtue of being white." Thus, we minimize and dilute the insidious nature of true racism by applying the same term to any utterance, regardless of its truth or falsity, that may have an upsetting effect on the hypersensitive. Some authors even go so far as to define racism as something only whites can be guilty of (Rothenberg, 1988:6). I define "true" racism as asserting consequential difference among races that are not supported by the evidence and then claiming racial superiority on the basis of those unproven differences.

9. Of course, aggregate national data such as these hide a plethora of contradicting factors; and the dangers of inferring individual characteristics from aggregate data are well known (the "ecological fallacy"). African-Americans *in general* may have realized a number of socioeconomic gains, but those who have made the gains are not necessarily those who are committing the crimes.

10. Jared Taylor offers many reasons for his belief that Asians have suffered as much as blacks in this country. Many Chinese coolies were bought and sold and were worked like slaves, were legally denied the rights and privileges of citizenship until 1943 (blacks were given it in 1870), and suffered many other disabilities that could have led to the same negative consequences so rife in the black community. Instead, Chinese and other Asian groups are overrepresented in the higher-income brackets in the United States and in the entrepreneurial, scholarly, and professional occupations (Taylor, 1992:Chapter 3).

11. Charges of racism would carry more weight if Rushton, Ellis, and others who believe the r/K model to be a useful heuristic for examining and ordering otherwise seemingly unconnected phenomena, were members of the favored "Mongoloid" race.

The Leslie (1990) article is the worst display of vituperative character assassination that I have ever read in a scholarly journal. Anyone wishing to assess the depth of feeling surrounding this issue will benefit from reading it.

12. Given the environmental effects on testosterone levels (Chapter 4), it may well be that the sexual opportunities available to black males due to the low sex ratio in that population may account for at least some of the difference between black and white male testosterone levels.

Chapter 9

Love, Marriage, and the Family

> A mother cradling her child, bent over in a posture of loving solicitude:
> If there is another image that will immediately be recognized by human
> beings of any age or culture and arouse in them comparable feelings of
> identification, we cannot think what it could be.
>
> —Brigitte and Peter Berger

The family is the basic unit of any society; it produces its new members and socializes them in its ways. Marriage is a legal contract conferring society's blessing on the reproductive couple and signifying the couple's pledge of fidelity to one another. Although there have been and are a myriad of marriage forms and motivations for marriage in different cultures and in different times, when not constrained by economic, political, or social considerations, the primeval motivation is love between man and woman. We have been fashioned by natural selection to pair-bond, and the epoxy of that bond is love.

There is something of a crisis in the nuclear family that concerns those who value it, but it is too rooted in human nature not to remain the predominant family form in the Western world and in much of the rest of the world also. Adjustments have been made to the nuclear family over the years, and others will be made according to environmental contingencies. Mating and parental patterns in all animal species have always been dependent on the interrelationships between organisms and their environments, with the general pattern being set by the ecology existing in their environments of evolutionary adaptation (Rees & Harvey, 1991).

No naïve claims are made that there are genes coding for a particular form of family system. Family forms and marriage patterns are cultural, with the dominant forms and patterns presumably offering the "best fits" with a particular culture's prevailing socioecology. However, a confluence of evidence strongly supports the thesis that the nuclear-family triad of man, woman, and offspring evolved from the ecological challenges to reproductive fitness faced by our hominid ancestors; and that it is still the most useful solution to the same challenges in the great majority of today's social ecologies.

THE EVOLUTION OF HUMAN PAIR-BONDING

In Chapter 4, we saw emotions described as "social energy" (Collins, 1984) and as "social glue" (Averill, 1992). The emotion that more than any other fully captures the essence of these descriptions is love. Love may be just as fundamental to the social organization patterns of *Homo sapiens* as the very sapience that gives our species its name. Human social organization may have taken a very different turn were it not for the evolution of what scientists call pair-bonding and which the more romantic among us call love. Indeed, there is evidence that the human species may not have remained viable were it not for the evolution of love (Mellen, 1981). As Hendrick and Hendrick (1991:211) argue, the whole thrust of evolutionary thinking "suggests that love is a crucial factor in human evolution."

Any scenario designed to account for the evolutionary origin and purpose of some species trait or characteristic is ultimately unverifiable, all the more so when we are speaking of the evolution of emotions, because they do not leave fossils behind. We can, however, muster evidence in support of a plausible scenario that corresponds with known data, fits those data into propositions which are internally consistent, and provides guidance for further exploration. The data for human evolutionary scenarios "include the fossil record of human evolution, non-human primate behaviour, and the present behavioural and morphological characteristics of our species" (Barkow, 1991:327).

There are a number of overlapping scenarios trying to account for human pair-bonding and the subsequent emergence of human social organization. Although all recent scenarios view human sexuality as the evolutionary foundation of human society, I rely primarily on C. Owen Lovejoy's (1981, 1984) provisioning–monogamy scenario as my framework. Lovejoy (1981:341) wrote in his influential *Science* article, "Evidence provided by the fossil record, primate behavior, and demographic analysis shows that the traditional view that early human evolution was a direct consequence of brain expansion and material culture is incorrect, and that the unique sexual and reproductive behavior of man may be the sine qua non of human origin." When all is said and done, successful evolution is measured by successful reproduction.

Lovejoy points out that the primate fossil record reveals an obvious trend toward an increasingly more K-selected reproductive strategy among the ancestors of modern primates, meaning that more and more human resources were being invested in child care. A strong bond between mother and offspring usually assures this investment and thus increases offspring survivability. Infant care comes with a price to be paid by the caregiver, so there is a tradeoff between the survivability of the infant and the survivability of the mother.

Infant mortality within many primate species is around 40 percent (Lovejoy, 1981:348). When we consider that the modern human infant mortality rate in even the most deprived of Third World countries is around 15 percent, and that it is under 1 percent in most developed nations (Hess, Markson, & Stein, 1988:501), this is truly a remarkably high figure. Although the chimpanzee mother–infant bond is "almost as lengthy and intense as that among humans" (P. Wilson, 1980:63), the inadequacy of the mother–infant bond and injuries caused by falling from the mother are major contributors to the high infant death rate (Lovejoy, 1981:344). Although chimpanzees are highly K-selected relative to other animals, an intensification of the mother–infant bond would make for a more viable species.

Thwarting strong selection pressures for further intensification are the reproductive (promiscuous) and feeding (self-provisioning) strategies of chimpanzees. Time spent in oversolicitous care of infants is time lost by mothers, who, in a species characterized by limited food sharing, must forage for themselves. The most common kind of food sharing among chimpanzees is in the form of "tolerated scrounging" by an offspring from its mother, with some male sharing with adult females when the females are in estrus. Food sharing is only well developed among monogamous primate species; and as is the case among the great majority of animal species, chimp parenting is an all-female affair (Clutton-Brock, 1991). Males in most primate species invest almost all their energy in determining dominance hierarchies, seeking mating opportunities, or feeding.

Evidence derived from paleontological demography suggests that hominid infant mortality during the Plio-Pleistocene period was even higher (estimated range of between 53 and 65 percent) than those of modern nonhuman primates (Mellen, 1981:141). Such a mortality rate suggests that early hominids (*Australopithecus afarensis, Homo habilis,* and *Homo erectus*) faced challenges to species survival more serious than those facing most modern primate species. A major challenge to maternal survival (and thus infant survival) during this period must have been the cephalopelvic disproportion problem discussed in Chapter 3.

Males are obviously a great untapped source of reproductive energy among many primate species. *Homo sapiens* is a successful species primarily because it was able to tap this energy source. Lovejoy (1984:28) suggests that the evidence favors the hypothesis that the major adaptive advantage of hominid bipedalism was that it allowed males to provision "sexually faithful females and their young." It would be a mistake, however, to view bipedalism as being selected "for" the resolution of one environmental challenge rather than as the result of a complex and holistic set of environmental changes and earlier behavioral and morphological adaptations. Being the quintessential "generalized" species (i.e., a species adaptable to almost any environment rather than to a narrow range of ecological niches), human uprightness and bipedalism seem to be the physical features best suited to exploit the widest range of environments.

Lovejoy thus ties feeding and reproductive strategies with the origin of biparental care among hominids. The relationship between mating and parenting patterns across the spectrum of avian and mammalian species is fairly straightforward: Female-only parenting is associated with polygynous mating systems; male-only parenting is not found among mammals (except among humans in atypical situations), and when it is found among birds, it is associated with monogamy or polyandry. Biparental care in avian and mammalian species is associated with monogamy (Clutton-Brock, 1991:152).

The scenario for the beginning of human male involvement in parenting takes place during the late Miocene–early Pliocene period when climactic changes caused the resource-rich rain forests to recede and the grassy, resource-limited savanna to expand. Obtaining food became more problematic and would have posed a particular, and potentially deadly, hardship for pregnant and lactating, self-provisioning females. The overarching adaptive challenge to be solved by these early hominoids and hominids was the provisioning of females and the young. Bipedal locomotion was one of the anatomical features that helped them meet this challenge. Bipedalism is an awkward and inefficient means of locomotion, but its major advantage is that it frees the hands. With free hands, food can be carried long distances from where it is killed or found and shared with females and the young. There is ample paleoanthropological evidence from many sites to suggest that sharing was fairly well established among our earliest ancestors (Shipman, 1986).

This scenario does not ignore evidence that meat constituted only about 20 percent of the hominid diet or that women gathered the bulk of the remainder of the diet (Potts, 1984). The focus of concern in Lovejoy's scenario is the provisioning of lactating or pregnant females who, now being relatively free of the necessity to forage for themselves during their most vulnerable periods, were better able to lavish more care on their young. Selection pressures for the intensification of the mother–infant bond could now proceed without the diverting concerns of maternal feeding. A division of labor could also develop in which mothers contributed to the male–female–child triad by gathering food located in familiar areas close to home, thus reducing risks to themselves and their offspring from predators while their mates hunted, gathered, and scavenged further afield.

What would induce our male ancestors to share food with females and their offspring rather than eating it where they found it, as most primates do today? Male provisioning of females, if this scenario is correct, contributed enormously to the survival of the hominid species; but natural selection works on individual genotypes, not on species.[1] Thus, food provisioning must have conferred a major reproductive advantage on specific males who selectively practiced it. However, the genes of males of any species are not candidates for selection if they contribute to the survival of offspring carrying another male's genes. Food provisioning would not have been selected for if males shared food with females and their offspring indiscriminately. It could only be selected for if the provisioned female was impregnated by the provisioning male.

If food provisioning was to become firmly entrenched in the behavioral repertoire of the species, both sexes required assurances of biological fidelity—males should provision only one female, and females should copulate with only one male (Lovejoy, 1984:30). Males and females who were faithful to this requirement had greater-than-average success in passing on their genes. Exceptions to this rule are permitted by the scenario; but fidelity, practiced by most of the actors in this drama most of the time, is required by the logic of natural selection.

Lovejoy's assertion of the need for monogamous bonding leads him to explore the role of the human loss of estrus. In promiscuous or polygynous mating systems, females in estrus are lavished with male attention, garnishing them extra food from their suitors and the genes of the most dominant males (Fisher, 1992:135). Overt ovulatory signals contribute to the reproductive success of females by attracting the "best genes" to them at the time they are most likely to conceive. Dominant males are likewise favored by ovulation signs because they point the way to mating partners currently offering them the best opportunity to push their genes into the future.

Concealed ovulation does not offer similar reproductive advantages for either males or females of species practicing communal or promiscuous mating and could only have been selected for *after* our ancestors no longer practiced it; otherwise, it would not be selected for (Smith, 1984).[2] This poses something of a "chicken-or-egg" dilemma for Lovejoy's scenario, but it should not overly concern us here. We know that evolutionary vectors sometimes conflict, and the intersection of the survival vector (selection for bipedalism) and the reproduction vector (selection against any variant deemphasizing overt signs of ovulation) may be another example of such conflict. Perhaps bipedalism and estrus loss were part of a holistic evolutionary "package" that included expanding brain size as part of strong selection for neoteny in the human species (Gould, 1977; Montagu, 1981; Feder & Park, 1989).[3]

Whatever the case may be, concealed ovulation, Lovejoy claims, discourages male cheating (which is otherwise under strong selection). Only frequent copulation with the same female over the length of her cycle will lead to a high probability of paternity. This strategy results in about the same probability of paternity as "complete promiscuity" (Lovejoy, 1981:211). Frequent copulations with the same female tends to cement the pair-bond via the development of emotional attachments; and with a roughly 1:1 sex ratio, it distributes copulation and reproduction opportunities more evenly among all males (reproduction opportunities are about equal for all females regardless of the mating system of a species). A fairly equal distribution means greater variability in the gene pool for natural selection to work on, which is an obvious evolutionary plus for any sexually reproducing population (Reynolds, 1991:63).

The emotional attachments that accrue from frequent copulations with the same woman is an important part of Lovejoy's scenario. Since human females are constantly sexually receptive, Lovejoy claims that far from having lost the external indicators of receptiveness, they display them all the time. Alone among the primates, humans display epigamic traits that are sex dependent (e.g., permanently enlarged breasts, hairless face, large rounded buttocks, everted lips) but not directly involved in the reproductive process (Lovejoy, 1984:30). Assuming that natural selection for bipedalism was taking place in concert with selection for loss of estrus, sight would have largely replaced smell as the impetus to mate, with youth and beauty offering the only readily recognizable signs of female fertility. These epigamic features facilitate sexual attraction over the female's entire cycle rather than confining it to her ovulatory period (Szalay & Costello, 1991). Sexual attraction would occasionally translate into an emotional closeness, especially if a couple enjoyed frequent copulations, leading to a pair-bond that would exist at least long enough to raise offspring to reproductive age.

Lovejoy (1981:348) views human pair-bonding as the beginning of the nuclear family, which he saw as a "prodigious adaptation central to the success of early hominids." Unlike earlier scenarios, Lovejoy's posits that material culture and the Pleistocene acceleration of brain development followed, rather than preceded, the hominid character system he describes. Thus, to the extent that Lovejoy's scenario is accurate, the tremendous importance of love in its many forms to the physical and mental health of human beings is anchored in millions of years of evolution. He is saying that humans are what they are because our distant ancestors learned to love. We are also what we are because we have culture and are intelligent, but love came first and made both possible. The doubling of mean cranial capacity from *Australopithecus* to *Homo erectus* (Bromage, 1987) meant a greater and greater degree of infant altriciality, which had to mean more intense selection pressure for stronger and more enduring mother–infant and adult male–female bonds.

Although Lovejoy's scenario has been criticized on specific points, his general proposition has found wide support (Foley & Lee, 1989; MacDonald, 1992). Evolution favored male–female bonds not for the emotional pleasure of adults per se—although such pleasure constitutes the actors' motivation and reinforcement—but rather because bonded males and females constituted a complementary pair with the mutually important goal of raising their offspring. "The function of attachment between adult lovers may be primarily to increase the likelihood of parental health, stability, and investment in offspring" (Shaver, Hazan, & Bradshaw, 1988:94). Those ancient hominids who did the better job of parenting were more reproductively successful, on average, than those who did not. Thus, the gene products that are the proximate causes (relative to evolutionary causes) of strong and stable bonding were passed on over the generations.

PROXIMATE MECHANISMS IN THE
EVOLUTION OF PARENTAL LOVE

Lovejoy's scenario extends over millions of years, during which time many biophysiological mechanisms for the intensification of mothering and for male–female emotional involvement were tried, added to, or discarded. These mechanisms need not have been selected "for" maternal intensification, that is, explicitly designed by natural selection to serve this particular function. This is equally true for the mechanisms underlying male–female bonding. Nature is parsimonious; it often makes one biological system or substance serve a variety of tasks. For intensification of the sexual or nurturant emotions, any biophysiological system that associated with feelings of joy or satisfaction, in whatever sense, could have been pressed into service.

The two kinds of affective bonds in Lovejoy's scenario are mother–infant and male–female. They are both quite similar, and quite different, from one another. They both involve an active concern for the well-being of another, but they also involve different motivational systems and goals. The mother–infant bond is primary and more primitive. Mother–infant bonds had to exist in prehominid times, albeit in less intensive forms; but prehominid mating was probably bereft of emotional involvement. Unlike male–female love, mother–infant love must be unconditional, for the infant is incapable of meeting any conditions, and it must be maintained among humans for much longer periods than among other primates due to the longer period of human dependency. Male–female love is very much conditional, and biologically speaking need not be maintained past a point where offspring survival is unproblematic.

For the sake of clarification, I will refer to mother–infant love as *attachment*, and male–female love as *attraction*. Attachment and attraction are not mutually exclusive, but they do seem to be facilitated by different neuropharmacologies. Because there are many forms of attachment, even dysfunctional forms, I limit my meaning of attachment to be similar to MacDonald's (1992:753) concept of *warmth*, which he defines as "a [biological] reward system which evolved to facilitate cohesive family relationships and parental investment in children." Panksepp (1992:559) augments MacDonald in viewing all kinds of human affective experience as emerging "from ancient neuro-symbolic systems of the mammalian brain that unconditionally promote survival."

The physiology of love, attraction or attachment, is poorly understood. Much of our knowledge about the importance of attachment for the normal development of primate infants has come from a variety of maternal-deprivation studies which point to consequences but say little about what the psychoneurohormonal mechanisms are that demand the formation of affectual bonds. Whatever the mechanisms may be, they will not be simple ones. They will be dependent on the permutation of several factors, probably organized by the birthing process itself, and then consolidated by mother–infant contact and interaction during the immediate postpartum period (Rossi 1984, 1987).[4]

A major candidate for such a mechanism is oxytocin, a neuropeptide syn-thesized in the hypothalamus (Insel, 1992; Svensson, 1992). Oxytocin is typi-cally synthesized in response to the birthing process, infant distress, breast feeding, and sexual behavior. A number of studies among a variety of mam-malian species have shown that administering exogenous oxytocin increases maternal behavior and that administering oxytocin antagonists reduces it (Insel, 1992). The process of breast feeding in the new mother, for instance, combines the panoply of sight, sound, smell, touch, and the tangible evidence in her arms that affirms her womanhood to stimulate the release of oxytocin, which intensifies the feelings that released it. As Montagu (1978:63) explains, "Physiologically, the nursing of her babe at her breast produces in the mother an intensification of her motherliness, the pleasurable care of her child. Psy-chologically, this intensification serves further to consolidate the symbiotic bond between herself and her child."

Love is more than a warm feeling; it is also a heightened sensitivity to its love object. The oxytocin (and perhaps other neuropeptides) released by breast feeding is related to reduced sensitivity to environmental stressors, which allows for greater sensitivity to the infant. Significant differences have been found in physiological responses to their infants among new mothers who were and were not breast feeding. Lactating mothers show significantly fewer stress responses to infant stimuli—determined by skin conductance and cardiac-response measures—than nonlactating mothers and show signifi-cantly greater desire to pick up their infants in response to all infant-presented stimuli (Weisenfeld, Malatesta, Whitman, Granrose, & Uili, 1985).

The neural distribution of oxytocin receptors appears to depend on the so-cial-organization patterns of the species being studied. For instance, prairie voles (small rodents) follow a monogamous mating system in which males and females share a nest and show high levels of parental care, while mon-tane voles, a closely related species, follow a polygynous mating system with no nest sharing and very little maternal investment. Maternal behavior in the montane vole only appears in the postpartum period, when there is a tempo-rary increase in oxytocin receptors. Prairie vole mothers, who are parental throughout their lives, maintain high concentrations of oxytocin receptors at all times (Shapiro & Insel, 1991; Insel, 1992).

Oxytocin may even have the effect of decreasing care-inhibiting testoster-one in new fathers in monogamous rodent species. Testosterone is respon-sible for significant sexual dimorphism in the medial preoptic area (MPOA), an area of the hypothalamus important in the control of maternal behavior in mammals. New fathers in one biparental rodent species (*Peromyscus californ-icus*) undergo changes in the MPOA that render it more anatomically similar to the female MPOA than to the same area in virgin males (Gubernick, Senge-laub, & Kurz, 1993). These findings do not mean that an analogous process occurs among human fathers or even among other biparental species. What they do mean is that natural selection works on mechanisms important to parenting in males to the degree that their participation in parenting (as a legacy of reproductive challenges faced by their ancestors in environments of evolutionary adaptation) is required to raise offspring to reproductive maturity. In this particular species, fathers are as parental as mothers, which is extremely rare among mammals (Gubernick, Sengelaub, & Kurz, 1993:200).

Proximate Mechanisms in the Evolution of Sexual Love

Unlike human sexuality, sexuality among nonhuman animals is almost entirely biologically determined by the ovulatory signals of the female. When these signals subside, so typically does the male's interest in the female. Although nonreproductive copulation does take place among some primate species with regularity, most animal mating is little more than a mechanistic reproductive dance, shorn of emotional intensity, and with very little indication that any pleasure is derived from the few seconds of intromission it takes them to ejaculate.[5] While humans can and do separate sex from that particular form of emotional intensity we call love, few of us would deny that sex with love is far more satisfying than the grunting urgency of casual copulation.

Bipedal hominids with forward-facing genitals evolved the practice of frontal intercourse, the preferred copulatory position in most cultures (Fisher, 1992:182). Frontal intercourse involves more skin contact than the general primate method of seizing the female from behind and staring off into space. Because of the intimate connection between the skin and the brain, human "naked apes" find tactile stimulation most pleasurable. We may assume that for our early ancestors frontal intercourse began more and more to recall the pleasures lovers once found in their mother's arms. The sucking of the lover's breasts, the warmth of skin contact, eye gazing and nose nuzzling, and the feeling that all is right with the world evoke deep unconscious memories of the mother–infant bond. Frontal intercourse mimicked and capitalized on the primary mother–infant bond, and elevated the sexual drive above simple genital pleasure. Nature has emotionally enriched the human reproductive impulse with love; and in doing so, it has immensely increased our enjoyment of both.

Frontal intercourse involves more of the human senses than are involved in the impersonality of belly–buttocks coupling. Evolving intellect and language skills enabled lovers to "know" each other by translating their physical and visual pleasures into words and to name each other. He or she is no longer simply a set of swollen genitals that look and smell like every other set but a unique individual capable of capturing and holding the imagination. This imagination no doubt allowed our ancestors, as it allows us, to replay previous sexual encounters with their lovers, to anticipate future ones, and to come to value sexual intercourse as the ultimate celebration of love. We might say that when emotionally involved men and women are making love, they are literally making (i.e., "creating") love.

At a biological level, romantic love—"attraction"—is a proprioceptive stimulus released by one or more encounters with a person whose unique characteristics have an anabolic effect on the hypothalamic–pituitary–gonadal axis.

Although mother love and sexual love have a great many differences, both involve the same axis for neurohormonal facilitation. In the long process of selection for pair-bonds, it was the male that nature had to capture in love. The female neurohormonal system was already equipped with mechanisms of infant attachment that could be co-opted for attachment to adult males. Nascent feelings of sexual love in males could build on memories of their early attachment to their mothers, which they could transfer to other females who, like their mothers, made them "feel good." Oxytocin is apparently the peptide that facilitates the feeling of sexual fulfillment and quiescence following orgasm (Fisher, 1992:340). The nude cuddling and nuzzling of our lovers is so physiologically similar to mother–infant interaction that it is reasonable to hypothesize that it would have been seized upon to also function as a releaser of attachment-facilitating oxytocin in adult lovers (in both cases, it stimulates nipple erection and uterine contractions).

Beyond the fleeting physical pleasures of sexual intercourse, how is it that the opposite sex makes us "feel good"? Being in love requires complex interactions of the cognitive and emotional centers of the brain as one analyzes and interprets feelings, images, thoughts, and social expectations, all of which arouse us to a kind of biological revolution. When this intensely exciting state strikes us, we become different people. Our perceptions are drastically altered, the loved one becomes the center of our universe, the whole world seems to be a better place, we smile at strangers, and we search for superlatives to describe the beloved. Sheer euphoria overcomes us; we feel more attractive, optimistic, and competent; we feel boundless energy; and we have less need for food, sleep, or for other pleasurable diversions.

This all sounds very much like a drug-induced high; and according to some authorities, that is what it is (Liebowitz, 1983; Sabelli, Fahrer, Medina, & Fragola, 1994). Stimulant drugs such as cocaine and the amphetamines have much the same effect as love's natural high. Whether we fall in love or take a stimulant drug, the upshot is increased limbic system activity in the form of increased neurotransmitter activity and neuroreceptor sensitivity. As MacDonald (1992) reminded us earlier, nature has chemically wired us to feel good when we do things that encourage reproductive success: the opiates that keep us safely attached as youngsters, and the stimulants that excite us when we experience sexual attraction as adults.

The primary action of the amphetamines is to prompt the release of the excitatory catecholamine neurotransmitters such as dopamine and norepinephrine and blocking their reuptake at synaptic terminals (Cloninger, 1986:209). The stimulant substance that probably mediates our experience of romantic love may be a naturally occurring, amphetamine-like, and mildly hallucinogenic substance called phenylethylamine (PEA) (Liebowitz, 1983). There is certainly enough clinical evidence that show PEA levels to be related to the ups and downs of romantic relationships and that treating "love addicts" and the lovesick with MAO inhibitors (thus retarding the breakdown of PEA) generally works (Liebowitz, 1983; Sabelli, Fahrer, Medina, & Fragola, 1994).

We have arrived at a point in which the human species, going back at least as far as *Homo habilis*, is characterized by two fundamental biological bonds: the mother–infant and the male–female bond. The mother–infant bond is paramount, the emotional male–female sexual relationship being arguably epiphenomenal to the primary bond. A third bond—that between father and offspring—is needed to complete the human relationship circle.

Most primate fathers are unable to identify their offspring, let alone form a bonded relationship with them (P. Wilson, 1980:48). Unlike the primarily mother–infant and adult male–female relationships, the father–offspring relationship is probably entirely cultural and is only possible by virtue of their common connection to the mother. If the human male was to contribute something to the species other than stud service, the species had to become sufficiently intelligent to recognize and grasp the abstract concept of *relationship*. With the ability to grasp such a concept came the integration of the two biological bonds (mother–infant and man–woman) with the cultural fatherhood bond. The result of the fusion of these basic bonds is the family, which served as a template for the evolution of ever more complex human relationships and bonds—kinship, clan, tribe, and on to society itself.

THE FAMILY AND MARRIAGE

For Peter Wilson (1980) the nuclear family is an evolutionary adaptation in the sense that hominids with the tendency to form them raised more offspring to sexual maturity, thus passing the tendency on. Lancaster and Lancaster (1987:188) see the nuclear family as a "specialized and very basic adaptation that greatly extended the investment parents could make in their offspring, especially furthering the survivorship of juveniles." All animals have social living arrangements that are species normal; the mother–father–offspring family is as normal and "natural" for humans as any of the other myriad social arrangements in the animal kingdom are for other animals.

Homo sapiens may be a pair-bonding species, but it is imperfectly so. The combination of permanently receptive females and ever-ready males has the potential for generating chaos in any social group without some form of control over who has legitimate sexual access to whom (Parker, 1987). After pair-bonding was well established in the human species, the next step in social evolution was probably to grant it the blessing of the larger social group by formally sanctifying it in marriage. Socially, marriage is more than a ceremony honoring the lovestruck; it is a mutual-aid contract that goes beyond the obligations that males and females owe to one another. Their obligations extend to their respective kin groups, their society, and most important, to their offspring. The contractual nature of marriage is perhaps, in part, a recognition that the mother–infant bond must be protected from the fragility of the male–female bond. No known human society has neglected to recognize the importance of the sexual pair-bond or neglected to set down rules governing it.

Cultural relativists will correctly point out that the majority of human cultures are polygynous, not monogamous. In Murdock's *Ethnographic Atlas* (1967) of 849 human cultures, it was shown that 709 (83.5%) of them were polygynous, 137 (16.1%) were monogamous, and 4 (0.047%) were polyandrous. These data do not in the least contradict the human propensity to pair-bond and reveal more about evolved male appetites for extrapair sex than about human pair-bonding propensities. Males of all species have generally been able to increase their fitness by increasing their number of mating partners, biparental care notwithstanding. Thus, when human males have the resources to marry polygynously, and their culture allows for it, many will do so. But because of either cultural proscriptions or lack of resources, most males do not. While it is true that most *cultures* in the world are polygynous, by far the most *marriages*, even within cultures allowing for polygyny, are monogamous (Wilson & Daly, 1992:309).

The various alternatives to monogamous marriage deserve a brief discussion because they do help to illuminate the sensitivity of reproductive patterns to socioecological conditions. Historical and anthropological evidence clearly shows that polygyny occurs mainly in the middle ranges of societal complexity—that is, in the agricultural stage between primitive hunting and gathering, in which monogamy was the dominant mating pattern, and modern industrial–postindustrial cultures, in which monogamy is again the dominant pattern (White & Burton, 1988:871). Monogamous marriage appears to be best adapted to egalitarian cultures in which there is relatively little accumulation of wealth and power by a few powerful males (Reynolds, 1991:73).

The inegalitarian nature of polygyny makes it highly unpopular both among males who are bereft of mating opportunities and, perhaps to a lesser extent, among females who have to share their husbands' attentions. The reproductive fitness of both males and females in relatively egalitarian cultures are logically optimized by pair-bonding. In rigidly stratified societies, female reproductive success may be best realized sharing the resources of one wealthy male with other wives than by living monogamously with a resource-poor peasant. As is the case in promiscuous animal mating systems, many males at the bottom of a polygynous social hierarchy have no opportunity to reproduce at all, which amounts to a species loss of genetic variation. For instance, Spurdle and Jenkins (1993) found reduced genetic diversity among polygynous Bantus, compared to monogamous San and Caucasoid populations in Africa. Monogamy admits more alleles into the gene pool and thus more raw material for natural selection. It is no surprise that increasing social equality brings with it the demise of polygyny.

Because polygyny is the dominant mating pattern among 97 percent of mammalian species (Fisher, 1989:347), we should not be surprised that human mammals are facultatively polygynous. However, the human practice of polyandry is something of a biological mystery, since humans are the only mammals known to practice it. Polyandry is typically, but not exclusively, fraternal—two or more brothers married to the same woman. All polyandrous cultures allow monogamous and polygynous marriages also. Among the Todas of southern India where fraternal polyandry is practiced by the lower classes, it is not uncommon for the upper classes to practice polygyny. Other cultures have practiced intermittent polyandry during periods in which the sex ratio was severely unbalanced with an abundance of males (Walsh, 1994:467).

Polyandry and polygyny should not be viewed as sexual mirror images. Sexual variety is undoubtedly a motivator for a man to take extra wives in polygynous cultures, and the choice to take on additional wives is his to make. Wives in cultures practicing fraternal polyandry have little or no say in the matter—if her husband has brothers, she is usually married to them also. In addition, and unlike wives in most polygynous cultures, a polyandrously married male can chose to leave the marriage and take his own wife if his resources allow. Sexual jealousy also appears to be more prevalent in polyandrous marriages than in polygynous ones (Beal & Goldstein, 1981).

What possible culturally adaptive function could polyandry serve? Among the Todas, where there are often two males for every female—a situation further exacerbated by the polygyny of the upper classes—polyandry can be viewed as a function of a shortage of women. Female shortage cannot explain the existence of polyandry in Tibet (the most populous polyandrous culture), where about 31 percent of women of childbearing age are unmarried (Goldstein, 1987). Polyandry functions in Tibet in the same way that primogeniture functioned in former times in England, that is, to retain family property. Just as primogeniture maintained family estates over the generations by permitting only one heir, fraternal polyandry accomplishes the same end by keeping brothers tied together with one wife and producing one set of heirs in each generation (Goldstein, 1987).

Polygyny is an opportunistic strategy of a basically monogamous species that provides polygynous males with a tremendous reproductive payoff, but polyandry is a strategy reluctantly engaged in and associated with extreme poverty, which severely reduces the reproductive fitness of polyandrous males. While some common gene transfer is assured by the fraternal nature of most polyandry (they might have no reproductive fitness at all if not part of the marriage), there is certainly some reproductive sacrifice for each brother in the family. From the female's point of view, it is useful in that the pooled resources of her husbands help to assure offspring survival; but she may not be any more reproductively successful than a polygynously married women (Fisher, 1992:71).

Given the genetic sacrifice, it is no surprise that polyandry is not a valued marriage form in the cultures where it is practiced. It is one born out of harsh economic conditions and female shortages. It may provide a "best fit" given the ecological conditions its practitioners find themselves in; but as economic

conditions improve, polyandry declines in favor of monogamy or, if culturally permitted, sometimes polygyny (Symons, 1979; Quale, 1988). Stated
differently, humans come to conform more to the mating norms of other
mammals and become either monogamous or polygynous when conditions
allow. We may view polyandry as an anthropological curiosity found only
among the truly destitute—destined for extinction if and when economic
conditions improve.

One further pattern of mating should be addressed, since it is found in many
primate species: communal or promiscuous mating or, among humans, group
marriage. This form of marriage is even rarer than polyandry and is found
geographically in the same area—the resource-poor mountainous areas of the
Indian subcontinent. It is probably a misnomer to refer to the kind of group
marriage found there as "promiscuous," for as van den Berghe (1979:53)
points out, it is "an adaptation to marginal agriculture, not an experiment in
promiscuity."

Although *Australopithecines* were apparently more promiscuous than later
hominids (Foley & Lee, 1989), the free promiscuity that anthropologists used
to think characterized early *Homo sapiens* probably never existed (Morris,
1983:137). Strong evolved patterns of human jealousy (very useful in the
maintenance of pair-bonds) render group marriages psychologically difficult
to sustain. Western experiments with group marriages have all ended as ab-
ject failures. A study of twenty-six group marriages by Constantine and
Constantine (1973), who advocated for them, showed them to be extremely
short lived. Despite the high education level and "sexual liberation" ideology of their members, these groups were rife with dissatisfaction and sexual
jealousy. Helen Fisher (1992:72) cites Margaret Mead on the topic of group
marriage: "No matter how many communes anybody invents, the family always creeps back," to which Fisher adds, "The human animal seems psychologically built to pair-bond with a single mate."

Given the ubiquity and robustness of the monogamous pair-bond among
humans, it is clear that there must be a number of biological, social, psychological, and economic benefits that make monogamous marriage the predominant form across time and place. Quale (1988:127–140) lists the following
benefits:

1. Almost all members of society have maximal opportunity to marry, with relatively
   few being left out.

2. A method of sexual gratification is provided for both sexes.

3. Intrasex jealousies and quarrels are minimized.

4. Emotional needs of both sexes are more easily fulfilled in a monogamous relationship than in other marriage forms.

5. Closer emotional bonds can exist between parents and children in a monogamous
   marriage.

6. Sociolegal issues such as inheritance, property rights, legitimacy, and lineage are
   less complicated than they are in other marriage forms.

In addition to the benefits listed by Quale, it might be added that the compact size of the nuclear family is best suited to life in industrial and postindustrial societies in which frequent geographical mobility is often required; and biologically, it maximizes the variety of alleles available for selection in the population. David Popenoe (1994:96), a leading family sociologist, states that the nuclear family "unquestionably works best . . . to produce offspring who grow up to be both autonomous and socially responsible, while also meeting the needs the adult needs for intimacy and personal attachment."

The Assault on the Nuclear Family

Despite this evidence, a number of sociologists on both sides of the ideological fence have pointed out that to support the nuclear family and the traditional values it embodies is a dangerous thing for anyone wanting to be thought of as a "good liberal" (Popenoe, 1993a; Glenn, 1993). Judith Stacey (1993:547) not only does not support it; but she wants to bury the ideology of "the family" (her sneer quotes) and implies that anyone who supports the nuclear family is classist, racist, sexist, and homophobic and further states that nontraditional family arrangements (single-parent, serial monogamy, same-sex) are preferable because they are "more egalitarian."

In taking such a position, Stacey and others like her betray a profound ignorance of the evolutionary drama that produced that which she decries. Alice Rossi (1977:2) argues that the kind of "egalitarianism underlying current research on, and advocacy of, 'variant' marriage and family forms is inadequate and misleading because it neglects some fundamental human characteristics rooted in our biological inheritance." Humanistic–symbolic interactionist sociologists Brigitte and Peter Berger are also cognizant of the evolutionary history of the family:

We do know enough about the biological constitution of *Homo sapiens* to be able to say that in many areas of behavior it acts as a tendency, rather than a compelling determinant—and there seems little doubt about a tendency toward the centrality of the father–mother–child triad. In other words, the triad may be biologically "natural" even though it is not institutionalized in the child-rearing practices of the Mumbumbu tribe, say in New Guinea, and of some lesbian communes in New Hampshire; all this would then mean is that the Mumbumbu and the lesbian communards, in "going against nature," may have to make an extra effort and perhaps have to pay an emotional or even a physical price. (Berger & Berger, 1984:188–189)

Perhaps one reason for intellectual attacks on the family is that it is the primary transmitter and defender of social values, and any institution performing such a function is always a prime target of those who do not subscribe to those values or who favor radical social change. If the family can be destroyed, radically altered, or greatly disvalued, then the society of which it is a part may be more easily molded to suit the ideology of the destroyers. A less sinister reason may be that the "family values" issue has been held captive for so long by right-wing religious fundamentalists and the Moral Majority (Popenoe, 1993b:38) that the antifamilism of some liberals may merely be reflecting a "friend-of-an-enemy" attitude.

Those who attack the nuclear family appear to be as ignorant of history as they are of biology. They would be well advised to explore the history of such attacks. The quintessential example occurred in the Soviet Union during the "war communism" and "new economic policy" periods from 1921 to 1928, when it was declared that the family was based on the "paternalistic" notion of bourgeois marriage, a property-based notion that exploited women. The Communist party passed legislation making abortion available on demand, legitimized unmarried cohabitation and the offspring of such, made divorce available for either party on demand (often accomplished simply by sending off a postcard requesting it), and encouraged "free love" as the "essence of communist living" (Hazard, Butler, & Maggs, 1977:470).

The human costs of these "reforms" were devastating, particularly for children and their mothers. The practice of "free love" (promiscuity) is incompatible with pair-bonding and biparental care throughout the animal kingdom and has been used in some societies in which marriages are largely arranged as a means of destroying love (Walsh, 1991b:173). The Soviets' destigmatization (indeed, the quasi encouragement) of sexual promiscuity, illegitimate births, and divorce resulted in hundreds of thousands of fatherless children roaming the streets who "formed into gangs, who would attack and rob people in the street, or even invade and ransack apartment blocks" (Hosking, 1985:213). This Russian tragedy is repeated with a vengeance every day in modern America, and for much the same reasons.

The Soviets soon learned that values cannot be selectively extirpated by undermining that which embodies them all at the most personal and meaningful level. After assessing the damage wrought by their antifamily policies, they responded by writing new laws extolling the family, the sanctity of marriage, the evils of divorce, and the joys of parenthood. Divorce became more difficult to obtain and very expensive, abortions could only be performed in cases of severe health risk to the mother (both the divorce and abortion laws became more liberal again in the 1960s), and the concepts of legitimacy and illegitimacy were restored to law (Hosking, 1985:214). Fletcher (1991:143) documents a similar derogation of the family in China after its revolution and the same rapid about-face when confronted with the consequences.

Breaking the Pair-Bond

Pair-bonding and monogamous marriage morally imply sexual exclusivity and permanence, but the implication lacks a reality base. Most avian and mammalian "monogamous" species are not monogamous in the normative human sense of the word (Rees & Harvey, 1991). Overwhelmingly, animal monogamy is serial monogamy and usually lasts only long enough to raise offspring of the bonded pair to independence; the next mating season will usually see new pair-bonds. Wherever pair-bonding is found in the animal kingdom, it is found because male parental investment is necessary for offspring survival, not for the joy and comfort of the bonded pair. The bonded pair certainly receive neuropharmacological rewards for staying together, but those rewards are the means to an end other than the pair-bond per se.

If monogamy in other species is generally limited to the period necessary for offspring survival, there is no reason to suspect that humans evolved any radically different strategy. Helen Fisher's (1989) study of divorce in fifty-eight cultures shows that it peaks at or around the fourth year of marriage and declines at an accelerating rate the longer the couple stays together. This finding is true regardless of the country's economic development or its rate of divorce. Fisher hypothesizes that this four-year period reflects the "natural" human period between successive births (the lactation period) and also marks the time at which the larger community in traditional societies begin to take a role in child care. When this occurs, she suggests, the complementary roles of the biological parents are no longer essential to the child's welfare.

Fisher (1989:349) speculates that serial monogamy has reproductive advantages for both sexes: Males could mate with younger females more likely to deliver viable young, and females in an unsatisfactory bond could form a better one with a male who could provide her with more resources for future offspring. If other members of the group assume some of the responsibility of child care after lactation, then the survival of children is not seriously compromised by the breakup of the nuclear pair. However, in modern societies, the *if* is a big one; and while sheer survival is indeed usually unproblematic, the quality of that life is generally not. This was amply demonstrated in the Soviet and Chinese experiences with family breakdown and, according to the Council on Families in America (CFA), is demonstrated in the United States every day. The CFA (1994:11), which consists of some of the top family scholars in the country, state that the "current disintegration of the well-functioning, two-parent family is a central cause of rising individual and social pathology: delinquency and crime (including an alarming juvenile homicide rate), drug and alcohol abuse, suicide, depression, eating disorders, and the growing number of children in poverty."

The probability that the average child will spend some significant proportion of his or her life in a single-parent situation—either because of divorce or illegitimate birth—is great. The current probability of the dissolution of a first marriage is 60 percent, and the proportion of single-parent children in 1990 was 24 percent for whites and 55 percent for blacks (Popenoe, 1993a:531–532). These figures are cause for alarm, and any extrapolation from current trends signals major exacerbations of current social problems.

There are those who will insist that some single-parent children are better off in all manner of ways than some biparental children, and of course they are right. But those who make such statements often confuse variation with central tendency. Some children now living in Sarajevo, perhaps even most of them, will grow up relatively healthy in mind and body; but child rearing in Sarajevo is not to be recommended. The consequences of not being reared in a nuclear family *range* from positive (if the family was very dysfunctional) to neutral to negative, but the *central tendency* is negative. A meta-analysis of ninety-two studies comparing children from divorced and intact homes found that mean levels of psychological adjustment, self-esteem, academic achievement, social relations, and conduct were significantly more negative for the children of divorce (Amato & Keith, 1991b). Another meta-analysis of thirty-three studies of adult children of divorced parents found them to have significantly poorer psychological adjustment and marital stability and to be lower on the socioeconomic scale than adults who grew up in intact homes (Amato & Keith, 1991a). The more marital transitions children experience, the poorer their adjustment (Capaldi & Patterson, 1991).

The cumulative picture obtained from meta-analyses such as these is clear: Divorce, no matter what advantages it may have for divorcing adults, is generally detrimental to children. This is not to deny that many divorces are desirable for all involved. Women and children should not have to remain in abusive homes, and divorce is to be encouraged under such circumstances. Indeed, a substantial proportion of the negative effects of divorce on children may be due to factors operating in the home prior to the divorce (Cherlin et al., 1991; but see Gill [1992] on this). For most academic critics of divorce, the primary problem is not divorce per se but rather "individualistic divorce" in which children are involved (Popenoe, 1994:102). Such divorces are the product of a decreasingly child-centered and increasingly self-centered society which looks upon "self-fulfillment" as a right. Love is generally considered to be the only acceptable reason for marrying today; so if one no longer loves one's partner, one is no longer being "fulfilled," and thus it is acceptable to terminate the relationship and take up another. Because "experts" stress that all family forms are equal, divorcing parents may feel that the children will be just as happy as they themselves hope to be in any new family arrangement.[6]

The self-fulfillment model has an unrealistic notion of the nature of love imbedded in it. If love is considered only to be the euphoric high one first experienced when one "fell" into it, then it is unrealistic not to expect to "fall" out of it. Such highs cannot be sustained indefinitely with the same partner, and it is probably not desirable that they should. Many "individualistic" divorcees may be "love junkies" who have developed a tolerance for PEA (resulting from the habituation of synaptic transmissions). Just as all drug addicts develop a tolerance for exogenous chemicals at some point, all lovers will sooner or later develop a tolerance for endogenous chemicals released in response to the stimuli presented by their partners.

When addicts find that the same amount of their drug no longer has the same affect on their feeling states, they take larger doses or take a short respite from it so that the brain becomes unhabituated. Married couples in constant proximity to one another cannot increase the amount of stimuli from their current spouse; and if one or both of them are disciples of the self-fulfillment ethos, they may decide that everything is over between them and seek out a new source of PEA. Michael Liebowitz (1983:90) suggests that the neuropharmacological basis of sexual love usually lasts (in ever-decreasing intensity) for no more than two to three years. Allowing time for the realization to sink in, for possible attempts to rekindle romance, for periods of "thinking about it," and for legal proceedings, the four-year mode for first-marriage duration fits the psychopharmacological model of love (Fisher, 1989:346).

Another unfortunate consequence of unrealistic expectations threatening the viability of marriage is the search for sexual novelty (for more PEA?) outside the pair-bond. Betzig's (1989) study of divorce in 160 different cultures found adultery to be the main cause across cultures. Divorce precipitated by adultery is consistent with Lovejoy's (1981, 1984) scenario positing that fidelity is necessary for successful pair-bonding. If extrapair-bond affairs had been tolerated with equanimity by our distant ancestors, successful pair-bonding may never have evolved; and we might be a quite different species, assuming we survived at all. As much as humans commit adultery, if we are victims rather than perpetrators we are aroused to the intensest of emotions.

Jealousy is an emotion useful for females in combating resource loss and for males in avoiding cuckoldry (Buss, 1989; Barkow, 1991). The severe reproductive costs incurred by cuckolded males suggests that natural selection for jealousy has operated more intensely on them than on females. Strong male jealousy is perhaps the primary reason why no culture considers male adultery to be as serious as female adultery and why female adultery, although much less common than male adultery, is more likely to put a marriage at risk in almost all cultures (Betzig, 1989; Wilson & Daly, 1992). Jealousy serves to reinforce the male sense of sexual proprietariness and induces him to cut his losses and depart when wifely infidelity threatens his genetic fitness. The seriousness with which adultery is taken by males can also be gauged by the fact that the overwhelming number of spousal homicides in the United States are fueled by male sexual proprietariness and jealousy (Daly & Wilson, 1988).[7]

Perhaps if those contemplating marriage were divested of unrealistic expectations of enduring bliss and of the narcissism implicit in the ethos of self-fulfillment, there might be less adultery and fewer divorces and hurt children. As the Fisher (1989) data indicate, for those who weather the storm of disappointment as "love highs" become less frequent and less intense, the probability of divorce decreases with each year. Herein lies the importance of choosing our lovers wisely so that we *like* them and will continue to do so after the sheer euphoria wears off. PEA tolerance does not spell the end of love; for most of us, it spells only a diminution of intense passion. Attachment, mediated by the same endorphins that facilitate the mother–infant bond, is a longer-lasting form of emotional relatedness well-chosen newlyweds can look forward to. Many people find the quiet security of companionate love (attachment) more emotionally satisfying than the mad gonadal helter-skelter of the attraction phase of love.

THE PROBLEM OF UNWED PARENTHOOD

Characterizing unwed motherhood as "the new American dilemma," Garfinkel and McLanahan (1986:1) assert that "few topics could be of greater importance to the nation's future." Unfortunately, the issue has been defined for many people by Dan Quayle's attack on the fictional Murphy Brown and the resulting brouhaha. The issue is much too important to be trivialized as a battle over sexual morality between the political right's "family values" and the political left's "sexual liberation." It is an issue that has found common cause among conservatives such as Dan Quayle, liberals such as Jesse Jackson, and centrists such as Bill Clinton. Almost all academic researchers of the topic, regardless of political persuasion, appear to reach the conclusion that in the vast majority of cases, unwed parenthood is destructive to both mother and child and immensely costly to society (Vinovskis, 1988; Plotnick, 1990; Moynihan, 1992; Hamburg, 1993; Vedder & Gallaway, 1993; J. Wilson, 1993; Herrnstein & Murray, 1994).

The "causes" of illegitimacy are a complex mixture of personal and environmental factors that feed on one another. The general breakdown on moral values, spearheaded by the "sexual revolution," may be cited as a cause. Evidence suggests that the sexual revolution was to be expected from the low sex ratio of the period, implying that moral breakdown is an effect of the sexual revolution rather than a cause. A number of researchers view the high illegitimacy rate as a function of male shortages (low sex ratio), which puts pressure on females to conform to male sexual strategies (e.g., Guttentag & Secord, 1983; Pedersen, 1991), but William J. Wilson (1987:Chapter 3) views black illegitimacy as a function of the dearth of *employable* black males, due to an increasingly deindustrialized economy rather than a dearth of males per se. It makes evolutionary sense that employment status should impact female epigamic choices, but Vinovskis (1988:91) points out that the black illegitimacy rate also increased in times of high black employment as it also did among whites.

Other researchers stress easy availability of welfare. As moral thresholds are lowered and the natural economic consequences of irresponsible reproduction are removed by well-meaning welfare programs, impulsive individuals find fewer reasons to deny their impulses (Garfinkel & McLanahan, 1986:59; Fletcher, 1991:148; Plotnick, 1990). Vedder and Gallaway (1993) point out that while the black family survived the trials of slavery, Reconstruction, Jim Crow laws, and segregation, it faced its most serious challenge to survival with the onset of the "Great Society." Prior to the onset of Great Society programs, the correlation between the unemployment rate and number of welfare cases was 0.91. After implementation, the correlation dropped precipitously and actually became *negative*; that is, as unemployment went down, new welfare cases went up (Moynihan, 1992:56).[8]

The availability of welfare clearly plays a part in explaining the illegitimacy rate, although, as Moynihan (1992:59) points out, the trend toward illegitimacy was already discernible before the Great Society; and other causes may be more important. Indeed, the 171-city study by Messner and Sampson (1991), discussed in Chapter 8, found that the sex ratio ($\beta = -0.60$) was almost five times more powerful (as determined by the squares of their respective standardized betas) in predicting the proportion of female-headed households in the black community than level of public assistance ($\beta = 0.27$).

Whether we view the crisis of illegitimacy as a function of a low sex ratio, deindustrialization, welfare availability, simple moral poverty, or some other "cause" or mixture of "causes," it cannot be denied that the problem is one impacting hardest on our most vulnerable citizens—young African-Americans. "If there is a single statistic that underlies the crime, poverty, and failure that beset blacks in America today, it is an illegitimacy rate of 66 percent," declares Jared Taylor (1992:305). Daniel P. Moynihan (1965:5) made much the same observation in his famous 1965 report in which he wrote: "At the heart of the deterioration of the fabric of Negro society is the deterioration of the Negro family," which he saw primarily in terms of the black illegitimacy rate of just under 25 percent in 1964.

Despite vitriolic liberal attacks on Moynihan's report (see especially William Ryan's *Blaming the Victim* [1971]), it received support from none other than Martin Luther King, who, citing the "alarming statistics on Negro illegitimacy," wrote that the black family had become "fragile, deprived, and often psychopathic" (quoted in Norton, 1987:53). Nevertheless, as William J. Wilson (1987:15) asserts, attacks on Moynihan's report led liberal social scientists to shy away from tackling the problems of the urban ghetto and even to redefine them as strengths, an exercise in double-speak soundly condemned by Wilson as destructive of his people.

Children born out of wedlock face enormous obstacles to meaningful participation in society from the very beginning. Their mothers tend to be younger than average, to be in poorer mental health, to have more antisocial personality traits, to have lower IQs, to be more abusive and neglectful, to suffer more stress, to be economically and educationally deprived, to have a propensity for an impulsive and risky lifestyle, and to lack a network of social support (Garfinkel & McLanahan, 1986; Zuravin, 1988; Hamburg, 1993; Vedder & Gallaway, 1993; Herrnstein & Murray, 1994). While most studies emphasize poverty and lack of social support for the many negative aspects of out-of-wedlock parenting, one recent study found mothers' antisocial personalities, a trait preceding both single pregnancy and its accompanying stresses, to be more important (Simons, Beaman, Conger, & Chao, 1993).

The plethora of negative experiences, combined with possible genetic material transmitted by typically impulsive, low-IQ, antisocial mothers (and probably fathers, although unwed fathers are not studied anywhere near as often as unwed mothers), puts many illegitimate children at high risk for many antisocial behaviors, including becoming unwed parents themselves. Karl Zinsmeister (1991:48) reports that most street-gang members, most adolescent murderers, and about 70 percent of juveniles in state reform institutions are from single-parent homes, and Leyton (1986:316) reports that the incidence of illegitimate birth among serial killers is far greater than is expected by chance. A British study of delinquents comparing legitimate and illegitimate boys concluded that "the boys born illegitimate were singularly delinquent prone" (West & Farrington, 1977:197), and Walsh (1991a) found illegitimate delinquents to be significantly more disadvantaged in every area of life measured. Moynihan (1992:56) sums up the situation well: "A community that allows a large number of young men to grow up in broken families, dominated by women, never acquiring any stable relationship to male authority, never acquiring any set of rational expectations about the future— that community asks for and gets chaos. Crime, violence, unrest, disorder . . . that is not only to be expected; it is very near to inevitable."

All of this again raises the issue of whether slavery, racism, and deprivation are adequate explanations of the many problems faced by the black community. Herbert Gutman's (1976) historical analysis of the black family essentially asks the following question: If slavery, racism, and deprivation are the "root causes" of the problems of black America, why are those problems getting worse as the "causes" grow weaker and more distant? If those causes were really causes, then surely their effects would have been more visible among the early post-Emancipation generations, when white racism was virulent and rampant and when Jim Crow laws were operative. As Gutman (1976:xviii) points out, such is not the case; the "tangle of pathology," as he puts it, was more severe in the 1950s and 1960s than it was 100 years earlier; and it is more severe today than it was in the period Gutman was concerned with.

Slavery and racism may not be direct causes of black crime, but perhaps they exert their influence indirectly via their effects on the black family, as the Moynihan report (1965) asserted. Again, this position runs up against demographic data that contradict it. Fatherless matrifocal black families, so often attributed to the effects of slavery, is far more typical in this last quarter of the twentieth century than in the corresponding period of the nineteenth century (Gutman, 1976:443). In New York City in 1925, 84 percent of black children lived in a two-parent family (Gutman, 1976:519); today less than 50 percent nationwide do (Popenoe, 1993a:531–532). Those who want to ascribe the pathology of the ghetto to slavery and racism, either directly or via their effects on the family, will have to explain to skeptics why these alleged transgenerational effects skipped several generations before revealing the full power of their alleged influence.

This is not to say that there were not or are not negative effects of slavery and racism, but more relevant to the issue of current pathology is current practice. As long as the black community tolerates the current rate of black illegitimacy, it will continue to suffer the consequences. Among the major consequences of bearing illegitimate children is a high probability of protracted welfare dependency and lifelong poverty for mothers and their children and a high probability of the same fate for many future generations. Black liberals such as William Wilson and Jesse Jackson are joining black conservatives such as Thomas Sowell, Glenn Loury, and Shelby Steele in the reasoned opinion that if a woman wishes to avoid poverty, she should avoid bearing illegitimate offspring. The thoughtless rhetoric of well-meaning liberals in the 1960s and 1970s which decoded concerns about unwed motherhood as "racism" and "genocide" and which even defined it as something positive probably did more harm to the African-American population than the KKK ever did or could.[9]

There is little doubt that Daniel Patrick Moynihan, Martin Luther King, and others who sounded the warning in the 1960s have been vindicated with a vengeance. The pathology they saw then has progressed along with the rate of illegitimacy, and there is an emerging consensus crossing all but the most radical of ideological lines that illegitimacy—not racism, discrimination, or the residual effects of slavery—is the prime mover in the development of the black underclass (W. Wilson, 1987; Vinovskis, 1988; Taylor, 1992; Conti & Stetson, 1993). The problem is not limited to blacks; the current illegitimacy rate among whites (about 23%) is perilously close to the black rate at the time of Moynihan's report (Gress-Wright, 1993:19). It is often claimed that the drug issue was ignored by the power structure until it burst out of the ghetto and began to impact middle-class whites; perhaps we will now see some meaningful efforts to combat the arguably more serious problem of illegitimacy.

CONCLUSION

This chapter has emphasized the evolutionary roots of the nuclear family and the necessity for huge investment of parental energy if children are to grow and flourish. Cascades of research have supported the centrality of love for the positive psychological and emotional development of children. *Homo sapiens* has evolved to expect and to thrive on love; the nuclear family is the setting most facilitative of it and is thus the setting in which the young of the human species best thrive. When a significant number of a society's children are raised outside of the species' "expected environment," large-scale pathology ensues.

Because the purpose of this book has been to examine familiar sociological issues from a biosocial perspective rather than social policy, I have resisted discussing social policy. Suffice it to say here that the family is so vital and fundamental to the well-being of the individual and to society that the nuclear family *must* be strengthened and illegitimacy strongly discouraged. Much of the policy implemented over the past three or four decades has contributed to the weakening of the nuclear family. No one can fault the concern and compassion of those who championed the policies of the Great Society. They were well-meaning individuals operating under the naïve assumptions of their theories, none of which predicted that the implemented policies would help to grind down the black community in two or three decades. Making essentially the same point, Morowitz (1979:167) adds, "The moral to be drawn is that we must work harder to make our knowledge commensurate with our compassion."

The moral Morowitz draws sums up the primary message of this book: *Sociology can no longer ignore knowledge about human nature available to it from the biological sciences.* Although I am concerned more about the progress of the discipline than its ability to guide social policy, sociology especially cannot afford to ignore the facts of human nature revealed by biology when recommending social policy if it is to avoid more fiascoes. Compassion is a commendable motive for implementing policy, but it often backfires by creating dependence and irresponsibility if not tempered with a broader view of the human nature of the recipients of our compassion. Broader views will only develop when mainstream sociology drops its antagonism toward biology and starts developing vertically integrated theories incorporating applicable biological principles.

NOTES

1. While most evolutionists agree that it is necessarily true that natural selection works on individual organisms by selecting advantageous alleles, the survival of individual phenotypes is dependent on the survival of other members of the species. Biologically, what is advantageous for the individual is advantageous for the group, and vice versa (Peres & Hopp, 1990). Other evolutionists (e.g., Gould, 1992), argue that selection operates simultaneously at several levels: genes, organisms, populations, and species.

2. Most authorities appear to agree that the earliest recognized hominids, *Australopithecus afarensis*, were harem builders. The evidence usually cited for this conclusion is the high level of sexual dimorphism for size and agonistic features typically found among polygynous animals. These features imply intense male–male competition for access to ovulating females, a competition in which reproductive success goes largely to the strongest and most aggressive males (Lovejoy, 1981; Foley & Lee, 1989). However, some authorities believe that sexual dimorphism among *australopithecines* may not have been as great as previously thought (McHenry, 1991).

3. The neotenous retention of the skull-to-spine orientation of newborn primates among humans may help us to understand the evolution of bipedalism and concealed ovulation (Feder & Park, 1989:144). This skull-to-spine orientation is necessary for protracted bipedal locomotion: Humans retain it; nonhuman primates lose it. Given that bipedalism was a fact among early hominids, female genitals would now be hidden between the legs. This would not only make the genitals less accessible to male eyes and nostrils, but it would make estrus swelling decidedly disadvantageous for locomotion. The human downward-tilting vagina exists in mammalian embryos; but

in all other species, it undergoes developmental rotation to lie parallel with the backbone (Montagu, 1981:25).

4. This is a process analogous, but not homologous, to the bonding process in some animals as described by ethologists. Although early mother–infant contact is considered extremely desirable, there is no time-restricted "critical" period governing the human bonding in which attachment must occur to assure species-normal development (Rossi, 1987).

5. Vervet monkeys may provide clues of an evolutionary stage intermediate of those of other nonhuman primates and humans. Females of this species do not advertise sexual receptivity via perineal swelling, and their receptivity extends well beyond ovulation. However, estrus is not concealed in the human sense, since females excrete in their urine a substance related to ovarian function that excites male interest. Thus, olfactory signals have replaced visual ones in this species (Andelman, 1987; Szalay & Costello, 1991). There is some evidence that weak pheromonal signs of ovulation remain among human females, but whether they constitute an (unconscious) excitant for human males is not known (Reynolds, 1991:62).

6. Studies of stepparenting in both the United States and Great Britain have concluded that children reared in stepfamilies are generally more poorly adjusted than children whose custodial parent (usually the mother) remains single (Amato, 1993; Popenoe, 1994). Despite the additional physical resources accrued by remarriage, the psychoemotional problems attending children's attempts to adjust to an alien intruder make second marriages difficult and even more likely to fail than first marriages (Amato, 1993). According to one data source of murdered children in Canada for the years 1974 to 1983, children run seventy times the risk of being killed by stepparents than by natural parents. This risk is greater the younger the child is (Fisher, 1991). Similar risk ratios for fatal abuse (overwhelmingly committed by stepfathers) have been found in the United States, Britain, and Australia (Daly & Wilson, 1988).

7. Males face lowered paternal certainty from spousal infidelity; females do not face maternal uncertainty, but they face the diversion of spousal resources. This suggests that males would be more troubled by sexual infidelity and females would be more troubled by emotional infidelity (alien gametes can be introduced by sexual infidelity with or without emotional infidelity, but resources are usually only diverted by emotional infidelity). Self-reported data and physiological arousal measures strongly confirm evolutionary predictions: Male jealousy is primarily sexual, and female jealousy is primarily emotional-commitment jealousy, although both sexes are distressed by both forms to the extent that one form signals the other (Buss, Larsen, Westen, & Semmelroth, 1992).

8. Those who stress welfare as a major facilitator of illegitimacy do not necessarily believe that all welfare is bad. They tend to object to long-term welfare dependency of able-bodied individuals, not to welfare for the chronically disabled or relief for those needing temporary help. Personally, I have long been an advocate of paid maternal leave and a comprehensive health-care system funded by taxation.

9. Income variability in the black community is significantly greater than it is within the white community and is primarily accounted for by the high rate of black illegitimacy. According to economists Vedder and Gallaway (1993), intact black families enjoyed a median income not significantly different from the white family median in 1990; but single-parent black families had a median income of only about one-third

of the income enjoyed by intact families of both races. They also show how welfare benefits, often considerably in excess of starting salaries for young women, can appear an attractive option to those with a limited time horizon. They also show that this initial economic advantage diminishes greatly over the years as work experience and responsibility are gained by the young woman who chose work over welfare.

References

Abitol, M. (1987). Obstetrics and posture in pelvic anatomy. *Journal of Human Evolution* 16:243–255.

Ackerman, S. (1992). *Discovering the brain.* Washington, D.C.: National Academy of Sciences Press.

Ader, R. (1983). Developmental psychoneuroimmunology. *Developmental Psychobiology* 16:251–267.

Adler, R., & Cohen, N. (1985). CNS-immune system interactions: Conditioning phenomena. *Behavioral and Brain Sciences* 8:379–394.

Agnew, R. (1992). Foundations for a general strain theory of crime and delinquency. *Criminology* 30:47–66.

Allen, W. (1988). Rhodes handicapping, or slowing the pace of integration. *Journal of Vocational Behavior* 33:365–378.

Amato, P. (1993). Children's adjustment to divorce: Theories, hypotheses, and empirical support. *Journal of Marriage and the Family* 55:23–38.

Amato, P., & Keith, B. (1991a). Parental divorce and adult well-being: A meta-analysis. *Journal of Marriage and the Family* 53:43–58.

Amato, P., & Keith, B. (1991b). Parental divorce and the well-being of children: A meta-analysis. *Psychological Bulletin* 110:26–46.

American Psychiatric Association. (1987). *Diagnostic and statistical manual of mental disorders: DSM-III-R.* Washington, D.C.: American Psychiatric Association.

Anastasi, A. (1976). *Psychological testing.* 4th ed. New York: Macmillan.

Anastasiow, N. (1986). *Development and disability.* Baltimore: Paul H. Brooks.

Andelman, S. (1987). Evolution of concealed ovulation in vervet monkeys (*Ceropithecus aethiops*). *American Naturalist* 129:785–789.

Andersen, M. (1988). *Thinking about women: Sociological perspectives on sex and gender.* New York: Macmillan.

Andreasen, N., Flaum, M., Swayze, V., O'Leary, D., Allinger, R., Cohen, G., Ehrhardt, J., & Yuh, W. (1993). Intelligence and brain structure in normal individuals. *American Journal of Psychiatry* 150:130–134.

Andrew, J. (1974). Delinquency, the Wechsler P > V sign, and the I-level system. *Journal of Clinical Psychology* 30:331–335.

Andrew, J. (1977). Delinquency: Intellectual imbalance? *Criminal Justice and Behavior* 4:99–104.

Andrew, J. (1980). Verbal IQ and the I-level classification system for delinquents. *Criminal Justice and Behavior* 7:193–202.

Applewhite, P. (1981). *Molecular gods: How molecules determine our behavior.* Englewood Cliffs, N.J.: Prentice-Hall.

Arnold, A., & Gorski, R. (1984). Gonadal steroid induction of structural sex differences in the central nervous system. *Annual Review of Neuroscience* 7:413–442.

Asso, D. (1983). *The real menstrual cycle.* New York: John Wiley.

Austin, R. (1981). I-level and rehabilitation of delinquents. In P. Kratcoski (Ed.), *Correctional counseling and treatment* (pp. 176–189). Monterey, Calif.: Duxbury.

Averill, J. (1992). Sociology becomes emotional. *Contemporary Psychology* 37:804–805.

Baekgaard, W., Nyborg, H., & Nielsen, J. (1978). Neuroticism and extraversion in Turner's syndrome. *Journal of Abnormal Psychology* 87:583–586.

Bailey, J., Gaulinn, S., Agyei, Y., & Gladue, B. (1994). Effects of gender and sexual orientation on evolutionary relevant aspects of human mating psychology. *Journal of Personality and Social Psychology* 66:1081–1093.

Bailey, J., & Pillard, R. (1991). A genetic study of male sexual orientation. *Archives of General Psychiatry* 48:1089–1096.

Bailey, J., Pillard, R., Neile, M., & Agyei, Y. (1993). Heritable factors influencing sexual orientation in women. *Archives of General Psychiatry* 50:217–223.

Baker, L., & Daniels, D. (1990). Nonshared environmental influences and personality differences in adult twins. *Journal of Personality and Social Psychology* 58:103–110.

Balazs, G. (1992). The older offender. In A. Walsh, *Correctional assessment, casework & counseling* (pp. 225–234). Laurel, Md.: American Correctional Association.

Barfield, A. (1976). Biological influences on sex differences in behavior. In M. Teitelbaum (Ed.), *Sex differences: Social and biological perspectives* (pp. 62–121). Garden City, N.Y.: Anchor.

Barkow, J. (1991). *Darwin sex and status: Biological approaches to mind and culture.* Toronto: University of Toronto Press.

Barnett, R., Zimmer, L., & McCormack, J. (1989). P > V sign and personality profiles. *Journal of Correctional and Social Psychiatry and Offender Treatment and Therapy* 35:18–20.

Baumrind, D. (1993). The average expected environment is not good enough: A response to Scarr. *Child Development* 64:1299–1317.

Beal, C., & Goldstein, M. (1981). Tibetan fraternal polyandry: A test of sociobiological theory. *American Anthropologist* 83:5–12.

Bell, A., Weinberg, M., & Hammersmith, S. (1981). *Sexual preference: Its development in men and women.* Bloomington: University of Indiana Press.

Belsky, J., Steinberg, L., & Draper, P. (1991). Childhood experience, interpersonal development, and reproductive strategy: An evolutionary theory of socialization. *Child Development* 62:647–660.

Berenbaum, S., & Hines, M. (1992). Early androgens are related to childhood sex-typed toy preferences. *Psychological Sciences* 3:203–206.

Berger, B., & Berger, P. (1984). *The war over the family: Capturing the middle ground.* Garden City, N.Y.: Anchor Press.

Bertenthal, B., & Campos, J. (1987). New directions in the study of early experience. *Child Development* 58:560–567.

Betz, N. (Ed.). (1988). Fairness in employment testing. *Journal of Vocational Behavior* 33(3): entire issue.

Betzig, L. (1989). Cause of conjugal dissolution: A cross-cultural study. *Current Anthropology* 30:654–669.

Black, J., & Greenough, W. (1986). Induction of pattern in neural structure by experience: Implications for cognitive development. In M. Lamb, A. Brown, & B. Rogoff (Eds.), *Advances in developmental psychology* (Vol. 4, pp. 1–50). Hillsdale, N.J.: Erlbaum.

Bloom, F. (1988). The neuropeptides. In R. Llinas (Ed.), *The biology of the brain: From neurons to networks* (pp. 114–130). New York: W. H. Freeman.

Blumstein, A., & Cohen, J. (1987). Characterizing criminal careers. *Science* 237:985–991.

Blumstein, P., & Schwartz, P. (1991). Intimate relationships and the creation of sexuality. In L. Kramer (Ed.), *The sociology of gender* (pp. 173–187). New York: St. Martin's.

Bouchard, T., Lykken, D., McGue, M., Segal, N., & Tellegen, A. (1990). Sources of human psychological differences: The Minnesota study of twins reared apart. *Science* 250:223–228.

Bouchard, T., & McGue, M. (1981). Familial studies of intelligence: A review. *Science* 212:1055–1059.

Bouchard, T., & Segal, N. (1985). Environment and IQ. In B. Wolman (Ed.), *Handbook of intelligence: Theories, measurements, and applications* (pp. 391–464). New York: John Wiley.

Boucher, C. (1985). A child development perspective on the responsibility of juveniles. In J. Sullivan & J. Victor (Eds.), *Criminal Justice 85/86*. Guilford, Conn.: Dushkin.

Boyar, R., & Aiman, J. (1985). The 24-hour secretory pattern of LH and the response of LHRH in transsexual men. *Archives of Sexual Behavior* 11:157–169.

Bradford, J. (1990). The antiandrogen and hormonal treatment of sex offenders. In W. Marshal, D. Laws, & H. Barbaree (Eds.), *Handbook of sexual assault: Issues, theories, and treatment of the offender* (pp. 297–310). New York: Plenum.

Bradley, R., & Caldwell, B. (1991). Like images refracted: A view from the interactionist perspective. *Behavioral and Brain Sciences* 14:389–390.

Brand, C. (1987). A touch of (social) class. *Nature* 325:767–768.

Bridgman, P. (1955). *Reflections of a physicist.* New York: Philosophical Library.

Brody, N. (1985). The validity of tests of intelligence. In B. Wolman (Ed.), *Handbook of intelligence: Theories, measurements, and applications* (pp. 353–390). New York: John Wiley.

Bromage, T. (1987). The biological and chronological maturation of early hominids. *Journal of Human Evolution* 16:257–272.

Bronfenbrenner, U., & Ceci, S. (1994). Heredity, environment, and the question "how"—A first approximation. In R. Plomin & G. McClearn (Eds.), *Nature, nurture, and psychology* (pp. 313–324). Washington, D.C.: American Psychological Association.

Broude, G., & Greene, S. (1977). Cross-cultural codes on twenty sexual attitudes and practices. *Ethnology* 15:409–429.

Brown, D. (1991). *Human universals.* New York: McGraw Hill.

Brown, G., & Goodwin, F. (1984). Diagnostic, clinical and personality characteristics of aggressive men with low 5-HIAA. *Clinical Neuropharmacology* 7:756–757.

Buchanan, C., Eccles, J., & Becker, J. (1993). Are adolescents the victims of raging hormones?: Evidence for activational effects of hormones on moods and behavior at adolescence. *Psychological Bulletin* 111:62–107.

Buikhuisen, W. (1982). Aggressive behavior and cognitive disorders. *International Journal of Law and Psychiatry* 5:205–217.

Buikhuisen, W. (1987). Cerebral dysfunctions and persistent juvenile delinquency. In S. Mednick, T. Moffitt, & S. Stack (Eds.), *The causes of crime: New biological approaches* (pp. 168–184). Cambridge: University of Cambridge Press.

Buikhuisen, W. (1989). Explaining juvenile delinquency from a biosocial developmental perspective. *International Journal of Offender Therapy and Comparative Criminology* 33:185–195.

Buikhuisen, W., Bontekoe, E., Plas-Koenhoff, C., & Van Buuren, S. (1984). Characteristic of criminals: The privileged offender. *International Journal of Law and Psychiatry* 7:301–313.

Bureau of the Census. (1993). *1990 census of the United States.* Washington, D.C.: U.S. Government Printing Office.

Buri, J., Kirchner, P., & Walsh, J. (1987). Family correlates of self-esteem in young American adults. *Journal of Social Psychology* 127:583–588.

Buss, D. (1989). Sex differences in human mate preferences: Evolutionary hypotheses tested in 37 cultures. *Behavioral and Brain Sciences* 12:1–49.

Buss, D. (1990). Toward a biologically informed psychology of personality. *Journal of Personality* 58:1–16.

Buss, D., Larsen, R., Westen, D., & Semmelroth, J. (1992). Sex differences in jealousy: Evolution, physiology, and psychology. *Psychological Science* 3:251–255.

Buss, D., & Schmitt, D. (1993). Sexual strategies theory: An evolutionary perspective on human mating. *Psychological Review* 100:204–232.

Byerley, W., & Mellon, C. (1989). Mapping genes for manic-depression and schizophrenia with DNA markers. *Trends in Neuroscience* 12:46–80.

Byrne, J. (1986). Cities, citizens, and crime: The ecological/non-ecological debate reconsidered. In J. Byrne & R. Sampson (Eds.), *The social ecology of crime* (pp. 77–107). New York: Springer-Verlag.

Cacioppo, J., & Bernston, G. (1992). Social psychological contributions to the decade of the brain. *American Psychologist* 47:1019–1028.

Campagnoni, A. (1985). Molecular biology of myelination: Gene expression of myelin basic protein. In C. Zomzely-Neurath & W. Walker (Eds.), *Gene expression in the brain* (pp. 205–233). New York: John Wiley.

Capaldi, D., & Patterson, G. (1991). Relation of parental transitions to boys' adjustment problems: I. A linear hypothesis. II. Mothers at risk for transitions and unskilled parenting. *Developmental Psychology* 27:489–504.

Capron, C., & Duyme, M. (1989). Assessment of effects of socio-economic status on IQ in a full cross-fostering study. *Nature* 340:552–554.

Cashdan, E. (1993). Attracting mates: Effects of paternal investment on mate attraction strategies. *Ethology and Sociobiology* 14:1–23.

Caspi, A., Lynam, D., Moffitt, T., & Silva, P. (1993). Unraveling girls' delinquency: Biological, dispositional, and contextual contributions to adolescent misbehavior. *Developmental Psychology* 29:19–30.

Caspi, A., Moffitt, T., Silva, P., Stouthamer-Loeber, M., Krueger, R., & Schmutte, P. (1994). Are some people crime-prone? Replications of the personality–crime relationship across countries, genders, races, and methods. *Criminology* 32:163–195.

Cattell, R. (1985). Intelligence and g: An imaginative treatment of unimaginative data. *Behavioral and Brian Sciences* 8:227–228.

Changeux, J. (1983). On the singularity of nerve cells and its ontogenesis. *Progress in Brain Research* 58:465–478.

Changeux, J. (1985). *Neuronal man: The biology of the mind.* New York: Pantheon.

Chase, T., Fedio, P., Foster, N., Brooks, R., Di Chiro, G., & Mansi, L. (1984). Wechsler adult intelligence scale performance: Cortical localization by fluorodeoxyglucose F 18 positron emission tomography. *Archives of Neurology* 41:244–247.

Chauchard, P. (1968). *Our need for love.* New York: P. K. Kennedy & Sons.

Cherlin, A., Furstenberg, F., Chase-Lansdale, P., Kiernan, K., Robins, P., Morrison, R., & Teitler, J. (1991). Longitudinal studies of effects of divorce on children in Great Britain and the United States. *Science* 252:1386–1389.

Chilton, R. (1986). Urban crime rates: Effects of inequality, welfare dependency, region, and race. In J. Byrne & R. Sampson (Eds.), *The social ecology of crime* (pp. 116–130). New York: Springer-Verlag.

Chisholm, J. (1993). Death, hope, and sex: Life-history theory and the development of reproductive strategies. *Current Anthropology* 34:1–24.

Cholst, S. (1990). *Finding love in a cold world.* New York: Beau Rivage.

Clarke, A. M., & Clarke, A. D. (1976). *Early experience: Myth and evidence.* New York: Free Press.

Cloninger, C. (1986). A unified biosocial theory of personality and its role in the development of anxiety stress. *Psychiatric Development* 3:167–226.

Cloninger, C., Reich, T., & Guze, S. (1975). The multifactorial model of disease transmission: II. Sex differences in the familial transmission of sociopathy (antisocial personality). *British Journal of Psychiatry* 127:11–22.

Clutton-Brock, T. (1991). *The evolution of parental care.* Princeton: Princeton University Press.

Cohen, L. (1987). Throwing down the gauntlet: A challenge to the relevance of sociology for the etiology of criminal behavior. *Contemporary Sociology* 16:202–205.

Coleman, J., & Cressey, D. (1987). *Social problems.* New York: Harper & Row.

Collins, R. (1984). The role of emotion in social structure. In K. Scherer & P. Ekman (Eds.), *Approaches to emotion* (pp. 385–396). Hillsdale, N.J.: Lawrence Erlbaum.

Constantine, L., & Constantine, J. (1973). *Group marriage.* New York: Macmillan.

Conti, J., & Stetson, B. (1993). The new black vanguard. *Intercollegiate Review* 28:33–41.

Cooke, W. (1945). The differential psychology of American women. *American Journal of Obstetrics and Gynecology* 49:457–472.

Cornell, D., & Wilson, L. (1992). The PIQ > VIQ discrepancy in violent and nonviolent delinquents. *Journal of Clinical Psychology* 48:256–261.

Coser, L. (1971). *Masters of sociological thought.* New York: Harcourt Brace Jovanovich.

Cosmides, L. (1989). The logic of social exchange: Has natural selection shaped how we reason? *Cognition* 31:187–276.

Cosmides, L., Tooby, J., & Barkow, J. (1992). Introduction: Evolutionary psychology and conceptual integration. In J. Barkow, L. Cosmides, & J. Tooby (Eds.), *The adapted mind: Evolutionary psychology and the generation of culture* (pp. 3–15). New York: Oxford University Press.

Coughlin, E. (1992). Sociologists confront questions about field's vitality and direction. *Chronicle of Higher Education*, August 12:A6–A8.

Council of Families in America (CFA). (1994). Family and child well-being: Eight propositions. *Family Affairs* 6:11–12.

Cox, O. (1940). Sex ratio and marital status among Negroes. *American Sociological Review* 5:937–947.

Crawford, C., & Anderson, J. (1989). Sociobiology: An environmental discipline? *American Psychologist* 44:1449–1459.

Crooks, R., & Baur, K. (1983). *Our sexuality*. Menlo Park, Calif.: Benjamin/Cummings.

Cunningham, M., & Barbaree, A. (1991). Differential K-selection versus ecological determinants of race differences in sexual behavior. *Journal of Research in Personality* 25:205–217.

Dabbs, J., & Morris, R. (1990). Testosterone, social class, and antisocial behavior in a sample of 4,462 men. *Psychological Science* 1:209–211.

Daitzman, R., & Zuckerman, M. (1980). Disinhibitory sensation seeking, personality and gonadal hormones. *Personality and Individual Differences* 1:103–110.

Daly, M., & Wilson, M. (1988). Evolutionary social psychology and family homicide. *Science* 243:519–524.

Das, M. (1989). Making sociology attractive. *Teaching Sociology* 17:356–359.

Dashkov, G. (1992). Quantitative and qualitative changes in crime in the USSR. *British Journal of Criminology* 32:160–165.

Davidson, R. (1992). Emotion and affective style: Hemispheric substrates. *Psychological Science* 3:39–43.

Dawkins, R. (1976). *The selfish gene*. Oxford: Oxford University Press.

Degler, C. (1991). *In search of human nature: The decline and revival of Darwinism in American social thought*. New York: Oxford University Press.

de Lacoste-Utamsing, C., & Holloway, R. (1982). Sexual dimorphism in the human corpus callosum. *Science* 216:1431–1432.

DeLozier, P. (1982). Attachment theory and child abuse. In C. Park & J. Stevenson-Hinde (Eds.), *The place of attachment in human behavior* (pp. 95–117). New York: Basic Books.

Denenberg, V. (1981). Hemispheric laterality in animals and the effects of early experience. *Behavioral and Brain Sciences* 4:1–49.

Diamond, M. (1984). Age, sex, and environmental influences. In N. Gerschwind & A. Galaburda (Eds.), *Cerebral dominance: The biological foundations* (pp. 134–146). Cambridge: Harvard University Press.

Dittman, R., Kappes, M. H., Kappes, M. E., & Borger, D. (1991). Congenital adrenal hyperplasia: I. Gender-related behavior and attitudes in female patients and sisters. *Psychoneuroendocrinology* 15:401–420.

d'Orban, P., & Dalton, K. (1980). Violent crime and the menstrual cycle. *Psychological Medicine* 10:353–359.

Dörner, G. (1976). *Hormones and brain differentiation*. Amsterdam: Elsevier.

Dörner, G., Rohde, W., Stahl, F., Krell, L., & Masius, W. (1975). A neuroendocrine predisposition for homosexuality in men. *Archives of Sexual Behavior* 4:1–8.

Doudna, C., & McBride, F. (1981). Where are the men for women at the top? In P. Stein (Ed.), *Single life: Unmarried adults in social context* (pp. 21–34). New York: St. Martin's.

Downey, J., Ehrhardt, A., Gruen, R., Bell, J., & Morishima, A. (1989). Psychopathology and social functioning in women with Turner syndrome. *Journal of Nervous and Mental Disease* 177:191–201.

Draper, P., & Harpending, H. (1982). Father absence and reproductive strategy: An evolutionary perspective. *Journal of Anthropological Research* 38:255–273.

Drigotas, S., & Udry, J. (1993). Biosocial models of adolescent problem behavior: Extension to panel design. *Social Biology* 40:1–7.

Duara, R., Grady, C., Haxby, J., Ingvar, D., Sokoloff, L., Margolin, R., Manning, R., Cutler, N., & Rapoport, S. (1984). Human brain glucose utilization and cognitive function in relation to age. *Annals of Neurology* 16:702–713.

Dufty, A. (1993). Personal communication [conversation].

Dumaret, A. (1985). IQ, scholastic performance and behavior of sibs raised in contrasting environments. *Journal of Child Psychology and Psychiatry and Allied Disciplines* 26:553–580.

Durant, W. (1957). *The story of civilization: Vol. 6. The reformation.* New York: Simon & Schuster.

Durden-Smith, J., & de Simone, D. (1983). *Sex and the brain.* New York: Arbor House.

Durkheim, E. (1951). *Suicide.* New York: Free Press.

Durkheim, E. (1982). *Rules of sociological method.* (S. Lukes [Trans.]). New York: Free Press.

Eckland, B. (1979). Genetic variance in the SES-IQ correlation. *Sociology of Education* 52:191–196.

Edelman, G. (1987). *Neural Darwinism. The theory of neuronal group selection.* New York: Basic Books.

Edelman, G. (1992). *Bright air, brilliant fire.* New York: Basic Books.

Edlin, G. (1990). *Human genetics: A modern synthesis.* Boston: Jones & Bartlett.

Ehrenkranz, J., Bliss, E., & Sheard, M. (1974). Plasma testosterone: Correlation with aggressive behavior and social dominance in man. *Psychosomatic Medicine* 36:469–475.

Ehrhardt, A., Evers, K., & Money, J. (1968). Influence of androgen and some aspects of sexually dimorphic behavior in women with late-treated adrenogenital syndrome. *Johns Hopkins Medical Journal* 123:115–122.

Ehrman, L., & Parsons, P. (1976). *The genetics of behavior.* Sunderland, Mass.: Sinauer Associates.

Ellis, B. (1992). The evolution of sexual attraction: Evaluative mechanisms in women. In J. Barkow, L. Cosmides, & J. Tooby (Eds.), *The adapted mind: Evolutionary psychology and the generation of culture* (pp. 267–288). New York: Oxford University Press.

Ellis, D., & Austin, P. (1971). Menstruation and aggressive behavior in a correctional center for women. *Journal of Criminal Law, Criminology, and Police Science* 62:388–395.

Ellis, L. (1977). The decline and fall of sociology: 1975–2000. *American Sociologist* 12:56–66.

Ellis, L. (1986). Evidence of neuroandrogenic etiology of sex differences from a combined analysis of human, nonhuman primate and nonprimate mammalian studies. *Personality and Individual Differences* 7:519–552.

Ellis, L. (1987a). Criminal behavior and r/K selection: An extension of gene-based evolutionary theory. *Deviant Behavior* 8:149–176.

Ellis, L. (1987b). Relationships of criminality and psychopathy with eight other apparent behavioral manifestations of sub-optimal arousal. *Personality and Individual Differences* 8:905–925.

Ellis, L. (1989). Evolutionary and neurochemical causes of sex differences in victimizing behavior: Toward a unified theory of criminal behavior. *Social Science Information* 28:605–636.

Ellis, L. (1989–1990). Sex differences in criminality: An explanation based on the concept of r/K selection. *Mankind Quarterly* 30:17–37, 399–417.

Ellis, L. (1990). Left- and mixed handedness and criminality: Explanations for a probable relationship. In S. Coren (Ed.), *Left-handedness: Behavioral implications and anomalies* (pp. 485–507). Amsterdam: Elsevier–North Holland.

Ellis, L. (1991). Monoamine oxidase and criminality: Identifying an apparent biological marker for antisocial behavior. *Journal of Research in Crime and Delinquency* 28:227–251.

Ellis, L., & Ames, M. (1987). Neurohormonal functioning and sexual orientation: A theory of homosexuality–heterosexuality. *Psychological Bulletin* 101:233–258.

Ellis, L., & Coontz, P. (1990). Androgens, brian functioning, and criminality: The neurohormonal foundations of antisociality. In L. Ellis & H. Hoffman (Eds.), *Crime in biological, social, and moral contexts* (pp. 162–193). New York: Praeger.

Ellis, L., & Nyborg, H. (1992). Racial/ethnic variations in male testosterone levels: A probable contributor to group differences in health. *Steroids* 57:72–75.

Elmer, E. (1977). *Fragile families, troubled children.* Pittsburgh: University of Pittsburgh Press.

Elshtain, J. (1991). What's the matter with sex today? In R. Francoeur (Ed.), *Taking sides: Clashing views on controversial issues in human sexuality.* Guilford, Conn.: Dushkin.

Emory, L., Cole, C., & Meyer, W. (1992). The Texas experience with DepoProvera: 1980–1990. *Journal of Offender Rehabilitation* 18:125–139.

Ernulf, K., Innala, S., & Whitam, F. (1989). Biological explanation, psychological explanation, and tolerance of homosexuals: A cross-national analysis of beliefs and attitudes. *Psychological Reports* 65:1003–1010.

Eshleman, J. (1988). *The family.* Boston: Allyn & Bacon.

Eysenck, H. (1977). *Crime and personality.* London: Routledge & Kegan Paul.

Eysenck, H. (1982). The sociology of psychological knowledge, the genetic interpretation of the IQ and Marxist–Leninist ideology. *Bulletin of the British Psychological Society* 35:449–451.

Eysenck, H. (1990). Genetic and environmental contributions to individual differences: The three major dimensions of personality. *Journal of Personality* 58:245–261.

Eysenck, H., & Gudjonsson, G. (1989). *The causes and cures of criminality.* New York: Plenum.

Eysenck, H., & Kamin, L. (1981). *The intelligence controversy.* New York: John Wiley.

Farley, J. (1990). *Sociology.* Englewood Cliffs, N.J.: Prentice-Hall.

Farrington, D. (1987). Implications of biological findings for criminological research. In S. Mednick, T. Moffitt, & S. Stack (Eds.), *The causes of crime: New biological approaches* (pp. 42–64). Cambridge: University of Cambridge Press.

Farrington, D. (1988). Social, psychological and biological influences on juvenile delinquency and adult crime. In W. Buikhuisen & S. Mednick (Eds.), *Explaining criminal behavior* (pp. 68–89). Leiden, The Netherlands: E. J. Brill.

Fay, R., Turner, C., Klassen, A., & Gagnon, J. (1989). Prevalence and patterns of same-gendered sexual contact among men. *Science* 243:338–348.

Feder, H. (1984). Hormones and sexual behavior. *Annual Review of Psychology* 35:165–200.

Feder, K., & Park, M. (1989). *Human antiquity.* Mountain View, Calif.: Mayfield.

Federal Bureau of Investigation. (1993). *Uniform crime report.* Washington, D.C.: U.S. Government Printing Office.

Fincher, J. (1982). *The human brain: Mystery of matter and mind.* Washington, D.C.: U.S. News Books.

Fischbach, G. (1992). Mind and brain. *Scientific American* 267:48–57.

Fischbein, S. (1980). IQ and social class. *Intelligence* 4:51–63.

Fishbein, D. (1992). The psychobiology of female aggression. *Criminal Justice and Behavior* 19:99–126.

Fishbein, D., & Pease, S. (1990). Neurological links between substance abuse and crime. In L. Ellis & H. Hoffman (Eds.), *Crime in biological, social, and moral contexts* (pp. 218–243). New York: Praeger.

Fisher, A. (1991). A new synthesis comes of age. *Mosaic* 22:2–17.

Fisher, H. (1989). Evolution of human serial pairbonding. *American Journal of Physical Anthropology* 78:331–354.

Fisher, H. (1992). *Anatomy of love: The natural history of monogamy, adultery, and divorce.* New York: W. W. Norton.

Flaherty, J., & Richman, J. (1986). Effects of childhood relationships on the adult's capacity to form social supports. *American Journal of Psychiatry* 143:851–855.

Fletcher, R. (1991). *Science, ideology and the media: The Cyril Burt scandal.* New Brunswick, N.J.: Transaction Publishers.

Flor-Henry, P. (1980). Cerebral aspects of the orgasmic response: Normal and deviational. In R. Forleo & W. Pasini (Eds.), *Medical sexology* (pp. 256–262). Amsterdam: Elsevier-North Holland.

Flor-Henry, P. (1987). Cerebral aspects of sexual deviation. In G. Wilson (Ed.), *Variant sexuality: Research and theory* (pp. 49–83). Baltimore: Johns Hopkins University Press.

Flor-Henry, P., Koles, Z., & Reddon, J. (1985). EEG studies of sex differences, cognitive and age effects in normals (age range 18–60 years). *Electroencephalography and Clinical Neurophysiology* 61:160–161.

Flowers, R. (1988). *Minorities and criminality.* New York: Greenwood.

Flynn, J. (1984). The mean IQ of Americans: Massive gains 1932 to 1978. *Psychological Bulletin* 95:29–51.

Foley, R., & Lee, P. (1989). Finite social space, evolutionary pathways, and reconstructing hominid behavior. *Science* 243:901–906.

Fortune, W. (1939). Apapesh warfare. *American Anthropologist* 41:22–41.

Fossett, M., & Kiecolt, K. (1993). Mate availability and family structure among African Americans in U.S. metropolitan areas. *Journal of Marriage and the Family* 55:288–302.

Fox, N., & Davidson, R. (1987). Electroencephalogram asymmetry in response to the approach of a stranger and maternal separation in 10-month-old infants. *Developmental Psychology* 23:233–240.

Frank, G. (1983). *The Wechsler enterprise.* New York: Pergamon.

Freedman, D. (1974). *Human infancy: An evolutionary perspective.* Hillsdale, N.J.: Lawrence Erlbaum.

Freedman, D. (1984). Ethnic differences in babies. In H. Fitzgerald & M. Walraven (Eds.), *Human development* (pp. 87–92). Guilford, Conn.: Dushkin.

Freud, S. (1961). *Civilization and its discontents.* New York: Norton.

Freud, S. (1965). *The new introductory lectures on psychoanalysis.* New York: Norton.

Frost, L., & Chapman, L. (1987). Polymorphous sexuality as an indicator of psychosis proneness. *Journal of Abnormal Psychology* 96:299–304.

Futuyama, D., & Risch, S. (1984). Sexual orientation, sociobiology, and evolution. *Journal of Homosexuality* 9:157–168.

Gagnon, J., & Simon, W. (1973). *Sexual conduct: The social sources of human sexuality.* Chicago: Aldine-Atherton.

Gangestad, S., & Simpson, J. (1990). Toward an evolutionary history of female sociosexual variation. *Journal of Personality* 58:69–96.

Garfinkel, I., & McLanahan, S. (1986). *Single mothers and their children: A new American dilemma.* Washington, D.C.: The Urban Institute.

Gaylin, W. (1986). *Rediscovering love.* New York: Penguin.

Geary, D. (1989). A model for representing gender differences in the pattern of cognitive abilities. *American Psychologist* 44:1155–1156.

Gelman, D. (1992). Born or bred. *Newsweek* (February 24):46–53.

Gerschwind, N. (1965). Disconnexion syndromes in animals and man. *Brain* 88:237–294.

Gerschwind, N. (1984). The biology of cerebral dominance: Implications for cognition. *Cognition* 17:193–208.

Gewertz, D. (1981). A historical reconsideration of female dominance among the Chambri of Papua New Guinea. *American Ethnologist* 8:94–106.

Gewertz, D., & Errington, F. (1991). *Twisted histories, altered contexts: Representing the Chambuli in a world system.* Cambridge: Cambridge University Press.

Gilder, G. (1976). *Sexual suicide.* New York: Bantam.

Gill, R. (1992). For the sake of the children. *Public Interest* 108:81–96.

Gladue, B., Green, R., & Hellman, R. (1984). Neuroendocrine response to estrogen and sexual orientation. *Science* 225:1469–1499.

Glasser, W. (1975). *Reality therapy.* New York: Harper & Row.

Glenn, N. (1993). A plea for objective assessment of the notion of family decline. *Journal of Marriage and the Family* 55:542–544.

Goelet, P., Castellucci, V., Schacher, S., & Kandel, E. (1986). The long and short of long-term memory. *Nature* 322:419–422.

Goldberg, S. (1974). *The inevitability of patriarchy.* New York: Morrow.

Goldberg, S. (1991). Reaffirming the obvious. In R. Francoeur (Ed.), *Taking sides: Clashing views on controversial issues in human sexuality* (pp. 4–8). Guilford, Conn.: Dushkin.

Goldman-Rakic, P. (1987). Development of cortical circuitry and cognitive function. *Child Development* 58:601–622.

Goldsmith, H. (1994). Nature–nurture issues in the behavioral genetics context: Overcoming barriers to communication. In R. Plomin & G. McClearn (Eds.), *Na-*

ture, nurture, and psychology (pp. 325–339). Washington, D.C.: American Psychological Association.

Goldstein, M. (1987). When brothers share a wife. *Natural History* 96:38–49.

Gonczol, K. (1993). Anxiety over crime. *Hungarian Quarterly* 129:87–99.

Goodman, R. (1987). Genetic and hormonal factors in human sexuality: Evolutionary and developmental perspectives. In G. Wilson (Ed.), *Variant sexuality: Research and theory* (pp. 21–48). Baltimore: Johns Hopkins University Press.

Goodman, R., Anderson, D., Bullock, D., Sheffield, B., Lynch, S., & Butt, W. (1985). Study of the effects of estradiol on gonadotrophin levels in untreated male-to-female transsexuals. *Archives of Sexual Behavior* 14:141–146.

Gordon, R. (1973). An explicit estimation of the prevalence of commitment to a training school, to age 18, by race and by sex. *Journal of the American Statistical Association* 68:547–553.

Gordon, R. (1976). Prevalence: The rare datum in delinquency measurement and its implications for the theory of delinquency. In M. W. Klein (Ed.), *The juvenile justice system* (pp. 201–284). Beverly Hills, Calif.: Sage.

Gordon, R. (1980). Research on IQ, race, and delinquency: Taboo or not taboo? In E. Sagarin (Ed.), *Taboos in criminology* (pp. 37–66). Beverly Hills, Calif.: Sage.

Gordon, R. (1986). Scientific justification and the race–IQ–delinquency model. In T. F. Hartnagel & R. A. Silverman (Eds.), *Critique and explanation: Essays in honor of Gwynne Nettler* (pp. 91–131). New Brunswick, N.J.: Transaction Books.

Gordon, R. (1987). SES versus IQ in the race–delinquency model. *International Journal of Sociology and Social Policy* 7:30–96.

Gordon, R., & Gleser, L. (1974). The estimation of the prevalence of delinquency: Two approaches and a correction of the literature. *Journal of Mathematical Sociology* 3:275–291.

Gordon, R., & Rudert, E. (1979). Bad news about intelligence tests. *Sociology of Education* 52:174–190.

Gorski, R. (1990). Interview with Roger Gorski. *Omni* 13:71–78, 132–140.

Gottfredson, L. (1986). Societal consequences of the *g* factor in employment. *Journal of Vocational Behavior* 29:379–410.

Gottfredson, L. (1987). The practical significance of black–white differences in intelligence. *Behavioral and Brain Sciences* 10:510–512.

Gottfredson, L. (1994). Egalitarian fiction and collective fraud. *Society* 31(3):53–59.

Gottfredson, M., & Hirschi, T. (1990). *A general theory of crime.* Stanford: Stanford University Press.

Gottlieb, G. (1983). The psychobiological approach to developmental issues. In M. Haith & J. Campos (Eds.), *Infancy and developmental psychobiology* (pp. 1–26). New York: John Wiley.

Gottlieb, G. (1991). Experiential canalization of behavioral development: Theory. *Developmental Psychology* 27:4–13.

Gottschalk, L. (1990). The psychotherapies in the context of new developments in the neurosciences and biological psychiatry. *American Journal of Psychotherapy* 44:321–337.

Gould, J., & Gould, C. (1988). *Sexual selection.* New York: Scientific American.

Gould, S. (1977). *Ontogeny and phylogeny.* Cambridge: Harvard University Press.

Gould, S. (1991). Exaptation: A crucial tool for an evolutionary psychology. *Journal of Social Issues* 47:43–65.

Gould, S. (1992). Ontogeny and phylogeny revisited and reunited. *Bioessays* 14:275–279.

Gove, W. (1985). The effect of age and gender on deviant behavior: A biopsychological perspective. In A. Rossi (Ed.), *Gender and the life course* (pp. 115–148). New York: Aldine.

Greenberg, M., & Schneider, D. (1994). Violence in American cities: Young black males is the answer, but what was the question? *Social Science and Medicine* 39:179–187.

Greenough, W., Black, J., & Wallace, C. (1987). Experience and brain development. *Child Development* 58:539–559.

Gress-Wright, J. (1993). The contraception paradox. *Public Interest* 113:15–25.

Gubernick, D., Sengelaub, D., & Kurz, E. (1993). A neuroanatomical correlate: Paternal and maternal behavior in the biparental California mouse (*Peromyscus californicus*). *Behavioral Neuroscience* 107:194–201.

Guterman, S. (1979). I.Q. tests in research on social stratification: The cross-class validity of the tests. *Sociology of Education* 52:163–173.

Gutman, H. (1976). *The black family in slavery and freedom, 1750–1925.* New York: Pantheon.

Guttentag, M., & Secord, P. (1983). *Too many women?: The sex ratio question.* Beverly Hills, Calif.: Sage.

Haier, R. (1990). The end of intelligence research. *Intelligence* 14:371–374.

Haier, R., Siegel, B., Nuechterlein, K., Hazlett, E., Wu, J., Paek, J., Browning, H., & Buchsbaum, M. (1988). Cortical glucose metabolic rate correlates of abstract reasoning and attention studies with positron emission tomography. *Intelligence* 12:199–217.

Halleck, S. (1971). *Psychiatry and the dilemmas of crime: A study of causes, punishment, and treatment.* Berkeley: University of California Press.

Hallman, J., Oreland, L., Edaman, G., & Schalling, D. (1987). Thrombocyte monoamine oxidase activity and personality traits in women with severe premenstrual syndrome. *Acta Psychiatrica Scandinavia* 76:225–234.

Hamburg, D. (1993). The American family transformed. *Society* 30:60–69.

Hammer, D., Hu, S., Magnuson, V., Hu, N., & Pattatucci, A. (1993). A linkage between DNA markers on the X chromosome and male sexual orientation. *Science* 261:321–327.

Harre, R. (1967). Philosophy of science, history of. In P. Edwards (Ed.), *The encyclopedia of philosophy* (Vol. 6, pp. 289–296). New York: Macmillan.

Haskett, R. (1987). Premenstrual dysphoric disorder: Evaluation and treatment. *Progress in Neuro-Psychopharmacology and Biological Psychiatry* 11: 129–135.

Hazard, J., Butler, W., & Maggs, P. (1977). *The Soviet legal system.* Dobbs Ferry, N.Y.: Oceana.

Hazen, R., & Trefil, J. (1991). *Science matters.* New York: Doubleday.

Heath, A., Berg, K., Eaves, L., Solaas, M., Corey, L., Sundet, J., Magnus, P., & Nance, W. (1985). Education policy and the heritability of educational attainment. *Nature* 314:734–736.

Hedblom, J. (1972). The female homosexual: Social and attitudinal dimensions. In J. McCaffrey (Ed.), *The homosexual dialectic* (pp. 31–64). Englewood Cliffs, N.J.: Prentice-Hall.

Heer, D., & Grossband-Shechtman, A. (1981). The impact of the female marriage squeeze and the contraceptive revolution on sex roles and the women's liberation movement in the United States, 1960 to 1975. *Journal of Marriage and the Family* 43:49–65.

Heim, N., & Hursch, C. (1979). Castration for sex offenders: Treatment or punishment? A review and critique of recent European literature. *Archives of Sexual Behavior* 8:281–304.

Heller, W. (1990). The neuropsychology of emotion: Developmental patterns and implications for psychopathology. In N. Stein, B. Leventhal, & T. Trabasso (Eds.), *Psychological and biological approaches to emotion* (pp. 167–211). Hillsdale, N.J.: Lawrence Erlbaum.

Hendrick, C., & Hendrick, S. (1991). Dimensions of love: A sociobiological interpretation. *Journal of Social and Clinical Psychology* 10:206–230.

Henggeler, S., Edwards, J., & Borduin, C. (1987). The family relations of female juvenile delinquents. *Journal of Abnormal Child Psychology* 15:199–209.

Herdt, G., & Davidson, J. (1988). The Sambian "turnim man": Sociocultural and clinical aspects of gender formation in male pseudohermaphrodites with 5-alpha-reductase deficiency in Papua New Guinea. *Archives of Sexual Behavior* 17:33–56.

Herrnstein, R. (1973). *IQ in the meritocracy.* Boston: Little, Brown.

Herrnstein, R. (1980). In defense of intelligence tests. *Commentary* 69:40–51.

Herrnstein, R. (1989). Biology and crime [National Institute of Justice Crime File, NCJ 97216]. Washington, D.C.: U.S. Department of Justice.

Herrnstein, R., & Murray, C. (1994). *The bell curve: Intelligence and class structure in American life.* New York: Free Press.

Hertzig, M., Birch, H., Richardson, S., & Tizard, J. (1972). Intellectual levels of school children severely malnourished during the first two years of life. *Pediatrics* 49:814–824.

Hess, B., Markson, E., & Stein, P. (1988). *Sociology.* New York: Macmillan.

Hinde, R. (1991). When is an evolutionary approach useful? *Child Development* 62:671–675.

Hindelang, M. (1979). Sex differences in criminal activity. *Social Problems* 27:143–156.

Hirschi, T. (1969). *Causes of delinquency.* Berkeley: University of California Press.

Hirschi, T., & Hindelang, M. J. (1977). Intelligence and delinquency: A revisionist review. *American Sociological Review* 42:571–587.

Hoffman-Plotkin, D., & Twentyman, C. (1984). A multimodal assessment of behavioral and cognitive deficits in abused and neglected preschoolers. *Child Development* 55:794–802.

Hook, E. (1973). Behavioral implications of the human XYY genotype. *Science* 179:157–175.

Horn, H., & Rubenstein, D. (1984). Behavioural adaptations and life history. In J. Krebs & N. Davies (Eds.), *Behavioral ecology: An evolutionary approach* (pp. 279–298). Sunderland, Mass.: Sinauer Associates.

Hosking, G. (1985). *The first socialist society: A history of the Soviet Union from within.* Cambridge: Harvard University Press.

Hoult, T. (1984). Human sexuality in biological perspective: Theoretical and methodological considerations. *Journal of Homosexuality* 9:137–155.

Hoyenga, K. B., & Hoyenga, K. T. (1979). *The question of sex differences: Psychological, cultural, and biological issues.* Boston: Little, Brown.

Huesmann, L., Eron, L., & Yarmel, P. (1987). Intellectual functioning and aggression. *Journal of Personality and Social Psychology* 52:232–240.

Hughes, R. (1993). *Culture of complaint: The fraying of America.* New York: Oxford University Press.

Humphreys, L. (1970). *Tearoom trade, impersonal sex in public places.* Chicago: Aldine.

Humphreys, L. (1986). Commentary. *Journal of Vocational Behavior* 29:421–437.

Humphreys, L. (1988). Trends in levels of academic achievement of blacks and other minorities. *Intelligence* 12:231–260.

Hunt, M. (1974). *Sexual behavior in the 1970s.* Chicago: Playboy Press.

Hutchinson, G. (1959). A speculative consideration of certain possible forms of sexual selection in man. *American Naturalist* 93:81–91.

Imperato-McGinley, J., Peterson, R., Gautier, T., & Sturla, E. (1979). Androgens and the evolution of male gender identity among male pseudohermaphrodites with 5 alpha-reductase deficiency. *New England Journal of Medicine* 300:1233–1237.

Insel, T. (1992). Oxytocin and the neurobiology of attachment. *Behavioral and Brain Sciences* 15:515–516.

Itzkoff, S. (1987). *Why humans vary in intelligence.* Ashfield, Mass.: Paideia.

Izard, C. (1992). Basic emotions, relations among emotions, and emotion–cognition relations. *Psychological Review* 99:561–565.

Jagger, A., & Rothenberg, P. (Eds.). (1984). *Feminist frameworks.* New York: McGraw Hill.

James, W. (1986). Hormonal control of sex ratio. *Journal of Theoretical Biology* 118:427–441.

James, W. (1987). The human sex ratio. Part 1. A review of the literature. *Human Biology* 59:721–752.

Jeffery, C. (1977). Criminology—Whither or wither? *Criminology* 15:283–286.

Jeffery, C. (Ed.) (1979). Biology and crime: The Neo-Lombrosians. In *Biology and crime* (pp. 7–18). Beverly Hills, Calif.: Sage.

Jeffery, C. (1990). *Criminology: An interdisciplinary approach.* Englewood Cliffs, N.J.: Prentice-Hall.

Jeffery, C. (1993). Obstacles to the development of research in crime and delinquency. *Journal of Research in Crime and Delinquency* 30:491–497.

Jencks, C. (1980). Heredity, environment, and public policy revisited. *American Sociological Review* 45:723–736.

Jensen, A. (1969). How much can we boost IQ and scholastic achievement? *Harvard Educational Review* 39:1–123.

Jensen, A. (1977). Cumulative deficit in IQ of blacks in the rural south. *Developmental Psychology* 13:184–191.

Jensen, A. (1980). *Bias in mental testing.* New York: Free Press.

Jensen, A. (1981). *Straight talk about mental testing.* New York: Free Press.

Jensen, A. (1985). The nature of the black–white difference on various psychometric tests: Spearman's hypothesis. *Behavioral and Brain Sciences* 8:193–263.

Jensen, A. (1992). Commentary: Vehicles of *g. Psychological Science* 3:275–278.

Jensen, A., & Faulstich, M. (1988). Differences between prisoners and the general population in psychometric *g. Personality and Individual Differences* 9:925–928.

Johnson, E., & Meade, A. (1987). Developmental patterns of spatial ability: An early sex difference. *Child Development* 58:275–740.

Jones, J. (1992). Can neuroscience provide a complete account of human nature? A reply to Roger Sperry. *Zygon* 27:187–202.

Joseph, R. (1982). The neuropsychology of development: Hemispheric laterality, limbic language, and the origin of thought. *Journal of Clinical Psychology* 38:4–33.

Joynson, R. (1989). *The Burt affair.* New York: Routledge.

Kagan, J., Reznick, S., & Snidman, N. (1987). The physiology and psychology of behavioral inhibition in children. *Child Development* 58:1459–1473.

Kalil, R. (1989). Synapse formation in the developing brain. *Scientific American* 261:76–85.

Kallmann, F. (1952). Twin and sibship study of overt male homosexuality. *American Journal of Human Genetics* 4:136–146.

Kandel, E. (1983). From metapsychology to molecular biology: Explorations into the nature of anxiety. *American Journal of Psychiatry* 140:1277–1293.

Kandel, E., & Hawkins, R. (1992). The biological basis of learning and individuality. *Scientific American* 267:79–86.

Kandel, E., Mednick, S., Kirkegaard-Sorensen, L., Hutchings, B., Knop, J., Rosenberg, R., & Schulsinger, F. (1988). IQ as a protective factor for subjects at high risk for anti-social behavior. *Journal of Consulting and Clinical Psychology* 55:224–226.

Kaplan, H. (1982). Prevalence of the self-esteem motive. In M. Rosenberg & H. Kaplan (Eds.), *Social psychology of the self-concept* (pp. 139–151). Arlington Heights, Ill.: Harlan Davidson.

Kaplan, R. (1985). The controversy related to the use of psychological tests. In B. Wolman (Ed.), *Handbook of intelligence: Theories, measurements, and applications* (pp. 465–504). New York: John Wiley.

Kaufman, A. (1976). Verbal-performance discrepancies on the WISC-R. *Journal of Consulting and Clinical Psychology* 5:739–744.

Keiser, T. (1976). Schizotype and the Wechsler digit-span test. *Journal of Clinical Psychology* 31:303–306.

Kemp, J. (1994). Blacks, Jews, liberals, and crime. *National Review* 46(May 16):40–42.

Kemper, T. (1990a). *Social structure and testosterone: Explorations of the socio-bio-social chain.* New Brunswick, N.J.: Rutgers University Press.

Kemper, T. (Ed.). (1990b). *Research agendas in the sociology of emotions.* Albany: State University of New York Press.

Kennedy, S., Glasser, R., & Kiecolt-Glasser, J. (1990). Psychoneuro-immunology. In J. Cacioppo & L. Tassinary (Eds.), *Principles of psychophysiology: Physical, social, and inferrential elements* (pp. 177–190). New York: Cambridge University Press.

Kenrick, D., Sadalla, E., Groth, G., & Trost, M. (1990). Evolution, traits, and the stages of human courtship: Qualifying the parental investment model. *Journal of Personality* 58:97–116.

Khan, A., & Cataio, A. (1984). *Men and women in biological perspective: A review of the literature.* New York: Praeger.

Kimura, D. (1985). Male brain, female brain: The hidden difference. *Psychology Today* 19(November):51–58.

Kimura, D. (1992). Sex differences in the brain. *Scientific American* 267:119–125.

Kimura, D., & Hampton, E. (1988). Sex differences and hormonal influences on cognitive brain function. Paper presented at the 1988 meeting of the Society for Neuroscience, Toronto, Canada.

Kinsey, A., Pomeroy, W., & Martin, C. (1948). *Sexual behavior in the human male.* Philadelphia: Saunders.

Kinsey, A., Pomeroy, W., Martin, C., & Gebhard, P. (1953). *Sexual behavior in the human female.* Philadelphia: Saunders.

Klinteberg, B., Levander, D., Oreland, L., Asberg, M., & Schalling, D. (1987). Neuropsychological correlates of platelet monoamine oxydase (MAO) activity in female and male subjects. *Biological Psychology* 24:237–252.

Klinteberg, B., Schalling, D., Edman, G., Oreland, L., & Asberg, M. (1987). Neurophysiological correlates of platelet monoamine oxydase (MAO) activity in female and male subjects. *Neuropsychobiology* 18:89–96.

Kochanska, G. (1991). Socialization and temperament in the development of guilt and conscience. *Child Development* 62:1379–1392.

Kolb, B., & Whishaw, I. (1985). *Fundamentals of human neurophysiology.* New York: W. H. Freeman.

Konner, M. (1982). *The tangled wing: Biological constraints on the human spirit.* New York: Holt, Rinehart & Winston.

Konner, M. (1990). *Why the reckless survive, and other secrets of human nature.* New York: Penguin.

Kornhauser, R. (1978). *Social sources of delinquency.* Chicago: University of Chicago Press.

Kraemer, G. (1992). A psychobiological theory of attachment. *Behavioral and Brain Sciences* 15:493–541.

Krebs, J., & Davies, N. (1993). *An introduction to behavioural ecology.* London: Blackwell.

LaFree, G., Drass, K., & O'Day, P. (1992). Race and crime in postwar America: Determinants of African-American and white rates, 1957–1988. *Criminology* 30:157–185.

LaFree, G., & Russell, K. (1993). The argument for studying race and crime. *Journal of Criminal Justice Education* 4:273–289.

Lancaster, J., Altmann, J., Rossi, A., & Sherrod, L. (Eds.). (1987). The biosocial perspective. In *Parenting across the life span: Biosocial perspectives* (pp. 1–12). New York: Aldine De Gruyter.

Lancaster, J., & Lancaster, C. (1987). The watershed: Changes in parental investment and family formation strategies in the course of human evolution. In J. Lancaster, J. Altmann, A. Rossi, & L. Sherrod (Eds.), *Parenting across the life span: Biosocial perspectives* (pp. 187–205). New York: Aldine De Gruyter.

LaTorre, R., & Wendenburg, K. (1983). Psychological characteristics of bisexual, heterosexual, and homosexual women. *Journal of Homosexuality* 9:87–97.

Laub, J. (1983). Urbanism, race, and crime. *Journal of Research in Crime and Delinquency* 20:183–198.

Leibowitz, L. (1978). *Females, males, families: A biosocial approach.* North Scituate, Mass.: Duxbury.

Lenski, G. (1977). Sociology and sociobiology: An alternative view. *American Sociologist* 12:73–75.

Leslie, C. (1990). Scientific racism: Reflections on peer review, science and ideology. *Social Science and Medicine* 31:891–912.

Lesser-Blumberg, R. (1983). Kibbutz women: From the fields of revolution to the laundries of discontent. In M. Palgi, J. Blasi, M. Rosner, & M. Safir (Eds.), *Sexual equality: The Israeli kibbutz tests the theories* (pp. 130–150). Norwood, Pa.: Norwood Editions.

LeVay, S. (1991). A difference in hypothalamic structure between heterosexual and homosexual men. *Science* 253:1034–1037.

LeVay, S. (1993). *The sexual brain.* Cambridge, Mass.: MIT Press.

Levenson, R., Ekman, P., Heider, K., & Friesen, W. (1992). Emotion and autonomic nervous system activity in the Minangkabau of West Sumatra. *Journal of Personality and Social Psychology* 62:972–988.

Levine, D. (1993). Survival of the synapses. *The Sciences* 33:46–52.

Levine, S., Halmeyer, G., Karas, G., & Denenberg, V. (1967). Physiological and behavioral effects of infant stimulation. *Physiology and Behavior* 2:55–59.

Lewontin, R. (1982). *Human diversity.* New York: Scientific American.

Leyton, E. (1986). *Hunting humans: Inside the minds of mass murderers.* New York: Pocket Books.

Liebowitz, M. (1983). *The chemistry of love.* New York: Berkley.

Linn, M., & Petersen, A. (1986). A meta-analysis of gender differences in spacial ability: Implications for mathematics and science achievements. In J. Hyde & M. Linn (Eds.), *The psychology of gender: Advances through meta-analysis* (pp. 67–101). Baltimore: Johns Hopkins University Press.

Llinas, R. (Ed.). (1988). Editor's introduction. In *The biology of the brain: From neurons to networks* (pp. vi–x). New York: W. H. Freeman.

Llinas, R. (1989). The intrinsic electrophysiological properties of mammalian neurons: A new insight into CNS functioning? *Science* 242:1654–1664.

Locurto, C. (1990). The malleability of IQ as judged from adoption studies. *Intelligence* 14:275–292.

Locurto, C. (1991). *Sense and nonsense about IQ: The case for uniqueness.* New York: Praeger.

Loehlin, J., Horn, J., & Willerman, L. (1989). Modeling IQ change: Evidence from the Texas adoption project. *Child Development* 60:993–1004.

Longstreth, L. (1981). Revisiting Skeels' final study: A critique. *Developmental Psychology* 17:620–625.

Loury, G. (1987). The better path to black progess: Beyond civil rights. In L. Barnes (Ed.), *Social problems.* Guilford, Conn.: Dushkin.

Lovejoy, C. (1981). The origin of man. *Science* 211:341–350.

Lovejoy, C. (1984). The natural detective: An anthropologist probes the myterious origins of bipedality. *Natural History* 93(10):24–30.

Luks, F., Hansbrough, F., Klotz, D., Kottmeier, P., & Tolete-Valcek, F. (1988). Early gender assignment in true hermaphrodism. *Journal of Pediatric Surgery* 23:1122–1126.

Lynam, D., Moffitt, T., & Stouthamer-Loeber, M. (1993). Explaining the relation between IQ and delinquency: Class, race, test motivation, school failure, or self control? *Journal of Abnormal Psychology* 102:187–196.

Lynch, G., & Baudry, M. (1984). The biochemistry of memory: A new and specific hypothesis. *Science* 224:1057–1063.

Lynn, M. (1989). Race differences in sexual behavior: A critique of Rushton and Bogaert's evolutionary hypothesis. *Journal of Research in Personality* 23:1–6.

Lynn, R. (1978). Ethnic and racial differences in intelligence: International comparisons. In T. Osborne, C. Noble, & N. Weyl (Eds.), *Human variation: The biopsychology of age, race, and sex* (pp. 261–286). New York: Academic Press.

Lynn, R. (1990). Testosterone and gonadotropin levels and r/K reproductive strategies. *Psychological Reports* 67:1203–1206.

Maccoby, E. (1988). Gender as a social category. *Developmental Psychology* 24:755–765.

Maccoby, E. (1991). Different reproductive strategies in males and females. *Child Development* 62:676–681.

MacDonald, K. (1992). Warmth as a developmental construct: An evolutionary analysis. *Child Development* 63:753–773.

Macionis, J. (1989). *Sociology.* Englewood Cliffs, N.J.: Prentice-Hall.

MacIver, R. (1960). Juvenile delinquency. In E. Ginsberg (Ed.), *The nation's children* (Vol. 3, pp. 103–123). New York: Columbia University Press.

Mackintosh, N. (1986). The biology of intelligence? *British Journal of Psychology* 77:1–18.

MacLean, P. (1973). *A triune concept of the brain and behavior.* Toronto: University of Toronto Press.

Magnusson, D. (1988). *Individual development from an interactional perspective: A longitudinal study.* Hillsdale, N.J.: Erlbaum.

Mandoki, M., Sumner, G., Hoffman, R., & Riconda, D. (1991). A review of Klinefelter's syndrome in children and adolescents. *Journal of the Academy of Child and Adolescent Psychiatry* 30:167–172.

Martineau, J., Tanguay, P., Garreau, B., Roux, S., & Lelord, G. (1984). Are there sex differences in averaged evoked responses produced by coupling sound and light in children and adults? *International Journal of Psychophysiology* 2:177–183.

Marx, J. (1982). Autoimmunity in left-handers. *Science* 217:141–144.

Marx, J. (1983). The two sides of the brain. *Science* 220:488–490.

Marx, K., & Engels, F. (1956). *The holy family, or critique of critical critique.* London: Foreign Language Publishing House.

Maslow, A. (1954). *Motivation and personality.* New York: Harper & Row.

Matarazzo, J. (1976). *Wechsler's measurement and appraisal of adult intelligence.* Baltimore: Williams & Wilkins.

Matarazzo, J. (1992). Psychological testing and assessment in the 21st century. *American Psychologist* 47:1007–1018.

Mawson, A., & Mawson, C. (1977). Psychopathy and arousal: A new interpretation of the psychophysiological literature. *Biological Psychiatry* 12:49–73.

Mazur, A. (1981). Biosociology. In J. Short (Ed.), *The state of sociology* (pp. 141–160). Beverly Hills, Calif.: Sage.

McCartney, K., Harris, M., & Bernieri, F. (1990). Growing up and growing apart: A developmental meta-analysis of twin studies. *Psychological Bulletin* 107:226–237.

McEwen, B. (1981). Neural gonadal steroid actions. *Science* 211:1303–1311.

McGue, M. (1989). Nature–nurture and intelligence. *Nature* 340:507–508.

McGue, M., Bacon, S., & Lykken, D. (1993). Personality stability and change in early adulthood: A behavioral genetic analysis. *Developmental Psychology* 29:96–109.

McHenry, H. (1991). Sexual dimorphism in *Australopithecus afarensis. Journal of Human Evolution* 20:21–32.

McLaren, A. (1990). What makes a man a man? *Nature* 346:216–217.

McLoughlin, M. (1990). Men vs. women. In K. Finsterbusch (Ed.), *Sociology 90/91* (pp. 55–61). Guilford, Conn.: Dushkin.

McNaughton, N. (1989). *Biology and emotion.* New York: Cambridge University Press.

Mead, M. (1935). *Sex and temperament in three primitive societies.* New York: Morrow.

Mead, M. (1949). *Male and female: A study of the sexes in a changing world.* New York: Morrow.

Mealey, L. (1990). Differential use of reproductive strategies by human groups? *Psychological Science* 1:385–387.

Mednick, S. (1979). Biosocial factors and primary prevention of antisocial behavior. In S. Mednick & S. Shoham (Eds.), *New paths in criminology* (pp. 45–53). Lexington, Mass.: Lexington Books.

Mednick, S., & Finello, K. (1983). Biological factors and crime: Implications for forensic psychiatry. *International Journal of Law and Psychiatry* 6:1–15.

Mellen, S. (1981). *The evolution of love.* San Francisco: W. H. Freeman.

Meltzer, H., & Zureick, J. (1987). Relationship of auditory hallucinations and paranoia to platelet MAO activity in schizophrenics: Sex and race interactions. *Psychiatry Research* 22:99–109.

Messner, S., & Sampson, R. (1991). The sex ratio, family disruption, and rates of violent crime: The paradox of demographic structure. *Social Forces* 69:693–713.

Meyer-Bahlburg, H. (1979). Sex hormones and female homosexuality: A critical examination. *Archives of Sexual Behavior* 8:101–119.

Meyer-Bahlburg, H. (1990–1991). Will prenatal hormone treatment prevent homosexuality? *Journal of Child and Adolescent Psychopharmacology* 1:279–283.

Miller, J. (1984). The development of woman's sense of self. Working paper, Stone Center for Developmental Services and Studies, Wellesley College, Wellesley, Massachusetts.

Miller, L. (1987). Neuropsychology of the aggressive psychopath: An integrative review. *Aggressive Behavior* 13:119–140.

Miller, L. (1988). The emotional brain. *Psychology Today* 22:34–42.

Moffitt, T. (1993). Adolescent-limited and life-course-persistent antisocial behavior: A developmental taxonomy. *Psychological Review* 100:674–701.

Moffitt, T., & Silva, P. (1988). IQ and delinquency: A test of the differential detection hypothesis. *Journal of Abnormal Psychology* 97:330–333.

Moir, A., & Jessel, D. (1991). *Brain sex: The real difference between men and women.* New York: Lyle Stuart.

Molenaar, P., Boomsma, D., & Dolan, C. (1993). A third source of developmental differences. *Behavior Genetics* 23:519–524.

Money, J. (1980). *Love and lovesickness: The science of sex, gender difference, and pair-bonding.* Baltimore: Johns Hopkins University Press.

Money, J. (1986). *Venuses penuses: Sexology, sexosophy, and exigency theory.* Buffalo: Prometheus.

Money, J. (1993). Specific neurocognitional impairments associated with Turner (45,X) and Klinefelter (47,XXY) syndromes: A review. *Social Biology* 40:147–151.

Money, J., & Ehrhardt, A. (1972). *Man and woman, boy and girl.* New York: New American Library.

Money, J., & Lewis, V. (1982). Homosexual/heterosexual status in boys at puberty: Ideopathic adolescent gynecomastia and congenital virilizing adrenocorticism compared. *Psychoneuroendocrinology* 7:339–346.

Money, J., Schwartz, M., & Lewis, V. (1985). Adult erotosexual status and fetal hormonal masculinization and demasculinization: 46,XX congenital virilizing adrenal hyperplasia and 46,XY androgen insensitivity syndrome compared. *Psychoneuroendocrinology* 9:405–414.

Montagu, A. (1974). *The natural superiority of women.* New York: Collier.

Montagu, A. (1978). *Touching: The human significance of the skin.* New York: Harper & Row.

Montagu, A. (1979). My conception of human nature. In T. Hanna (Ed.), *Explorers of humankind* (pp. 90–105). New York: Harper & Row.

Montagu, A. (1981). *Growing young.* New York: McGraw Hill.

Morell, V. (1993). Evidence for a possible "aggression" gene. *Science* 260:1722–1723.

Morowitz, H. (1979). *The wine of life.* London: ABACUS.

Morris, R. (1983). *Evolution and human nature.* New York: Avon.

Mosley, J., & Stan, E. (1984). Human sexual dimorphism: Its cost and benefit. In H. Reese (Ed.), *Advances in child development and behavior* (Vol. 18, pp. 147–185). Orlando, Fla.: Academic Press.

Moynihan, D. (1965). *The Negro family: The case for national action.* Washington, D.C.: U.S. Department of Labor.

Moynihan, D. (1992). How the Great Society "destroyed the American family." *Public Interest* 108:53–64.

Murdock, G. (1967). *Ethnographic atlas.* Pittsburgh: University of Pittsburgh Press.

Murray, L. (1987). Sexual destinies. *Omni* 9:100–128.

Naftolin, F. (1981). Understanding the bases of sex differences. *Science* 211:1263–1264.

Nass, R., & Baker, S. (1991a). Androgen effects on cognition: Congenital adrenal hyperplasia. *Psychoneuroendocrinology* 16:189–201.

Nass, R., & Baker, S. (1991b). Learning disabilities in children with congenital adrenal hyperplasia. *Journal of Child Neurology* 6:306–312.

National Science Board. (1987). *Science and engineering indicators, 1987.* Washington, D.C.: U.S. Government Printing Office.

Nettler, G. (1982). *Explaining criminals.* Cincinnati: Anderson.

Nielsen, J., & Christensen, A. (1974). Thirty-five males with double Y chromosome. *Journal of Psychological Medicine* 4:38–47.

Noel, B., & Revil, D. (1974). Some personality perspectives of XYY individuals taken from the general population. *Journal of Sex Research* 10:219–225.

Norton, E. (1987). Restoring the traditional black family. In L. Barnes (Ed.), *Social problems.* Guilford, Conn.: Dushkin.

Nyborg, H. (1984). Performance and intelligence in hormonally different groups. *Progress in Brain Research* 61:491–508.

Nyborg, H., & Boeggild, C. (1989). Mating behavior: Moves of mind or molecules? *Behavioral and Brain Sciences* 12:29–30.

O'Connor, L., & Fischette, C. (1987). Hormone effects on serotonin-dependent behaviors. *Annals of the New York Academy of Sciences* 512:437–444.

Oliver, M., & Hyde, J. (1993). Gender differences in sexuality: A meta-analysis. *Psychological Bulletin* 14:29–51.

Ornstein, R., & Thompson, R. (1984). *The amazing brain.* Boston: Houghton Mifflin.

Oxenkrug, G., & McIntyre, I. (1985). Stress-induced synthesis of melatonin: Possible involvement of the endogenous monoamine oxidase inhibitor (tribulin). *Life Sciences* 37:1743–1746.

Panksepp, J. (1992). A critical role for "affective neuroscience" in resolving what is basic about basic emotions. *Psychological Review* 99:554–560.

Parker, S. (1987). A sexual selection model for hominid evolution. *Human Evolution* 2:235–253.

Parks, R., Loewenstein, D., Dodrill, K., Barker, W., Yoshii, F., Chang, J., Emran, A., Apicella, A., Sheramata, W., & Duara, R. (1988). Cerebral metabolic effects of a verbal fluency test: A PET scan study. *Journal of Clinical and Experimental Neuropsychology* 10:565–575.

Pearsall, P. (1987). *Superimmunity.* New York: Fawcet.

Pedersen, F. (1991). Secular trends in human sex ratios: Their influence on individual and family behavior. *Human Nature* 2:271–291.

Pedersen, N., Plomin, R., & McClearn, G. (1994). Is there G beyond *g*? (Is there genetic influence on specific cognitive abilities independent of genetic influence on general cognitive ability?) *Intelligence* 18:133–143.

Peres, Y., & Hopp, M. (1990). Loyalty and aggression in human groups. In J. van der Dennen & V. Falger (Eds.), *Sociobiology and conflict* (pp. 123–130). London: Chapman & Hall.

Phillips, K. (1990). Why can't a man be more like a woman . . . and vice versa? *Omni* 13:41–68.

Phillis, D., & Gromko, M. (1985). Sex differences in sexual activity: Reality or illusion? *Journal of Sex Research* 21:437–448.

Piattelli-Palmarini, M. (1989). Evolution, selection, and cognition: From "learning" to parameter setting in biology and the study of langauge. *Cognition* 27:1–52.

Pinker, S., & Bloom, P. (1992). Natural language and natural selection. In J. Barkow, L. Cosmides, & J. Tooby (Eds.), *The adapted mind: Evolutionary psychology and the generation of culture* (pp. 451–493). New York: Oxford University Press.

Plato. (1960). *The republic and other works.* (B. Jowett [Trans.]). Garden City, N.Y.: Dolphin.

Plomin, R. (1989). Environment and genes: Determinants of behavior. *American Psychologist* 44:105–111.

Plomin, R. (1990). The role of inheritance in learning. *Science* 248:183–188.

Plomin, R., & Bergeman, C. (1991). The nature of nurture: Genetic influences on environmental measures. *Behavioral and Brain Sciences* 14:373–427.

Plomin, R., Chipuer, H., & Loehlin, J. (1990). Behavioral genetics and personality. In L. Pervin (Ed.), *Handbook of personality theory and research* (pp. 225–243). New York: Guilford Press.

Plomin, R., & Daniels, D. (1987). Why are children in the same family so different from one another? *Behavioral and Brain Sciences* 10:1–60.

Plomin, R., & DeFries, J. (1980). Genetics and intelligence: Recent data. *Intelligence* 4:15–24.

Plomin, R., DeFries, J., & McClearn, G. (1980). *Behavioral genetics: A primer.* San Francisco: W. H. Freeman.

Plomin, R., McClearn, G., Smith, D., Vignetti, S., Chorney, M., Chorney, K., Venditti, C., Kasarda, S., Thompson, L., Detterman, D., Daniels, J., Owen, M., & McGuffin, P. (1994). DNA markers associated with high versus low IQ: The IQ quantitative trait loci (QTL) project. *Behavior Genetics* 24:107–118.

Plomin, R., & Neiderhiser, J. (1991). Quantitative genetics, molecular genetics, and intelligence. *Intelligence* 15:369–387.

Plotnick, R. (1990). Welfare and out-of-wedlock childbearing: Evidence from the 1980s. *Journal of Marriage and the Family* 52:735–746.

Pollock-Byrne, J. (1990). *Women, prison, and crime*. Pacific Grove, Calif.: Brooks/Cole.

Popenoe, D. (1993a). American family decline, 1960–1990: A review and appraisal. *Journal of Marriage and the Family* 55:527–542.

Popenoe, D. (1993b). A new familism: Renewing families. *Current* 350:36–40.

Popenoe, D. (1994). The family condition of America: Cultural change and public policy. In H. Aaron, T. Mann, & T. Taylor (Eds.), *Values and public policy* (pp. 81–111). Washington, D.C.: The Brookings Institute.

Potts, R. (1984). Home bases and early hominids. *American Scientist* 72:338–347.

Prescott, J. (1975). Body pleasure and the origins of pleasure. *Bulletin of the Atomic Scientist* 31:10–20.

Purifoy, F., & Koopmans, L. (1980). Androstenedione, testosterone, and free testosterone concentration in women of various occupations. *Social Biology* 26:179–188.

Quale, G. (1988). *A history of marriage systems*. New York: Greenwood Press.

Raine, A., Venables, P., & Williams, M. (1990). Relationships between central and autonomic measures of arousal at age 15 years and criminality at age 25 years. *Archives of General Psychiatry* 47:1003–1007.

Ramey, C. (1992). High-risk children and IQ: Altering intergenerational patterns. *Intelligence* 16:239–256.

Rees, J., & Harvey, P. (1991). The evolution of animal mating systems. In V. Reynolds & J. Kellett (Eds.), *Mating and marriage* (pp. 1–45). New York: Oxford University Press.

Reinisch, J. (1977). Prenatal exposure of human foetuses to synthetic progestin and oestrogen affects personality. *Nature* 226:561–562.

Reinisch, J. (1981). Prenatal exposure of human foetuses to synthetic progestins increases potential for aggression among humans. *Science* 211:1171–1172.

Reite, M. (1987). Some additional influences shaping the development of behavior. *Child Development* 58:596–600.

Restak, R. (1979). *The brain: The last frontier*. New York: Warner.

Restak, R. (1986). *The infant mind*. Garden City, N.Y.: Doubleday.

Restak, R. (1992). See no evil: Blaming the brain for criminal violence. *The Sciences* (July-August):16–21.

Reynolds, V. (1991). The biological basis of human patterns of mating and marriage. In V. Reynolds & J. Kellett (Eds.), *Mating and marriage* (pp. 46–89). New York: Oxford University Press.

Ribchester, R. (1986). *Molecule, nerve and embryo*. Glasgow: Blackie.

Rice, R. (1977). Neurophysiological development in premature infants following stimulation. *Developmental Psychology* 13:69–76.

Ricketts, W. (1984). Biological research on homosexuality: Ansell's cow or Occam's razor? *Journal of Homosexuality* 9:65–93.

Roberts, J., & Gabor, T. (1990). Lombrosian wine in a new bottle: Research on race and crime. *Canadian Review of Criminology* 32:291–313.

Roche, J. (1986). Premarital sex: Attitudes and behavior by dating stage. *Adolescence* 31:107–121.

Rogawski, M., & Barker, K. (1985). *Neurotransmitter actions in the vertebrate nervous system*. New York: Plenum.

Rohner, R. (1975). *They love me, they love me not: A worldwide study of the effects of parental acceptance and rejection.* New York: Hraf.

Rose, R., Bernstein, L., Judd, H., Hanisch, R., Pike, M., & Henderson, B. (1986). Serum testosterone levels in healthy young black and white men. *Journal of the National Cancer Institute* 76:45–48.

Rose, R., Holaday, J., & Bernstein, R. (1971). Plasma testosterone, dominance rank and aggressive behavior in male rhesus monkeys. *Nature* 231:366–368.

Rosenberg, M., & Kaplan, H. (1982). *Social psychology of the self-concept.* Arlington Heights, Ill.: Harlan Davidson.

Rosenzweig, M., Bennett, E., & Diamond, M. (1973). Brain changes in response to experience. In W. Greenough (Ed.), *The nature and nurture of behavior: Developmental psychobiology* (pp. 117–124). San Francisco: W. H. Freeman.

Rossi, A. (1964). Equality between the sexes: An immodest proposal. *Daedalus* 93:607–652.

Rossi, A. (1977). A biosocial perspective on parenting. *Daedalus* 106:1–31.

Rossi, A. (1984). Gender and parenthood: American Sociological Association, 1983 presidential address. *American Sociological Review* 49:1–19.

Rossi, A. (1987). Parenthood in transition: From lineage to child self-orientation. In J. Lancaster, J. Altmann, A. Rossi, & L. Sherrod (Eds.), *Parenting across the life span: Biosocial perspectives* (pp. 31–81). New York: Aldine De Gruyter.

Rothenberg, P. (1988). *Racism and sexism: An integrated study.* New York: St. Martin's.

Rowe, D. (1992). Three shocks to socialization research. *Behavioral and Brain Sciences* 14:401–402.

Rowe, D., & Osgood, D. (1984). Heredity and sociological theories of delinquency: A reconsideration. *American Sociological Review* 49:526–540.

Rubin, R. (1987). The neuroendocrinology and neurochemistry of antisocial behaviour. In S. Mednick, T. Moffitt, & S. Stack (Eds.), *The causes of crime* (pp. 239–262). Cambridge: Cambridge University Press.

Ruse, M. (1982). Are there gay genes? Sociobiology and homosexuality. *Journal of Homosexuality* 6:5–34.

Rushton, J. (1988a). Epigenetic rules in moral development: Distal–proximal approaches to altruism and aggression. *Aggressive Behavior* 14:35–50.

Rushton, J. (1988b). The reality of racial differences: A rejoinder with new evidence. *Personality and Individual Differences* 9:1035–1040.

Rushton, J. (1990a). Race and crime: A reply to Roberts and Gabor. *Canadian Journal of Criminology* 32:315–334.

Rushton, J. (1990b). Sir Francis Galton, epigenetic rules, genetic similarity theory, and human life history. *Journal of Personality* 58:117–140.

Rushton, J. (1991). Race differences: A reply to Mealey. *Psychological Science* 2:126.

Rushton, J. (1994). Comment on life-history evolution. *Current Anthropology* 35:41–42.

Rushton, J., & Bogaert, A. (1989). Population differences in susceptibility to AIDS: An evolutionary analysis. *Social Science and Medicine* 28:1211–1220.

Rushton, J., Fulker, D., Neale, M., Nias, D., & Eysenck, H. (1986). Altruism and aggression: The heritability of individual differences. *Journal of Personality and Social Psychology* 50:1192–1198.

Rutter, M., & Giller, H. (1984). *Juvenile delinquency: Trends and perspectives.* New York: Guilford.

Ryan, W. (1971). *Blaming the victim*. New York: Vintage.

Sabelli, H., Fahrer, R., Medina, R., & Fragola, E. (1994). Phenylethylamine relieves depression after selective MAO-B inhibition. *Journal of Neuropsychiatry and Clinical Neurosciences* 6:203.

Sagarin, E. (1980). Taboo subjects and taboo viewpoints in criminology. In E. Sagarin (Ed.), *Taboos in criminology* (pp. 7–21). Beverly Hills, Calif.: Sage.

Salzinger, S., Kaplan, S., Pelcovitz, D., Samit, C., & Kreiger, R. (1984). Parent and teacher assessment of children's behavior in maltreating families. *Journal of the American Academy of Child Psychiatry* 23:458–464.

Sampson, R. (1985). Race and criminal violence: A demographically disaggregated analysis of urban homicide. *Crime and Delinquency* 31:47–82.

Sanderson, S., & Ellis, L. (1992). Theoretical and political perspectives of American sociologists in the 1990s. *American Sociologist* 23:221–231.

Scarr, S. (1981). *Race, social class, and individual differences in IQ*. Hillsdale, N.J.: Lawrence Erlbaum Associates.

Scarr, S. (1988). Race and gender as psychological variables. *American Psychologist* 43:56–59.

Scarr, S. (1992). Developmental theories for the 1990s: Development and individual differences. *Child Development* 63:1–19.

Scarr, S. (1993). Biological and cultural diversity: The legacy of Darwin for development. *Child Development* 64:1333–1353.

Scarr, S., & Carter-Saltzman, L. (1986). Gentics and intelligence. In R. Sternberg (Ed.), *Handbook of human intelligence* (pp. 792–896). Cambridge: Cambridge University Press.

Scarr, S., & McCartney, K. (1983). How people make their own environments: A theory of genotype ——> environment effects. *Child Development* 54:424–435.

Scarr, S., Pakstis, A., Katz, S., & Barker, W. (1977). The absence of a relationship between degree of white ancestry and intellectual skills within a black population. *Human Genetics* 39:69–86.

Scarr, S., & Weinberg, R. (1978). The influence of "family background" on intellectual attainment. *American Sociological Review* 43:674–692.

Scarr-Salapatek, S. (1971). Race, social class, and IQ. *Science* 174:1285–1295.

Scarr-Salapatek, S., & Williams, M. (1973). The effects of early stimulation on low-birth-weight infants. *Child Development* 44:94–101.

Schalling, D. (1987). Personality correlates of plasma testosterone levels in young delinquents: An example of person-situated interaction? In S. Mednick, T. Moffitt, & S. Stack (Eds.), *The causes of crime: New biological approaches* (pp. 283–291). Cambridge: Cambridge University Press.

Schiavi, P., Theilgaard, A., Owen, D., & White, D. (1988). Sex chromosome anomalies, hormones, and sexuality. *Archives of General Psychiatry* 45:19–24.

Seligman, D. (1992). *A question of intelligence: The IQ debate in America*. New York: Birch Lane.

Selye, H. (1956). *The stress of life*. New York: McGraw Hill.

Selye, H. (1970). The evolution of the stress concept. *American Journal of Cardiology* 26:289–299.

Senger, H. (1993). Human rights and crime. Paper presented at the 11th International Congress on Criminology, August 22–28, Budapest, Hungary.

Shallis, T. (1991). Precis of *From neuropsychology to mental structure. Behavioral and Brain Sciences* 14:429–469.

Shapiro, L., & Insel, T. (1990). Infant's response to social separation reflects adult differences in affiliative behavior: A comparative developmental study in prairie and montane voles. *Developmental Psychobiology* 23:375–394.

Shaver, P., Hazan, C., & Bradshaw, D. (1988). Love and attachment: The integration of three behavioral systems. In R. Sternberg & M. Barnes (Eds.), *The Psychology of Love* (pp. 68–99). New Haven: Yale University Press.

Shields, W. (1992). An intellectual meal with many courses. *Politics and the Life Sciences* 11:124–126.

Shipman, P. (1986). Scavenging or hunting in early hominids: Theoretical framework and tests. *American Anthropologist* 88:27–43.

Sieff, D. (1990). Explaining biased sex ratios in human populations: A critique of recent studies. *Current Anthropology* 31:25–48.

Simons, R. (1978). The meaning of the IQ–delinquency relationship. *American Sociological Review* 43:268–270.

Simons, R., Beaman, J., Conger, R., & Chao, W. (1993). Stress, support, and antisocial behavior traits as determinants of emotional well-being and parenting practices among single mothers. *Journal of Marriage and the Family* 55:385–389.

Simons, R., & Blyth, D. (1988). *Moving into adolescence: The impact of pubertal change and school context.* Hawthorn, N.Y.: Aldine de Gruyter.

Simpson, M. (1980). The sociology of cognitive development. *Annual Review of Sociology* 6:287–313.

Singer, T. (1987). Perspectives in MAO: Past, present, and future. *Journal of Neural Transmission* 23:1–23.

Skinner, B. (1966). The phylogeny and ontogeny of behavior. *Science* 157:1205–1213.

Smith, D. (1993). Brain, environment, heredity, and personality. *Psychological Reports* 72:3–13.

Smith, M. (1987). Research on developmental sociobiology: Parenting and family behavior. In K. McDonald (Ed.), *Sociobiological perspectives in human development* (pp. 271–292). New York: Springer.

Smith, R. (Ed.). (1984). Human sperm competition. In *Sperm competition and the evolution of animal mating systems* (pp. 601–659). New York: Academic Press.

Smith, T. (1991). Adult sexual behavior in 1989: Number of partners, frequency of intercourse and risk of AIDS. *Family Planning Perspectives* 23:102–107.

Snyderman, M., & Rothman, S. (1988). *The IQ controversy, the media and public policy.* New Brunswick, N.J.: Transaction Books.

Solomon, R. (1980). The opponent-process theory of acquired motivation. *American Psychologist* 35:691–712.

South, S., & Trent, K. (1988). Sex ratios and women's roles: A crossnational analysis. *American Journal of Sociology* 93:1096–1115.

Sowell, T. (1983). *The economics and politics of race: An international perspective.* New York: William Morrow.

Sperry, R. (1991). Search for beliefs to live by consistent with science. *Zygon* 26: 237–258.

Spiro, M. (1975). *Children of the Kibbutz.* Cambridge: Harvard University Press.

Spiro, M. (1980). *Gender and culture: Kibbutz women revisited.* New York: Schocken.

Spoont, M. (1992). Modulatory role of serotonin in neural information processing: Implications for human psychopathology. *Psychological Bulletin* 112:330–350.

Spurdle, A., & Jenkins, T. (1993). Complex polymorphisms are revealed by Y chromosome probe 49a with BglIII, HindIII, PstI and SstI. *Annals of Human Genetics* 57:41–55.

Stacey, J. (1993). Good riddance to the "family": A response to David Popenoe. *Journal of Marriage and the Family* 55:545–547.

Stark, R. (1987). Deviant places: A theory of the ecology of crime. *Criminology* 25:893–909.

Stattin, H., & Klackenberg-Larsson, I. (1993). Early language and intelligence development and their relationship to future criminal behavior. *Journal of Abnormal Psychology* 102:369–378.

Steelman, L., & Doby, J. (1983). Family size and birth order as factors on the IQ performance of black and white children. *Sociology of Education* 56:101–109.

Sternberg, R. (1983). How much gall is too much gall?: A review of *Frames of the mind: The theory of multiple intelligence. Contemporary Education Review* 2:220–221.

Stoller, R., & Herdt, G. (1985). Theories of origins of male homosexuality: A cross-cultural look. *Archives of General Psychiatry* 42:399–404.

Strange, M. (1980). *The durable fig leaf.* New York: William Morrow.

Strickland, S. (1971). Can slum children learn? *American Education* 7:3–7.

Stringer, C. B., & Andrews, P. (1988). Genetic and fossil evidence for the origin of modern humans. *Science* 239:1263–1239.

Suomi, S. (1980). *A touch of sensitivity.* Boston: WGBH Educational Foundation.

Sutaria, S. (1985). *Specific learning disabilities: Nature and needs.* Springfield, Ill.: Charles C. Thomas.

Svensson, T. (1992). A psychopharmacologist's view of attachment. *Behavioral and Brain Sciences* 15:524.

Swaab, D., & Fliers, E. (1985). A sexually dimorphic nucleus in the human brain. *Science* 228:1112–1114.

Symons, D. (1979). *The evolution of human sexuality.* New York: Oxford University Press.

Symons, D. (1987). If we're all Darwinians, what's all the fuss about? In C. Crawford, M. Smith, & D. Krebs (Eds.), *Sociobiology and psychology: Ideas, issues, and applications* (pp. 121–146). Hillsdale, N.J.: Lawrence Erlbaum.

Symons, D. (1992). On the use and misuse of Darwinism in the study of human behavior. In J. Barkow, L. Cosmides, & J. Tooby (Eds.), *The adapted mind: Evolutionary psychology and the generation of culture* (pp. 137–159). New York: Oxford University Press.

Szalay, F., & Costello, R. (1991). Evolution of permanent estrus displays in hominids. *Journal of Human Evolution* 20:439–464.

Tallal, P. (1991). Hormonal influences in developmental learning disabilities. *Psychoneuroendocrinology* 16:203–211.

Tambs, K., Sundet, J., Magnus, P., & Berg, K. (1989). Genetic and environmental contributions to the covariance between occupational status, educational attainment, and IQ: A study of twins. *Behavior Genetics* 19:209–222.

Tarter, R., Hegedus, A., Winsten, N., & Alterman, A. (1985). Intellectual profiles and violent behavior in juvenile delinquents. *Journal of Psychology* 119:125–128.

Tavris, C. (1992). *The mismeasure of woman*. New York: Simon & Schuster.

Taylor, G. (1979). *The natural history of the mind*. New York: E. P. Dutton.

Taylor, J. (1992). *Paved with good intentions: The failure of race relations in contemporary America*. New York: Carroll & Graff.

Taylor, L. (1984). *Born to crime*. Westport, Conn.: Greenwood Press.

Teitelbaum, M. (1976). *Sex differences: Social and biological perspectives*. New York: Anchor.

Tellegen, A., Lykken, D., Bouchard, T., Wilcox, K., Segal, N., & Rich, S. (1988). Personality similarity in twins reared apart and together. *Journal of Personality and Social Psychology* 36:1031–1039.

Terkell, J., & Rosenblatt, J. (1972). Hormonal factors underlying maternal behavior at parturition: Cross transfusions between freely moving rats. *Journal of Comparative and Physiological Psychology* 80:365–371.

Theilgaard, A. (1983). Aggression and XYY personality. *International Journal of Law and Psychiatry* 6:413–421.

Thiessen, D. (1976). *The evolution and chemistry of aggression*. Springfield, Ill.: Charles C. Thomas.

Thio, A. (1979). *Deviant behavior*. Boston: Houghton Mifflin.

Thomas, A., & Chess, S. (1977). *Temperament and development*. New York: Brunner/Mazel.

Thompson, J. (1988). *The psychobiology of emotions*. New York: Plenum.

Thornhill, R., & Thornhill, N. (1992). The evolutionary psychology of men's coercive sexuality. *Behavioral and Brain Sciences* 15:363–421.

Tooby, J., & Cosmides, L. (1990). On the universality of human nature and the uniqueness of the individual: The role of genetics and adaptation. *Journal of Personality* 58:17–67.

Tooby, J., & Cosmides, L. (1992). The psychological foundation of culture. In J. Barkow, L. Cosmides, & J. Tooby (Eds.), *The adapted mind: Evolutionary psychology and the generation of culture* (pp. 19–136). New York: Oxford University Press.

Tracy, P., Wolfgang, M., & Figlio, R. (1990). *Delinquency careers in two birth cohorts*. New York: Plenum.

Trasler, G. (1987). Some cautions for the biological approach to crime causation. In S. Mednick, T. Moffitt, & S. Stack (Eds.), *The causes of crime: New biological approaches* (pp. 7–24). Cambridge: Cambridge University Press.

Trivers, R. (1972). Parental investment and sexual selection. In B. Campbell (Ed.), *Sexual selection and the descent of man 1871–1971* (pp. 136–179). Chicago: Aldine.

Trunnell, E., Turner, C., & Keye, W. (1988). A comparison of the psychological and hormonal factors in women with and without premenstrual syndrome. *Journal of Abnormal Psychology* 97:429–436.

Udry, J. (1988). Biological predispositions and social control in adolescent sexual behavior. *American Sociological Review* 53:709–722.

Udry, J. (1990). Biosocial models of adolescent problem behaviors. *Social Biology* 37:1–10.

Udry, J., & Talbert, L. (1988). Sex hormone effects on personality at puberty. *Journal of Personality and Social Psychology* 54:291–295.

Utain, W. (1980). *Menopause in modern perspectives*. New York: Appleton-Century-Crofts.

Vandenberg, S., & Volger, G. (1985). Genetic determinants of intelligence. In B. Wolman (Ed.), *Handbook of intelligence: Theories, measurements, and applications* (pp. 3–58). New York: John Wiley.

van den Berghe, P. (1979). *Human family systems: An evolutionary view*. New York: Elsevier.

van Praag, H., Kahn, R., Asnis, G., Wetzler, S., Brown, S., Bleich, A., & Korn, M. (1987). Denosologination of biological psychiatry or the specificity of 5-HT disturbances in psychiatric disorders. *Journal of Affective Disorders* 13:1–8.

Vedder, R., & Gallaway, L. (1993). Declining black unemployment. *Society* 30:57–63.

Venables, P. (1987). Autonomic nervous system factors in criminal behavior. In S. Mednick, T. Moffitt, & S. Stack (Eds.), *The causes of crime: New biological approaches* (pp. 110–136). Cambridge: University of Cambridge Press.

Vernon, P. (1991). Studying intelligence the hard way. *Intelligence* 15:389–395.

Vila, B. (1994). A general paradigm for understanding criminal behavior: Extending evolutionary ecological theory. *Criminology* 32:311–358.

Vinovskis, M. (1988). Teenage pregnancy and the underclass. *Public Interest* 93:87–96.

Virkkunen, M., DeJong, J., Barkto, J., Goodwin, F., & Linnoila, M. (1989). Relationship of psychobiological variables to recidivism of violent offenders and impulsive fire setters. *Archives of General Psychiatry* 46:600–603.

Virkkunen, M., & Linnoila, M. (1990). Serotonin in early onset, male alcoholics with violent behaviour. *Annals of Medicine* 22:327–321.

Vold, G., & Bernard, T. (1986). *Theoretical criminology*. New York: Oxford University Press.

Wadsworth, M. (1976). Delinquency, pulse rates, and early emotional deprivation. *British Journal of Criminology* 16:245–256.

Walker, S. (1992). *The police in America*. New York: McGraw Hill.

Walsh, A. (1986). Love and human authenticity in the works of Freud, Marx, and Maslow. *Free Inquiry in Creative Sociology* 14:21–26.

Walsh, A. (1991a). *Intellectual imbalance, love deprivation and violent delinquency: A biosocial perspective*. Springfield, Ill.: Charles C. Thomas.

Walsh, A. (1991b). *The science of love: Understanding love and its effects on mind and body*. Buffalo: Prometheus.

Walsh, A. (1991c). Self-esteem and sexual behavior: Exploring gender differences. *Sex Roles* 25:441–450.

Walsh, A. (1992). Genetic and environmental explanations of juvenile violence in advantaged and disadvantaged environments. *Aggressive Behavior* 18:187–199.

Walsh, A. (1993). Love styles, masculinity/femininity, physical attraction and sexual behavior: A test of evolutionary theory. *Ethology and Sociobiology* 14:25–38.

Walsh, A. (1994). Polyandry. In V. Bullough & B. Bullough (Eds.), *Human sexuality: An encyclopedia* (pp. 467–469). New York: Garland.

Walsh, A. (1995). Genetic and cytogenetic intersex anomalies: Can they help us to understand gender differences in deviant behavior? *International Journal of Offender Therapy and Comparative Criminology* 39:151–166.

Walsh, A. (In press). Parental attachment, drug use, and facultive sexual strategies. *Social Biology*.

Walsh, A. (Submitted). Gender differences in sexual dreaming, sensation-seeking, and number of coital partners.

Walsh, A., & Balazs, G. (1990). Love, sex, and self-esteem. *Free Inquiry in Creative Sociology* 18:37–41.

Walsh, A., Petee, T., & Beyer, J. (1987). Intellectual imbalance and delinquency: Comparing high verbal and high performance IQ delinquents. *Criminal Justice and Behavior* 14:370–379.

Walsh, A., & Walsh, G. (1993). *Viva la difference: A celebration of the sexes.* Buffalo: Prometheus Books.

Wang, Z. (1994). An exploratory analysis of the "China trail": Causations, methods, and policy implications. *CJ International* 10(May-June):11–14.

Watters, J., & Stinnett, N. (1971). Parent–child relationships: A decade review of research. *Journal of Marriage and the Family* 33:70–103.

Wechsler, D. (1958). *The measurement and appraisal of adult intelligence.* Baltimore: Williams & Wilkins.

Weisenfeld, A., Malatesta, C., Whitman, P., Granrose, C., & Uili, R. (1985). Psychophysiological response to breast- and bottle-feeding mothers to their infant's signals. *Psychophysiology* 22:79–86.

West, D. (1982). *Delinquency: Its roots, careers and prospects.* Cambridge: Harvard University Press.

West, D., & Farrington, D. (1977). *The delinquent way of life.* New York: Crane Russak.

Weyler, W., Hsu, Y., & Breakfield, X. (1990). Biochemistry and genetics of monoamine oxidase. *Pharmacotherapy* 47:391–417.

Wheeler, D. (1992). Meeting on possible links between genes and crime canceled after bitter exchange. *Chronicle of Higher Education,* September 16:A7–A8.

Whitam, F. (1987). A cross-cultural perspective on homosexuality, transvestism and trans-sexuality. In G. Wilson (Ed.), *Variant sexuality: Research and theory* (pp. 176–201). Baltimore: Johns Hopkins University Press.

White, D., & Burton, M. (1988). The causes of polygyny: Ecology, economy, kinship, and warfare. *American Anthropologist* 90:871–887.

Whitman, D., & Friedman, D. (1992). The war over "family values." *U.S. News & World Report* (June 8):35–36.

Whitman, S. (1993). The crime of black imprisonment. In J. Sullivan & J. Victor (Eds.), *Criminal Justice 93/94* (pp. 212–214). Guilford, Conn.: Dushkin.

Whitney, G. (1990). On possibile genetic bases of race differences in criminality. In L. Ellis & H. Hoffman (Eds.), *Crime in biological, social, and moral contexts* (pp. 134–149). New York: Praeger.

Whybrow, P. (1984). Contributions from neuroendocrinology. In K. Scherer & P. Ekman (Eds.), *Approaches to emotion* (pp. 59–72). Hillsdale, N.J.: Lawrence Erlbaum.

Wickett, J., Vernon, P., & Lee, D. (1994). In vivo brain size, head perimeter, and intelligence in a sample of healthy adult females. *Personality and Individual Differences* 16:831–838.

Widom, C. (1989). Child abuse, neglect, and violent criminal behavior. *Criminology* 27:251–271.

Wilbanks, W. (1987). The myth of a racist criminal justice system. *Criminal Justice Research Bulletin,* Vol. 3. Criminal Justice Center, Sam Houston State University, Huntsville, Texas.

Willerman, L., Schultz, R., Rutledge, J., & Bigler, E. (1991). In vivo brain size and intelligence. *Intelligence* 15:223–228.

Williams, J., & Jacoby, A. (1989). The effects of premarital heterosexual and homosexual experience on dating and marriage desirability. *Journal of Marriage and the Family* 51:489–497.

Wilson, E. (1978a). Academic vigilantism and the political significance of sociobiology. In A. Caplan (Ed.), *The sociobiology debate* (pp. 291–303). New York: Harper & Row.

Wilson, E. (1978b). Foreword. In A. Caplan (Ed.), *The sociobiology debate* (pp. xi–xiv). New York: Harper & Row.

Wilson, E. (1978c). *On human nature.* Cambridge: Harvard University Press.

Wilson, E. (1990). Biology and the social sciences. *Zygon* 25:245–262.

Wilson, G. (1983). *Love and instinct.* New York: Quill.

Wilson, G. (1987). An ethological approach to sexual deviation. In G. Wilson (Ed.), *Variant sexuality: Research and theory* (pp. 84–115). Baltimore: Johns Hopkins University Press.

Wilson, J. (1991). *On character: Essays by James Q. Wilson.* Washington, D.C.: AEI Press.

Wilson, J. (1993). On gender. *Public Interest* 112:3–26.

Wilson, J., & Herrnstein, R. (1985). *Crime and human nature.* New York: Simon & Schuster.

Wilson, M., & Daly, M. (1992). The man who mistook his wife for chattel. In J. Barkow, L. Cosmides, & J. Tooby (Eds.), *The adapted mind: Evolutionary psychology and the generation of culture* (pp. 289–322). New York: Oxford University Press.

Wilson, P. (1980). *Man: The promising primate.* New Haven: Yale University Press.

Wilson, W. (1987). *The truly disadvantaged.* Chicago: University of Chicago Press.

Wilson-Perkins, M. (1981). Female homosexuality and body build. *Archives of Sexual Behavior* 10:337–345.

Witelson, S. (1976). Sex and the single hemisphere: Specialization of the right hemisphere for spacial processing. *Science* 193:425–426.

Witelson, S. (1987). Neurobiological aspects of language in children. *Child Development* 58:653–688.

Witkin, H., Mednick, S., Schulsinger, R., Bakkestrom, E., Christiansen, K., Goodenough, D., Hirschorn, K., Lundsteen, C., Owen, D., Philip, J., Rubin, D., & Stocking, M. (1976). Criminality in XYY and XXY men. *Science* 193:547–555.

Wolfgang, M., Figlio, R., & Sellin, T. (1972). *Delinquency in a birth cohort.* Chicago: University of Chicago Press.

Wolman, B. (Ed.). (1985). Intelligence and mental health. In *Handbook of intelligence: Theories, measurement, and applications* (pp. 849–872). New York: John Wiley.

Woodger, J. (1948). *Biological principles.* London: Routledge & K. Paul.

Woodward, V. (1992). *Human heredity and society.* St. Paul: West.

Wu, F., Bancroft, J., Davidson, D., & Nicol, K. (1982). The behavioural effects of testosterone undecanoate in adult men with Klinefelter's syndrome: A controlled study. *Clinical Endocrinology* 16:489–497.

Zald, M. (1991). Sociology as a discipline: Quasi-science and quasi-humanities. *American Sociologist* 22:165–187.

Zeller, R., & Carmines, E. (1980). *Measurement in the social sciences: The link between theory and data.* Cambridge: Cambridge University Press.

Zigler, E., & Seitz, V. (1986). Social policy and intelligence. In R. Sternberg (Ed.), *Handbook of human intelligence* (pp. 586–641). Cambridge: Cambridge University Press.

Zinsmeister, K. (1991). Growing up scared. In K. Finsterbusch (Ed.), *Sociology 91/ 92* (pp. 46–54). Guilford, Conn.: Dushkin.

Zomzely-Neurath, C., & Walker, W. (1985). *Gene expression in the brain.* New York: John Wiley.

Zuckerman, M. (1987). All parents are environmentalists until they have their second child. *Behavioral and Brain Sciences* 10:42–44.

Zuckerman, M. (1990). The psychophysiology of sensation-seeking. *Journal of Personality* 58:314–345.

Zuckerman, M., & Brody, N. (1988). Oysters, rabbits and people: A critique of "Race differences in behaviour" by J. P. Rushton. *Personality and Individual Differences* 9:1025–1033.

Zuckerman, M., Buchsbaum, M., & Murphy, D. (1980). Sensation seeking and its biological correlates. *Psychological Bulletin* 88:187–214.

Zuravin, S. (1988). Child maltreatment and teenage first births: A relationship mediated by chronic sociodemographic stress? *Journal of Orthopsychiatry* 58:91–103.

Name Index

Subject Index

ABOUT THE AUTHOR

ANTHONY WALSH is currently Professor of Criminal Justice at Boise State University in Idaho. His research interests include any social-psychological topic that can be informed by biological concepts, particularly IQ and crime. Walsh is the author or coauthor of nine other books and more than sixty journal articles or essays.

ISBN 0-275-95328-9

EAN

9 780275 953287

90000>

HARDCOVER BAR CODE